ALSO BY DENNIS McNALLY

Desolate Angel: Jack Kerouac, The Beat Generation, and America
On Highway 61: Music, Race and the Evolution of Cultural Freedom
Jerry on Jerry: The Unpublished Jerry Garcia Interviews
A Long Strange Trip: The Inside History of the Grateful Dead

How Bohemians Became Hippies and Created the Sixties

THE LAST GREAT DREAM

DENNIS MCNALLY

DA CAPO

New York

Copyright © 2025 by Dennis McNally

Jacket design by Milan Bozic. Jacket image by Robert W. Klein/Associated Press.
Jacket copyright © 2025 by Hachette Book Group, Inc.

Hachette Book Group supports the right to free expression and the
value of copyright. The purpose of copyright is to encourage writers
and artists to produce the creative works that enrich our culture.

The scanning, uploading, and distribution of this book without permission
is a theft of the author's intellectual property. If you would like permission to
use material from the book (other than for review purposes), please contact
permissions@hbgusa.com. Thank you for your support of the author's rights.

Da Capo Press
Hachette Book Group
1290 Avenue of the Americas, New York, NY 10104
grandcentralpublishing.com
@grandcentralpub

First Edition: May 2025

Da Capo Press is an imprint of Grand Central Publishing. The Da Capo Press
name and logo are registered trademarks of Hachette Book Group, Inc.

The publisher is not responsible for websites (or their content)
that are not owned by the publisher.

The Hachette Speakers Bureau provides a wide range of authors for speaking
events. To find out more, go to hachettespeakersbureau.com
or email HachetteSpeakers@hbgusa.com.

Da Capo Press books may be purchased in bulk for business, educational, or
promotional use. For information, please contact
your local bookseller or the Hachette Book Group Special Markets
Department at special.markets@hbgusa.com.

Library of Congress Control Number: 2025931395

ISBNs: 978-0-306-83566-7 (hardcover), 978-0-306-83568-1 (ebook)

Printed in the United States of America

LSC-C

Printing 1, 2025

To my favorite hippie, Susana Millman

CONTENTS

Introduction   ix

1   The Poets Gather   1

2   The San Francisco Art Scene   11

3   Los Angeles and the Émigrés   17

4   Post–World War II Greenwich Village   25

5   The Village in the '50s   31

6   San Francisco in the Early '50s   39

7   Mainstream America and San Francisco's First Resistance   49

8   City Lights, the Place, and Marin   57

9   The Beats and "Howl"   65

10   Changes Become Visible—Civil Rights and Rock 'n' Roll   75

11   Baghdad by the Bay and Its Artists   81

12   England Awakens—Skiffle and Style   91

13   Los Angeles: Wallace Berman, Ferus, and Venice Beach   101

14   New York in the Late '50s   109

15   Asian Thought and America   119

16   Four Freshmen, the Rise of Student Activism,
and New Options for Women   125

17   The Folk Scare   133

18   The Tape Music Center and Its Cohorts   143

19   The Church on Capp Street: A New Culture Blossoms   151

Contents

20 The Arc of the Moral Universe—Civil Rights in the South, San Francisco, and Berkeley **161**

21 London, No Longer Dull **171**

22 Transformation via LSD **181**

23 The Village in the Mid-'60s **191**

24 Los Angeles and Folk-Rock **199**

25 More Changes: 1965 in San Francisco and Thereabouts **209**

26 The Trips Festival and What Followed **219**

27 Posters and Light Shows and Really Transitional Sexual Politics **231**

28 London, Psychedelicized **241**

29 The Diggers and the Love Pageant Rally **249**

30 The *Oracle* and Digger Ritual **257**

31 Hippie in New York **265**

32 The Be-In **275**

33 After the Be-In **281**

34 Pilgrims Overrun the Haight **289**

35 A New Guitar Hero in London—*Sgt. Pepper* **299**

36 Monterey Pop **309**

Afterword **319**

Acknowledgments **323**

Glossary of Names **325**

Bibliography **349**

Notes **385**

Index **405**

INTRODUCTION

By the middle of the 1960s, San Francisco's Haight-Ashbury neighborhood was home to several hundred colorful refugees from the conventional. They had created the world's first psychedelic neighborhood, an alchemical chamber for social transformation. They called themselves *freaks*, a term taken, with so much else, from African American jazz culture. Uncomfortable with the term, the media would rename them *hippies*. This evolution did not take place only in San Francisco, of course; other people and cities are distinctly part of this story. But for clear reasons of geography and history, San Franciscans went further and deeper.

Collectively, these freaks stood for a series of values. In an uneven, unsystematic, not-fully-digested way, they rejected a large part of the mythology that was and largely remains the substructure of the conventional American identity. They began by dismissing the founding lie of American exceptionalism as expressed by Bob Dylan's "With God on Our Side" and the assumed innocence and explicit racial superiority enshrined in the partial humanity allotted to slaves by the Constitution. They rejected the consumerist materialism that was the presumed quasi-divine reward for service to the Protestant work ethic. They upheld creativity against competition. They opposed violence, and the gentle males among them undermined conventional gender roles. They wrote off the Western world's notions of mind-body separation and in doing so anticipated both the elimination of sexual repression and an understanding of nature in which humans were part of the planetary life cycle, not warriors out to conquer it.

Introduction

Their ideas were not original but part of a long tradition. America has always celebrated the flag of freedom, but it has always denoted two realms. The most popular option was the freedom to make as much money as possible. Freedom of thought and religion, freedom to question the shadow side of American culture in the manner of Thoreau was less accepted but no less essential. The citizens of the Haight were decidedly committed to the latter course.

Starting in World War II–era San Francisco, a thread of artistic discourse focused on freedom coalesced into a subculture. It began with poets—Kenneth Rexroth and Robert Duncan initially, to be followed by many more—and blossomed among students at the San Francisco Art Institute like Mel Weitsman and Wally Hedrick and Jay DeFeo and the allied artist Bruce Conner, then electronic composers like Ramón Sender and radical theater people like Herbert Blau and Ronnie Davis. East Coast transplants like Lawrence Ferlinghetti and Allen Ginsberg nurtured the burgeoning phenomenon. Different forms of popular music, from rock to folk, helped generate a parallel youth culture. It was not premeditated, ideological, or planned; it simply happened. By the '60s, the addition of widespread access to the psychedelic experience would be the final, catalytic touch.

What was remarkable about the Haight scene was that it took the insights of a small group of avant-garde artists and made them accessible to the better part of a generation through music and culture, with ripples of influence that in many cases have only grown since 1967. As James Baldwin once remarked, "The great force of history comes from the fact that we carry it within us." The psychedelic experience left the pioneers of the Haight feeling free to begin anew, to choose a history that did not assume that the Judeo-Christian tradition was the sole appropriate spiritual path and that Cartesian rationality did not address every question.

A note about this study: Cultural connections and influences are ultimately impossible to prove. Correlation is not causation, but it is often the best available evidence in these matters. I can only promise a scrupulous commitment to fairness. After all, one of the threads in this book is surrealism—which is only one of many rabbit holes that I've explored.

Introduction

*   *   *

It was entirely reasonable that their path led to San Francisco, where the visual beauty and proximity to nature were unique among American cities. Moreover, its orientation on the far edge of the North American continent at the beginning of the Pacific Rim made it a place somewhat apart from the rest of the nation, "the westward edge of dreams," as Robert Duncan put it.

The city began as a fantasy. The word *California* (and until well into the twentieth century, this largely connoted San Francisco) was created by the author Garci Rodríguez de Montalvo in the early-sixteenth-century popular novel *The Adventures of Esplandián* to describe the land now known by that name, although Rodríguez de Montalvo's imaginary California was an island inhabited by Black Amazon warriors.

The subsequent social madness known as the gold rush of 1849 was hardly more orthodox. The '49ers were marginalized rejects from the Eastern US, Chilean, and Cantonese mainstreams, gamblers chasing dreams, unlike the more orthodox bourgeois strivers who built most other American cities. Even as the city grew and acquired churches and a conventionally corrupt political system, it would acknowledge its slightly delirious origins by paying homage to a madman who'd dubbed himself Emperor Norton. Other cities have their lunatics, but few East Coast restaurateurs would have accepted his self-inscribed "Emperor Norton Bank Notes" as legitimate currency the way San Franciscans did.

Just as with the name *California*, the city also adopted another essential part of its collective identity from fiction, most notably the ambience of Dashiell Hammett's Continental Op and his 1929 magnum opus, *The Maltese Falcon*.

The Depression that came to the city was inarguably real, and among its primary effects was to add leverage to the efforts by longshoremen to unionize. Led by a charming, canny Australian named Harry Bridges, the longshoremen and the sailors struck in 1934, and when two of their number were killed by police, the majority of the city joined them in a general strike, perhaps the largest and most effective left-wing political action in US history.

The ensuing war with Japan was fought from San Francisco's Presidio and the naval headquarters on the man-made Treasure Island, guaranteeing that the war was omnipresent in the city, to the point that all its schoolchildren were issued identity tags, like soldiers' dog tags, in anticipation of air raid casualties. Artillery flanked the Golden Gate Bridge, and their test rounds were audible for miles around.

After much vacillating and absent any credible evidence of disloyalty from the target population, the local commandant, Lieutenant General John DeWitt, persuaded the president to sign Executive Order 9066 on February 19, 1942, which called for the internment of all Japanese Americans on the West Coast, a tragedy particularly felt in California.

The American war effort produced victory, but the atomic bombs that obliterated Hiroshima and Nagasaki had deeper and grislier implications as well. Along with the horror of the Nazi concentration camps so viscerally documented by Margaret Bourke-White's ghastly *Life* photographs, the bomb was literally unnerving. The poet Richard Meltzer later wrote that "it was the Bomb / Shoah / it was void / spirit crisis disconnect." As the broadcaster H. V. Kaltenborn covered the Japanese surrender, he invited his audience to "think of the mass murder which will come with World War III." The bomb, wrote the lyricist John Barlow many years later, left "a soupçon of pure nihilism" in the minds of the generation born during and after the war.

Having united to defeat a palpably evil enemy, the ensuing realization that, by catalyzing the end of several European empires, the victory had triggered much more change than most had initially realized came first as a shock, followed by a sense of betrayal. Few could attribute the Cold War to the blind course of history; people wanted identifiable traitors—Communists, it was commonly held—to explain the ambiguous ending of the war.

It was in the war's end atmosphere of hollow joy and mortal fear that San Francisco poets like Kenneth Rexroth and Robert Duncan would explore alternatives to a world that could incinerate more than one hundred thousand humans in the blink of an eye.

1

The Poets Gather

Newly returned to the Bay Area in 1942, a young man named Robert Duncan came to visit Kenneth Rexroth at his home on Potrero Hill. Having been charmed by the "crotchety" letters with which Rexroth had been peppering the magazines *Partisan Review* and *View*, he was very much the younger poet seeking counsel. Impressed that Rexroth was working in an underground way to support newly interned Japanese Americans, Duncan found a mentor who would soon enough be a colleague.

They were a distinctly odd couple in many ways. Rexroth was of medium size and pugnacious; Duncan was tall and talkative, with a very large head, a small mouth, and noticeably crossed eyes. His open gayness and Rexroth's intermittent homophobia somehow didn't matter, and they would become the nucleus of a remarkably powerful gathering of poets over the next decade.

Assuming the mantle of poet outside academia inherently propels the claimant out of conventional society into an artistic subculture where money is no longer the sine qua non. In fact, both these men were consciously anarchistic in the philosophical rather than bomb-throwing sense, and these views would not only permeate the community that gathered around them but affect San Francisco's arts culture as a whole well into the era of Haight-Ashbury in the 1960s.

Born in Chicago in 1905, Rexroth was a truant hostile to authority and pursued his education in the literary ferment known as the Chicago Renaissance that gathered around Theodore Dreiser, Vachel Lindsay, Harriet Monroe's *Poetry*, and Margaret Anderson's *Little Review*.

As a teen, he met all these people and more, particularly Bill Haywood, the leader of the Industrial Workers of the World (IWW). He studied left-wing politics and also the cutting edge of avant-garde writing, the dadaist Tristan Tzara and the surrealist poet Robert Desnos, then found the Green Mask, a bohemian tearoom on State Street, which connected him to Chicago's flourishing African American cultural scene, from the music of Alberta Hunter and Jimmy Yancey to the poetry readings of people like Langston Hughes, Countee Cullen, and Claude McKay. Rexroth's Chicago was a highly creative social, sexual, cultural, and political free-for-all, and he soaked it all in.

Briefly an IWW recruiter and then a newspaper reporter, he married Andrée Schafer, a painter. They packed their meager possessions into rucksacks and in the spring of 1927 headed for San Francisco, where the relaxed Mediterranean atmosphere of what he termed *dolce far niente* (sweet doing nothing) persuaded him that they were home. An unerring instinct for what would later be called *networking* quickly brought them to the door of a poet named Elsa Gidlow, an extraordinary woman who'd published overt lesbian odes in the 1910s. Her untroubled certainty in her orientation would make her an icon when the times began to catch up with her.

For the next decade, the focus of Rexroth's life apart from poetry was political activism with the Communist Party, although he was insufficiently doctrinaire to be a successful party member. He organized an Artists and Writers Union, which facilitated the painting of historic frescoes at San Francisco's Coit Tower, but was chastised by the party for working with the petit bourgeois rather than the proletariat. When he sensibly reached out to Black churches as part of organizing Black workers on behalf of the Unemployment Council, the party lectured him about the opiate of the masses. After he wrote a play about the Paris Commune, the party ordered him to "abandon formalist Trotskyite petty bourgeois bohemianism."

As war approached, he abandoned the party and turned toward pacifism and philosophical anarchism, joining the Fellowship of Reconciliation and working with the American Friends Service Committee to support the victims of Japanese American internment. His was an anarchism built on what is known as *political personalism*, in which the personal *is* political, in which the moral and the spiritual precede the social and political, and the fundamental emphasis is on the dignity of the individual. Anti-hierarchical, it advocates participatory rather than representative democracy. Personalism would be at the core of social and civil rights activism in America for the next several decades.

His poetry fused his progressive politics and an appreciation for wild nature with an elegiac feel that recognized life after Hiroshima as damaged, yet still permeated with the immanent presence of the divine. Such a sacramental faith was wildly divergent from the dominant East Coast "New Critics" approach that advocated a detached, unemotional poetry.

It was poetry itself as a force for social good that he truly believed in, and his friendship with Robert Duncan fed that. Both men shared a similar politics; Duncan added a mystical streak from his personal metaphysics. Orphaned at birth and raised across the bay from San Francisco in Alameda by a matriarchal family that believed in astrology, Atlantis, Rosicrucianism, Theosophy, and reincarnation, Duncan particularly cherished his grandmother Mary, the family head, who proclaimed an affection for Christ, Lao Tzu, and *Azoth: The Occult Magazine*. His aunt Fay responded to an early poem of his with the remark, "This is very lazy of you. You have been a poet already in so many lives."

"His conversation," said his poet/filmmaker friend James Broughton— and the flow of words rarely ceased—"was a bewildering tour of hermetic philosophy, astrology, linguistics, Celtic myth, the Zohar, Whitehead, medieval history, family history, and many other zones freely retranslated by his mental hopscotch."

Duncan was essentially a shaman who wanted to conjure magic out of language by interweaving ancient, mythic mysteries with his own personal ones, and with the apocalypse that had consumed Hiroshima. One biographer wrote that "his true devotion…was to human freedom generally."

In Duncan's poetry, the sexual and the spiritual were both sacramental, and he felt that his particular duty was to free men from their sexual prisons.

He pioneered open gay culture with a 1944 *Politics* essay, "The Homosexual in Society," not only identifying himself as gay but also rejecting an emerging camp culture. The essay seemingly shut him off permanently from America's East Coast–based intelligentsia.

Both he and Rexroth generally lived within the bohemian tradition that traced back to the Paris of Henri Murger's *Scènes de la vie de Bohème*, in which art replaced conventional expressions of religion, although his friend Rexroth had been baptized an Anglican and never disavowed it. In terms of throwing off sexual repression, both men were enthusiastically promiscuous all their adult lives.

Rexroth and Duncan were two of the more prominent members of the substantial circle of poets that mysteriously cohered around San Francisco at this time. One major poet had preceded them. The Big Sur region 150 miles to the south was so extraordinarily beautiful and dramatic a meeting of land and sea that it seemed to encourage mysticism. As such, it was exactly the right destination for Robinson Jeffers, who had settled in Carmel in 1914. He dubbed his commitment to the overwhelming impact of Big Sur "inhumanism," and against that natural backdrop, he would set narrative poems based on Greek mythology that touched on frequently brutal and sexual themes like incest, fratricide, and bestiality. Politically conservative and ultimately rather Calvinist in his preoccupation with sin and suffering, Jeffers's resolute submission to nature would be one of the essential elements in the future thinking of California.

Big Sur attracted a second key figure during the war, when in 1944 the bohemian avatar Henry Miller moved there to paint. As a pacifist who'd also just condemned American materialism in his book *The Air-Conditioned Nightmare*, his views were appropriately outside the norm. His aim, he wrote in *The Cosmological Eye*, "is to establish a greater REALITY…I am against pornography and for obscenity and violence. Above all for imagination, fantasy, for a liberty as yet undreamed of…I believe that man can exist, and in an indefinitely better, larger way, without 'civilization.'"

From the north, a flock of poets, artful printers, and theater people descended on Rexroth and San Francisco from Camp Angel, a conscientious objectors' (CO) facility in Waldport, Oregon. During the war, roughly six

The Poets Gather

thousand conscientious objectors were sent to prison, but a consortium of traditional "peace" churches like the Quakers and Mennonites managed the placement of around twelve thousand more in 151 public service camps to plant trees, build roads, and fight fires.

The religious bureaucracy found artists challenging and settled many of them at Camp Angel, which consequently had the only fine arts program in the system. It also had a printing press and a poet-printer inmate named William Everson. A farmer from Fresno and the son of a printer, Everson had discovered Robinson Jeffers in college and read him so profoundly that it became, he said, his "intellectual awakening" and his "first religious conversion, all in one."

Everson's early work conjoined Jeffers-style pantheism with a cosmic sexuality taken from D. H. Lawrence, and in 1935, he printed up his first poems, *These Are the Ravens*, and sent them to Rexroth. It would be an important relationship for Everson, who later acknowledged that Rexroth "saw me as a sacramental man before I knew I was one." Later in his life, Everson would join the Dominican order and become Brother Antoninus.

He entered Camp Angel in 1943. His fellow inmates ranged from adherents to authoritarian religious beliefs who entirely rejected the day-to-day world, to anarchists and the extremely idealistic. Given that Waldport averaged seventy inches of rain a year, the hard work plus the gray deluge ensured that losing oneself in creative projects was a welcome diversion. The artists dismissed the camp's official newsletter, the *Tide*, as bureaucratic pap; their own, the *Untide*, was considerably more engaging.

Soon it became the Untide Press, and Everson and others were publishing a magazine called *Illiterati*, another called *Compass*, and a book of Everson's poetry, *War Elegies*. The pacifist network spread the word, and before long, an issue of *Illiterati* included a fragment of Miller's *The Air-Conditioned Nightmare* and three poems by Kenneth Patchen, whose *An Astonished Eye Looks Out of the Air* also became an Untide book. As 1944 passed, the camp also absorbed a number of veterans of the cooperative, peace-oriented Hedgerow Theatre near Philadelphia. As the war wound down and the inmates were released, many of them drifted down the coast to look in on Rexroth.

His status as chief macher of San Francisco poetry had been firmly established with the 1944 publication of his second book of poetry, *The*

Phoenix and the Tortoise, which received outstanding reviews, including a gem from William Carlos Williams in the *Quarterly Review of Literature*: "Strong meat and drink written in a verse which is clear as water."

The title poem depicted Rexroth and his second wife, Marie (Andrée had died of a seizure in 1940), camping on the shore on Easter week, where they found the body of a Japanese sailor. On the beach, they stood between society and the cosmic world. History, the sailor, brought death; poetry was the life force, although they were one, united in nature. "The State is the organization / Of the evil instincts of mankind. / History is the penalty / We pay for original sin." Opposed to this is Eros, not just sexuality but love for all beings, which in Buddhism is called the *Boddhisattva vow*.

More poets began to seek out Rexroth. Philip Lamantia had been the wunderkind of surrealist poetry, having left San Francisco for New York in 1942 at the age of fifteen to become André Breton's protégé and be published in the surrealist journal *View*. In November 1946, still only nineteen, he published his *Erotic Poems*, which was fittingly celebrated at Rexroth's home on Potrero Hill in the company of Duncan, the poet Muriel Rukeyser, and Rexroth's close friend, New Directions publisher James Laughlin.

The poets found an outlet for their work in a Berkeley-based journal called *Circle*, edited by a cabbie and bookstore owner named George Leite and designed by Bern Porter, who'd published Lamantia's *Erotic Poems*. Anti-war, experimental, and anarchist, *Circle* featured contributions from the local poets as well as Henry Miller, Anaïs Nin, and William Carlos Williams, plus work from the avant-garde composers Harry Partch and Darius Milhaud. Between 1944 and 1948, they put out ten issues with an expansive credo: "When a technique becomes a school, death of creation is the result. Eclecticism is the only approach to Art in which there is no death. *CIRCLE* is completely eclectic."

Meantime, Rexroth had convened yet another anarchist group, the Libertarian Circle, to succeed his wartime pacifist Randolph Bourne Council. They met on Wednesday nights in the top floor of a house on Steiner Street that they rented in cooperation with the Arbeiter Ring (Workmen's Circle), a left social democratic group. The price of admission was a bottle of red wine, about forty-nine cents. Reading Kropotkin, Proudhon, Engels, Lenin, Lao Tzu, Plato, Aristotle, and Bacon, they were all, said Duncan, "brought up on Daddy Rexroth's reading list."

The Poets Gather

A genuine if unconventional teacher, Rexroth would have his greatest influence on the poetic community in an ongoing series of salons held in his own home, mixing scatological humor, gossip, and a profound knowledge of poetry and anarchist philosophy. It was all a great deal more intellectual than what would flower on Haight Street twenty years later, but the spirit would remain true.

The Libertarian Circle was allied with a new publication, the *Ark*, edited by Lamantia and Sanders Russell. Personal conflicts doomed it to a single issue in 1947, but it included the Bay Area regulars as well as New Yorkers Paul Goodman, e. e. cummings, William Carlos Williams, and Ammon Hennacy of the Catholic Workers. Assertively anarchist, it argued that "the integrity of the personality [is] the most substantial and considerable of values…the validity if not the future of the anarchist position is more than ever established. It has become the polished mirror in which the falsehoods of political models stand naked."

They certainly should have been confident of their impact after *Harper's* that year ran "The New Cult of Sex and Anarchy," a distinctly scurrilous attack by a freelance writer named Mildred Brady. After dismissing the poets as a mere revival of '20s modernism, she savaged her primary target, Wilhelm Reich, then sank to the bottom by smearing the poets' seeking after mystic revelations as "uncomfortably reminiscent of the glorification of instincts and urges, the subjective absolutism of the famed [pre-Nazi] Stefan George circle." "Not to pin a label" of fascism on them, she wrote, it was no surprise (unnamed) people murmured "neo fascist" about them.

The article was followed by a four-episode hit piece in the Hearst flagship *San Francisco Examiner*, which described Big Sur as a "colony of hate." "Their philosophy is the doctrine of doom that characterizes the limp wrist, surrealist school of thought." Any criticism of America would corrupt the children, thought the *Examiner*, a right-wing trope that would endure.

In 1946, Duncan returned to UC Berkeley. The next year, he took up with a student named Gerald Ackerman, who lived in a boardinghouse at 2208 McKinley Avenue with the poet Jack Spicer (and also, curiously, the future science fiction writer Philip K. Dick and Duncan's old friend from college, a nascent film critic named Pauline Kael). That year, he also published his first book of poetry, *Heavenly City, Earthly City*, an allegorical and mythological transmutation of his personal life.

A highly charged erotic circle gathered around him, most notably Jack Spicer and Robin Blaser. Their aesthetic was based on magic, polytheism, and sexual freedom, and Duncan preached this gospel in weekly literary salons. His studies were in medieval history, and what emerged was the pursuit of a utopian polis, a genuine community of poetry.

The English department's presiding poet, Josephine Miles, encouraged the trio to give workshops, but her professional attitude was much more conventional; after all, her doctoral dissertation involved the systematic counting of syllables of emotion in Wordsworth. Duncan, said James Broughton, was a "poet who lived poetically because poetry lived him."

By the late '40s, San Francisco and Berkeley had become, said Broughton, "a whirlpool of maverick poets." *Maverick* was well chosen; they were a diverse bunch. At the age of three, Broughton himself had been told by an angel named Hermy that he was a poet; he would receive instruction from Hermy for the rest of his life. He discovered Ezra Pound in college at Stanford. In 1947, seeking to merge his passions for poetry and dance into "something magical," he attended an experimental film series at the San Francisco Museum of Art, and with the teacher as his cinematographer, then produced two well-regarded avant-garde short films, *Mother's Day* and *The Adventures of Jimmy*. He used poems as his shooting scripts: "I had always wanted to dance impossible dances."

Broughton also joined a small poetry reading group, Devotees of the Maiden, which included Duncan, Madeline Gleason, and the group's founder, Helen Adam, a mystic poet and sorceress from Scotland who wrote of women fulfilled not by men but by supernatural forces. Women were noticeably prominent in the emerging San Francisco poetry community.

Gleason, Broughton related, "lived to read poetry aloud and hear it read." Born in Fargo, North Dakota, she had come to San Francisco in 1935 and briefly worked with Rexroth on a Works Progress Administration (WPA) arts project. Supporting her poetry with a job as a runner in the financial district, her hair dyed bright red to match her equally vivid lipstick, she lived on Telegraph Hill with her lover, "a teacher lady," an orange cat, "and a red velvet armchair," recalled Broughton, "devoted to tea and whisky and the Virgin Mary." Indefatigable, she "bullied museums, galleries, and bookshops" into sponsoring readings.

Gleason's earliest success was the 1947 Festival of Modern Poetry readings at the Labaudt Gallery, 1407 Gough Street, which featured Rexroth, Everson, and Duncan, along with the more academically oriented Berkeleyites Josephine Miles and Thomas Parkinson, and Stanford professor Yvor Winters. They formed the Poetry Guild, and the readings continued at the museum and at SF State—which in 1954 opened its Poetry Center, directed by Ruth Witt-Diamant.

In explicit contrast to the consciously hermetic literary approach of the Easterners, San Francisco poetry had become a performance art. They had found their voice.

2

The San Francisco Art Scene

The poets soon had company in their pursuit of an alternate path of creativity. The visual arts would be an essential thread in the developing culture, and the California School of Fine Arts (CSFA, later the SF Art Institute) would be a particularly fertile seedbed for divergent artists for a decade and more to come.

San Francisco was quite a long way from the art world's New York center, but two administrators made it a more sophisticated place than it had any reason to be. The first was Grace McCann Morley, the visionary founding director of the San Francisco Museum of Art, later the Museum of Modern Art, then located in the Veterans Memorial next to the city's opera house. Under Morley, it was always a modern museum. It was also democratic, staying open evenings to widen access. Morley hosted programs with the Scouts (Boy and Girl), the Amalgamated Clothing Workers, and the Window Cleaners Union, and pointedly displayed the work of Japanese American artist Miné Okubo in at least two separate shows in 1940 and 1941.

Traveling exhibits brought Kandinsky, Klee, Matisse, and Picasso to provincial San Francisco. But these artists were to varying degrees famous and an easy sell; to exhibit American abstract expressionists like Arshile Gorky (1941), Clyfford Still (1943), Jackson Pollock (1945), Robert Motherwell (1946), and Mark Rothko (1946) so early in their careers was the work of great perception. Excepting Rothko, each event was the artist's first solo museum show.

The city's other main nexus of the visual arts was CSFA, whose small, beautiful campus, complete with a gracious courtyard and an elegant tower, was perched on the side of Russian Hill overlooking North Beach and the bay. The war had taken its students and income, and in 1945, it verged on collapse. In July, its board reached out to one of Grace Morley's associates, a thirty-two-year-old curator named Douglas MacAgy, and invited him to be the new president.

Progressive and experimental, he demanded and received a free hand, and he transformed the place. He cut requirements, kept studios open twenty-four hours a day so students could work on their own schedules, added photography and later film to the curriculum, and hired a world-class faculty that among other things brought abstract expressionism to the campus in the persons of the painter Clyfford Still and, for two summers, Still's friend Mark Rothko.

In parallel with Kenneth Rexroth's motivating facility as a teacher, Still inspired a succession of CSFA students with lessons that remained vital long after he'd departed. His studio was a damp room in the cellar at the base of the school tower, and it became a seat of revelation. There he preached the gospel of Art, not as a mode of communication but as a record, he said, "of the artist in the act of creation." Still presented an austerity, a purity, a concentration that was monk-like. His message, combined with an astonishing student body, catalyzed a storm of energy that changed the sensibilities of the San Francisco art world.

Anti-materialist and anti-conformist, Still was profoundly concerned with encouraging artists to maintain their own integrity. He wrote that "I held it imperative to evolve an instrument of thought which would aid in cutting through all cultural opiates, past and present, so that a direct, immediate, and truly free vision could be achieved, and an idea be revealed with clarity."

One of his students, a working-class marine corps veteran named Mel Weitsman, remembered Still as "a guy unto himself. A strange man. Very tall

The San Francisco Art Scene 13

and intellectual. There was a kind of split in his personality. His wild, on-the-edge paintings, and his intellectual straight-laced-ness. Sometimes he wore spats. He had a Jaguar."

"Painting can blow the world apart, blow your world apart," Still told another student. He did not teach painting but rather the spirit of freedom and the need for a nearly hermetic dedication to the pursuit. Yet another student, Wally Hedrick, reflected that Still's persona "instilled in the people and the students that became attached to him, and followed him, a tremendous feeling of purpose." A decade later, a teenaged student of Wally's by the name of Jerry Garcia would come to grasp that "art isn't what you do but who you are" and carry that understanding into the world of the Haight-Ashbury of the '60s.

Still's message met an ideal audience. The CSFA student body in the late '40s, 70 percent of whom were veterans, was every teacher's dream. Men and women who'd endured war and regimentation now applied themselves with equal energy to art with what one of their instructors, an army air corps veteran named Elmer Bischoff, called "a sense of urgency about things" with "a religious character" to their efforts. "They were like a community of monks, all praying, but each in his own way." They were genuinely there to learn. No wonder MacAgy kept the studios open all night.

Students like Weitsman and Hedrick were both veterans who'd decided to leave the "normal" world behind and follow the muse. They would move through the various arts scenes of the city for the next decade and more, popping up in different contexts but always carried by the same drive to create on their own terms. In highly differing ways, both would succeed mightily.

A sometime drummer, MacAgy began the old-timey New Orleans–style Studio 13 Jass Band, which would perform into the 1960s and contribute much to the school's sense of community; Hedrick played banjo. MacAgy also opened the school to photography, bringing in the already-famous San Franciscan Ansel Adams to establish what would be the first fine art photography program in the nation.

Abstract art was by no means the whole of the curriculum, and the figurative painter David Park became a faculty mainstay. But for many of the students, abstract expressionism was the pathway to the grail. Just as the US had emerged from the war as the world's leading power, its painters had created an extraordinary new form. Consummately personal, abstract expressionism reflected the postwar existential reality; it followed no rules because there didn't seem to be any left. It was a new way of seeing.

Thanks in part to the support of *Chronicle* critic Alfred Frankenstein, the new approach was as popular among San Francisco artists as in New York, although the San Francisco version unsurprisingly reflected an approach much closer to nature than Manhattan's. It had, said painter Jorge Goya-Lukich, "a more earthy organic quality about it than the New York school, which was more intellectual."

Surrealism was one of the new mode's fundamental sources, founded on the revolt against conventionality that was Dada, which had begun in 1916. Exploring sources that included Freud and psychoanalysis, the mystic and the occult, Asian religion, Native American and other so-called primitive cultures, found objects, and above all dreams and free association, the surrealists sought to explore the liminal space between sacred and profane and find the sacred in the present moment. As with dreams, much of their method was spontaneous, seemingly random, and certainly rooted in chance.

Revolted by the butchery of World War I, they brought together religion, Eros, and the imagination to fashion an altered state that went beyond realism to...surrealism. Though the movement would bog down in manifestos, excommunications, and political infighting, surrealism set the arts on a path that would be endlessly fertile, if often otherwise labeled, for many decades.

Surrealism came to CSFA in 1949, when a faculty member named Clay Spohn put on a show called *Museum of Unknown and Little Known Objects* that was so well received it stayed up for a month. A set of mixed-media constructions like the assemblages of Marcel Duchamp—one was a jar containing dust bunnies, another a watch with attached wires titled "Starter for a Rat Race"—it was also a commentary on consumerism and the commodification of art.

One leading expression of surrealism was the collage, which would become the preferred medium for a number of CSFA faculty and students. As the '50s passed, students like the collagist Jess (who was known by the single name) and Wally Hedrick came to be leading practitioners of assemblage, sometimes called *funk art*.

Another faculty member, Jean Varda, also worked with collage, but touched young artists even more with his personality and lifestyle. Having already stirred things up by inviting Henry Miller to visit Big Sur, Varda in 1949 recruited the wealthy British surrealist painter Gordon Onslow Ford to finance the purchase of an iron-hulled ferry boat, the SS *Vallejo*, which they docked in Sausalito, just north of San Francisco. Half of it was to be Varda's home and studio, the other half Ford's studio. Varda had known Braque and Picasso in Paris in the '20s and brought cubist/surrealist aesthetics to CSFA.

A natural-born bohemian, he lived for art, love, and wine. His friend Anaïs Nin said of him, "His collages taught how to remain in a state of grace of love, extract only elixirs, transmute all life into lunisolar fiestas, and all women, by a process of cutouts, to aphrodisiacs."

Ford was a formal member of the surrealist movement, the last person to be officially acknowledged by Breton in Paris. With the *Vallejo* as a gathering spot, he and Varda became the locus of a blossoming scene in Sausalito, just across the Golden Gate Bridge from San Francisco. The town resembled an Italian coastal village, white and pastel homes climbing up a steep hillside above an active waterfront dotted with moored sailboats.

Six CSFA students, including Richard Diebenkorn, who would become a faculty member the next year, had settled in the town and dubbed themselves "the Sausalito Six." In 1948, the Six took part in a show at the Sausalito gallery Schillerhaus, which was owned by an unusual man named Bern Porter, already the publisher of Lamantia's *Erotic Poems*, the Berkeley magazine *Circle*, and Robert Duncan's first book, *Heavenly City, Earthly City*. He'd also taken part in some of Kenneth Rexroth's Libertarian Circle meetings.

Porter was a true polymath, who spent his intellectual life trying to reconcile science and art. A graduate degree in physics from Brown had established his scientific credentials, and when war came, his draft board sent him to Princeton, where he became part of the Manhattan Project. Earlier, in 1936, he'd attended the first comprehensive gathering of surrealist works, a show at the New York Museum of Modern Art titled *Fantastic Art, Dada, Surrealism*. It consumed his imagination, and he began to create what he called "Founds," much like Marcel Duchamp's "Readymades."

He also became obsessed—his inclinations tended to the extreme—with Henry Miller's writing, publishing several Miller pieces and setting himself the task of creating a Miller bibliography.

In a truly bizarre contrast, he was visiting the anarcho-pacifist Miller in Big Sur on weekends while spending the workweek at the Berkeley laboratories of the Manhattan Project. How this escaped the notice of the lab security team is a mystery, although an invitation to a leftist union gathering that he did not attend made him the subject of attention by the FBI for a decade after the war. He had not really known the aim of the project, and the news of Hiroshima so devastated him that he resigned that day. After acting as publisher and gallery owner later in the decade, he grew deeply troubled and made up his mind to vanish, departing for Guam.

By 1950, Douglas MacAgy had concluded that the extraordinary commitment of the immediate postwar student body was dribbling away, and he left CSFA. Although there would be many more exceptional students over the ensuing decade, his decision was in touch with what was going on in America at that time. The creative excitement of the San Francisco poetry and art circles was in stark contrast to the atmosphere of the rest of the country.

Among the consequences of the war was a general suspicion of progressive thinking commonly called—though by no means the sole work of the senator—*McCarthyism*, primarily inculcated in loyalty programs directed against labor, civil rights activists, atheists, gay people, and anyone else who deviated from the norm.

One of the war's other legacies was the Servicemen's Readjustment Act (also known as the GI Bill), which made college education and home ownership available to an enormous swath of formerly working-class veterans. Now that so many more could afford a private home, it became enshrined as the ultimate expression of American individualism and love of family.

The paranoid mistrust at the root of McCarthyism met the sanctified notion of the home and was beautifully summed up in a 1953 speech made by Elizabeth Gordon, editor of *House Beautiful*. She informed her listeners that only the single-family suburban home was democratic, a "bulwark against communist infiltration." Large, modern apartment buildings were "a design for living that we associate with totalitarianism" because a "few, strategically placed, block leaders could check on all movements and conduct classes of ideological indoctrination."

In an era when *Life* magazine could list Albert Einstein and Dorothy Parker as "Dupes and Fellow Travelers," it was clear that any line of thought that diverged from the national norms placed the thinker in grave danger. Deviant artists like Rexroth and Varda were rare birds indeed.

3

Los Angeles and the Émigrés

San Francisco was not alone in producing cultural outliers. Los Angeles's endless buttery-yellow sunshine attracted orange growers and immigrants while the city sprawled out for miles in all directions to welcome newcomers chasing the American dream. Some of those immigrants would pursue unconventional spiritual paths in highly influential ways.

Given that it had been founded by priests and then settled in the early twentieth century by generally conservative midwestern Protestants and Latin immigrants, Los Angeles had no particular heritage of freedom-seeking in the San Francisco mold. Instead, and for no obvious reason, it became fertile ground for nonmainstream religious and occult thinking. The city also played a part in introducing other esoteric cultural phenomena to America, from avant-garde art and music to health foods and vegetarianism. In this context, its most important contribution would prove to be Aldous Huxley's discovery of the psychedelic experience. All these constructs would find their way to San Francisco.

The Last Great Dream

In 1931, the folklorist Joseph Campbell visited Los Angeles and found himself repulsed by the "blithe spirit of Californian mysticism, that perennial feature of the culture-mind of West Coast America." He wrote of his apartment building that "this household is a sanctuary of 'mystic' belief—astrology, palmistry, reincarnation—it is in that way perfectly typical of Southern California as a whole."

Theosophy had a presence in San Diego from 1897 to 1942. Annie Besant, who practiced a blend of Hindu thought and Madame Blavatsky–style Theosophy, opened a retreat center in Ojai, in the process anointing Jiddu Krishnamurti as the new savior/world teacher/messiah. Displaying a humble wisdom beyond that of his sponsors, Krishnamurti declined the honor in 1929, asserting that "truth is a pathless land, and you cannot approach it by any path whatsoever, by any religion, by any sect." He would remain a teacher, but on a purely individual basis.

In 1931, a Zen teacher named Nyogen Senzaki settled in Los Angeles and established what he called the "floating zendo," a teaching space wherever he happened to be, working with both Japanese and Western students. He called himself a "mushroom monk," because unlike most Zen teachers, he had no roots, no branches, and no flowers (he was not part of a formal lineage). Still, he worked with Paul Reps to translate the Japanese koan (spiritual teaching puzzles) text *The Gateless Gate* into their version, *Zen Flesh, Zen Bones*, which would touch many minds in the coming years.

He also worked with a much more Los Angeles–style mystic, Manly P. Hall, an esoteric philosopher in the occult tradition who would establish the Philosophical Research Society and its library in 1934 and write *The Secret Teachings of All Ages*, bringing together, Hall said, "ancient mathematics; alchemical formulas; Hermetic doctrine; pagan rites; Hebrew number mysticism; the geometry of ancient Egypt; Native American myths; the uses of cryptograms; an analysis of the Tarot; the symbols of Masonry and Rosicrucianism; the esotericism of the Shakespearean dramas."

For reasons mixing both the sunny weather and this receptivity to mysticism, three English pacifists—Gerald Heard, Christopher Isherwood, and Aldous Huxley—fled the impending carnage in Europe and came to Los Angeles in the late 1930s.

Los Angeles and the Émigrés

Huxley was the best known and most influential. Tall, slender, stylish, and courtly in manner, he had been born to be a golden child of the English ruling class, but circumstance and inclination changed all that when he lost his mother at the age of fourteen and his brother to suicide a few years later. There was considerable angst beneath his elegant appearance.

While a student at Oxford, he had been made welcome at the country home of upper-class bohemia in England, Garsington Manor, the home of Lady Ottoline Morrell and the country retreat of the Bloomsbury group of artists and writers—among many others, Huxley would meet Bertrand Russell, Virginia Woolf, and D. H. Lawrence there. As was sometimes the case in the higher social reaches of England, their rejection of conventional values was primarily confined to a publicly discreet but privately ferocious exploration of unorthodox sexuality. There Huxley met and soon after married Maria Nys, whose bisexuality and propensity for sharing her lovers with Huxley made for an unconventional but happy and long-lived partnership.

At first a poet, Huxley turned to novels to express his reservations about British society, most notably with the dystopian masterpiece *Brave New World*. As European politics began to churn, Huxley's inner demons pushed him into depression, and he turned to spiritual explorations. In 1929, he met the polymath Gerald Heard, who shared Huxley's pacifism and suggested that studying Ouspensky and Gurdjieff might be therapeutic.

Heard was yet another of the pivotal characters in this story—he would later be described as the "godfather of New Age thinking"—who were gay. Born to Irish gentry, his sexual orientation and his rejection of Christianity led him to a breakdown that exempted him from service in World War I. While working at the BBC, he spent a decade in the Bloomsbury/bohemian/gay subculture of London with men like Lytton Strachey, Isherwood, W. H. Auden, and E. M. Forster before a further spiritual conversion in the late 1930s led him to embrace celibacy and committed him to a formal meditation practice.

Their mutual pacifism and despairing certainty that war would soon engulf Europe sent Huxley and Heard westward (Isherwood would follow later), and on April 7, 1937, Heard and his lover Christopher Wood, Huxley and Maria, and their son, Matthew, sailed for America. Settling in Hollywood, Huxley found work in the film studios through his friendship with Anita Loos, although his writing style was not really suited to script writing. Along with a Hollywood social life that included Charlie Chaplin, Greta Garbo, and Harpo Marx, he studied yoga with Jiddu Krishnamurti, and with Heard and later Isherwood explored Hindu philosophy at the white-domed temple of the Vedanta Society.

Vedanta had begun in the 1800s among followers of a Bengali mystic named Ramakrishna Paramahamsa and then come to America via his disciple, Swami Vivekananda, who took part in the 1893 Parliament of the World's Religions in Chicago. Among the swami's first American disciples was a woman named Carrie Mead Wyckoff, later Sister Lalita, who happened to live in Southern California.

The swami died in 1902, but Sister Lalita carried on and in 1938 helped open the Hollywood Vedanta temple, something of a miniature Taj Mahal, just in time for Huxley and Heard to add enormous energy to their cause. Vedanta would be central to Heard's life for some years, editing the society's journals until his doubts about the swami's holiness cost him his faith. More skeptical, Huxley would feel greater affinity for the independent Krishnamurti, who had remained in Ojai despite parting ways with the Theosophists.

In 1941, Heard and Isherwood established a nonsectarian and nondogmatic spiritual commune called Trabuco College south of Los Angeles in Orange County. It mixed pantheism, Buddhism, yoga, and Quakerism and welcomed guest lecturers like Huxley, Zen scholar D. T. Suzuki, and Walter Evans-Wentz, an American Theosophist who had returned from travels in Asia with a translation of the Tibetan *Bardo Thos Grol*, which he rather fancifully dubbed *The Tibetan Book of the Dead*, publishing it at Oxford in 1927.

Eventually, the job of actually running Trabuco fell to Heard, who was not qualified, and he closed it in 1947. As he explored religions at Trabuco, Huxley did the same from a shack in Llano, a spot on the map in the desert northeast of Los Angeles, and worked on his book *The Perennial Philosophy*, which traced the common aim of all religions, "liberation from prevailing conventions of thought, feeling and behavior."

In addition to religion, esoteric "classical" music was one of the more influential elements of alternative culture in Los Angeles. On April 23, 1939, a married couple—Frances Mullen, a pianist, and Peter Yates, an amateur pianist who dabbled in poetry, philosophy including Krishnamurti, and

Los Angeles and the Émigrés 21

aesthetics—put on the first of an ongoing series of concerts called Evenings on the Roof. Tickets for the all-Bartok show were fifty cents; nineteen attended. They would go on to present chamber music from contemporary avant-garde (Charles Ives) to very old to Bach with the slogan, "The concerts are for the pleasure of the performers and will be played regardless of audience."

Their timing was fortuitous, because the war brought exiles like Arnold Schoenberg, Igor Stravinsky, and Arthur Rubinstein to Southern California, all of whom would attend and at times contribute to the series. Drawing on top-line performers from the Los Angeles Philharmonic and the film studios, Yates pushed his performers to be as free as possible.

One of the composers Mullen and Yates programmed was named John Cage, who would influence art music in America for the next fifty years. Born in Los Angeles in 1912, he was a child of the modern, a young piano student equally interested in Gertrude Stein's writing style and the work of Marcel Duchamp. Among his earliest musical influences were the compositions of Henry Cowell, who'd grown up on the edge of San Francisco's Chinatown and whose music reflected Asian microtones.

In his twenties, Cage became part of the intellectual scene surrounding the collector/dealer/painter Galka Scheyer, who had founded the Blue Four artists' group that included Paul Klee and Wassily Kandinsky. Scheyer's circle embraced the photographer Edward Weston, the art collectors Walter and Louise Arensberg, Bertolt Brecht, Charlie Chaplin, Greta Garbo, and Marlene Dietrich, a very heady atmosphere indeed for a talented young man.

As Cage focused on music, he studied the Italian futurist painter and composer Luigi Russolo, whose *The Art of Noises* was particularly important to him. Given Schoenberg's prominence in the Los Angeles music world, it was inevitable that Cage would try out the twelve-tone system, but he had no feeling for the sound of it, nor for harmony in general, which meant that his early work tended toward percussion. Schoenberg wouldn't listen to Cage's compositions, but the dancers Cage wrote for liked them.

In 1938, Cage went off to the Bay Area to attend Mills College, where he met the San Francisco avant-garde composer Lou Harrison, introducing himself with the comment, "Henry Cowell sent me." Not long after, Cage moved on to Seattle, where he met the dancer Merce Cunningham. The two would come to widening cultural influence over the next several decades.

22 **The Last Great Dream**

* * *

The dry, sunny climate that had made Los Angeles a refuge for TB patients as early as the turn of the century, along with the development of Hollywood and the film industry, seemed to invite a concern for beauty and bodies, for health and diet. Soon after, Los Angeles became the home to alternative medicine such as naturopaths and chiropractors and then to dietary missionaries, advocates for alfalfa sprouts and wheat germ and vegetarianism. By the 1950s, vegetarian restaurants like the Aware Inn and the Health Hut were thriving.

The most colorful and charming of these phenomena were imports, German followers of *Lebensreform* (life reform) called the *Naturmenschen* (nature men and women). Long-haired and bearded, they advocated free love and a mix of "Germanic myth and Rousseauian nature worship." Their legend crested with Nat King Cole's 1948 hit song "Nature Boy," written by Eden Ahbez, who was one.

In the end, it would be one of Aldous Huxley's many esoteric pursuits—he'd practiced vegetarianism and also studied parapsychology—that would have the deepest and widest impact on American life: the study of psychedelic drugs. Peyote and psychoactive mushrooms had been available so long as humans had existed, but it was the work of Albert Hofmann, who had discovered the psychedelic properties of lysergic acid diethylamide (LSD) in 1943, that would come to be of special importance.

Synthesizing derivatives from ergot fungus in search of an analeptic, a restorative to treat depression, ADHD, or respiratory inhibition, he'd made the twenty-fifth derivative in 1938. Five years later, acting on what he called a "peculiar presentiment," he made a fresh batch and accidentally ingested the tiniest amount through his skin. He found himself in a new world, one of a "remarkable but not unpleasant state of intoxication…characterized by an intense stimulation of the imagination and an altered state of awareness of the world." Two days later, he deliberately tossed down 250 micrograms and became entirely incapacitated. It was just a few weeks after Enrico Fermi had achieved fission in Chicago. Gerald Heard would later quip that LSD was simply "God's way of saving man from the Bomb."

The psychedelic experience was one of the fundamental elements that would create the counterculture of the 1960s. It was clearly a manifestation of what one might term the Old Religion (shamanism, paganism) and the Mysteries as against doctrinal Christianity or the objectivist reliance on the measurable.

Ironically, although Western drug experimentation had a history going back at least to the English romantic poets Samuel Taylor Coleridge and Thomas De Quincey, in postwar America the Central Intelligence Agency would assume the role. Working from the assumption that the drug could potentially be used as a truth serum, it began studying LSD in 1953 with a program called MK-ULTRA, having already recruited some of the German scientists who'd studied the peyote derivative mescaline under Nazi auspices.

Using a wide-ranging network of both psychologists and CIA operatives, they tested it on subjects who had given permission and were aware of what was happening...and those who had not given permission and were entirely unaware why life had suddenly become peculiar. Perhaps the ripest example of the latter was the Midnight Climax program in San Francisco, run by a Federal Bureau of Narcotics agent named George White, who observed bordello customers who'd unknowingly been slipped LSD by their hostesses. The agency's psychologists termed LSD a *psychotomimetic*, in the belief that it replicated the experience of schizophrenia, which in the case of White's victims was perhaps not entirely unreasonable.

On the more ethical side, Dr. Humphry Osmond was studying the possible therapeutic use of hallucinogens on alcoholism and wrote about his work in a 1952 article in the *Journal of Mental Science*, "Schizophrenia: A New Approach." Huxley read the article and wrote to Osmond suggesting that mescaline might not be mimicking psychosis but might help people understand mystical enlightenment by "permitting the 'other' world to rise into consciousness."

Osmond visited Los Angeles for an American Psychiatric Association gathering and came equipped. On May 4, 1953, sitting in his study on La Brea Avenue in West Hollywood, Huxley proceeded to swallow four-tenths of a gram of mescaline dissolved in half a glass of water. When it had taken effect, he looked at three flowers and understood that he was "seeing what Adam had seen on the morning of his creation—the miracle, moment by moment of naked existence...a transience that was yet eternal life, a perpetual perishing that was at the same time pure Being, a bundle of minute, unique particulars in which, by some unspeakable and yet self-evident paradox, was to be seen the divine source of all existence." The survival needs of evolution, he came to understand, had imposed a sort of reducing valve on the brain's sensory intake. The drug loosened the valve.

Being Huxley, he immediately wrote about it, dashing off in a month an essay he named after the image in William Blake's poem *The Marriage of Heaven and Hell*: "If the doors of perception were cleansed every thing would appear to man as it is, infinite." The intrinsically prejudicial expression *psychotomimetic* gave way to a new nomenclature coined by Osmond—*psychedelic*, mind-manifesting. Two years after the mescaline experience, Gerald Heard introduced Huxley to a former OSS captain named Al Hubbard, one of the mysterious spooks who floated around the fringes of the LSD world. At Christmas 1955, Huxley took LSD for the first time, learning, in Osmond's words, "what came through the closed door was the realization...the direct, total awareness, from the inside, so to say, of Love as the primary and fundamental cosmic fact."

The Doors of Perception was published in 1956. His reflections wandered through art history and the philosophy of education: "In a world where education is predominantly verbal, highly educated people find it all but impossible to pay serious attention to anything but words and notions." He concluded, wisely, "Systematic reasoning is something we could not, as a species or as individuals, possibly do without. But neither, if we are to remain sane, can we possibly do without direct perception, the more unsystematic the better, of the inner and outer worlds into which we have been born."

Though poorly reviewed, *The Doors* sold well, and across the country, those inclined to explore consciousness learned of a new and astonishingly efficient accelerant for these inner travels. The seeds that would blossom in the Haight-Ashbury neighborhood were beginning to germinate.

4

Post-World War II Greenwich Village

Greenwich Village had been the capital of American freethinking at least since Walt Whitman held court at Pfaff's tavern in the 1850s, and it played host to such important examples of the modern twentieth century as Max Eastman's the *Masses* and Margaret Anderson and Jane Heap's *Little Review*. As early as 1914, the Village was the site of a peyote ritual conducted by Mabel Dodge Luhan as "an experiment in consciousness." She had a wonderful time, floating "filled with smug laughter for all the 'facile enthrallments of humanity…anarchy, poetry, systems, sex, society.'" Decades later, the Village was still home to the experimental.

Several phenomena dominated Village culture after World War II, most notably psychoanalysis, abstract expressionism, and jazz, which was the soundtrack to Village life throughout the decade of the '50s. The style that mattered most had its birthplace at the Hotel Cecil on 118th Street. Henry Minton was a saxophonist and the first Black delegate to Local 802 of the American Federation of Musicians (AFM) when he opened Minton's Playhouse in the hotel. His official status sheltered the room from union rules that banned unpaid public jam sessions, and young players like Dizzy

Gillespie, Thelonious Monk, Charlie Parker, and Kenny Clarke gathered there to experiment with the fundamentals of music and incubate a musical revolution. For the first time, young Black players began to create a music that was not first oriented to entertainment and dancing. The new style was art music that required virtuoso abilities and a new sensibility.

They called it *bebop*; fans shortened it to *bop*. It was, wrote a white fan named John Clellon Holmes, "not merely expressive of the discords and complexities we were feeling, but specifically separated us from the times just passed, for even our jazz idols of the thirties mostly loathed it." As Holmes's friend Allen Ginsberg, another of the young white fans who were deeply moved and inspired by bop, paraphrased Plato, "When the mode of the music changes, the walls of the city shake."

Thanks especially to the efforts of Harry Anslinger, the head of the Federal Bureau of Narcotics, bop would always be associated with drugs, both marijuana and heroin. Anslinger in turn linked drugs to race, using the specter of demonic Negro jazz musicians to pass the marijuana tax in 1937 and thereafter staging selective arrests of musicians—Louis Armstrong, Dizzy Gillespie, and Billie Holiday among them—to maintain the fiction that the bureau was keeping the nation pure and uncorrupted by alien substances and influences.

In the 1940s and into the next decade, the remarkable fertility of jazz attracted a significant subset of young white bohemians interested in alternatives, men like the writer Jack Kerouac, turned on to life by jazz and to marijuana by the legendary Lester Young, who would be deft not only with his horn but his language, contributing the expressions *cool*, *I got eyes for that*, *bread*, *crib*, and *dig* to American slang—code words for an emerging subculture.

The other exciting music of New York in the late 1940s and the '50s was also consciously progressive. As a composer, John Cage operated from a truly singular premise that included silence as part of the span of music. He also valued rhythm above the other primary elements of music (pitch, timbre, amplitude, and duration), since duration alone applied to both sound *and* silence. Modern music, he thought, sought the liberation of dissonance. But the newest music, his music, was "the attempt to liberate all audible sound from the limitations of musical prejudice."

One day, he had to compose a piece for dancers in a tiny space that could hold only a piano, an instrument he was not fond of that was also not ideal for choreography. Recalling his teacher Henry Cowell's example in reaching into the body of the piano to strike and pluck the strings, Cage wedged bolts and erasers between the piano strings and turned it into a percussion instrument, the prepared piano.

He also spent time with the painters Morris Graves and Mark Tobey and the author Nancy Wilson Ross. All were serious students of Buddhism and specifically Zen—Tobey had just spent a month in a monastery in Kyoto—and their talk of emptiness (as paired with form) confirmed for him the inclusion of silence as a fundamental element of his art.

Moving on to New York City in 1942, Cage and his wife, Xenia, stayed first at the home of Peggy Guggenheim, the owner of the leading modern gallery Art of This Century. A jealous diva, she evicted them when he performed at the rival Museum of Modern Art, and they moved into the apartment of the scholar and folklorist Joseph Campbell and his wife, dancer/choreographer Jean Erdman, who were away for the summer while Erdman taught at Bennington College. Grateful, Cage began to compose for her, putting his art at the center of what was au courant in the Village. His friend Merce Cunningham had been recruited by Martha Graham, for whom dance was movement rather than storytelling. In kind, Cage thought sound was sound, not an expression of something else.

Although the surrealist refugees (as well as simpatico intellectuals like the Villager Claude Lévi-Strauss) and abstract expressionist painters who prowled the Village during the war largely gathered at the Cedar Tavern, the Village's true bohemian HQ was the San Remo Café at 189 Bleecker Street. It was, wrote a young socialist activist named Michael Harrington, "a sort of Village United Nations. It was straight and gay; black, white, and interracial; socialist, communist, Trotskyist, liberal, and apolitical; literary, religious, pot smoking, pill popping, and even occasionally transvestite." The young poet Allen Ginsberg, "Cage, Miles Davis, Mary McCarthy, Delmore Schwartz, James Agee…Julian Beck and Judith Malina…[and] the editors of the *Partisan Review*" all frequented the place.

Around this time, Cage parted from Xenia and focused on his relationship with Cunningham, although they would not live together for another sixteen years. Cage also spent time with his San Francisco composer friend Lou Harrison, who'd pursued a lover to New York but had ended up bereft.

Harrison was very much of a piece politically with the gathering alternative culture, taking part in the boycott of a restaurant that discriminated against Black people and seeking new vistas in religion by studying Vedanta. Like so many other creative personalities of this era leaning into a divergent point of view, he was gay. Deeply spiritual and humanist, his sensibilities were very San Francisco versus the über-modern Cage. The sheer volume of street noise in New York City disturbed him, and eventually Lou would return to the Bay Area, where he belonged.

The music of Henry Cowell had connected the two young men during the period when Cage was in San Francisco, and their shared interest in percussion as the focus of their composing and their mutual openness to improvised instruments and thus unconventional sounds made them musical cohorts.

In the fall of 1938, Harrison had moved to North Beach and became close friends with the poet Elsa Gidlow, who would attend rehearsals for shows Cage and Harrison would put on a couple of years later at Mills College, across the bay in Oakland. She was fascinated by their arrangement of "brake drums… buffalo bells, [and] a dozen other exotic instruments." Harrison set several of Gidlow's poems to music, including "May Rain" (1941), in which the solo voice is accompanied by a tam-tam (a type of gong) and a prepared piano. By the time they met again in New York, Cage's and Harrison's composing styles had somewhat diverged, but they would remain close friends.

One night at the San Remo, Lou fell in with two people, Julian Beck and Judith Malina, who would be among the nexus points of Village alternative life for the next thirty years. They had met in 1943, she working as the hatcheck girl and sometime performer at Valeska Gert's Beggar Bar, he a painter and student at Yale. Although Beck was at least as attracted to men as women, they had fallen in love, the beginning of a long and frequently tumultuous relationship that lasted until his death in 1985.

Perhaps inspired by Gert, who had been Polly Peachum in the film of Brecht's *The Threepenny Opera*, Malina became a student at Brecht associate Erwin Piscator's Dramatic Workshop at the New School in 1945. The workshop faculty featured Group Theatre veterans Stella Adler and Lee Strasberg. Completely consumed by the notion of a theater of liberation, Malina and Beck began to scheme for what, some years later, would become the Living Theatre. She would learn much from Piscator, although her political orientation was never doctrinaire.

Post–World War II Greenwich Village

Even before meeting Beck, she had joined a group of poets on Wooster Street for a group reading and learned about philosophical anarchism, for which she felt an immediate affinity. Her next anarchist group included Beck, the writer Paul Goodman, the poet/composer Jackson Mac Low, and Robert Duncan, briefly in New York during the war. By no means a gang of bomb throwers, this was an anarchism modeled more on what one scholar identified as "a respect for the autonomy of all individuals."

In a journal entry reflecting on the night she'd met Beck, Malina wrote, "We are determined to shock the world and succeed in shocking ourselves. But the constant shock keeps us constantly awake." Their romance was a rocky one. In April 1944, Beck took up with a painter named Bill Simmons and spent the summer with him in Provincetown, Massachusetts, with Tennessee Williams writing *The Glass Menagerie* next door, Tennessee's former lover Paul Goodman around the corner, and the poet and anarchist Harold Norse and his lover Chester Kallman (who'd go on to be W. H. Auden's endlessly frustrating object of desire) also nearby. When drunk or angry with his future wife, Lee Krasner, Jackson Pollock would sample the gay scene as well.

Malina and Beck would finally marry in the fall of 1948, and their son, Garrick, would be born the following year. Their lives were an ongoing cultural banquet, with Malina's journal recording seeing Judith Anderson in Robinson Jeffers's adaptation of *Medea*—"She is a beast, half goddess, half hunted wolf"— the Broadway opening of T. S. Eliot's *The Cocktail Party*, and Dylan Thomas reading at the Ninety-Second Street YMHA, mixed with passing phases of interest in J. B. Rhine and his parapsychology experiments, working a Ouija board with their friend Harold Norse, and "reading L. Ron Hubbard...And Proust." They responded to the beginning of the Korean War by typing up five thousand labels and pasting them on mailboxes and signposts: "1) Answer War. Resist It Gandhi's Way. 2) Don't Let Politics Lead You to War. 3) War Is Hell." As she recovered from giving birth, Malina read *The Hero with a Thousand Faces*, Joseph Campbell's central contribution to Greenwich Village intellectual reading. Largely apolitical and personally conservative, Campbell was something of a joker in the Village deck; he was isolationist and anti–New Deal because he thought Roosevelt a warmonger.

But his work gave scholarly heft and depth to the emerging Village culture by giving voice to ancient myths and to a fundamental teaching—

that no culture, and certainly not the dominant Judeo-Christian culture of America—was superior to any other. Ultimately, he was a pantheist.

His marriage to Jean Erdman ensured his place at the center of Village life because the arts intersected in dance. As Elaine de Kooning would observe, "Artists, in fact, seemed to be the built-in audience for modern dancers, poets, and composers in the forties—and even more so in the fifties." Thus Erdman would perform percussion in Cage's first New York concert, Campbell would further introduce Cage to Eastern religion, and Cage would later bring together Campbell and his teacher D. T. Suzuki.

Hero was published in 1949 and spent a year on the bestseller list; Malina was not the only Villager who devoured it. As his biographer noted, "Campbell's thought is Apollonian in its classical sources and formal elegance, and Dionysian in its wild intoxication with the mysteries of transformation and transcendence." The newly emerging twentieth-century disciplines of religious history and folklore studies derived from the work of Freud and even more so of Jung, and Campbell worked as an art historian to document Jung's concepts of synchronicity, archetypes, and the collective unconscious, his scholarship arising from the same sources as the art of the surrealist émigrés who'd also settled in New York.

Campbell came to see the art of his neighbors, the abstract expressionists, as "function instead of proportion, operation instead of construction, dynamics instead of statics, infinite space instead of limited body." Rather like Buddhism, in fact. "The role of the artist I now understood as that of revealing through the world-surfaces the implicit forms of the soul, and the great agent to assist the artist in this work was the myth." "What Campbell sought to elucidate in his books and in all of his teaching," wrote his biographer, "was a spiritual method for the West, one equivalent to the great Eastern paradigm of spiritual awakening."

Malina wrote of Campbell in her journal, "He is under the delusion that he is a kind of a scientist, but he is a kind of poet, and if he were brave he would be a kind of sage." His work in introducing an appreciation for all cultures would have a significant impact across America, from the Village to San Francisco's North Beach.

5

The Village in the '50s

Larry Rivers was so deeply immersed in such a variety of the Village's arts and social patterns that he might serve as an icon for the place and time. He began as a pot-smoking white bebopper baritone saxophonist—"Though white-skinned we had black heart"—and shared classes at Juilliard with Miles Davis. Larry's closest friend was a pianist named Jack Freilicher, whose cousin was Chester Kallman, who would later live upstairs from Larry with his lover W. H. Auden.

More importantly, Jack's wife, Jane, was an artist, which inspired Larry. By 1947, he was taking lessons from the Village's painting mentor, Hans Hofmann. Soon, Rivers's work was taken up by John Bernard Myers, a partner in the Tibor de Nagy gallery, and Rivers had his first solo show there (as did Red Grooms, Grace Hartigan, and Helen Frankenthaler—Jane was one of a number of notable women who cracked the New York painters' boys club).

But perhaps one of the most interesting aspects of Rivers's life was his affair, despite his lifelong behavior as a heterosexual, with Frank O'Hara, a charismatic poet who seemed to embody the emerging openness to gay life of the '50s in the Village. Reflecting on it later, Larry told his Village friend

John Gruen that "there was something about homosexuality that seemed too much, too gorgeous, too ripe. I later came to realize that there was something marvelous about it because it seemed to be pushing everything to its fullest point."

This expressed, Rivers continued, "the 1950s exuberance of the Every-minute Theater of Gay Life starring my close friends. The stage changed every night....The cast was never the same. What remained the same were the gestures, the arms, fingers, lips, eyebrows, eyes, tossing heads. And the content of the short verbal bursts and abundant name and phrase dropping to signal how much Mallarmé and Valéry and Reverdy you'd read, in the original." It was a common trope to suggest that psychoanalysis and sexuality were the central thread of postwar New York creative intellectuals. Here was evidence.

It was unsurprising that O'Hara was his object of desire; he was enormously attractive to many people. "Larry Rivers once said there are at least forty people who could say Frank O'Hara was his best friend. So I was one of those," the poet Bill Berkson told John Gruen. Berkson recalled O'Hara "running to the theater, always in a hurry to get there, always out of breath getting out of a taxi, being at the New York City Ballet. Bursting into tears there. Just going wild—and those tremendous palpitating discussions out in the lobbies and in the bars across the street."

Gruen, a former head of publicity for Grove Press, was himself an interesting anomaly in Village sexual politics. Virgil Thomson, the composer and *Herald Tribune* music critic, hosted a largely gay salon in his rooms at the Chelsea Hotel. Having come to some fame by collaborating with his friend Gertrude Stein in the 1934 opera *Four Saints in Three Acts*, he would endear himself to penurious young composers like Lou Harrison (and Cage, Paul Bowles, and Elliott Carter) by giving them work as music reviewers. The salon also welcomed Leonard Bernstein, Tennessee Williams, and Frank O'Hara. Gruen was not only a guest of the salon but became a *Tribune* art and music critic, even though he was heterosexual, married to the painter and sometime model Jane Wilson. Along with Rivers and Larry's mentor Jane Freilicher, they were part of O'Hara's New York Poets cohort.

Gruen said of Freilicher that she had "the kind of hypersensitive but noncommittal personality that matched John's [Ashbery] and Frank O'Hara's generally offhand, intellectual style. The ground rule of their relationship was

The Village in the '50s

Wit At Any Cost." They were an interesting bunch, deeply engaged with the arts both intellectually and emotionally. Early on, Ashbery had decided that he could no longer write. Then he went to hear John Cage's *Music of Changes*. He told Gruen that it was "disjointed chords. It had very little rhythm and it just went on and on until you sort of went not *out* of your mind but *into* your mind. It seemed that anything was possible after listening to that."

The dance critic Edwin Denby remarked that "Frank O'Hara was a catalyst for me, although I was much older. But then, he was everybody's catalyst." O'Hara would make his mark not only as a poet but also with his day job, which began as a ticket seller at the Museum of Modern Art, moved on to an editorial job at *Art News*, and returned to MOMA as a curator.

Like most of the modern painters, Rivers was naturally a habitué of what he called the "G-spot of the art scene," the Cedar Tavern, at 24 University Place, as well as the Club, a loft on Eighth Street where the abstract expressionists gathered for serious discussions. "At the club there were no doubts about the necessity of being modern. It was inarguable. It was so inarguable that it wasn't even mentioned." None of the new painters had achieved any great commercial success in the early '50s, so that "it was like belonging to a church. Not receiving any rewards for making art somehow made the concerns even stronger. Art was not a career. Not yet." Eventually, Rivers's art would mix abstraction and narrative elements, to the point that he would be dubbed the godfather of '60s pop art.

The leading abstract expressionist painters—Pollock, de Kooning—had all endured the depression with aid from the WPA, then encountered the European masters who had fled the Nazis. Now they responded with something new. Using unconventional materials and modes in large, colorful works that reflected their New Deal mural training as well as the city itself, they produced a message of anti-conformity with what was ineluctably great art.

The media focused on the booze-fueled wild man aspects of Pollock's personality, although as his widow would observe he mostly worked. "And when he worked, he never drank. His drinking came in cycles, and it would always start before or after a painting period, never during."

*   *   *

In 1951, John Cage visited the anechoic chamber at Harvard so that he could truly experience silence, and it was a revelation; he learned that there was "no split between spirit and matter," as his biographer wrote; no dualism, in the words of the Zen scholar D. T. Suzuki, whose class Cage was attending at Columbia University. Everything is connected; all is one. His path was sound, but just as Zen teaches that emptiness is the same as the world of form, silence is part of music. The result was his revolutionary, disturbing composition "4'33"," which was not actually silent but presented the sound of the room and the audience. It was the ultimate minimalist statement and would challenge conventional notions of music for decades to come.

"4'33"" was an apotheosis that would befuddle many and put Cage into the "lunatic artist" category of popular culture, but it had been preceded by a performance that shook the artists quite as much. In May 1951, Cage put on "Imaginary Landscape #4," which involved twelve radios, twenty-four performers, including Lou Harrison, Harold Norse, and Jean Erdman, and lots of silence. Judith Malina thought it was "like a seashell's enigmatic perfection....Sitting through the concert wishing it were done with and wishing it would be there forever." Anti-atonalists hissed in the balcony. Harrison was a stagehand in an elegant dark suit for Virgil Thomson's "Capitals, Capitals." Harrison's "Canticle Number 3 for Five Percussionists" featured gongs, brake drums, cowbells, guitar, and lengths of pipe. He conducted, transformed; his hands were "like miraculous birds."

Around this time, Harrison gave Cage a copy of the *I Ching*, the Chinese method of divination, and Cage's compositional model shifted into the use of random chance, a process he thought would remove the ego, a further reflection of his studies in Zen. Not making decisions but asking questions, his music was, he said, "an affirmation of life—not an attempt to bring order out of chaos nor to suggest improvements in creation, but simply a way of waking up to the very life we're living."

Malina had especially focused on Harrison at the "Imaginary Landscape" show because she'd fallen in love with him, as she did with a succession of men. She later told Harrison's biographer that "we were an artistic community, striving to make sense of things...on the verge of tremendous social change" in a period of transition from the old Village bohemia to a newer version. Consequently, and

The Village in the '50s

for one of the very few times in his life as a generally gay man, Harrison woke up in bed with a woman. In a bit of a panic, he called her husband and asked him what to do. "Feed her breakfast and send her home," said Julian.

As many lovers as Malina took on, and there were times when she was only content when she returned home at dawn, her heart's desire was to establish the Living Theatre, a drive so essential that they created Theater in the Room for audiences of twenty in their living room. Their program for August 15, 1951, included a comic invention from Paul Goodman, a didactic play by Brecht, and Gertrude Stein's *Ladies' Voices*.

When Julian inherited some money, they were able to rent the Cherry Lane Theatre for a few months, finally opening the Living Theatre on a stage on December 2, 1951, with Gertrude Stein's *Doctor Faustus Lights the Lights*. They would receive a much-cherished love letter of praise for the effort from the poet William Carlos Williams, although the play was, put mildly, challenging. Its language was beyond dense. Far too long at three hours, it was "a sort of frozen sleepwalk through the classical period," wrote one scholar. Julian Beck thought Stein was the greatest playwright of the twentieth century.

Later that month they put on Kenneth Rexroth's *Beyond the Mountains*, and it did not go well. As Phaedra, Malina was carried onto the stage on a palanquin moaning Rexroth's stilted lines. "I freeze! I burn! I am hot! I am cold." At length, she burst into giggles, then shouted to pull down the curtain, but there wasn't one. (In Malina's version, it was an oboe player who laughed.)

Whoever laughed, it was a painful time for her. She resolved to enter therapy three days a week with the poet/playwright/social critic Paul Goodman, who had written *Gestalt Therapy* from Fritz and Lore Perls's notes and had undergone analysis with Lore. At least as promiscuous as Malina, Goodman advocated complete openness about sexuality and had earlier experienced Reichian therapy.

What made him a very poor choice as a therapist was that he was overwhelmingly patriarchal. A few years later, he would write the brilliant but lamentable post-Marxian social critique of the American educational system, *Growing Up Absurd*, directing it only at young men because women, he opined, could easily find all necessary fulfillment by giving birth.

When she told Goodman one day that she was "addled," he replied, "You are better that way." On another day, she wrote in her journal, he told her that there are "no woman artists…because a woman is too much concerned with her own body."

At least one of his recommendations was sound, although she did not take him up on it; he told her about Black Mountain College, near Asheville, North Carolina. Since the bulk of their friends would attend or teach at Black Mountain, it was not surprising that Goodman would bring it up. Founded in 1933 by refugees from a loyalty pledge debacle at Rollins College, Black Mountain was experimental, anti-hierarchical, interdisciplinary, and focused on the arts. There were no grades, requirements, or degrees. Its students would spread across the continent; many, like Ruth Asawa and John Ryan, landed in San Francisco.

Some of the most interesting minds in America would pass through the faculty. The Bauhaus designer Josef Albers and his wife, Anni, who worked in textiles, arrived in 1933. In the next twenty years, they were joined, for differing periods, by Walter Gropius, Willem de Kooning, and Robert Motherwell. Buckminster Fuller would teach and build his first large-scale geodesic dome there. Merce Cunningham formed his dance company there. The poet Charles Olson came to teach in 1948 and later became rector. His "militant insistence on subjectivity, self-expression, self-exposure" struck at least one student as "revolutionary." In the mid-'50s, Robert Duncan would teach there, and Olson and Robert Creeley would put out the *Black Mountain Review*.

It was at Black Mountain in the summer of 1952 that John Cage presented "Theater Piece #1," generally acknowledged as the first "happening." A multi-genre collective effort involving the poets M. C. Richards and Olson and the pianist David Tudor, it was a theater piece in which each performer had an amount of time to do something of their own choosing, without a rehearsal or script. Robert Rauschenberg draped the room in white, and Franz Kline added a black-and-white painting. Standing on ladders, the poets declaimed, and Cage read from a lecture on Zen and then the Bill of Rights and the Declaration of Independence. All the while, Merce Cunningham danced and films played. It was a theater not of narrative but of juxtaposition.

In spirit, it was what Malina and Beck dreamed of. At this point, however, the Living Theatre was longer on manic energy than almost anything else. Earlier in 1952 *Desire Trapped by the Tail* had generated enthusiasm and sold tickets with a cast that included "Bow-wows" John Ashbery and Frank O'Hara wearing dog costumes and simulating buggery.

The Village in the '50s

At the same time, Malina had taken up with cast member Philip Smith, and Beck had paired off with one of the actresses. Paul Goodman, Malina's therapist, was on the premises because they were about to begin rehearsals on his play *Faustina*, somewhat delayed because Goodman and Smith were screwing in the dressing room.

Creditors hounded them, cast members fell away, and in August, an authority, either ConEd regarding unpaid utilities bills or the fire marshal about almost anything, forced them to close.

Nothing loath, Malina took up with a new lover, James Agee, a self-confessed drunk then putting away a quart of whiskey a day, even as he managed to work on his masterful *A Death in the Family*. Malina clearly liked to dance with demons. At a dinner party one night, she fell into conversation with "unsettlingly handsome Joseph Campbell." Their conversation coursed over "arts, morality, Hindu sculptures, Lola Montez, witchcraft, insanity." Campbell, she wrote, believed in power and encouraged her to explore the dark arts. "There can be no real power," she attributed to him, "unless it is used for evil first." "He lies."

On June 19, 1953, Julius and Ethel Rosenberg were executed by the US government. At 2:00 a.m. the next day, Malina and Beck rose and took the subway to a Brooklyn funeral home to pay their respects. The Korean War ended with an armistice. They got out of town that September and visited Walden, Malina perceptively noting that "it was Thoreau's intense commitment to the actual that made him a visionary." In October, they rented a loft for a theater at One Hundredth and Broadway. Dylan Thomas died in November; Agee followed two years later. She tried mescaline.

In the end, the true poet's comment on the Village of the mid-'50s was made by Ted Joans, a young, trumpet-playing poet who also painted. Influenced by André Breton and Langston Hughes, he said, "Jazz is my religion, and Surrealism is my point of view." On March 12, 1955, he reacted to the premature death of his former roommate, Charlie "Yardbird" Parker, by sorrowfully going out into the Village night to leave a simple two-word graffiti that expressed mourning, respect for creativity, and love.

"Bird Lives!"

6

San Francisco in the Early '50s

In 1953, Lou Harrison wearied of living in New York City and returned to the Bay Area. One of his motivations was that life for a gay man was better in San Francisco. Post-Prohibition, the regulation of bars in California had been assumed by the State Board of Equalization, whereas in New York it fell to a separate State Liquor Authority. Tax people wanted sales and thus more tax revenue and did not concern themselves overmuch with the social milieu of the bars. The State Liquor Authority tended to criminalize gay behavior. As we have already seen, this clearly did little to slow the pursuit of partners, but the San Francisco model certainly made for greater ease.

San Francisco had been sexually loose from its inception. Largely male in the nineteenth century, it had been governed by a succession of corrupt city governments that protected the sex trade, gay or straight, and culminated in the de facto legalized prostitution of the Barbary Coast. Founded in 1908, the Dash was the first notorious gay bar there, with cross-dressing waiters who, for a sum, were available for services other than delivering drinks.

Since it was owned by a judge's clerk, it prospered until a combination of the approaching war and social "cleanup" efforts closed the district in 1917.

Prohibition was essentially ignored in San Francisco; the board of supervisors passed a resolution in 1926 barring the police department from enforcing it. Bars that welcomed gay men and lesbians began to emerge in the 1930s, most notably the Black Cat (initially a progressive bohemian hangout), directly across the street from police headquarters at the Hall of Justice. Lesbians went to Mona's 440, which opened in 1939 at 440 Broadway, complete with male impersonators as the waitstaff.

The military police brought heat during the war, arresting the bartender of the Black Cat in 1943, but the California Supreme Court would eventually decide for the bartender, affirming the civil right of gay people to assemble peacefully. After the war, Black Cat waiter and singer José Sarria would nurture the development of a conscious, politically engaged community with drag performances that, in the midst of McCarthyism, celebrated gay life with show-closing singalong performances of "God Save Us Nelly Queens."

Along with a more relaxed sexual atmosphere, San Francisco welcomed Lou home with a number of creative social institutions, including Robert Duncan's King Ubu Gallery, hip theater from the Interplayers, the uniquely left-wing/pacifist radio station KPFA, and the only-in-San-Francisco American Academy of Asian Studies.

In 1949, Robert Duncan moved into a cottage in the Berkeley Hills to help care for Jaime de Angulo, a legend of California alternative culture. Born in Paris of Spanish descent, de Angulo came to America to be a cowboy and became one of the first settlers on Partington Ridge in Big Sur. He got a medical degree from Johns Hopkins University, then became a significant linguistic anthropologist under the tutelage of the distinguished Alfred Kroeber at UC Berkeley, immersing himself so deeply in Native American culture that he would also tutor Duncan in shamanism. De Angulo would die in 1950.

Shortly before, Duncan had met his life partner, Burgess Collins, whose artist's nom de brush was simply Jess. A chemist with a degree from Cal Tech, Jess had worked on aspects of the Manhattan Project, but an apocalyptic

San Francisco in the Early '50s

dream awakened him to the horrors, and he left chemistry for art, enrolling at CSFA in the late 1940s to study with Clyfford Still, Elmer Bischoff, and others. He settled on collage, which he called "paste-ups," as his medium, and his aesthetic, wrote the *Chronicle* critic Alfred Frankenstein, was "romantic, visionary, literary." It was a medium, said Duncan, "for the life of the spirit."

Jess lived at 1350 Franklin Street, a building known as the Ghost House. Halfway between CSFA and North Beach and the jazz joints of the Fillmore, the Ghost House housed a fascinating collection of residents, including the poet Philip Lamantia, the artist Wally Hedrick, and a bebop musician, name forgotten, whom Rexroth would sometimes visit. It had a mysterious and potent ambience, said Hedrick, where "Thelonious Monk or Miles Davis might drop in, where drugs and parties were common." It was distinctly not like the rest of America. On January 1, 1951, Jess and Duncan shared what they described as "marriage vows." Duncan would never be monogamous, but their relationship would last.

Later that year, the filmmaker James Broughton fled McCarthyism for England, subletting his flat at 1758 Baker Street to Duncan and Jess. They were soon joined by filmmaker Stan Brakhage, who worked as their houseboy while attending CSFA. A little while later, the filmmaker and Aleister Crowley devotee Kenneth Anger began to visit.

Toward the end of 1952, Duncan, Jess, and another friend, the painter Harry Jacobus, opened the King Ubu Gallery at 3119 Fillmore Street. Over the next year, they would mount fifteen shows, with work by CSFA faculty members Bischoff, David Park, and Hassel Smith, Jess, Jacobus, and others as well as early Brakhage films. The first exhibitor was Still's student Mel Weitsman. It was a "casual and artist-involved gallery," observed Lyn Brown Brockway, the wife of one of the artists. The art filled the room haphazardly, not necessarily in the conventional simple eye-level horizontal line.

King Ubu was one of several alternative institutions that popped up in San Francisco in the early '50s. The Interplayers, a theater company formed out of friendships that began at Camp Angel in Waldport, was another. Martin Ponch had been part of a co-op theater group near Philadelphia, then became a conscientious objector and landed at Camp Angel, where he grew friendly with Kermit Sheets and Adrian Wilson, who visited San Francisco after the war and sensed that it was receptive to new ideas. The three of them, plus Adrian's wife, Joyce Lancaster, formed the theater group. They rehearsed at the (Quaker) Friends' Center on Sutter Street and put on work by Chekhov, Lorca, Shaw, Sartre, Stein, and James Broughton at various venues around the city.

Maintaining a theater group is a torturous challenge, and the group broke up in 1954. Wilson would go on to a distinguished career in fine-art printing, as did his erstwhile theatrical partner Sheets, who had founded the Centaur Press with James Broughton. Centaur published poetry and drama by Broughton, Anaïs Nin, and Duncan, whose *Medieval Scenes* attracted considerable notice.

The most significant gift of the conscientious objector world to Bay Area culture was the creation of "free speech radio" station KPFA. A CO named Lewis Kimball Hill had become head of the American Civil Liberties Union's (ACLU) National Committee on Conscientious Objectors during the war and decided that advancing the cause of pacifism in modern times called for the use of modern media like radio. The only place he could imagine such a thing happening was the Bay Area, and he arrived in 1946 to begin work.

One of his first recruitment stops was a meeting of Rexroth's Libertarian Circle. His pitch began poorly, with too much sociology; Rexroth dismissed radio as turning everything into "kitsch." "How? Why?" asked Hill, who wore him down with his passion, eventually gaining ground with the audience. His best first-day convert would be Eleanor McKinney, who had covered the United Nations conference in San Francisco for NBC radio. A student of Jung and Gurdjieff (Theosophy was another favorite topic of the early KPFA group), McKinney was a regular at the Black Cat and, per one friend, a "pre-1960s flower child."

Inevitably, there had been compromises. Forced out of the mass-audience AM world by wavelength saturation, they chose the more available realm of FM, which played well to the Berkeley faculty who would be their initial audience. Opposed to both the US military-industrial security state and the Stalinist US Communist Party and lacking a viable pacifist audience, KPFA became more a sanctuary for personal freedom and high culture than a vanguard for peace, less an "agent of change," wrote the station's historian, and more "a refuge from the storm" of McCarthyism.

The refugees could stay home and listen to classical music played by Alan Rich, jazz from a young record collector and California Labor School student

San Francisco in the Early '50s

named Phil Elwood, folk music from Gert Chiarito, who began the long-running Saturday night show *Midnight Special*, and opera on *Golden Voices*, hosted by a "beer-drinking, card-playing, pulp fiction editor" named Anthony Boucher.

Taking appropriate notice of the postwar tidal wave of babies, they put together a children's show that featured tapes of Jaime de Angulo, who'd turned his ethnography studies into a well-received collection of Native American stories, *Indian Tales*. One knowledgeable critic would cite it as "thoroughly Indian and a real tale told, not written." A man who'd changed identities throughout his life, de Angulo was the ideal person to present what KPFA's historian called "a forgiving world of limitless possibilities" for their youngest audience members. For more sophisticated minds, said one observer, he was an avatar who represented "an escape from the conventional and the discovery of *dharma* on the Big Sur coast."

Three voices would embody KPFA to most listeners: Kenneth Rexroth, Pauline Kael, and Alan Watts. "Each," as the station's historian put it, "in his or her unique fashion tried to show Cold War America a way out." Rexroth's program, *Books*, mixed Buddhism and Asian thought with a sophisticated, wide-ranging knowledge of world politics and literature. One of his shows, for instance, covered the "Bloomsbury group, imperialism, Lenin, and Trotsky in one breath and [then told] his listeners what to get their Scout nephew or niece for Christmas in the next" (a book about fossils).

Kael brought popular culture, specifically film, to KPFA. After living with James Broughton, she had moved out and given birth to their daughter, Gina, then married a man who owned twin repertory cinemas in Berkeley. There she selected and annotated the programs, a job that carried her to her radio show before going on to glory at the *New Yorker* as perhaps the nation's greatest film critic.

The station's first PR director was Gerd Stern, a Black Mountain College dropout and sometime poet ("My poetry is not of a very acceptable style, it's too abstract and obscure for most people") who would have more of a personal impact later in the decade as a visual artist. One of his greatest contributions to the station was to convince the philosopher Alan Watts to begin a show on Buddhism and Eastern thought that ran from 1953 until Watts's death in 1973. In many ways, Watts introduced Buddhism and kindred notions to an American mass audience.

Locke McCorkle, in coming years a key figure in the scene, saw Watts as the root voice of the era. He "gave us a whole different way of looking at reality." Never doctrinaire, he "thought everybody in the religious business was an entertainer"—and he was certainly entertaining. There was, thought one friend, more than a little of the Native American trickster folk figure Coyote in Watts's persona. He was ethically ambiguous and unconventional, at times highly dignified, at times a drunken fool.

Born in England, Watts had become interested as a teen in Asian culture through the writings of Sax Rohmer and Lafcadio Hearn. A mentor gave him Buddhist books and introduced him to the heart of Buddhism in England, a man named Christmas Humphreys, and he began to study. Either as an act of resistance or a failure of nerve, Watts botched the process for entering university and set out on what his biographer called a "career as an outsider."

What Watts himself termed his fundamental stance as an "unrepentant sensualist" brought him closest to the Taoist tradition of drunken hermit monks. In the 1930s, he met Frederic Spiegelberg, a German scholar of Asian thought who'd studied with Tillich, Heidegger, and Jung. Spiegelberg set Watts to reading Vedanta, Christian mystics, and Jung; Watts would spend the rest of his life connecting Buddhism and Christianity and the healing effects of psychotherapy.

In 1937, Watts met a wealthy student of Zen named Ruth Fuller Everett and her daughter, Eleanor, whom he married the next year, grateful for the comforts that came from being part of their social stratum. Fleeing the coming war, in 1938 they all moved to New York, where Mrs. Everett continued her Zen studies with Shigetsu Sasaki, an artist, laborer, and independent Buddhist teacher of many decades who'd founded the Buddhist Society of America. Watts studied with Sasaki as well.

Now widowed, Ruth married Sasaki and set up the First Zen Institute of America in 1941, but soon lost her husband to internment. Though she managed to secure his release, incarceration had ruined his health, and he died in 1945.

Since Watts needed a job, he decided—a "sincere, but not serious" choice—to become an Episcopalian priest. He tap-danced his way into the seminary with the help of a sympathetic bishop, read his way through graduate school, and was ordained in 1944. He would concede that it was a mistake: "To be precise, I am not so much a priest as a shaman. The difference is that whereas a priest is a duly ordained corporate officer and caste member in an agrarian culture, a shaman is a loner who gets his thing from the wilds and is usually found in hunting cultures."

His belief in sexual pantheism and opposition to monogamy—and, according to one biographer, his English boarding school taste for flagellation—brought his marriage to an end in the late 1940s, and after briefly studying with Joseph Campbell in New York, Watts came to San Francisco in 1951 to take up a position at possibly the most interesting of all the San Francisco alternative institutions, the American Academy of Asian Studies (AAAS). Pipe-smoking, with a mellifluous English accent, he was a smallish man who wore a short goatee. Somehow, he was perfect for the academy.

It could only have taken shape in San Francisco, the place where Asia truly touched the continental US via the immigration of many thousand Cantonese to Gum Saan, Gold Mountain. Chinatown there was not a tourist fantasy but home, where Sacramento Street was Tong Yun Gai (Street of the Chinese).

The only thing in Chinatown that was movie-set-like was the architecture, which was part of a canny maneuver on the part of local merchants. After the 1906 earthquake and fire leveled much of the city, the board of supervisors made plans to move Chinatown to the southeast part of the city. The merchants Look Tin Eli and Tong Bong planned and swiftly built an "Oriental" dream of a district with elaborate pagoda-like decorations. The positive reception made moving Chinatown out of the question.

The AAAS was initially the vision of Louis Gainsborough, a San Francisco businessman with Asian interests who thought Americans should know more about the world across the Pacific. He primarily wanted a school that would train emissaries to do business there, although he accepted that a deeper understanding of the cultural differences was required. He chose Frederic Spiegelberg, by now teaching at Stanford, to put it together. Spiegelberg in turn invited Haridas Chaudhuri, a professor of philosophy and student of Sri Aurobindo, and what Gainsborough got was a laboratory for multiculturalism and East–West fusion. The faculty added Watts, then Sir C. P. Ramaswamy Aiyar, Rom Landau in Islamic studies, and a Thai scholar and princess, Poon Pismai Diskul.

They established themselves at 2030 Broadway Street and arranged sponsorship as a graduate school with the College of the Pacific in Stockton. Accreditation meant students and funds, but as Watts acknowledged, their actual program concerned "the practical transformation of human consciousness, with the actual living out of the Hindu, Buddhist, and Taoist ways of life at the level of high mysticism."

"In retrospect one can see that the Academy of Asian Studies was a transitional institution emerging from the failure of universities and churches to satisfy spiritual needs," wrote Watts. "Thus our participatory approach to these cultures was as strange to Orientalists at the University of California as it was disturbing to Methodists at the College of the Pacific."

While it lasted, it was an exceptionally fertile garden of learning. Watts would recall that one of his colloquia was attended by a remarkable group of painters, including Mark Tobey, Gordon Onslow Ford, Lee Mullican, and Jean Varda. Among the students were Michael Murphy and Richard Price, who would go on to establish the New Age center of consciousness exploration, the Esalen Institute.

Chaudhuri introduced yogic concepts of holistic healing to American culture at AAAS. Hodo Tobase, the priest at Sokoji, San Francisco's Japantown community temple, taught calligraphy, in particular to Gordon Onslow Ford, who found in calligraphy a metaphysical sense of the spirit that surrealism lacked for him. D. T. Suzuki, the Zen scholar teaching at Columbia University, visited and spoke, as did Watts's former mother-in-law, Ruth Fuller Sasaki. Watts met the Japanese artist and theoretician Saburo Hasegawa and immediately convinced him to come and teach.

Two AAAS students, fledgling poets Philip Whalen and Gary Snyder, would go on to make their own marks on the local and even national culture. Seven years older, Whalen would be Snyder's *kalyanamitra* (noble friend) and older brother. They had met at Reed College in the late '40s, and they were learned and smart. But Whalen was "kind of nuts," said Snyder. He "never adapted to reality, quite." He simply could not bear the normal, tedious consequences of working at jobs, all of which he hated beyond reason.

Snyder, on the other hand, was practical. Raised on a hardscrabble farm north of Seattle, he had an intimate relationship with the land, both as food source—he fished, clammed, picked berries—and as spiritual stimulus, climbing Mount Hood and other Cascade peaks by his early teens. Around the age of twelve, he saw Chinese sumi-e landscape paintings in the Seattle art museum and soon began to explore Asian philosophy, a pursuit he and Whalen would share for the rest of their lives.

He graduated from Reed College in 1951 with a major in Native American studies, and while hitchhiking to graduate school in folklore at Indiana University, he read D. T. Suzuki's *Essays in Zen Buddhism*. Graduate school convinced him that the academic world was not for him, and when he read Kenneth Rexroth's *The Signature of All Things*, he decided that San Francisco was.

There he reconnected with Whalen. They shared a place in North Beach while Snyder took classes in Chinese and sumi-e painting at UC Berkeley, and less formal classes by regularly attending Rexroth's weekly salon. Though Broughton would note Rexroth's sometimes prickly demeanor in teaching social anarchy and a formal approach to writing, Snyder observed that while Rexroth did not invite too many people, he rarely told anyone to go away. And people like Duncan certainly felt no obligation to fall into line with Rexroth's opinions.

Snyder and Rexroth shared profound interests in environmentalism, anarchism, and Asian philosophy, but where Rexroth used the natural world as a setting for "personal and philosophical allegories," Snyder's poetry would give nature considerably more autonomy. Such differences did not interfere with their mutual appreciation for the salon as a rich and satisfying place. Snyder would recall that the poets there "nourished each other in a grand way." He supported himself by working as a fire lookout in the summers of 1952 and 1953 in the North Cascades in Washington.

One day at AAAS, Snyder met Ruth Fuller Sasaki, who had by now established a study and translation center at the Zen monastery complex Daitoku-ji in Kyoto. She invited him to join the work there, and his classes now became preparations for studying in Japan. He would depart the Bay Area in May 1956.

By 1957, the College of the Pacific would withdraw its support, and AAAS would collapse financially; Chaudhuri would take what remained and eventually create the California Institute of Integral Studies. That year, Watts would publish his book *The Way of Zen*, a significant element in the introduction of Zen to America that truly began his career as a freelance shaman.

7

Mainstream America and San Francisco's First Resistance

It would be useful to consider the mainstream America of 1954 that the poets, artists, and students of AAAS inhabited.

Gary Snyder was not able to work as a fire watcher in 1954 because his union membership had tagged him as suspect, and he couldn't get a security clearance. He was one of thousands. Though linked to a particular senator as "McCarthyism," the virulent anti-Communist ideology of the era was seated in a fear of the modern that had erupted after World War I as the "Red Scare" and had never gone away. Mixed with xenophobia and hatred of atheism—"godless communism"—it defined patriotism as Americanism, and Americanism as support for bare-knuckle capitalism, Christianity, and the nuclear family.

An essential if unspoken aspect of the anti-Communist hysteria of the '50s lay in the Right gaining revenge for the New Deal, visible in the House Un-American Activities Committee's (HUAC) first report, which defined

50   **The Last Great Dream**

as un-American a belief in "absolute social and racial equality." But the hunt for deviations from the norm took on a life of its own in the first Eisenhower administration when his Executive Order 10450 announced that "alcoholism, drug addiction, communism, sexual deviation, mental illness [and] membership in a nudist colony" were sufficient to disqualify one from government service. Ten thousand people lost their government jobs under Eisenhower, at least half of them due to their sexual identity. No spy was ever found in federal employ.

The obsession with loyalty twisted the very policies meant to deal with real threats. Senator Joseph McCarthy was a morphine addict whose drug supplier was Federal Bureau of Narcotics boss Harry Anslinger—the two men had agreed that the chance of this news leaking would be harmful to American interests. At the same time, Anslinger and McCarthy were attributing opiate traffic in the US to the Chinese, although they both knew the source was the Mafia. Since FBI director J. Edgar Hoover would not even publicly acknowledge the existence of the Mafia, the authorities were happy, in an Orwellian sort of way.

Simultaneously, the Central Intelligence Agency had shifted from its mandated intelligence-gathering function to covert paramilitary operations, toppling regimes identified as anti-American in Iran and then Guatemala. America had become a full-blown empire. The nation's absolute military superiority, combined with its stunning prosperity and the admiration of much of the world, served to confirm the bedrock notion of national exceptionalism, the idea that the US was uniquely—as though ordained by God—virtuous and deserving of its good fortune.

That this carried with it an implicit sense of racial superiority went largely unspoken. The religious aspect was much more overt. Though he'd never attended church before, Eisenhower regarded his role as president as the minister in chief of the American people, with a clear bias in favor of a vaguely Protestant and explicitly Christian slant: in his words, "Recognition of the Supreme Being is the first, the most basic, expression of Americanism."

On February 7, 1954, as a traditional part of honoring Abraham Lincoln's birthday, Eisenhower attended services in the Lincoln pew at Washington's New York Avenue Presbyterian Church. The minister's sermon observed that there was no religious reference in the Pledge of Allegiance and that the phrase *under God* had been part of Lincoln's Gettysburg Address. A bill to insert the phrase was passed and signed into law in June. Within two years, *Under God* had replaced *E Pluribus Unum* (from many, one) as the national slogan imprinted on currency.

Public opinion so completely linked Christianity to American patriotism that 60 percent of respondents in one survey said they would not permit a book by an atheist in a public library. Eighty-four percent opposed allowing atheists the right to teach. And although the only thing about Communists respondents were absolutely sure of was that "the Commies" were against religion, 89 percent favored firing Communists from college teaching posts.

Even more closely attuned to the American mood, Norman Vincent Peale preached *The Power of Positive Thinking* as a pathway to wealth. A shallow fusion of Babbitt-like self-persuasion and the gospel of gold, it sat atop the bestseller list for 112 weeks.

Uneasy academic intellectuals dismissed the idea of competing interests and expounded the notion of an American consensus. Richard Hofstadter argued that the populism of the 1890s was a psychological response to anxiety rather than anything to do with class conflict. Since Joe McCarthy was seen as a populist rather than as the cat's-paw of a resurgent Republican Party, populism was anathema. It was time, thought academics, for the elite to be in charge.

That opinion spilled over into literature, where the New Critics stressed expertise, nuance, and the displacement of art from any social or political context. Silence followed. "The young complacent of America," wrote one of the rare remaining social critics, C. Wright Mills, "the tired old fighters, the smug liberals, the shrill ladies of jingoist culture—they are all quite free. Nobody locks them up. Nobody has to. They are locking themselves up."

Coming after an apocalyptic depression, the social fact of great prosperity had led to a near worship of the corporate economy and the hasty conclusion that class conflict was at an end. The notion that pretty much everyone was middle class grew, as the writer Tom Wolfe would smirk a few years later: "After all, this is a nation that, except for a hard core of winos at the bottom and a hard crust of aristocrats at the top, has been going gloriously middle class for two decades." That this was arrant nonsense, as Michael Harrington's *The Other America* would soon document, was a distinctly minority opinion.

In the course of the '50s, family income did in fact nearly double. America was awash in chrome and Formica, and in all manner of new goodies. As one historian summed it up: "TV and hi-fi, frozen, low-calories, and instant foods, aerosol containers and electronic garbage disposals, power steering and power transmission, the entire field of synthetic chemistry." Another new item, credit cards, made it all possible. Thrift was obsolete, and debt was normalized. Americans got what they wanted when they wanted it.

Keeping the empire's internal economic engine running became the job of television, which, by the end of the decade, was in 90 percent of American homes. Primarily a vehicle for advertising, television sold the basic notion that one couldn't be happy (or sexy or popular) without buying...fill in the blank. This went beyond simple capitalism to a deification of consumerism, with advertising that gave absolution for buying luxury items—and going into debt. The other television fundamental was violence, which was always punished but was simultaneously celebrated as the focal point of "dramatic" television.

The era's comedies followed suit. Cloaked in rigid censorship that permitted nothing that might offend Southern stations, and certainly nothing that could be seen as anti-capitalist, it taught stereotypes: Smoking is good for you, men run things, women are intellectually limited, and life is to buy. In the world of *Leave It to Beaver* and *Father Knows Best*, there were no class divisions, no ethnic variety, no divorce, no alcoholism, no mental illness or conflict in marriage. It was the America of Eisenhower's dreams.

If one sought out some shred of emotional realism in '50s American culture, it would have to be in the theater. Congruent with the postwar Manhattan focus on psychoanalysis, American acting had embraced the Method, a series of exercises designed to access feelings, which had been developed by Konstantin Stanislavski in the 1920s. Established in America by Lee Strasberg, Harold Clurman, and Cheryl Crawford as the Group Theatre, it would morph into two schools, Strasberg's the Actors Studio, and Stella Adler's version, the Studio of Acting at the New School. Working from the slogan "Don't Act, Behave," she would teach Rod Steiger, Shelley Winters, Ben Gazzara, and the ne plus ultra of Method actors, Marlon Brando.

The Cold War had frozen America's emotions in fear, and the new style of theater would be an implicit protest. Brando would be, said his biographer, the "macho outsider, the American male who cares so deeply he must pretend not to care at all."

On December 3, 1947, *A Streetcar Named Desire* opened at the Barrymore Theatre, presenting in Brando a whirlwind of desire, sensitivity, and brutality, eight shows a week. A "wild, sexy rebel," Camille Paglia wrote of him; "Mumbling, muttering, flashing with barbaric energy, [he] freed theatrical emotion from its enslavement by words...all mute and surly bad attitude, [he] prefigured the great art form of the Sixties generation: rock and roll." *The Wild One* wrapped him in black leather and burnished his erotic, defiant, hipster persona: "What are you rebelling against?" "Waddya got?"

James Dean followed the same intuitive path, brilliantly illuminating the screen with a persona that was equal parts disillusioned, alienated youth and master actor. His meteoric career encompassed just three films, most notably *Rebel Without a Cause*, the third work not even released when he died at the wheel of his Porsche on September 30, 1955.

In addition to these films, San Franciscans had another source for serious theater, the Actor's Workshop (AW), not to be confused with New York City's, though both shared roots in the Group Theatre. Two professors at SF State, Jules Irving and Herbert Blau, were married to two actresses, Priscilla Pointer and Beatrice Manley, respectively.

Initially, Blau had seen their theater group as a salve for his marital insecurities and a way to hold on to his wife. It was not long before he realized that they were also trying to develop "a counter-atmosphere in which the special properties of the dramatic form, devoted to crisis, are enlisted against the epidemic of mystifications (i.e., the Cold War)" in a way that was not polemical but "communal, playful, protestant, and life-giving." Their mission, Blau wrote, was to "fight the barbarians at every turn" and come to "an act of communion at the risk of outrage."

As the AW progressed from its start in 1951, those involved came to understand that their work was founded on social responsibility and the inherent principles of ensemble or repertory theater, which, Blau wrote, "directs itself, by inviting diversity of viewpoint, to whatever is most civic and civil in man, to his essential brotherhood, his social intelligence, and his instincts for secular communion....There are occasions when the theater must do its work against what passes for common consent, to appear to say, 'To hell with society.'"

The Last Great Dream

At a time when Americans were being told that atomic war was an acceptable risk, that fallout from the 122 nuclear weapons tests between 1951 and 1958 was negligible, that hiding under a desk would protect schoolchildren from a nuclear blast, the AW sought to speak truth to power.

Their initial productions—a one-act satire, Lorca, Tennessee Williams, and Isherwood—were by invitation only, and the exclusivity began to build a reputation for them.

Moving to larger quarters at the Elgin Theater, an abandoned warehouse at 123 Valencia Street, they produced their first theater (versus studio) play, *Lysistrata*, which Blau thought was their "first minor step toward identity." At the very nadir of McCarthyism, the play had "the courage to insist, in defiance of the demagogues, that each citizen be given the right to judge."

The Crucible came in 1954. The next year, they signed a contract with Actors' Equity, the first ever awarded outside New York City, and began to produce plays at the Marines' Memorial Theatre on Sutter Street downtown. Sustained by some seventy volunteers who took supporting roles, built scenery, sewed costumes, and staffed the box office, the AW became part of the city's fabric. The shows themselves came equipped with Blau's production notes, which made the drama, wrote one observer, "part of public discourse, a challenge to McCarthyism's lies and petty tyrannies."

The AW came of age in 1956 when it introduced Brecht's *Mother Courage* to America. They had evolved from Cold War alienation to "a more provocative sense of mission, the kind of theater I'd been hoping for," wrote Blau. He continued, "The zero-sum lesson from the tribunal of *Mother Courage* was what it remains today: beware of ideology, even when it looks like Brecht's."

The next year, they topped themselves with what was only the second American production of Samuel Beckett's *Waiting for Godot*, which Blau termed "that existential or absurdist non sequitur of a drama, [which] would turn out to be the most consequential *political* play of the period, a prologue to the Sixties, with its activism set off by passive resistance." Capturing the very essence of the charnel house that was postwar Europe, Beckett made existential philosophy into a feasible schema for acting.

Godot's opening line: "Nothing to be done." True enough, but salvation was just barely possible. It is a comedy, after all, and a call for a sense of wonder before all that is absurd, which is to say, life. The production went on

Mainstream America and San Francisco's First Resistance   55

to a standout six-week run in New York City, but even more exquisitely, the AW took the play across the bay to San Quentin State Prison, where it was so well received that the prisoners would later put on their own production. Few humans knew more about waiting.

Designed by Robin Wagner, who would later do the same for *Hair*, *Dreamgirls*, and *The Producers*, *Godot* also featured a soundtrack created by the electronica composer Morton Subotnick, and so excited the painter Robert LaVigne that he would collaborate as scene designer for later productions of Beckett's *Endgame* and Jean Genet's *The Balcony*. Having grown considerably, the AW brought in two assistant directors as collaborators: Lee Breuer (and his partner Ruth Maleczech) and Ronnie Davis. Breuer and Maleczech would go on to acclaim in New York City. Davis would initiate the San Francisco Mime Troupe and be an essential part of the unfolding drama that was the '60s in the city.

In 1964, Blau and Irving were hired away by the newly opened Lincoln Center in New York. Blau later reflected that they had made their mark because they followed what Yeats established as his conditions for the Abbey Theatre: "Not what you want but what we want."

8

City Lights, the Place, and Marin

ostwar San Francisco exerted an interesting social magnetism, attracting people from the East Coast who would become important contributors to an emerging bohemian community. A bookstore and a couple of bars were the essential elements.

One day in 1953, a painter and poet named Lawrence Ferlinghetti was driving up Columbus Avenue in San Francisco and noticed a man working on a shop window. His name was Peter Martin, and he was about to open America's first all-paperback bookstore, City Lights. Ferlinghetti knew Martin slightly, so he pulled over and they talked. Soon Ferlinghetti was a partner, and when Martin wanted to move on to New York City, Ferlinghetti bought him out.

Despite a wrenching childhood in which he was orphaned and left with a succession of foster parents, Ferlinghetti was a stable and gifted man. Tall, angular, balding, and benign in manner, he'd graduated from the University of North Carolina before serving in the navy during the war, where he commanded a subchaser as part of D-day. He got his master's at Columbia

57

with Mark Van Doren, then used his GI benefits to earn a doctorate at the Sorbonne.

He wanted to live in a real city, and in 1951, he boarded the Union Pacific's California Zephyr for San Francisco. When he got to North Beach, he found, he said, "anarchism, pacifism, and a wide-open, non-academic poetry scene, provincial but liberating." Having become a pacifist after seeing Nagasaki mere weeks after the war's end, he'd come home. He settled in a flat on Chestnut Street, near the California School of Fine Arts, and began to frequent Rexroth's salon.

Shigeyoshi Murao was a North Beach citizen who fell in love with City Lights, working for free until Ferlinghetti could afford to pay him. Open from early morning until midnight, they encouraged browsing, held packages for people to pick up, provided a bulletin board for notes, and swiftly became the nexus of a community. Paperbacks had only surfaced in America in 1939 with the launch of Pocket Books, but for the Francophile Ferlinghetti, they were quite normal; after all, the first edition of *Ulysses* had been a paperback.

The store prospered, and in 1955, also in the French tradition, it established the in-house City Lights Press to publish the Pocket Poets series. The first release was Ferlinghetti's own *Pictures of the Gone World*, the second was a translation by Rexroth, and the third was Kenneth Patchen's *Poems of Humor & Protest*. The basic jacket design of the book and of the series from then on was taken from Patchen's *An Astonished Eye Looks Out of the Air*, published at Camp Angel by Kemper Nomland, who had stripped blocks of color down to the fundamental quality of contrast. The Pocket Poets were now instantly recognizable as well as a convenient fit.

City Lights was just a few doors down from the intersection of Columbus Avenue and Broadway, which was the boundary between Chinatown and the Italian neighborhood of North Beach. There was an alley next to the store, and on the other side of the alley was the bohemian institution the Vesuvio Café, founded in 1948 as an artists' hangout by Silvio Velleman, a Swiss man who claimed to have danced in the chorus line of *No, No, Nanette*. He also said that his immigration officer had told him that when his visa lapsed, he should just change his name and disappear. He did change his name, to Henri Lenoir, and was part of the poetry scene even before he opened Vesuvio, selling Rexroth's book *The Phoenix and the Tortoise* just

City Lights, the Place, and Marin

59

after the war at his first place in San Francisco, a bar on Montgomery Street called the Iron Pot.

The bookstore's neighbors also included the lesbian bar just across Columbus Avenue at 12 Adler Place and the hungry i (for "id"), a club founded in 1950 just down the block by Eric "Big Daddy" Nord. City Lights fit right in. Three blocks down Columbus Avenue sat the Montgomery Block, at one time the biggest building in America west of the Mississippi and home to artist studios and bohemian hideaways since the era of Mark Twain.

"It was as if North Beach had a kind of dome over it," said one young poet, Michael McClure. "A touch of the anarchist, of the philosopher, a kind of romance of narrow streets leading into Chinatown—all that was North Beach." In 1953, bohemian HQ was the brand-new bar called the Place at 1564 Grant Avenue. Founded by two veterans of Black Mountain College, it was decorated by the art pouring out of CSFA. The bartender, John Ryan, was also a CSFA student. He and his fellow students Jay DeFeo and Wally Hedrick were among those who had one-person shows there. There was a piano, and local musicians Paul Desmond and Brew Moore played there. Like City Lights, it became a community center, with packages held for regulars and a bulletin board that posted relevant clippings and messages.

Mondays were dubbed "Blabbermouth Night," in which everyone at least nominally became a poet. Poetry was returning to its oral roots—and in a highly entertaining way. Those voted as presenting the best rant would win a bottle of presumably cheap champagne. Robert Duncan's protégé Jack Spicer made the Place his headquarters and became the primary organizer of Blabbermouth Night. An exceedingly vocal critic of everything that he perceived as commercial, he was the ideal choice.

Other hangouts began to sprout on Grant Avenue. A mixed bar and deli, the Co-Existence Bagel Shop, opened at 1398. It became the home of Bob "Bomkauf" Kaufman, one of the street's legendary characters, and the tragic subject of abuse from Officer William Bigarini, who apparently had a major problem with the mixed-race Kaufman and his Anglo wife. After several police-administered beatings, Bob produced a poem written down by his wife—Kaufman was a purely oral poet and had left his poems largely on the wind—that compared Bigarini to Hitler. She posted it in the window of the bagel shop, and when Bigarini came in to tear it down, he became aware that Kaufman was urinating on his leg, which doubtless earned Kaufman further damage. In later years, Kaufman adopted a vow of silence, perhaps in self-defense.

Mel Weitsman, once Clyfford Still's student, was another North Beach regular. Painting in the day and driving a cab at night, he had taken up with a fascinating poet named ruth weiss (she spelled her name without capital letters). A refugee from Vienna, she'd grown up in Chicago and had left home in her teens to move into the Art Circle, an arty boardinghouse. There she discovered jazz. As she was writing one day, a friend suggested she come upstairs to listen to a jam session. She showed him the poem, and he said they should hear it. When she began to read, "instead of listening," she said, "they just started playing behind me."

A natural-born free spirit, she hitchhiked to San Francisco because it had a reputation for diversity. She visited the Rexroth salon but found it "too cerebral—a lot of literary preening." Instead, she spent time at a largely gay hotel on Polk Street, the Hotel Wentley, where she met a writer from New York named Jack Kerouac. There was no physical spark between them, but they regularly exchanged haikus all night before Kerouac's friend Neal Cassady would arrive and take them to Potrero Hill to watch the sunrise.

Her relationship with Weitsman was more romantic, and they began living together, eventually in an apartment on Cumberland Street across from Mission Dolores Park that was near a former orphanage called Hill Haven. Millie, the landlady, was married to Johnny Elgin, a jazz pianist ruth knew from New Orleans. Hill Haven came equipped with a boiler room that was effectively soundproofed, and Elgin, Sonny Nelson or Will Carlson on drums, Jack Minger on trumpet, Max Hartstein on bass, and occasionally Brew Moore on tenor saxophone adopted it for jam sessions. Motivated by the scene, Mel took up the trumpet as well. In 1956, Nelson, Minger, and Carlson decided to formalize the jams and opened a bar in North Beach called the Cellar at 576 Green Street. Most nights, ruth waited tables, and on Wednesday, she read poetry backed by jazz. Unlike Rexroth and Ferlinghetti, she would never record her jazz poetry, but she seemingly introduced the practice to the neighborhood.

Bohemians gathered in several places in Northern California aside from San Francisco. In the postwar period, quite a number of artistically inclined

City Lights, the Place, and Marin   61

veterans settled in the footsteps of Robinson Jeffers and Henry Miller in Big Sur. Miller noted that the communal impulse of the nineteenth century had been supplanted by individuals in the twentieth, young artists "indifferent to reward, fame, success...not concerned with undermining a vicious system but with leading their own lives—on the fringe of society."

Describing the time and place in his book *Big Sur and the Oranges of Hieronymus Bosch*, he connected their quest with Bosch's, who wanted to see through the phenomenal world. "One's destination is never a place but rather a new way of looking at things...there are no limits to vision." It was apt that such a quest would come to Big Sur, where the staggering beauty seemed to demand a profound response. "Paradise or no paradise, I have the very definite impression that the people of this vicinity are striving to live up to the grandeur and nobility which is such an integral part of the setting. They behave as if it were a privilege to live here."

Not quite so magnificent but hardly less wonderful, Sausalito continued to attract artists seeking to live on the fringes, with Jean Varda still the shining example. In Anaïs Nin's telling, "Magic must predominate. Varda's attitude in life was that of a Merlin, the enchanter, who must constantly enchant and seduce, fascinate and create...the alchemist searching only for what he could transmute into gold." In Varda's own words, "Man is nourished by what's marvelous," and "Color is ecstasy, and everything but ecstasy is vanity."

Varda was briefly joined on the Sausalito waterfront by one of the more extraordinary composers of the twentieth century, Harry Partch. His music was so divergent from the norm that he had little influence, either on other composers or the public, but the fact that he did his best work there is revealing.

As a composer, he felt a deep connection to what he called "the old ways," a form that long preceded the mainstream Western classical tradition of eighteenth- and nineteenth-century European music. Instead, he pursued the music of Pythagoras, called *just intonation* (versus the modern tempered intonation with its sharps and flats). Having burned his first work, he began in 1930 to work with the human voice and the viola, which did not require a fixed pitch.

It was no ordinary viola. He had a craftsman build an instrument with the fingerboard of a cello to make what he called an Adapted Viola, and wrote music with twenty-nine tones to the octave. Striving for absolute, celestial freedom, his music became a liquid glide. Much of his energy for the rest of his life would center on creating new instruments that could play his very special music.

Homeless and sleeping in an ancient car, he attended a party in January 1953 and met Gordon Onslow Ford and Ford's wife, Jaqueline, who connected with him on the subject of instrument building. Adopting him, Jacqueline nursed him to health, put up with his whining, and took him around the local artist circles. She found a man who rented an enormous shed to Partch—instrument-building required room—at 3030 Bridgeway, also known as Gate 5, just down from Ford's studio on the *Vallejo*. There he built a Diamond Marimba, a Marimba Eroica, Cloud-Chamber Bowls, and a Quadrangularis Reversum. He was a twentieth-century alchemist.

Various locals banded together to sell subscriptions to the Harry Partch Trust Fund. Young musicians began to gravitate to him, and the Gate 5 Ensemble was born. For a little while, Partch's art received a warm and genuine response. His privately released *Plectra and Percussion Dances* was reviewed by the local newspapers and *High Fidelity*—and the reviews were good. The piece was broadcast in November 1953 on KPFA. The station's public relations manager, Gerd Stern, began to assist him with instrument construction as well as fundraising.

Always vulnerable to a greener-pastures syndrome, Partch received a modest offer from Peter Yates of the Evenings on the Roof series in Los Angeles and blew it up into something much larger, went off to Los Angeles, and then impatiently decided Yates was insincere and rejected him. Distrust of those who could help him was a regular pattern of his life, and self-sabotage was the inevitable result.

Just up the road from Sausalito lay the town of Mill Valley, where Gary Snyder had settled late in 1955 in anticipation of departing for Japan in May 1956. Locke McCorkle, a carpenter whom he'd met at an Alan Watts lecture at AAAS, had invited him to stay in the back house on the property at 340 Montford Avenue that Locke was renting for twenty-five dollars monthly.

The house was a shack up the hill from where Locke lived with his wife and two children, and it became Marin-An, Gary's home and a meditation center for his friends. While there, he finished his long poem *Myths and Texts* and spent time with Alan Watts, both on the *Vallejo* in Sausalito and at Alan's home, just down Montford. On one of his visits, he and Locke introduced Watts to marijuana.

Gary's shack attracted quite a number of people. One of them was a vagabond writer from back East named Jack Kerouac, who'd connected with Gary in the fall of 1955. He spent the spring of 1956 with Gary before following in Snyder's footsteps to work as a fire watcher in the Cascades in Washington State that summer. The two spent many hours in meditation and in hiking around Mount Tamalpais, which rose directly above their home. Marin-An was a peaceful and spiritually happy place.

As Gary's departure approached, they threw a three-day party, a blowout that attracted a wide selection of the Bay Area's literary scene. Midway through it, Gary and Jack took off walking around Mount Tam. Gary's journal recorded their route, from Montford Avenue up a canyon onto Edgewood Road, then along a series of trails with names like Pipeline, Troop 80, and Bootjack, to the amphitheater near the summit, and eventually home. They talked about the teachings of the Buddha, the dharma—Jack was something of an apprentice monk to Gary—and how it might change the world. Jack recorded Snyder saying, "East'll meet West anyway....Think of what a great world revolution will take place when East meets West finally, and it'll be guys like us that can start the thing."

Some weeks later, on board his ship the *Anita-maru*, Gary wrote in his journal:

I advocate the overthrow of all governments by peace & quiet,
—The subtle revolution of non-consumption: when everybody will quit buying foolish (but not frivolous or beautiful) things. Governments depend, for their existence, on fostering & exploiting ignorance...
—As expounded to Jack on Troop 80 trail.

Tracing their path on the side of Mount Tam, a paradisical slice of beauty looming just a few miles north above San Francisco, they looked toward the city and saw strange things. Perhaps five miles south of Marin-An, the

Cold War had come home to the San Francisco Bay Area in 1954 with the installation of Nike Hercules rockets on the Marin Headlands overlooking the Golden Gate. Twenty-seven feet long with a range of seventy-five miles, they were designed to attack incoming aircraft at altitudes from 1,000 to 150,000 feet. Men and dogs prowled the hills to guard them.

Gary concluded his journal note with:

—Now looking up at the radar station barracks—that fragile world—two men camping by a creek makes modern history silly.

9

The Beats and "Howl"

Allen Ginsberg, yet another migrant from the East Coast, arrived in San Francisco in 1954. It would be his destiny to be the lightning rod for a bolt of poetic creativity that would illuminate the American decade. Along with his friend Jack Kerouac's *On the Road*, his poem "Howl" would punch a hole in the American culture, and nothing would be quite the same afterward.

In 1943, he was a bright, curious, closeted Columbia University freshman and fledgling poet, all glasses and chatter. One day in December, he heard *Brahms' First* coming from a nearby dormitory room. He knocked on the door and met Lucien Carr, a handsome young man who was an instinctive rebel and iconoclast, and they bonded instantly, becoming the nucleus of a growing circle. As Ginsberg recalled, "Know these words, and you speak the Carr language: fruit, phallus, clitoris, cacoethes, feces, foetus, womb, Rimbaud."

Ginsberg had grown up poor, his family impoverished by the expense of his mother Naomi's recurring psychiatric care. He had a profound sympathy for the underdog, perhaps in reaction to his mother's pain and her leftist political opinions. He also had a healthy ego, at least in the privacy of his journal: "I'll be a genius of some kind, probably in literature."

By contrast, Lucien had come from St. Louis gentry, a family prosperous enough to finance his quest, which was apparently to be expelled from every school he attended. His fascination with Rimbaud was a sensualized urban revisiting of the spiritual pursuits of the American transcendentalists of a century before. Their literary and philosophical inquiries were in vivid contrast to Columbia, where the poetry taught stopped pretty much at 1902. Soon after, the *Partisan Review* would declare that "the jobless, wandering artist is almost extinct...the death of bohemianism." Carr and Ginsberg begged to differ.

They were joined by a St. Louis friend of Carr's, a slightly older Harvard graduate named William Burroughs, grandson but not an heir to the man who had invented the adding machine. A prosperous childhood did not divert him from a lifelong feeling of alienation, of being possessed by what he would call an "ugly spirit." Perhaps even more importantly, his ambivalent recognition of his own gay sexual orientation led him to adopt a persona of invisibility.

He studied New England witchcraft with George Lyman Kittredge at Harvard, then attended medical school in Vienna, simultaneously a pedophile's dream and an ideal site to observe the rise of Nazism. An allowance from his parents financed his studies in Mayan archeology at Harvard University, and later of semantics with Count Alfred Korzybski. His ghostly persona became genuine; he was without ambition, direction, or purpose. Brief jobs as a private detective and then exterminator seemed to be in character.

Burroughs had a friend from St. Louis named David Kammerer who had been obsessed with Lucien Carr since the latter was a teen, a passion that had led Kammerer to pursue the beautiful young man from Phillips Andover to Bowdoin to Chicago and now to New York. Following David, Burroughs came to New York and met Lucien and then Ginsberg and another member of their inner circle, a French Canadian ex-Columbia football player named Jack Kerouac. Handsome, muscular, a bit naïve, passionately devoted to writing and Thomas Wolfe, Kerouac had a certain charisma that matched Carr's. An injury had forced him off the team, and he showed no inclination to return to conventional student life.

Provoked by Carr, they began to discuss what they came to call, in Yeats's phrase, the "New Vision," which contained elements of Nietzsche, Rimbaud,

The Beats and "Howl"   67

Rilke, and Dostoevsky. Their Vision boiled down to an updated chapter in the ongoing bohemian rejection of conventional morals as applied to sexuality and consciousness by way of an art created by the derangement of the senses. Along with the local bars, they spent more and more time in apartment number 62 at 421 West 118th Street, home to Joan Vollmer and Edie Parker, Kerouac's girlfriend. As knowledgeable about philosophy and literature as the men, Joan served as muse and hostess of the New Vision.

Their scene shattered in August 1944 when Carr and Kerouac plotted to escape Kammerer by working their way to Europe. That night, Carr would kill Kammerer, reportedly in defense against rape. He'd be sentenced to two years in the Dannemora prison. Kerouac, who'd helped conceal evidence of the deed, would marry Parker so that her family would bail him out of jail. It was not a marriage meant to last. Though primarily gay, Burroughs would move in with Joan.

He would also introduce a rougher crowd to the scene, including a bright but somewhat demented prostitute named Vickie Russell (real name Priscilla Arminger) who turned them all on to Benzedrine, which very rapidly became the entirety of Joan's world. That fall, Burroughs brought around a Times Square hustler and addict named Herbert Huncke, who would introduce Ginsberg and Kerouac to the multiple pains and joys of the Times Square underworld. Friends of Huncke's soon introduced Burroughs to his own path to oblivion; he experienced morphine and almost immediately had a simple overwhelming purpose in his life, that of satisfying his drug addiction.

Much later, Ginsberg would conclude that their use of drugs in 1945 had "accelerated a process that had begun the year before, a process of cultural and personal deconditioning. Boundaries began to dissolve between us." Having taken up marijuana, he concluded that a great deal of the American social model "was some public hallucination that simply had no relationship to reality."

Late in 1946, their last great inspiration arrived in New York City. Neal Cassady was the object of Ginsberg's desire and the brother Kerouac had longed for since his elder brother, Gerard, had died when Jack was four. Cassady was an illuminated con man, an antisocial hustler from Denver who stole cars, pursued multiple women (and occasionally shared some of himself with Ginsberg), and to many observers appeared quite mad. For Kerouac, always a witness of life, he seemed a man completely involved in the moment, whether it was driving a car, talking, or seducing someone—or all three simultaneously. He seemed more alive than Kerouac had ever imagined it was possible to be.

Over the next decade, Cassady drove Kerouac back and forth across the United States as Kerouac learned how to write the way jazz was played and Cassady drove, ultimately composing the book called *On the Road*. Burroughs tried growing pot in Texas, shot and killed Joan Vollmer in Mexico City while drunk, and dove even deeper into his addiction in Tangiers. Ginsberg stayed in New York and experienced a vision of William Blake that sent him in a tortured pursuit of cosmic oneness. Life wore away at all of them, and eventually, Kerouac would remark to a friend that "I guess you might say we're a *beat* generation," a recognition of exhaustion, of seeing through the façade of American optimism, or perhaps something beatific, as he would later suggest. His friend John Clellon Holmes wrote an article about "Beat" for the November 16, 1952, *New York Times Magazine*, and there the matter rested.

After years of stasis, Ginsberg left New York in 1954, first to explore Mayan ruins in Mexico before settling in San Francisco. Still pursuing a dream of conventionality, he got work as a market researcher and began a relationship with an aspiring jazz singer named Sheila Williams Boucher. He began to meet the local poets but found Robert Duncan "domineering." Kenneth Rexroth was more simpatico, and Ginsberg attended the salon regularly. The city itself was appealing. *All in all a very active cultured city the rival of New York for general relaxation and progressive art life*, he thought.

On October 17, 1954, Ginsberg's life began a tectonic shift. He took peyote in Boucher's apartment at 755 Pine Street on the side of Nob Hill, and in the foggy mist, the top-floor windows of the Sir Francis Drake Hotel below looked to him like an inhuman robot skull, like Moloch, the biblical eater of souls. The image would linger with him.

After a major argument with Boucher, their relationship seemed over, and the next day, he had his first psychotherapy session with Dr. Philip Hicks. Some months later, the good doctor asked him what he really wanted to do. Ginsberg recalled his reply: "'Doctor, I don't think you're going to find this

The Beats and "Howl" 69

very healthy and clear, but I really would like to stop working forever…and do nothing but write poetry and have leisure to spend the day outdoors and go to museums and see friends. And I'd like to keep living with someone—maybe even a man—and explore relationships that way. And cultivate my perceptions, cultivate the visionary thing in me. Just a literary and quiet city-hermit existence.' Then [Dr. Hicks] said, 'Well, why don't you?'"

Set free in May 1955, Ginsberg told the market research firm to replace him with a computer, began to collect unemployment benefits, moved into an apartment at 1010 Montgomery Street, and spent lots of time just down the block at City Lights Books.

He enrolled in graduate school at UC Berkeley, and then on August 25, something wonderful happened. He wrote in his journal, "I saw the best mind angel-headed hipsters damned." With "Lester Leaps In" on the record player, he sat down at the typewriter, the first time he'd tried to write poetry that way. He thought back to all the souls he'd witnessed wounded by America—Carl Solomon, with whom he'd spent time in the New York psychiatric facility, Huncke, Cassady, Burroughs's friend Bill Garber, Philip Lamantia, whom he'd known in New York, Julian Beck and Judith Malina, Kammerer…He wrote the first section of a new poem in one sitting, telling Kerouac that "the first time I sat down to blow, it came out in your method, sounding like you, an imitation practically."

A blend of resistance to the inhuman, destructive values of Moloch and tender sympathy for the victims, the poem was, Ginsberg later wrote to a critic, "an act of sympathy, not rejection…I have taken a leap of detachment from the Artificial preoccupations and preconceptions of what is acceptable and normal and given my yea to the specific type of madness listed in the Who section.…I am talking about *realization* of love. LOVE." Ginsberg sent it off to Kerouac, then in Mexico, who replied with what he thought was the appropriate name. He called it "Howl."

The site of the poem's first public reading had its own exceptional history. A cluster of art student friends from Los Angeles who'd attended Pasadena Junior College in the late 1940s heard about the California School of Fine Arts and set their sights on attending. In 1949, John Ryan, Hayward King, Deborah

Remington, and David Simpson began to work with Jean Varda, David Park, and Elmer Bischoff. Jack Spicer, a poet associate of Robert Duncan's, later a CSFA teacher and the master of Blabbermouth Night at the Place, would be part of their group, as well as Wally Hedrick, who'd had to serve in the military first to be able to afford tuition. Having mockingly dubbed themselves the Progressive Art Workers back in Pasadena, they stuck together. Greatly disappointed when the King Ubu Gallery had folded, they reopened it on Halloween 1954, under the rubric of their group, the 6 Gallery, since each of them contributed ten dollars a month toward the sixty-dollar rent.

Ryan and Hedrick "installed wall panels and a large, matte-black plywood '6' over the garage doors along the street....We also had a combination lock," Ryan said, "which Wally Bill set to '6666.'" It was a long, narrow space that somewhat resembled a bowling alley, with a larger room, complete with a stage, in back. As much a social gathering spot as any sort of business— "Selling our work at the 6 Gallery never really occurred to us," recalled Simpson—it attracted other artists and different sorts of events. As Ryan saw it, "It was exactly what we wanted. Anything that we wanted to have happen could happen." More practically, recalled Hedrick, "we started it because there was no place else in the city that would show our work."

In a nod to their predecessors, one of the first events at the 6 was a play by Robert Duncan, *Faust Foutu* ("Faust Fucked"), a comic portrait of Cold War bohemian culture whose cast included Duncan, the poet of the supernatural Helen Adam, a young poet named Michael McClure, Jack Spicer, and Jess. Ginsberg was in the audience that night, January 20, 1955, having been invited when he ran into Duncan at the Place.

They put on various art shows but wanted to do more, "to improvise organized polyphony from one media to the next," said Hedrick. That fall, they agreed a poetry reading would be ideal. They asked McClure to organize it, but he was too busy and passed the idea to Ginsberg. The poet who'd once thought about being a labor organizer was the ideal man for the job. He talked with Rexroth and came up with a lineup.

Ginsberg had met McClure at a W. H. Auden reading at the SF State Poetry Center in the fall; Ginsberg had known Philip Lamantia since he'd been a teenaged surrealist in New York. Rexroth suggested Gary Snyder, and in the course of an introductory meal, he and Ginsberg bonded immediately.

The Beats and "Howl" 71

Snyder mentioned his friend Phil Whalen. The same day as they talked, Ginsberg's friend Jack Kerouac had arrived at Ginsberg's place in Berkeley. They naturally invited him to read, but he was too shy and declined. Rexroth would emcee.

To promote their show, Ginsberg drafted a postcard that read: "6 Poets at 6 Gallery / Philip Lamantia reading mss. of late John Hoffman—Mike McClure, Allen Ginsberg, Gary Snyder & Phil Whalen—all sharp new straightforward writing—remarkable collection of angels on one stage reading their poetry. No charge, small collection for wine and postcards. Charming event. / Kenneth Rexroth, M.C. / 8 PM Friday Night October 7, 1955." He sent out one hundred cards.

The place was packed, foretelling a community that awaited a catalyst; the ubiquitous Mel Weitsman was among them. Surreal sculptures, orange crates swathed in muslin and dipped in plaster of Paris, hung behind the stage. Lamantia opened. In his first public reading, McClure delivered "Point Lobos: Animism" and "For the Death of 100 Whales," which reflected his intimate engagement with biology, the poet as a mammal. His view would be an important contribution to the rising tide of environmental awareness to come. Whalen followed with the sly, witty "Plus Ça Change," in which a man becomes a bird, and then "The Martyrdom of Two Pagans," which dismissed organized Christianity and argued for "the sacredness of plant, animal, human and god realms." It was a live audience, Whalen thought, that was "really interested."

After an intermission, a slightly tipsy Ginsberg—his friend Kerouac had taken up a collection and bought wine, which loosened the gathering up considerably—took the podium. He sobered as he read, Kerouac chanting, "Go, go," in support, and both he and the audience were swept up in a moment of connection so powerful it could only be described as transcendent. As he would recall it many years later, he was "surprised at his own power...driving forward with a strange ecstatic intensity, delivering a spiritual confession to an astounded audience—ending in tears which restored to American poetry the prophetic consciousness it had lost since the conclusion of Hart Crane's *The Bridge.*"

They had, thought McClure, "gone beyond a point of no return...none of us wanted to go back to the gray, chill, militarist silence, to the intellectual void—to the land without poetry—to the spiritual drabness…we wanted voice and we wanted vision." Snyder brought the evening to a close with his "Berry Feast," appositely about the loss of community in the modern world on the night when a very real new community manifested itself.

A diverse lot, the poets shared a poetics of immanence, a spiritual platform in which the poems came directly from the author and the form was dictated by the poem itself, all very different from the New Critics who then ruled academic critic-speak, whose permanent mantra was "ambiguity, tension, irony, and paradox." That night at the 6 declared the revival of publicly performed poetry in America for poets not from Wales. Years later, a critic would rather querulously point out that the "best minds" Ginsberg wrote about were from New York, missing the point that Ginsberg had to leave New York and go to San Francisco to be able to write the poem—and find an audience that would appreciate it fully.

After adding further sections, including the Moloch passage, and after eighteen drafts of polishing, *Howl and Other Poems* was published on November 1, 1956. On March 25, 1957, San Francisco collector of customs Chester MacPhee seized 520 copies of the second printing (done in England), although 1,000 copies got through. In May, *Chronicle* book editor William Hogan defended the poem, and a few days later, MacPhee released the seized books, the US attorney having declined prosecution.

This outraged William Hanrahan, captain of the San Francisco Police Department's Juvenile Bureau, and he proceeded, along with MacPhee, to give twentieth-century American poetry its greatest single promotional boost. On June 3, 1957, his police arrested City Lights clerk Shigeyoshi Murao for selling obscenity; soon after, they added Ferlinghetti to their haul. In September, the case went before a Sunday school teacher and judge named Clayton Horn.

Well before publication, Ferlinghetti had called the ACLU to ensure that he had support, and the union's Albert Bendich called in an even heavier weapon, San Francisco's legendary Jake "the Master" Ehrlich. With expert witnesses like UC Berkeley professor Mark Schorer, SF State's Walter Van Tilburg Clark, *San Francisco Examiner* book editor Luther Nichols, Kenneth Rexroth, and Actor's Workshop director Herbert Blau, among others, they made mincemeat of the two prosecution witnesses. Judge Horn concluded his decision by citing the aphorism, "Honi soit qui mal y pense." "The defendant

The Beats and "Howl" 73

is found not guilty." The *Chronicle*, which had headlined the original arrest MAKING A CLOWN OF SAN FRANCISCO, celebrated the result with an editorial: "'Howl' Decision Landmark of Law"—"decision sound and clear, foursquare with the Constitution."

Howl was a large rock dropped into the still pond of American poetry. Ginsberg's Columbia classmate John Hollander labeled it "the ravings of a lunatic fiend" in *Partisan Review*. More thoughtfully, John Clellon Holmes wrote that it was "a new *kind* of poetry (or, rather, the oldest kind): it was incantatory, hymnal, purging in its repetitions; it marked the entry of the Whitman breath and vision, as a major influence, into American poetry at last...it was also far better poetry than most of us realized in our first excitement over the fact that it had been written at all." There were a few insightful responses like Holmes's, but Hollander's views were more common.

Not least of the reasons that the critics dismissed Ginsberg and his friends was their sheer success in penetrating the media and finding a warm reception in a mass audience. One reason for the ease with which the Beat poets attracted so much (generally ill-informed) media attention was the simple word *Beat*; it was a highly effective brand name. *Beat*, and later *beatnik*, was an intricate and multilayered coded label that allowed slapdash journalists to pack all manner of connotation into four letters.

Alongside their innate elitism, the literary critics rejected the implicitly political content of Ginsberg's mystical personalist poetics, which were anti-consumption and anti-authority. The mainstream assumption was that politics only meant power and voting, whereas Ginsberg argued that his poetry was an extension of his personhood and that everything in the latter belonged in the former—which made the critics crazy.

Since to many critics the only other deviation from the American consensus seemed to be juvenile delinquency (the concerns of women, the sexually nonmainstream, African Americans, and so forth apparently did not exist), they found violence where none existed, most fabulously in the writing of Norman Podhoretz, who declared in *Partisan Review*'s "The Know-Nothing Bohemians" that *Howl* and later Ginsberg's friend Kerouac's work "worships primitivism, instinct, energy, 'blood.'" Thirty years later, he would trot out the same tropes: "In its glorification of madness, drugs, and homosexuality, and in its contempt and hatred for anything and everything generally deemed healthy, normal, or decent, Ginsberg's poem simultaneously foreshadowed and helped to propagate the values of the youth culture of the 1960s."

Shortly after the trial, Ginsberg would write to his father that "people keep seeing destruction or rebellion [in the Beats]…but that is [a] very minor element, actually; it only seems to be so to people who have accepted standard American values as permanent. What we are saying is that these values are not really standard or permanent, and we are in a sense I think ahead of the times."

Perhaps the most remarkable thing about *Howl* was that it was only the beginning.

10

Changes Become Visible—Civil Rights and Rock 'n' Roll

acial politics and the civil rights movement were essential elements in what would develop in the culture of the new Haight-Ashbury. A profound desire to transcend racism and take seriously the lessons of Black culture was a fundamental value and a key to the later 1950s and the '60s, largely through the music called *rock 'n' roll*.

Despite the best efforts of the American power structure to ignore the realities of white supremacy in '50s America—the title of Ralph Ellison's *Invisible Man* was supremely appropriate—social change began to gain momentum. Thurgood Marshall, the NAACP's brilliant lead attorney, brought the case of Linda Brown against the Topeka Board of Education to the US Supreme Court, and the chief justice, Earl Warren, though not especially liberal, used his considerable political skills to ensure the court made a unanimous decision.

76   **The Last Great Dream**

Brown v. Board of Education of Topeka would declare "separate but equal" illegal in a 9–0 decision issued in May 1954. It was epochal, but also only the beginning. Led by senators like James Eastland, the South united to resist school integration, closing public schools and aiding private ones.

When a fourteen-year-old Black boy from Chicago named Emmett Till was kidnapped and lynched for supposedly flirting with a white woman in August 1955, it was business as usual in central Mississippi. At the funeral in Chicago, his mother insisted that his casket be open, and thousands saw the gruesome brutality the killers had inflicted on him, galvanizing the Black community in a very special way. The national press descended on the trial of his murderers and saw the all-white, all-male jury deliberate for sixty-seven minutes—at the request of the incoming sheriff, they had actually slowed down their considerations to put a better face on "justice" in Mississippi—to deliver a not guilty verdict.

On December 1, 1955, Rosa Parks refused to move to the back of the bus in Montgomery, Alabama, an action that would send ripples across the South and the nation. In an astonishing display of solidarity produced by savvy political organizing by E. D. Nixon and inspirational speaking by the young Martin Luther King Jr., the Black people of Montgomery brought off a yearlong boycott that was a milestone in nonviolent resistance. As King put it in an elegant paraphrase of Boston abolitionist Theodore Parker's wordier version, "The arc of the moral universe is long, but it bends toward justice." The arc bent in Montgomery.

In November 1956, the US Supreme Court declared bus segregation illegal. On December 21, Nixon got on the bus. "It was the best ride I ever had in my life, just riding through downtown and out to the west and back again, going nowhere but feeling like we was heading to heaven."

Just as Black people began to move, young white artists moved by Black culture stepped into the spotlight. In September 1957, something remarkably fortunate for Jack Kerouac manifested itself: Orville "Prissy" Prescott was on vacation, and so Gilbert Millstein, a young editor at the *New York Times*, got the assignment to review Kerouac's *On the Road*. He lauded it as a generational statement on par with *The Sun Also Rises*, and it leaped up the bestseller lists.

Five years before, Millstein had commissioned a piece on Beat from Kerouac's friend John Clellon Holmes. "Beat," Holmes wrote, was "an instinctive individuality, needing no bohemianism or imposed eccentricity to express it."

Unsurprisingly, the mass media's coverage of Beat tended toward the hysterical ("They worship blood") or the patronizingly silly (the most famous "beatnik" was a television sitcom character named Maynard G. Krebs, who would tremble and collapse when he heard the word *work*). More perceptively, Holmes wrote in *Esquire* the next year that improvisatory jazz, "the music of inner freedom," was the root of *On the Road* and that "Howl" was "clearly a defense of the human spirit in the face of a civilization intent on destroying it."

The spirituality at the root of the two best-known Beat writings was largely ignored. So was the fact that they were the only two samples of avant-garde art that were ever genuinely popular in their time. Ginsberg would write in his journal that "the Beat Generation, a decisive moment in American consciousness—henceforth the horses' heads are headed toward eternity. No group as weird before...The elements were present before in Poe, Dickinson, Melville—Whitman—then Crane—An evolution of human consciousness—'Widen the area of consciousness.'"

Just after the publication of *On the Road*, Norman Mailer's "The White Negro: Superficial Reflections on the Hipster" made a considerable splash. Largely a product of the Manhattan-in-the-'50s obsession with psychoanalysis, the essay had come about because Mailer had spent time in Harlem in the company of his housekeeper. Since Kerouac had drawn well-deserved mockery for his naïve desire to be a Negro in *On the Road*, one might think Mailer had gone deeper with the subject.

But Mailer himself, though correctly tagging Kerouac as "sentimental as a lollipop," had admitted that he'd read *Road* with "a sinking heart. We were very competitive back then. I was thinking, Oh shit, this guy's done it. He was there, living it, and I was just an intellectual, writing about it." He wrote, wisely, that "to judge his worth it is better to forget about him as a novelist and see him instead as an action painter or a bard." Their contemporary, Dan Wakefield, added, "Perhaps it was as a bard that his freedom song appealed." And that was spot-on. Because the root of *On the Road* was jazz, the meeting place of African American culture and young white bohemians, and that was indeed a subject Kerouac grasped deeply.

In San Francisco, two high school art students in a Saturday class at CSFA asked their teacher, Wally Hedrick, what *Beat* meant. "You're Beat," he said and sent them down to City Lights bookstore to buy *On the Road*. One of those students was a young local named Jerry Garcia, who would take up guitar in part because of the Big Bill Broonzy records that Hedrick played while they painted. He would read Kerouac and absorb the bohemian code, that a life of art and spirituality was preferable to money and the pursuit of power. He'd follow the path of Kerouac and guitars the rest of his life, not least when he was among the most visible people in the Haight-Ashbury a decade later.

On the Road was not the only cultural artifact in which Black culture touched young white people. During World War II, Black music had morphed at lightning speed into at least three distinct modes—bebop, Chicago-style electric blues, and rhythm and blues. R & B had begun, among other sources, with Illinois Jacquet's solo on Lionel Hampton's "Flying Home." With Louis Jordan's shuffle boogie animating hit after hit, by the end of the war, R & B had captured sufficient attention that white musicians began to get interested.

Bill Haley was a country music disc jockey with a band called the Saddlemen until he heard Ike Turner's "Rocket 88" in 1951 and shortly after changed the band's name to the Comets. Picked up by a major record company, Decca, and working with Jordan's producer, Milt Gabler, they recorded "Rock Around the Clock," a B-side until the movie *Blackboard Jungle* put it high up the charts for the bulk of the summer of 1955.

Jordan's true heir was Charles Edward Anderson "Chuck" Berry, who established rock guitar with a blend of western swing (Bob Wills's "Ida Red") and the backbeat at the core of all Chess Records songs. They released "Maybellene" in July 1955, "Roll Over Beethoven" in 1956, and the primal rock guitar song, "Johnny B. Goode," in 1958. A slightly feral reformatory veteran, Berry incurred the displeasure of his hometown St. Louis establishment and, in an archetypically racist show trial followed by appeals and more trials, was eventually sent to prison for Mann Act violations in 1962.

Sun Records producer Sam Phillips wanted a white boy who could sing Black and found him in Elvis Presley, although the guitar playing on his records had to come from Scotty Moore. By early 1956, RCA had purchased Elvis's contract and released "Heartbreak Hotel," which went almost immediately to number one. "Don't Be Cruel," backed by "Hound Dog," came out in July, and on September 9, Presley appeared on *The Ed Sullivan Show*, the camera focused firmly above his waist and swiveling hips, and 80 percent of the American television audience watched him. He recorded hit after hit for the next few years—fourteen consecutive gold records, in fact—but his manager entombed him in a lifetime career of bad movies that made the manager more money than Elvis and offered Presley none of the satisfactions of live performance.

As a business matter, '50s rock 'n' roll succeeded because television had made radio stations specialize. The major record companies stuck to pop and Broadway, and so it was small specialty labels that worked with street smarts rather than predictability and fed hits to the radio. The result was R & B labels and then stations that played music that was more energetic and sexually honest than '50s pop tripe ("How Much Is That Doggie in the Window?"). Thus, Little Richard could produce the frenzied, orgiastic "Tutti Frutti," and the Dominoes their "Sixty Minute Man."

The major record companies reacted to the new music by issuing bland white pop covers, most notoriously with Pat Boone, who built a career with vapid do-overs of Little Richard songs. Though he played genuine R & B music and banned white covers from his show, Alan Freed popularized the phrase *rock and roll* (soon supplanted by the grittier *rock 'n' roll*), which suggested a white alternative to R & B. The racial overtones of liking rock 'n' roll led to a general adult suspicion of the genre, connecting it to juvenile delinquency, in good part due to the movie *Blackboard Jungle*, along with media coverage of rock "riots," which quite frequently mostly involved dancing in the aisles.

In the South, the concern about race mixing was more open. In the spring of 1956, Asa Carter, the executive secretary of the North Alabama Citizens Council, an offshoot of the White Citizens' Council (WCC), started a campaign to ban rock from jukeboxes in Birmingham and Anniston. To Carter, rock was "the basic, heavy-beat music of Negroes. It appeals to the base in man, brings out animalism and vulgarity." Southern shows that used a rope down the middle of the dance floor to segregate the races frequently resulted in a rope on the floor and the sight of Black and white youth dancing together, with a predictable reaction from local "adults." Perhaps even more to the point, by 1956, half of all records were being bought by teens.

Rock 'n' roll had created, wrote the journalist Jeff Greenfield, "a world of citizens under sixteen...we were the first to have a music rooted in uncoated sexuality." Though erotic, it remained apolitical. Children of McCarthyism, the majority of rock fans thought that censorship was acceptable, that left-wingers were suspicious, that the theory of evolution was suspect. They were conformist, sexually conservative, and silent. But the sensuality of dancing to loud music would be yet another step toward a generational split that would become a chasm in just a few years.

One of the other things that they believed was that women should not hold elected office…as usual, women had the worst of it. "They were stereotyped, singled out as different, discriminated against on the basis of alleged differences, and treated almost as a separate caste," wrote one historian. "Like blacks, women were alleged to be mentally and emotionally unstable, irresponsible, weak, and submissive."

When boys rebelled, it was often seen as protest; when young women did so, they were seen as having psychiatric problems. Joyce Johnson was just such a rebellious young woman, a child of New York City who'd begun hanging out in the Village at thirteen, had an affair with a married man at eighteen, had already sold a novel of her own, and happened to be Jack Kerouac's girlfriend on the day he read Gilbert Millstein's *New York Times* review.

Well before *On the Road*, women like Johnson and the Village poet Diane di Prima had stepped out of the marriage-and-two-point-four-children straitjacket. "Naturally, we fell in love with men who were rebels," wrote Johnson. "We did not expect to be rebels all by ourselves; we did not count on loneliness. Once we had found our male counterparts, we had too much blind faith to challenge the old male/female rules. We were very young and in over our heads. But we knew we had done something brave, practically historic. We were the ones who had dared to leave home."

In Kerouac, she had a lover thirteen years older than her twenty-one, a man who was already very tired. As she later put it, she believed "in the curative powers of love as the English believe in tea or Catholics believe in the Miracle of Lourdes." But love could not conquer his ambivalence about all women other than his mother. "I hate Jack's woman-hatred, hate it, mourn it, understand, and finally forgive." Kerouac showed her a picture of his daughter, Jan, even as he denied that he was the father, and Joyce thought of the child she'd not had because of an abortion. "For me, too, freedom and life seemed equivalent." Social pioneering is arduous.

11

Baghdad by the Bay and Its Artists

Interestingly, as the institutions of an artistic subculture developed in mid-'50s San Francisco, its mainstream culture loosened considerably, ultimately becoming even more hospitable to the subculture.

Despite its general toleration of eccentricity and the implicitly radical support of the general strike of 1934, San Francisco was by no means exempt from the larger American culture. Mayors tended to be Republican and conservative. The postwar penchant for technocratic urban planning commissions led to urban renewal, also known as Negro removal, which destroyed the core of the (Black) Fillmore District. A considerable swath of the original San Francisco was transformed into the gleaming, soulless but indubitably modern Golden Gateway and Embarcadero Centers. And only the determination of a society matron named Friedel Klussmann prevented the city fathers from eliminating the cable cars.

Intermittent puritanism, like mid-'50s mayor George Christopher's crusades against prostitution, gambling, and gay bars, reflected the conventional side of the city. So did the color line, which meant that Oscar Peterson and Sammy Davis Jr. had to sleep outside of downtown, west of Van Ness Avenue.

82 **The Last Great Dream**

But the city's mainstream culture was undergoing a momentous shift. The touchstone of provincial San Francisco had been the 1906 earthquake and fire; the more cosmopolitan San Francisco that was revealed as the '50s passed was built on memories of World War II, and its voice and amanuensis was named Herbert Eugene Caen. The enduring columnist for the *San Francisco Chronicle*, Herb Caen conjured up the expression "Baghdad by the Bay" to describe an enchanted city so beautiful that it wasn't entirely real. As such, it stood as an alternative to the rest of America. Year after year, in column after column, he documented his love affair with the city and became quite simply the best item columnist in the history of American journalism.

His employer helped. The *Chronicle* was merely the city's third-largest newspaper—the *Examiner* had even lured Caen away in 1950—when Scott Newhall became the *Chronicle*'s executive editor in 1952. He had old San Francisco roots, but "his wartime experiences, his savoir faire and ironic approach to life," wrote California historian Kevin Starr, "his Tory bohemianism" and "his conviction that the San Francisco Bay Area was the most favored place on earth" made him the right man in the right place. He would make the *Chronicle* an outlet that defined and celebrated San Francisco as "a chosen place, as Baghdad by the Bay."

Emphasizing features and good writing, he brought in a slew of columnists. Most importantly for the young artists, he hired Thomas Albright to cover the visual arts and Ralph Gleason to be the first full-time jazz critic for an American daily. Their support of the emerging arts, both painterly and musical, would be profoundly encouraging to the bohemians in the coming years.

And, of course, in 1958, Newhall orchestrated the triumphant return of Herb Caen to the *Chronicle*. By the time he was done, Caen was truly the personification of the city—left liberal, a union man, sentimental, open to anything that seemed to glorify the city, wild about food and drink and pleasure, sophisticated, and very, very funny. His sixteen thousand columns of a thousand words each, wrote Pat Conroy, were "the richest portrait of a city ever conceived by an American writer."

One of the jewels of the city that the *Chronicle* covered was the California School of Fine Arts (CSFA, in 1961 renamed the San Francisco Art Institute, SFAI),

Baghdad by the Bay and Its Artists

which in the late '50s had an astonishing collection of students. Over the years, quite a few of them lived in a four-apartment building above a ground-floor store, Barry's for Pets, at 2322 and 2330 Fillmore Street, up the hill from the 6 Gallery. A superb book by Anastasia Aukeman took from the poet and onetime resident Michael McClure the moniker *Painterland*, although at least one former resident swore that she'd never heard the expression used there.

Among the most important reasons for remembering the place was the work of Mary Joan "Jay" DeFeo, who lived in 2322 for many years (at first in the second-floor flat, later in both that and the third floor) with her husband, Wally Hedrick, by now a teacher at CSFA/SFAI, the banjo player in the Studio 13 Jass Band, and a seminal practitioner of assemblage, also known as *funk art*.

The only child of a failed marriage, Jay found her life rescued by her grade school art teacher, Mrs. Emery, a surrogate mother who exuded an Isadora Duncan–style bohemianism. After Jay earned a master's degree at UC Berkeley, she began to attract notice with a show at the Place in 1954 and another at the new San Francisco Dilexi Gallery in 1955.

By 1957, she was featured at the first show at the cutting-edge Ferus Gallery in Los Angeles. Both she and her husband were among the *Sixteen Americans* selected by New York's Museum of Modern Art in 1959, along with future stars like Jasper Johns, Robert Rauschenberg, Louise Nevelson, and Frank Stella. True bohemians, neither she nor Wally attended the show's reception, rejecting it as careerist, although she also said later that they simply didn't realize how important it was. Always relatively reclusive in contrast to her husband, who ran the 6 Gallery as well as the night school at CSFA, Jay withdrew from anything resembling the business of art in 1958 when she began work on what would become her masterpiece.

Around her, the various occupants of her building went about changing San Francisco's arts culture. After the painter Sonia Gechtoff moved to New York, the painter Joan Brown and her husband, Bill, moved in, to be succeeded by the poets Michael and Joanna McClure. Upstairs at 2330 was Jim Newman, a supermarket chain heir from Nebraska who'd attended Stanford in the early '50s until he discovered that the Black jazz players he wanted to book into the college theater weren't welcome, and transferred to Oberlin.

While at Stanford, he met Walter Hopps, who would transfer to UCLA for the same reason, and they remained close. They opened the Syndell Gallery

84   The Last Great Dream

in Los Angeles in 1954, just three years after the county board of supervisors had banned modern art as a tool of Communist infiltration; fortunately, the law does not seem to have been enforced. When Newman moved to San Francisco in 1955, Hopps closed the Syndell, opening the Ferus Gallery in Los Angeles in 1957. Newman had a friend named Bob Alexander, who managed the Jazz Workshop at 473 Broadway, and they joined forces to open the Dilexi Gallery above the Jazz Workshop in 1958. Along with the 6 and the Ferus, the Dilexi became a receptive, catalytic home for modern art ranging from abstract expressionist to assemblage/funk to pop over the next decade.

Newman, said DeFeo, "was totally engaged. He cared for the artists... [he] came along with something that was an absolute original. He was in a position not to be commercial but to be selective in the artists that he chose to handle, and because of that he was totally unique from the so-called more commercial schlocky kind of galleries that will always prevail, I suppose."

Like the 6, the Dilexi was as much an expression of community as any sort of commercial enterprise. Among the other elements of that community were the regular parties at Wally and Jay's apartment. As the head of the night program at CSFA/SFAI, Wally felt "paternal" toward the students, Jay thought, and they joined the poet friends of the McClures in an ongoing and cheerful social life at 2322.

Hedrick was a gregarious and influential presence in the art scene and a pioneering source of many developments in art, ranging from kinetic sculpture to funk/assemblage, pop art, and conceptual art. He'd come to San Francisco from the Southern California car culture, and he would be among the first artists at CSFA to work exclusively with metal. Rather than be either figurative or an abstract expressionist, he created his own path, which was an individualized form of Dada that centered on puns.

A Beat with a sense of humor, he was not above exploiting the emerging stereotype costume of beards, turtleneck, and sandals by accepting pay to sit in the window of the Vesuvio Café and sketch, attracting the tourists who were now crowding North Beach looking for beatniks. His military service in Korea had left him a firm antiauthoritarian, and some of his strongest work in the future would rail against the coming war in Vietnam. He was also an anti-fame-and-money purist; when asked why he declined museum shows, he replied that they only brought attention and money, and then "I would just have

Baghdad by the Bay and Its Artists
85

too much to drink....I know what happens when I get a little money. So I don't need that stuff." He would withdraw entirely from the art business in his late thirties, although he would make art for the rest of his life.

The poet Michael McClure had a friend from his childhood days in Wichita named Bruce Conner, whom he deluged with letters urging him to flee Kansas for Baghdad by the Bay. (Another of his Wichita targets was poet and printer Dave Haselwood, then in the military in Germany. Dave would come to San Francisco in 1958 and be a significant publisher for the poets.) On September 1, 1957, Conner and his brand-new wife, Jean Sandstedt, arrived at the McClure apartment. His arrival was much anticipated: for a long time, said DeFeo, "there was this marvelous talk that 'Bruce is coming, Bruce is coming.'"

After staying with the McClures, the Conners moved around the corner from Painterland to Jackson Street, where their neighbors included Wallace and Shirley Berman and their son, Tosh.

Wallace was an artist from Los Angeles and the publisher of the magazine *Semina*. The *Chronicle*'s Albright described Wallace as a "slight, self-effacing, and yet strangely charismatic figure." Joan Brown thought him "mystical." Visiting San Francisco a few years earlier, he had met Robert Duncan, and they'd fallen into an intense afternoon's conversation. Duncan would later write of his kinship with Berman: "In our conscious alliance with the critical breakthrough of Dada and Surrealism as in our alliance with the Romantic Movement writ large, we began to see ourselves as fashioning unnamed contexts, contexts of a new life way in the making, a secret mission."

Conner was distinctly part of that alliance. As he put it, he'd "always been involved in mysticism—Zen, alchemy, magic, all that stuff." He also had considerable experience with psychedelics. His art was at this point classified as assemblage, although he might well have thought of it as funky. As Albright pointed out, funk was not then a formal style—by the time it became a style, it was stagnant and commercialized—but "a constellation of attitudes and ideas" that originated outside CSFA/SFAI on the street, as it were. It expressed late '50s futility, isolation, and withdrawal, building on sources like Samuel Beckett, Hermann Hesse, and Zen. For Hedrick, the funkiest piece created in this period was Joan Brown's *Rat*.

In correct critic-speak, Conner's method was assemblage, and his most notable early piece was *Child*, a small skeleton in a high chair, which was created to protest an execution; Conner in fact carried it around city hall as part of demonstrations there. He worked with film as well, exploring what Aukeman identified as "primal angst and spiritual yearning—of our mortal fears, joys, pain and pleasures, and our aching need to transcend them." All his work expressed the altered consciousness he'd experienced with peyote, a dislocation from conventional thinking that was pretty much universal among these artists. He was as anti-careerist as Hedrick, stopping his highly successful assemblage work only six years after arriving in San Francisco and treating all his work as subject to revision and essentially incomplete.

Perhaps his most successful artwork was conceptual, the creation of the Rat Bastard Protective Association (RBPA). Thomas Albright thought of the pseudo-organization as a take on Antonin Artaud's "living theater" and "culture in action." A few months after Conner's arrival, he "sent letters out to Joan Brown and Manuel Neri and Wally Hedrick and Jay DeFeo and…[t]old them that they were members of the organization and I was the founder and president, and that they should pay their dues right away. The next meeting was next Friday at my house and that we would have meetings every three weeks at a different person's house." The gatherings were also frequently held at the 6 Gallery, although many of the parties at 2322 began as RBPA meetings.

The name was a mocking play on the Pre-Raphaelite Brotherhood. combined with the city's trash collectors' group, the Scavengers Protective Association. Somewhat later, Conner told a curator that the name was fitting because both he and his artist friends and the garbage workers were "people who were making things with the detritus of society, who themselves were ostracized or alienated from full involvement with society."

By way of example, his first film, *A MOVIE*, was a collage of found film taken from stunt and disaster newsreels, B movies, a German propaganda film, and soft pornography. Ultimately, all his art was a dark, gleeful joke, rooted in Dada, as when his 1959 exhibit at the Spatsa Gallery was publicized with a small card with black borders that read "Works by the Late Bruce Conner."

It was not surprising that the San Francisco artists never became nationally famous; when recognition loomed, they generally walked away. Joan Brown, who had entered CSFA purely on impulse, was featured in a post–*On the*

Baghdad by the Bay and Its Artists 87

Road feature in *Holiday* magazine on "North Beach Poet-Makers." She soon found that success bred a pressure to succeed some more, and opted out, disconnecting from her New York gallery representative. The New York poet Diane di Prima visited San Francisco in 1961, staying with the McClure family at 2330. She found the local artists just as passionate about their work as her fellow New Yorkers, but without the Manhattan hustler's edge. In the west, it seemed to her, it was "possible to have it all," art and a homelife as well. In fact, it was just as important to live one's art as to sell it.

Which was why the Batman Gallery, which opened in 1960 at 2222 Fillmore Street, only a block away from Painterland, was important even though it sold very little, not least because founder Billy "Batman" Jahrmarkt was not always able to make it out of bed to open the gallery. The creativity was there. Bruce Conner had given it black matte walls and assembled ninety-nine pieces of work for his gallery-opening show. *Chronicle* critic Alfred Frankenstein applauded the effort, noting that it was not improvised but a serious gallery, a "magic grotto." The showstopper was Conner's *BLACK DAHLIA*, about the famed Los Angeles murder, a sort of crucifixion that assembled an ostrich plume and nails, "a dialogue between the victim and her murderer." As fellow artist Carlos Villa reflected, "Bruce was in it for a soul journey…there were secrets there."

The Batman would close in 1965, done in by a rent hike that affected 2322 and 2330 Fillmore Street as well, leading to the eviction of Jay DeFeo and Wally Hedrick…and of DeFeo's masterpiece, *The Rose*, arguably the most important work of art in the entire '50s San Francisco scene.

She'd begun it as *The Death Rose* in 1958 in the front room of the downstairs flat at 2322. Year after year, she painted, then scraped off the paint and began again. She would later tell the Smithsonian, "I wanted to create a work that was just so precariously balanced between going this way or that way that it maintained itself." It was both formal and "funky or primitive." Overtly abstract expressionist, it was loosely a mandala, which is to say a psychic map for a pathway to the cosmic.

As it grew, it became as much a sculpture as a painting. Layer after layer of paint on the eleven-by-eight-foot canvas built to a depth of eleven inches; it eventually weighed 1,850 pounds. Eighteen rays surged out from a center point, "a burst of white light in the darkness, like the auras reported by those

88 **The Last Great Dream**

who have returned from the threshold of death," wrote one critic, who noted that in the Kabbalah, eighteen represents *chai*, life.

Bruce Conner watched it being painted and said, "The room itself was the work. The stool, the floor, was covered in chunks of almost flesh-like paint that would be scraped off the canvas. She also mixed powder with the paint that had a mica-like sparkle to it. So walking into this room was like walking into a temple, it was almost alive." In fact, for many years, the paint didn't quite harden and would respond to body heat when people stood close.

Her friend Michael McClure wrote, "She was dealing with paint as the assemblage-ists would deal with worn materials. She was part of a vision, of a new way of seeing. She was beat, she was elegant, she was worn, and she was glimmer. DeFeo is the visionary of the assemblage-ists." Thomas Hoving placed *The Rose* in his *Greatest Works of Art of Western Civilization*, where it was the most chronologically recent choice and the only one by a woman.

One of the most perceptive observations came from Dave Getz, one of the last new artist residents of 2330 Fillmore Street, a student and later teacher at SFAI and the drummer in the Studio 13 Jass Band. Soon after the rent hikes chased them all out in November 1965, he would join a rock band called Big Brother and the Holding Company. An enthusiastic psychedelicist who was unmistakably a part of the mid-'60s countercultural scene, he reflected later that "*The Rose* itself was something that really was a psychedelic piece. In some way, it kind of heralded the new consciousness."

When Walter Hopps learned that the work would have to move—it took a considerable crew from the Bekins Company and a forklift as well as some emergency carpentry to remove part of the bay window and lower the painting to a truck—he offered the painting a refuge in Pasadena, where DeFeo continued to work on it. Eventually, it would be sealed behind a wall at SFAI for twenty years. On November 9, 1995, thirty years after the Bekins truck came, it found a permanent home at the Whitney Museum in New York. DeFeo had died six years before.

Meantime, as she began work, sensualists in pursuit of heightened audio and visual satisfaction in San Francisco had a brand-new experience to enjoy, one that would yield further developments in the 1960s. Jordan Belson had studied painting at CSFA before attending a surrealist film series, *Art in*

Baghdad by the Bay and Its Artists

Cinema, at the SF Museum of Art, when his aim shifted to presenting abstract art in film, beginning in 1947 with a piece fittingly called *Transmutation*.

Henry "Sandy" Jacobs was a KPFA engineer who played what came to be called *world music*. He also began to experiment with tape recorders and ambient sounds, which morphed into musique concrète, frequently served with a large helping of his hipster sense of humor. In 1955, Folkways Records released his *Radio Programme No 1: Henry Jacobs' Music and Folklore*, followed in 1958 on World Pacific by *The Wide Weird World of Shorty Petterstein*.

Early in 1957, Sandy persuaded the management of the Morrison Planetarium at the California Academy of Sciences in Golden Gate Park to present music inside the dome. Built in 1952, the Morrison was the seventh major planetarium in the US and used the very latest technology, developed in part for the navy during World War II. For Jacobs, "simply being in that dome was a holy experience. The entire theatre was like an exquisite instrument." He went to work with the venue's own engineers, placing thirty-six loudspeakers clustered in groups of three around the dome and in the center of the room.

A few weeks later, he joined forces with Belson, and the presentation grew even more extraordinary. Under Belson's supervision, the engineers added special interference-pattern projectors to the hundreds of projectors already there.

They debuted on May 28, 1957, under the name *Vortex*, and it was beyond spectacular. "We could tint the space any color we wanted to," said Belson. "Just being able to control the darkness was very important. We could get it down to jet black and then take it down twenty-five degrees lower than that, so you really got that sinking-in feeling...we masked and filtered the light, and used images that didn't touch the frame lines. It had an uncanny effect: not only was the image free of the frame, but free of space somehow. It just hung there three-dimensionally because there was no frame of reference....We were able to project images over the entire dome, so that things would come pouring down from the center, sliding along the walls. At times the whole place would seem to reel."

They presented forty shows over the next two years using music like Luciano Berio's *Omaggio a Joyce*, Karlheinz Stockhausen, John Cage, and Afro-Cuban drumming, set to images of the cosmos—suns, stars, galaxies—and Buddhist iconography. The *Chronicle's* Alfred Frankenstein particularly applauded the sense of space their work and the dome created: "limitless, incomprehensively vast, and awe-inspiring in its implications."

The scholar David McConville observed that *Vortex* explored "the effects of a spatialized, synaesthetic, and omnidirectional gestalt on audience perceptions. The overwhelming audience response anticipated the quest for new modes of experience that would become prevalent throughout the following decade."

Some of those new modes of experience undoubtedly included transforming consciousness with cannabis before entering the planetarium. In any case, Jacobs later recalled, planetarium management found that some of the clientele attracted to the shows made them uncomfortable, and after two years, they canceled the series.

The explorations that Belson and Jacobs had so beautifully initiated would continue. Building on Beat affirmation of spirituality and rejection of the bourgeois, a rough beast of a subculture was taking shape in San Francisco.

12

England Awakens— Skiffle and Style

Five thousand miles away from the planetarium in London, kindred waves of new social rules began to move through English life. Bound by an overweening class system, much of Britain's so-called previous bohemianism had been largely upper class, private, and personal, usually sexual, which did not seem to have had any great social effect.

World War II not only ended the empire, it also helped set loose African American music that British youth would embrace, part of a wider postwar trend toward loosening class barriers. Musically basic and rather homely, skiffle would have a remarkable impact.

In the decade after the war, England was economically stagnant. The rationing of seemingly everything—petrol, meat, sugar, sweets, cheese, even tea—made Britain seem gray. The economies of Germany and Japan were booming, but England lagged. America had youth, Paris had existentialists, Italy had la dolce vita. It wasn't yet obvious, but British youth had hope. America had sent not only armaments but music as well, and England was going to adapt and transform the latter.

"Trad"—in English slang, traditional New Orleans jazz—found an early home in 1943 in George Webb's Bexleyheath & District Rhythm Club in the back bar of the Red Barn pub, opposite Barnehurst railway station. By 1948, there were enough kindred spirits that the London Jazz Club was able to move to a long-term situation at the 100 Club at 100 Oxford Street in Soho.

One of the jazz club fans, Ken Colyer, had grown up in Soho in the 1930s and found himself being Americanized by the movies and by the jazz his elder brother, Bill, never stopped playing. When Bill went off to war, the family left Soho for suburban Cranford, and Ken took up the trumpet and dove into the blues and New Orleans jazz on tunes like "Alabama Bound," "Matchbox Blues," "How Long Blues," and "It's Tight Like That."

Joining the merchant marine after the war, Ken got to New York and went straight to the shrine of New Orleans music there, Eddie Condon's club in Greenwich Village. Soon after, he jumped ship in Mobile and headed to New Orleans to play with one of his heroes, clarinetist George Lewis. He was ecstatic, though he was swiftly deported back to London.

His first group in England, the Crane River Jazz Band, had taken shape at the White Hart pub back home in Cranford. At first, their manager, his brother, Bill, played some of his treasured 78s during set breaks, tunes from Jelly Roll Morton and King Oliver. Along with classic jazz, they liked country blues and a variant that they called "breakdown music," which in America would be better known as jug band music, although at the White Hart they used a kazoo rather than a jug. Lead Belly's "Midnight Special" was a favorite, along with Leroy Carr, Big Bill Broonzy, and Lonnie Johnson's "Careless Love." In their hands, the Mississippi Sheiks' "Corinna, Corinna" became "Crane River Woman."

In 1953, having returned from his adventure with George Lewis, Ken joined forces with Chris Barber, who'd grown up next to an American air base near Cambridge. Chris, too, had become besotted by a wide range of African American music, learning trombone after listening to Duke Ellington, Tampa Red, Slim Gaillard, the Golden Gate Quartet, and Louis Jordan on the Armed Forces Network.

While Colyer was at sea, Barber started a new band with Tony "Lonnie" (for Lonnie Johnson) Donegan on banjo and Monty Sunshine, once of the Crane River unit, on clarinet. They debuted on Christmas Eve 1952 at

England Awakens—Skiffle and Style

the Creole Club in Soho and were a triumph. Early in 1953, they lost their trumpet player, but they heard rumors from New Orleans, and in March, when Ken arrived back at Waterloo Station, he was greeted by both his brother and Chris Barber. Their meeting would have consequences.

Billed as "Ken Colyer's Jazzmen" and with Bill as manager, the band debuted on April 25, 1953, at the London Jazz Club, the basement of a church a block away from Marble Arch, working there until September. They were very good and soon had a recording contract with Decca, which released their first record in February 1954. From the beginning, they played folk blues at the intervals with Colyer on trumpet and Barber on bass and Lonnie on guitar and vocals.

At Bill's suggestion, they named the interval music *skiffle*, in homage to an obscure group called Dan Burley & His Skiffle Boys. Burley was actually a significant figure in African American journalism, the editor of the *New York Age* and *Amsterdam News*, and later *Ebony* and *Jet*. He'd gotten his start as a pianist in Chicago Depression-era rent parties and then recorded some sides for the producer Rudi Blesh in 1945. Bill Colyer was clearly a serious collector to know Burley's name, since Dan and the Skiffles never developed much of a following, even though the group included the legendary Pops Foster on bass along with Brownie McGhee and his brother, Stick.

Ken was a superb player but a difficult man and a heavy drinker, which made him more difficult still. In May 1954, Ken and Bill began to talk about firing the rhythm section. Instead, the rest of the band fired them.

Skiffle was about to ride to popularity through yet another innovation in English life. Though England will eternally be thought of as the home of tea drinkers, one of the essential elements of English youth culture from 1953 on was something new: coffee bars. Fleeing their own depressed economy with its 30 percent unemployment, many Italians had sought work in England, and one of them was a traveling dental equipment salesman named Pino Riservato. He sensibly disdained the local version of coffee, and he just happened to be related to a director of the Gaggia company, which made imposing, steam-blasting espresso machines. Riservato added the machines to his sales inventory, and when English cafés didn't respond, he opened the first English coffee bar, the Moka, at 29 Frith Street in Soho. It boomed.

In addition to improving the quality of coffee, the bars became a second home for youth—and skiffle. The Gyre & Gimble, at 31 John Adam Street near Charing Cross Station, was a basement joint whose owner put out handbills that read, "London's rendezvous for its famous bohemians, artists, models, and musicians." The regulars included prostitutes, merchant seamen, students from Saint Martin's School of Art, and occasionally their models. Soon after, the all-night club Nucleus opened on Monmouth Street, which gave musicians whose gigs ended after the tube stopped running a place to hang out until transport resumed in the morning. Then Orlando's on Old Compton Street began to host a skiffle group called the Ghouls.

On May 31, 1954, Chris Barber's Jazz Band debuted at the 100 Club, and six weeks later recorded *New Orleans Joys* (intriguingly, it was just eight days after Elvis Presley had recorded "That's Alright, Mama," a rhythmically similar, high-energy version of an original). They included two skiffle tunes, "Rock Island Line" and "John Henry." Decca was not overwhelmed and delayed releasing it until January 1955. Later that year, Fats Domino's "Ain't That a Shame" hit the charts, followed by the October arrival in theaters of *Blackboard Jungle*, which sent "Rock Around the Clock" to the top of the British charts for the last seven weeks of the year.

Hoping to capitalize on the popularity of American music, Barber released a second album in November 1955, which went nowhere, nor did another album, *Backstairs Session*, credited to Lonnie Donegan. But in January 1956, a bright lad at Decca, which had dropped Barber, smelled the interest in skiffle and released Donegan and Barber's rendition of Lead Belly's "Rock Island Line" as a single under Donegan's name. It entered the charts at number eight (joining "The Ballad of Davy Crockett" and Tennessee Ernie Ford's "16 Tons") and rose from there.

Skiffle exploded. Played on guitar, tea chest bass, and washboard, it was cheap at a time when instruments in England were scarce and expensive, and relatively simple music that seemingly everyone could play. Music historian Pete Frame wrote of skiffle that "it was history, it was romance, it was offbeat and rebellious, it was unpalatable and incomprehensible to old fogies, a generation gap widener. What's more it swung like crazy and tore through the room like a tornado....We could do this! The washboard was the key." Suddenly, frantic dancing had become a feature of trad jazz.

England Awakens—Skiffle and Style

Yet another Soho pub, the Roundhouse, began to feature skiffle in the fall of 1955, with a house act led by Bob Watson, who'd gotten his start in skiffle as an audience member listening to the Crane River Jazz Band at the White Hart. With regular sit-ins by blues harmonica player and Lead Belly student Cyril Davies and the highly knowledgeable Alexis Korner, the Roundhouse became an institution.

Korner brought along a political edge with his music. "Although it came to nothing, some of us were convinced that we were on the edge of breaking down the British three-class system, that we could create a fourth class made up of refugees from the other three, and then say, 'Fuck the class system altogether.' Jazz was one of the ways of doing that, as far as we were concerned." Nor was he alone. Banjoist John Hasted, who taught nuclear physics at University College, was a party member who bridged the world of skiffle with the nascent English anti–nuclear weapons movement.

They were social as well as political deviants. Johnny Pilgrim, a member of the skiffle band the Vipers, recalled, "We were beatniks before the term was invented and ours was a world where sex and jazz and drinking and having a good time wasn't wrong."

One very good time came on July 14, 1956, when John Hasted and Redd Sullivan from the Gyre & Gimble grabbed Vipers Wally Whyton and Johnny Pilgrim and inveigled them onto a flatbed truck to play as part of a parade for the Soho Fair. The parade ended at 59 Old Compton Street, in front of the 2i's coffee bar. The four of them went in to grab some coffee and played a little, and the owner invited them to take up musical residence. Although the stage at the 2i's was in the basement and nothing to brag about, merely planks laid on top of milk crates, the Vipers took the gig. And, Pete Frame declared, "all British rock history starts that day."

England wasn't initially an easy sell for rock. Very little American rock or R & B was released in Britain, and British covers of American songs were generally poor. But American movies were welcome, even cheap exploitation flicks like *Rock Around the Clock*. English fans went wild over it, and in the fall of 1956 it became a Big Deal when the ever-restrained English tabloid press portrayed the fan response—some vandalism, dancing in the aisles and even onstage, sixty arrested—as the entire country in chaos. Behind it all was the sultry, seemingly dangerous image of Elvis Presley, although he would never perform in England.

96 **The Last Great Dream**

At first, *Melody Maker* and the BBC refused to acknowledge rock, the Beeb intoning, nose in air, "It is not autocracy, but wisdom, that suggests a policy of broadcasting on the basis of giving people what they should like and will come to like." Unsurprisingly, young Britons ignored such opinions, and by June 1957, the BBC Light Programme had begun a weekly *Saturday Skiffle Club* show. The frozen monolith that was English social custom had begun to thaw.

One of the other handicaps for the new young British rockers was the paucity of equipment in England. Mo Foster, one of those rockers, also cited the primitive state of sound systems in venues, such that "it was lucky anyone in the audience heard a note before well into the '60s. Around 1960, it became possible to import American goods built for the purpose."

The first British rock performer was an attractive if not overly gifted vocalist named Tommy Hicks, who sat in on "Heartbreak Hotel" with the Vipers at the 2i's in the fall of 1956. Within months, he'd become Tommy Steele, the protégé of the promoter Larry Parnes. His first song, "Rock with the Caveman," did well, and a string of weak imitations would follow. More credible music came with Buddy Holly and the Crickets, who toured England in March and April 1958 to considerable acclaim. Hard on their heels was the Killer, Jerry Lee Lewis, accompanied by his thirteen-year-old cousin and newlywed wife, Myra. On May 26, 1958, the *Daily Mirror*'s front page read POLICE CHECK UP ON CHILD BRIDE, and after three shows, the tour was canceled.

Soon after Holly's tour, British youth had their own rock star. Born in India, Harry Webb came to England as part of the dissolution of the Empire. After seeing Bill Haley & His Comets, he started a skiffle group, then formed an Elvis Presley–style trio, the Drifters—his resemblance to the King had not escaped notice. In 1958, they were joined by Ian Samwell, and on May 3, they debuted at the 2i's as Cliff Richard and the Drifters (by 1959, they were the Shadows, to avoid legal conflict with the American Drifters).

Their agent gave them a piece of junk, "Schoolboy Crush," to record, with permission to do what they liked on the B-side. Annoyed by a *Melody Maker* article that pronounced rock dead, Samwell produced a very good rockabilly song called "Move It." No one much liked "Schoolboy Crush," but TV producer Jack Good, who'd fled the BBC to form the show *Oh Boy* on

England Awakens—Skiffle and Style

independent television, loved the B-side, and it became a hit, the first genuine British rock song.

As the new decade came on, signs of a further loosening of class structure and moral strictures abounded, melted by music and dancing. The birth control pill arrived in 1961. The year before, the Crown had prosecuted the publication of *Lady Chatterley's Lover* for obscenity; after three hours of deliberation, the jury's response was "Not guilty." A week later, a new edition sold two hundred thousand copies in a day. Satire was set free, and Peter Cook, Jonathan Miller, Alan Bennett, and Dudley Moore presented the savagely hilarious *Beyond the Fringe*, first in Edinburgh in August 1960 and then in the West End of London. After a great review from Kenneth Tynan, it sailed into legend. The magazine *Private Eye* followed, and then the television series *TW3* (*That Was the Week That Was*).

The trend toward freedom came not only in matters of popular culture but at the more conventionally sociopolitical level. The Campaign for Nuclear Disarmament (CND) began in February 1958 and held the first of a number of galvanizing marches on Easter weekends from 1958 until well into the next decade. The first march started from Trafalgar Square in London and proceeded fifty-two miles west to Aldermaston, home of the Atomic Weapons Research Establishment, in "bitter cold, incessant rain, and the first Easter snow for a century," reported Pete Frame. Ken Colyer's Jazzmen played along the route, as well as the City Ramblers—no surprise, as John Hasted of the Gyre & Gimble was the march's music director. The next year and after, they reversed direction, aiming now at the seat of power.

The marchers were a varied lot. Sue Miles, who with her husband, Barry, would be at the center of London's alternative culture for the next decade and longer, thought of them as "vaguely left-wing and brown rice and lentils, hand-made pottery mugs." There were trade unionists, pacifists, Quakers, and beatniks—from the looks of it, the coffee bars were empty that weekend. The marches brought hundreds and then thousands of young people out of small towns and connected them to people in London, leading to a quickening of alternative opinion around the country. The marches also catalyzed a great realization: "Contrary to our headmasters' propaganda," wrote one marcher, "we weren't the only freaks around, there were actually *thousands* of us. And that was wonderful."

The Last Great Dream

*   *   *

The other new cultural opening for English youth came in the realm of fashion and the arts. Born in 1934, Mary Quant was an émigré from suburban Blackheath attending Goldsmiths' College, an art and technical school. She recalled that "I grew up not wanting to grow up. Growing up seemed terrible. It meant having candy-floss hair, stiletto heels, girdles and great boobs. To me it was awful; children were free and sane and grown-ups were hideous." Instead, she married the free spirit Alexander Plunket Greene, heir to a family of eccentrics connected to Paul Robeson, Bertrand Russell, and Evelyn Waugh. Late in 1955, she and Greene opened Bazaar, a clothing and jewelry boutique at 128 King's Road.

Bazaar was funded by Archie McNair, who'd just opened Fantasie, the first coffee bar outside Soho. Fantasie, Bazaar, Finch's Pub, and Archie's studio swiftly became the home ground—pubs, clubs, and coffee bars along King's Road—for what was termed *the Chelsea Set*. The set was the first divergent youth group in London since the '20s; upper-class, aristocratic, trust fund babies who rejected the postwar malaise.

Quant's talents went far beyond running a shop. At night, she whipped up fashions in her home, offering them for sale the next day. Sexy, casual, young, and free, the clothing epitomized her and her customers. Until Quant came along, Britain and fashion had been limited to elegant men's suits from Savile Row and cashmere twin sets and pearls for women. She would change all that.

As the new decade began, an actor and a photographer would join her as the new faces representing England. Terence Stamp was a complete East Ender (the socially déclassé Cockney side of London), the sort of person afraid of nothing except being accused of putting on airs. He earned a scholarship to the Webber Douglas Academy of Dramatic Art and studied hard. Mentored by the slightly older Peter O'Toole, he began to move in a world where people read novels, studied film, and then talked about it all in coffee bars. In 1961, he got the lead in Peter Ustinov's *Billy Budd*, and when he received an Oscar nomination for his work, he became the symbol of a new and modern Britain. "We work hard and we play hard," he told the press. "We have no class and no prejudice. We're the new swinging Englishmen. And it's people like me who are spreading the word."

England Awakens—Skiffle and Style

Born east of the East End, David Bailey, along with Terence Donovan and Brian Duffy, shot to fame as one of a trinity of British fashion photographers. Though dyslexic, he refused to be categorized as a working-class yob (British slang for an uncultured lout). RAF service in Singapore turned his life around; he picked up a camera and became enamored of bohemian life through reading. Released in 1958, he found a sponsor in the photographer John French, who liked his style, which featured, in one historian's words, "Cuban-heeled boots, jeans, leather jacket, and hair over the ears, all before the Beatles."

Equipped with the outsider/East Ender belief that life was a joke and the conventional world absurd, he sold pictures to the tabloid *Daily Express*, which led to job offers from John Parsons, art director of the British *Vogue*. He turned down the first offer but took the second, and by February 1961, he was shooting covers. He began using a 35 mm Pentax and dispensed with a tripod, injecting movement and energy into his shots. The act of shooting became an erotic dance, and his models loved the results. A serious workaholic, he also held true to his East End roots, playing the Cockney court jester with his upper-class editors. Cheek, they called it.

East End cheek now seemed attractive. The magazine *Queen* changed from staid coverage of the royal family to articles about the new creators like Quant, and tripled in size to accommodate all the advertising that poured in.

Rationing was over. Suddenly, England seemed to be youth and energy and fun.

13

Los Angeles: Wallace Berman, Ferus, and Venice Beach

Los Angeles's contribution to the evolving bohemian culture during the late '50s was most powerful in the world of avant-garde painting, notably Walter Hopps's Ferus Gallery, which would put on Andy Warhol's first one-man show. Later, Hopps produced the first major Duchamp retrospective, and before the label had even come into existence, he presented the first pop art show, called *New Painting of Common Objects*.

Hopps had help from his friend Wallace Berman. "[Ed] Kienholz was my partner, but Berman was my intellectual guide." He remarked that Berman was "spiritually misty." He'd be walking rather slowly, and when asked how he was doing, reply, "I'm waiting for a message to come in on the ether." When asked who was on the ether, he'd answer, "The dead poets are speaking to me."

The actor Dennis Hopper, a regular in the Ferus scene as a collector and photographer, said of Berman that he was "always a mystery to me, and he was very glamorous. He was a quiet, gentle, humble person, and he had this strange aura about him that was removed, yet not hostile—he was a guy you couldn't really reach...we all deferred to him because he had a very spiritual quality. He was the guy. Wallace was the guru."

Growing up in Los Angeles's Fairfax district, Berman had an early affinity for African American life; his closest high school friend was Sammy Davis Jr. Berman came of age in the postwar bebop and dance culture, so that Hopps first saw him in a jazz joint, a "short, angular white man with dark glasses in a baby-blue zoot suit moving through the room with a blonde in a tight black dress, about a foot taller than him." Berman was a serious music fan, hanging out for hours at Ross Russell's Tempo Music Shop on Hollywood Boulevard, so much a regular that he was able to attend one of Russell's earliest recording sessions for Dial Records. The session would inspire Berman to create his first art piece, the cover for the 1947 Dial release *Be-Bop Jazz*.

After being expelled from high school for gambling, he was arrested for possession of cannabis and offered the choice of jail or the navy. His service was tolerable enough until he was forced to take part in the killing of dolphins and had an emotional breakdown, which led to an honorable discharge. Soon after, he was ejected from art school. By now, he had a clear, fixed taste for life outside the mainstream and a desire to be anonymous as far as the conventional world was concerned. He had a driver's license because it was impossible to live in Los Angeles without one, but he never voted or had his name on a lease or mortgage. His son thought that he "craved anonymity like it was air."

In 1955, he began the ongoing artwork that would be his primary legacy, an unusual magazine called *Semina*. Over the next decade, he would create nine issues, each an envelope that held poems, pictures, and *objets*, a work of assemblage that was also greatly inspired by poets. Berman in fact operated at the nexus of the assemblage art world and the current new poetry being written by people like Michael McClure and Robert Duncan and their friends, as well as older surrealists like Jean Cocteau and Antonin Artaud. It was no wonder that Hopps described Berman as "crucial to me as an interpreter of what was going on in art and literature." Art was his entire persona. As Joan Brown put it, Berman "just stood, for me, for the whole idea of the individual."

Because there was a significant element of chance in how one removed the items from the envelope, the cards that carried the poems and pictures, it

Los Angeles: Wallace Berman, Ferus, and Venice Beach   103

was something of a game, perhaps an homage to Hesse's *The Glass Bead Game*, which he revered, or perhaps the tarot. The first issue included Hesse's "To a Toccata by Bach" from "Poems of Knecht's Student Days" in the *Bead Game*, along with Cocteau's "The Detective," a poem by the young David Meltzer, and a Walter Hopps photograph of a big band tenor player. An issue of *Semina* was not an object but an element in a relationship that demanded a response, if only in how one laid out the cards.

An enigma wrapped in mystery, *Semina* was "both ocular and occultic," wrote Meltzer. "It was both revealed and concealed which gives it an interesting edge....You have to translate it in a different way than looking at an Altoon gestural painting...." One likely source for *Semina* as an art container was Duchamp's "The Box in a Valise." Yet another was *View*, the surrealist journal of the 1940s.

Berman's goal, said one scholar, was "to transcend the 'monster' of postwar meaninglessness." It was an art, said one curator, "infused with nostalgia, lyricism, and feeling," which neatly reflected its community ethos, since it was mailed to friends and not usually offered for sale. It also contained an ethos of exploration that included drugs, ranging from a Cocteau sketch of an opium smoker to a picture of Bob Alexander (Jim Newman's partner at the Dilexi, an addict) shooting up. Berman himself was an enthusiastic pot smoker.

More creatively, an early issue included McClure's "Peyote Poem"—quite fitting, since Berman had given McClure the peyote buttons. As McClure told a historian later, "We were not taking peyote to get high, we were taking it for personal and alchemical reasons. We were damned serious." His poem shimmered: "Light is eternity. Breathing is music made in space and looms like a physical object. Creakings and rustlings are Noh plays....The crisp edge and light on all things is vast and true. Colors are all bright and are new in Timelessness." McClure would see and celebrate the flesh as inherently spiritual, and the peyote trip forever confirmed what one critic called his "biological mysticism."

Along with Berman, Walter Hopps had grown up deeply invested in the jazz/ R & B music of Los Angeles, but the visual arts were his life's passion. A high school program led him to a transformational visit with the renowned collectors of surrealist and Dada art, Walter and Louise Arensberg. Their home was simply stuffed with paintings, he recalled in his brilliant memoir, *The Dream Colony*. "They were used in any way decoratively and they took precedence over the furniture: chairs, desks, tables, anything associated with the normal activities of life was in second position. The art was hung edge to edge—it was everywhere and in every room. You could open a coatroom door and there would be pictures hung on the inside of the door. Or on both sides."

Hopps also connected with the LA avant-garde world by attending the Evenings on the Roof concerts organized by Peter and Frances Yates. When Hopps went off to Stanford, he found time to observe Clyfford Still at CSFA and also hang around a warehouse with many loft studios at 9 Mission Street, where Richard Diebenkorn, Hassel Smith, and Lawrence Ferling (he would soon reclaim his entire name) worked.

Transferring to UCLA, Hopps organized in 1955 the first West Coast abstract expressionist show, *Action One*, more often known as the *Merry Go Round* show, since it was held at the carousel on Santa Monica Pier. Stretching tarps around the carousel poles, they hung one hundred paintings from forty artists that included San Franciscans Rothko, Still, Diebenkorn, and DeFeo.

After opening and closing the Syndell Gallery, Hopps partnered with painter Ed Kienholz to open the Ferus Gallery at 736 La Cienega Boulevard in March 1957. Their first show, *Objects on the New Landscape Demanding of the Eye*, featured work by several of the *Action One* group. Most of the later shows were one- and two-person shows by artists Hopps described as "dark-side-of-the-moon assemblage artists and the lyric abstract people." The most important show, he said, was Wallace Berman's, his first solo show.

It had a piece called *Homage to Hermann Hesse*, an environmental enclosure called *Temple*, a third sculpture, *Cross*, and, scattered on the floor, the contents of *Semina 1*. That's where the trouble began and the LAPD came calling. One element of the *Semina* issue was a line drawing of a woman mounted from behind with a snake tongue sticking out of her mouth. It had been drawn by Cameron—Marjorie Cameron Parsons Kimmel, among other things a follower of Aleister Crowley's Thelema movement and later, with Anaïs Nin, a star in Kenneth Anger's *Inauguration of the Pleasure Dome*. The picture was not even visible, which lends credence to the theory that someone seeking press coverage of the gallery, perhaps Ed Kienholz, had called the police and encouraged the arrest.

Los Angeles: Wallace Berman, Ferus, and Venice Beach 105

A member of the vice squad called that morning and said the gallery could clear things out if they wanted, but Berman declined. Certainly, the Cameron drawing did not suggest obscenity to him; he thought of it as white magic. At trial, Berman testified that an angel of God had told him to marry a good woman and have a child and devote himself to goodness. The judge was unpersuaded of his virtue, found him guilty, and fined him $150, which a friend covered. For a man so devoted to privacy, the arrest was shattering, although the *Los Angeles Times*, which never did cover Ferus, ignored the case. He burned *Temple* and *Cross* and moved to San Francisco for the next three years.

The gallery did much better. Kienholz withdrew to resume painting and was replaced by Irving Blum, who found an angel to improve finances and generally made it a more professional operation. A New Yorker, Blum connected the gallery to the rising stars in the east, and shows with Jasper Johns, Roy Lichtenstein, and Frank Stella joined work by the Los Angeles regulars, soon including Ed Ruscha. Piqued by the proximity to Hollywood, Andy Warhol made his solo gallery show debut at Ferus in 1962 and contributed his *Campbell's Soup Cans*, which garnered notoriety but almost no sales. In the end, Blum bought the lot on time for $1,000 at $100 dollars a month. Thirty years later, he sold it to New York's MoMA for $15 million.

One of the reasons Warhol had been interested in Ferus was that Blum had assured him that movie stars frequented the gallery. When Warhol returned for a second visit in 1963, Blum delivered on his promise, thanks to their real Hollywood connection, Dennis Hopper.

Stagestruck from childhood, Hopper had landed a part as an epileptic in the television show *Medic*, where he apparently did a good job of portraying a seizure. He began to get studio offers and early on established a well-earned reputation for being difficult when he told the autocratic head of Columbia, Harry "King" Cohn, to fuck off. Deeply moved by James Dean's genius, Hopper reached an early peak with his performance in *Rebel Without a Cause*, but soon slid into B-movie status. One of his friends was the Ferus painter Billy Al Bengston, and Hopper became a regular at the gallery.

Warhol was impressed by meeting the man he remembered as Billy the Kid, "Billie the Maniac," from an episode of the television series *Sugarfoot*. When Hopper put him up at the Beverly Hills Hotel and threw a party that included his friends Peter Fonda, Troy Donahue, Dean Stockwell, and Suzanne Pleshette, Warhol was thrilled.

The Ferus group pointed the way to a new and individualized mode of seeing art. The literary side of the Los Angeles scene was more problematic, not least because it had an explicit leader, which inevitably grated against the inherent anarchism of the Beat sensibility.

Although the leader was sincere, he was ultimately quite clueless about the meaning of Beat. Lawrence Lipton came from the same left-wing Chicago bohemian circle that had produced Kenneth Rexroth, and with Rexroth was coauthor of the Dada-esque "Escalator Manifesto," which declared, "Escalator is the backfire of the hindbrain / against the conflagration of reason...the moon in a puddle of mud."

He would advocate anarchism and the bohemian for the rest of his life, while being simultaneously trapped in a conundrum, for as a writer, he was a very competent hack. "I was capable of doing the very thing I had the most contempt for," he told a friend, "and doing it well." Although his wife was given the credit, he was coauthor of a successful series of detective stories.

Lipton wanted to be a shamanic poet, a pagan new barbarian directly transmitting experience, but he had to acknowledge that his *Rainbow at Midnight* was "not so much a book of poems as a long essay written in verse *about* poetry." "Sentimental," "bookish," "too many long words," said his friend Rexroth.

Venice was an inexpensive soft landing for those no longer interested in the American rat race, and by 1954 or so, twenty or thirty bohemians had settled there, most notably poets Stuart Perkoff, Tony Scibella, Alexander Trocchi, and Charles Foster. Lipton began a salon, lecturing on history and preaching the cause of "disaffiliation"—*alienation* smacked too much of the *Partisan Review.* Perhaps *preach* was the relevant word. Most of Lipton's followers lacked great talent and frequently came accompanied by dire handicaps like drug addiction (Perkoff, Trocchi) or psychotic episodes (John Altoon, who would grace the cover of Lipton's magnum opus, the novel *The Holy Barbarians*).

Before he fell prey to heroin addiction, Perkoff was by far the most interesting of the group, and his *The Suicide Room* was their best piece of work. Born in St. Louis, he had turned up in Judith Malina's anarchist

Los Angeles: Wallace Berman, Ferus, and Venice Beach 107

circles in 1950, and after debuting in Cid Corman's *Origin* had published in *Semina* and kindred magazines in San Francisco and New York. Historian John Maynard described Perkoff as having a true shamanic approach, poems written "not to be spoken, but *as if* spoken."

In contrast, Lipton was only intellectually a bohemian. His salons included jazz, since that was what was happening in San Francisco and New York. He forbade pot smoking, which seems odd. When Perkoff's wife, Suzan, broke down under the influence of pot, sex, Benzedrine, and cosmic self-exploration, she sought counsel from Lipton. As he wrote about it, her problem was not so much that she had taken on far too much to handle but that she had not listened carefully enough to Lipton's lectures on the various subjects. When Allen Ginsberg famously challenged an apparently drunken heckler by disrobing and telling him, "Come and stand here, stand naked before the world. I dare you! The poet always stands naked before the world," Lipton tut-tutted that there were women and children upstairs.

Lipton compounded this disconnect with his personal ambition to make Venice a scene that would top that of his old friend and now rival Rexroth. To do that, he produced *The Holy Barbarians*, a fictionalized history of the Venice scene and an easily digested popularization of the ideas that *Howl* and *On the Road* had floated. Eager to link Venice to a wider revolution, he applied the term *Beat* to the Venice scene, although none of the locals had used it to that point.

What was truly embarrassing was Lipton's breathless sales pitch to the media, announcing to one journalist that he was "Mentor of the Holy Barbarians. They call me *The Shaman of the Tribe*. I interpret their way of life to the public." Television was dubious about Ginsberg, who might well say something difficult. But as he waited backstage at *The Jack Paar Show*, Lipton told a reporter from *Saturday Review*, "The Holy Barbarians are the conscience of the world....You've got to swing with that idea, or you're still in Squaresville."

Sincere but oblivious, Lipton promoted poverty and art as though, said his biographer, it was "like any other consumer product. Thus his enduring gifts to the movement...were oversimplification, a nearly incestuous relationship with the commercial media, and, most of all, the hard sell."

14

New York in the Late '50s

As bohemia matured in the late '50s Village, it mixed existential drama, a hip publishing company, poetry, jazz, the Catholic Workers, and a prophetic comedian into a rich, fascinating gumbo.

In the fall of 1956, Samuel Beckett's *Waiting for Godot* became famous on Broadway, but it had come to America, logically enough, via Barney Rosset's Grove Press, soon to be an iconic part of Village culture. Rosset had married the painter Joan Mitchell, part of the Cedar Tavern art circle, who told him about a publishing firm for sale on Grove Street. Under Rosset, Grove Press was a most informal place, a hangout as well as a publishing firm; Allen Ginsberg got to know Elsa Dorfman, the Grove secretary, because they had the first copying machine in the neighborhood and she let him use it.

Reading about *Godot* in the *Times*, Rosset read it in French, then met Beckett and for a $200 advance published it in 1954. After an abortive premiere billed as a "laugh sensation" at the Coconut Grove Dinner Playhouse (what *were* they thinking?), it opened on Broadway on April 19, 1956, with Bert Lahr as Estragon and E. G. Marshall as Vladamir. The first words, "Nothing to be done," announced not only the characters' "existential impasse," wrote critic John Lahr, but also "the author's aesthetic attack—no context, no exposition, no admonitions, no answers, no common ground." Doing is pointless; one can only be. Thus "the compulsion to narrate our meaninglessness *is* our meaning."

If he had only brought the most important play of the twentieth century to America, Rosset would be worthy of celebration. Of course, Grove did much more, joining James Laughlin's New Directions in the pantheon of significant avant-garde Greenwich Village publishers (the latter was a part of Village intellectual culture, albeit located just above the Village's northern border). In 1936, Ezra Pound had told a well-fixed Harvard undergraduate named Laughlin to "do something useful," and he responded with a library's worth of modern poetry and prose, from Wallace Stevens, James Agee, and Rexroth to Pound, Tennessee Williams, and William Carlos Williams.

One of Rosset's editors was Don Allen, who had studied at Berkeley, worked at New Directions, and then helped edit Grove's house journal, *Evergreen Review*, which, in its second issue, spring 1957, helped define the San Francisco scene nationally with a truly remarkable collection of work: all the 6 Gallery poets plus Kerouac, Duncan, Ferlinghetti, and Henry Miller, as well as a report on the jazz scene by Ralph Gleason and splendid photography of the poets by Harry Redl. It was so astonishingly good that Allen then enlarged his range and curated Grove's definitive anthology, *The New American Poetry*.

Godot and poetry were important, but the middle-late '50s in the Village meant jazz. Modern (bop) jazz had begun in Harlem, then moved to Fifty-Second Street, but it settled in for life at the mother church of jazz in America, the Village Vanguard, at 178 Seventh Avenue South, Max Gordon, proprietor. Gordon had come to the Village after graduating from Reed College in 1924. In 1932, he opened Village Fair, a place to hear poets. Oddly enough, the club drew an audience that wanted to listen to old-school declaimers like Joe Gould and Maxwell Bodenheim. By the end of the decade, it was the Village Vanguard, with folk music by Lead Belly as its first attraction.

Then Lorraine Lion, née Stein, arrived. A committed jazz fan, she had gone to work for and then married Alfred Lion, the cofounder of Blue Note Records. As the '40s passed, Gordon had increasingly booked small group

New York in the Late '50s

jazz, and in between importuning Gordon to book the Blue Note artist Thelonious Monk, she fell in love with Gordon. After divorcing Lion, she married Max Gordon, a marriage of some forty years; her romance with the Vanguard lasted another thirty.

By the mid-'50s, their place was joined by several more Village jazz clubs, from Café Bohemia, where Miles Davis made a newly sober return to New York in 1956 after his triumph at the 1955 Newport Jazz Festival, to the funky little bar in the Bowery called the Five Spot that became home to Monk for some six months starting in the fall of 1957, to the Village Gate in 1958, where simply everyone in jazz would play, above all John Coltrane.

Jazz was the soundtrack for hip Village life, a part of an increasingly conscious group. One of those people was the young poet Diane di Prima. She estimated, rather conservatively, that there were forty or fifty people in New York, perhaps the same number in San Francisco, "who knew what we knew: who raced about in Levi's and work shirts, made art, smoked dope, dug the new jazz, and spoke a bastardization of black argot....But our isolation was total and impenetrable, and we did not try to communicate with even the small handful of our confreres. Our chief concern was to keep our integrity... and to keep our cool."

One night, a friend walked in as she was cooking and handed her a copy of *Howl*. She read the first line, walked away from the stove, and sat down by the Hudson to absorb it. Allen had "broken ground for all of us....The poem put a certain heaviness in me, too....For I sensed that Allen was only, could only be, the vanguard of a much larger thing."

She had already committed herself to an unconventional life, seduced into poetry by Cocteau's *Blood of a Poet*: "In the striving, get-ahead thrust of America 1950, where nothing existed beyond the world of the senses, the clearest way to turn from materialism was to turn to the arts. To be an outcast...was the calling. Not fame or publication. Keeping one's hands clean, not engaging. By staying on the outside we felt they weren't our wars, our murders, our mistakes."

She was one of the people in the audience at Café Bohemia or the Five Spot, but she also participated in the new culture, helping the dancer Jimmy Waring stage-manage the Living Theatre. Her affair with LeRoi Jones was further consummated in poetry when they founded the *Floating Bear* (named for Winnie the Pooh's "boat," an upturned umbrella), a biweekly mimeographed poetry journal.

The *Bear* was another community effort; the pianist Cecil Taylor helped run the mimeo machine, and everyone addressed envelopes. It was not sold but mailed free to subscribers, which did not prevent the FBI from arresting Jones for obscenity—one recipient was in prison, and the warden turned them in. Charles Olson would tell di Prima that he cherished this fresh ability to send her a new poem and have 150 artists, many of them his friends, read it within a few weeks, perhaps reflecting his work in theirs in something like a vast jam session.

It was, after all, New York City, which meant that there were dozens of scenes at all times. Writers held forth at the White Horse Tavern and the San Remo, painters at the Cedar Bar. The knowing patronized Barron Bruchlos, an Ayn Rand enthusiast who kept a shop at 306 East Sixth Street and sold peyote buttons imported from Moore's Orchid Farm in Laredo, Texas. Eventually, the FDA noticed and shut him down, but not before people like the musician Peter Stampfel, later with the Holy Modal Rounders, and the novelist Robert Stone had paid Barron for what Stone called "a glimpse of wonders beyond description."

The White Horse Tavern was the nursery for the Village's own local newspaper, the weekly *Village Voice*, which began in October 1955, cost a nickel (a year's subscription was two dollars), and counted as its main draw a regular column by Norman Mailer. He began by telling his readers, "Given your general animus to those more talented than yourselves, the only way I see myself becoming one of the cherished traditions of the Village is to be actively disliked each week." The longer-lasting impact of the *Voice* was in the realm of arts coverage, with Jill Johnston (dance), Nat Hentoff (jazz), and Andrew Sarris (film) setting new standards.

John Cage remained an influence, both as a composer—his chaotic 1958 New York City Town Hall *Concert for Piano and Orchestra*, in which each musician made their own decisions, made him even more notorious—and as a teacher at the New School, where his students included Allan Kaprow, who would find fame as a performance artist by creating "happenings," and a young Yoko Ono, part of the avant-garde Fluxus group.

One of the exceptional influences on Village life was Dorothy Day of the Catholic Worker Movement, America's most successful anarchist group. Day had begun as a socialist, writing for the *Masses* and associating with Mike Gold, Max Eastman, and Eugene O'Neill, reportedly able to drink any of them under the table at their favorite bar, the Hell Hole.

Converting to Roman Catholicism but troubled by the church's lack of social consciousness, she met the French peasant-intellectual Peter Maurin, and in 1933, they founded the Catholic Workers, at first focusing on labor relations. They espoused voluntary poverty and gathered followers in houses of hospitality, where basic needs could be met while people dedicated themselves to service. Always anti-violence, whether from war, the nation-state, or either capitalist or Marxist economies, the Workers came to focus on pacifism. In truth, said Day, the Workers preached meeting the world with love...no matter what. "A practice of loving, a learning to love, a paying of the cost of love."

Their weekly newspaper, the *Catholic Worker*, grew to have print runs of over one hundred thousand, although their anti-war message cost them followers during the Spanish Civil War and then World War II. They influenced many, not all of them Roman Catholic: Hannah Arendt, Michael Harrington, the Berrigan brothers, Noam Chomsky, Robert Coles, and Julian Beck and Judith Malina.

Beginning in 1955, Day and her group began an annual protest of the air raid drills that implicitly supported the atomic warfare industry that was the US military. By 1961, the nation possessed 100 intermediate and intercontinental missiles, 1,700 intercontinental bombers, and 1,000 supersonic land-based fighters, all armed with nuclear weapons.

In the preceding decade, there had been 122 atomic bomb tests, mostly in Nevada. Popular culture reflected this grim reality with science fiction movies depicting mutant creatures, but far more frightening was Herman Kahn's tome *On Thermonuclear War*, which contemplated acceptable levels of civilian deaths and popularized phrases such as *thinking about the unthinkable* and *doomsday machine*.

Allying with the pacifist groups Fellowship of Reconciliation and the War Resisters League, the Workers refused to participate in the annual nationwide Operation Alert civil defense drill. Arrested and convicted, they received no sentence in 1955, as the judge wanted to avoid making martyrs of them.

114 **The Last Great Dream**

In 1956, they received five days, in 1957, thirty. By 1960, Norman Mailer, Dwight Macdonald, and Nat Hentoff were among a thousand demonstrating, and in 1961, it was two thousand—at which point the drills ceased.

Before that, the inimitable Judith Malina had joined Day in getting arrested. When she was committed to Bellevue Hospital, she shouted that the judge was a "rude young man," then jumped on a bench to elude the bailiffs. The judge channeled Herman Kahn and Lewis Carroll and said of Malina and the Workers, "These people, by their conduct and behavior, contributed to the utter destruction of the three million theoretically killed in our city."

The Village led the way in knocking down other walls. In 1959, Grove Press sued the post office for confiscating copies of *Lady Chatterley's Lover*. Their prospects seemed dim, since just two years before, in *Roth v. US*, the Supreme Court had ruled that obscenity was not protected. Grove's attorney, Charles Rembar, had never argued a case before, but when he read *Roth*, he noticed the phrase "redeeming social importance" and proceeded to drive a truck through it. The judge ruled for Grove, and the post office was no longer in the censorship business. The legal notion of obscenity remained, and in the next few years, Rosset would sue on behalf of Henry Miller's *Tropic of Cancer* and William Burroughs's *Naked Lunch* and effectively surmount that barrier.

Live spoken comedy was a very different category, and Lenny Bruce did not do as well as Rembar. In fact, from his first arrest (of thirty, all misdemeanors) in 1961 to his death in 1966, Lenny Bruce underwent a slow-motion crucifixion that ended quite literally in martyrdom. His comedy routines were blasphemous, mocking the church, American sexual mores, and American exceptionalism among other targets, but he was charged with obscenity. The frequently Roman Catholic district attorneys of several American cities lined up to silence him.

One of the few cases he won was in San Francisco, where Herb Caen defended him: "They call Lenny Bruce a sick comic—and sick he is. Sick of the pretentious phoniness of a generation that makes his vicious humor meaningful." Bruce was intellectually subversive: "What I want people to dig is the lie."

Run out of Los Angeles, he moved on to Chicago, where the head of the vice squad, Captain McDermott, told Gate of Horn manager Alan Ribback, "If [Bruce] ever speaks against religion, I'm going to pinch you and everyone in here....[H]e mocks the pope—and I'm speaking as a Catholic—I'm here to tell you your license is in danger." In the courtroom one Ash Wednesday, the judge, the two prosecutors, and all twelve jurors wore their faith on their foreheads. Bruce was not there, or he could have made a brilliant bit out of it. In New York, where the district attorney was Frank Hogan, a Roman Catholic and a prig, Bruce and the club owner were arrested before the show even began.

Bruce had many supporters in New York, but the most simpatico was undoubtedly Paul Krassner, who had progressed from the satirical *Mad* magazine to his own publication, the *Realist*. A beacon of free speech, the *Realist* published interviews with a variety of thinkers, from Bruce and Alan Watts to the iconic atheist Madalyn Murray and the humorist Jean Shepherd. In 1962, Krassner ran an interview with an anonymous Pennsylvania abortionist, which led to Krassner's sideline as a referral service when women began to call and beg for information. Joseph Heller caught the essence of the magazine when Krassner confessed that he had not yet read *Catch-22* and the author responded, "If you haven't read it yet, there's no hurry—you practically write *Catch-22* with every issue of *The Realist*."

After more than a decade of trying, Julian Beck and Judith Malina began to gain traction. In June 1957, they discovered an abandoned department store at Fourteenth Street and Sixth Avenue, which became the home of the Living Theatre. It immediately became a de facto arts center, hosting poetry readings (Gregory Corso, Frank O'Hara, LeRoi Jones), art shows (Franz Kline, Willem de Kooning, Joan Mitchell, Helen Frankenthaler, Larry Rivers) and music performances in the David Tudor/John Cage realm.

Then they found a winner. In April 1958, a young writer named Jack Gelber brought Malina a script for a play called *The Connection*. Lacking any conventional plot, it was driven by the tension of addicts waiting for their drugs. Beck and Malina wanted a theater of such extreme realism that it challenged the audience's concept of their own existence: theater as shock treatment. When one of the actors actually shot up onstage, they had succeeded. Yet at the core of the play was the recognition that addicts were not pariahs but human and that addiction was not a personality disorder but was, Beck said, "symptomatic of the errors of the whole world." It opened in June 1959, and though the *Times* sneered, other critics were more generous, and a fascinating mix of famous names began to attend, ranging from Lauren Bacall to Dag Hammarskjöld of the United Nations.

The Living Theatre had become the center of a thriving arts community. When the troupe was invited to a Theatre des Nations festival in Paris, they raised money with an arts auction that included work by de Kooning, Kline, Robert Rauschenberg, Jasper Johns, and others, as well as the original manuscript of Allen Ginsberg's "Kaddish." The Living Theatre went to Paris and triumphed at the festival, toured Europe, and earned a response that would nurture them for the next decade. In the years to come, their play *The Brig*, in which actors switched roles from prisoners to guards, saw the troupe morph into a gestalt that was part political discussion and part psychotherapy encounter session. Their *Paradise Now* (1968) would bring the audience into the play.

The latecomer to Beat publishing and the capstone of early 1960s bohemian literature, William Burroughs's *Naked Lunch* represented the third and grimmest of the Beat triumvirate of writing that had begun with *Howl* and *On the Road*. Haunted by his addiction, Burroughs had come to realize the diseased elegance of it all: "The junk merchant doesn't sell his product to the consumer, he sells the consumer to his product. He does not improve and simplify his merchandise. He degrades and simplifies the client."

Published in 1962, the story takes place in Interzone, which began as a vision from Ginsberg's Lower East Side apartment window of fire escapes and backyards with laundry lines, many levels, all interconnected—so Interzone was "a great labyrinth of alleyways and passages, squares and tunnels" with an unnerving soundtrack of insect wings thrumming over larvae about to be born. But even the Village didn't have the demonic Dr. Benway, orgasms from broken necks, talking rectums, and a dildo named Steely Dan.

In Interzone, said one critic, "telling is equated with selling, appearance with deception, authority with power." It's an attack on all reality, a multi-dimensional fantasy/science fiction version of anarchism, "a point," Burroughs

New York in the Late '50s

wrote in a letter to Ginsberg and Kerouac, "where three-dimensional fact merges into dream, and dreams erupt into the real world."

Though Burroughs was often portrayed as terrifying, he was in fact tortured by his memories of killing his wife, Joan, in a drunken replaying of William Tell, along with other aspects of his life. His willingness to explore his nightmares had an enormous impact on the rising artists of the new decade, from David Bowie and Bob Dylan to Donald Fagen and Walter Becker.

15

Asian Thought and America

An interest and openness to Asian thought would be an essential element of the Haight-Ashbury community. Though plagued by appropriation and Orientalist fantasizing, the root of white America's interest in Asian religious thought is clearly based on a genuine perception of wisdom. Where most of Western thought is crippled by the separation of mind from body and of humans from nature, the Buddhist recognition of the interconnectedness of all beings and what historian Rick Fields called its "nontheistic mode of contemplation" is a valuable, healing corrective.

Buddhism entered American thought with Elizabeth Palmer Peabody's translation from the French of the introduction to the Lotus Sutra, "The Preaching of the Buddha," published in the last issue of the transcendentalist journal the *Dial*. Henry David Thoreau edited the article, and his life and future thought, including *Walden*, would reflect a deep affinity for Asian spirituality.

Though he formally remained a Christian, Kenneth Rexroth contributed mightily to a growing understanding of the US as part of the

Pacific Rim, a mélange resting on wilderness, anarchism, and Buddhism that is most clear in his poem "In What Hour." As poetry anthologies go, his *One Hundred Poems from the Japanese* (1954) was a bestseller, as was its 1971 successor with Chinese work. The West Coast was now understood, in Lawrence Ferlinghetti's view, as "not only the last frontier but also the place where the Orient begins, where the Far East begins again."

Kerouac's first new book after *On the Road*, *The Dharma Bums* (1958), was a portrait of Gary Snyder that reflected not only Kerouac's personal admiration for Snyder but their shared interest in Buddhism. Mired in depression in 1953, Kerouac had read *Walden* and then Ashvaghosha's *The Life of the Buddha*, where he found the phrase "Repose Beyond Fate." It inspired several years of serious study. Though much of his Buddhism was clearly an overlay on his childhood Catholicism, his sincerity was unquestioned. However doctrinally wobbly, *The Dharma Bums* would introduce a large group of young Americans to Buddha's message, the dharma.

Alan Watts's best-selling *The Way of Zen*, published in 1957, had an even greater impact. Ironically, Watts was by nature more a Taoist, and the best information in *The Way* traces the development of Ch'an (Zen in Japan) in China that resulted from the encounter of Mahayana Buddhism from India and the original Chinese spiritual practice of Taoism. The Tao, or way, was something that one could only experience with a calm, ungrasping, receptive awareness. The resulting liberated person sees the same world as before, but without superimposed concepts. Clarity is the goal rather than mystic transcendence.

As the decade passed, Watts increasingly spent time at Druid Heights, a former ranch and now informal commune on the side of Mount Tamalpais overlooking the Pacific, named in tribute to the Celtic mythologist Ella Young. There was a piquant balance there between the two primary tenants, Roger Somers and Elsa Gidlow. Somers, a jazz musician and carpenter-architect, incarnated Pan for Watts, "if you can imagine Pan based on a bull instead of a goat...physique is formidable, his grizzly hair sticks out like short horns, and his energy is endless. He plays the saxophone, the oboe and all kinds of drums. He dances—free form—like a maniac, and his shrieks of delight can be heard all over the hill."

Watts's relationship with Gidlow was more philosophical. Her lesbian orientation obviated the need for the usual sexual tension; "we were to meet

Asian Thought and America

121

on the green and not the red band of the spectrum, where intense friendship lies between vermillion lust and violet agape...she was to fulfill exactly in my life the role that would have been taken by a very companionable elder sister." Their minds met at a subtle intellectual nexus, and they eventually established the Society for Comparative Philosophy for "studies of humanity's relation to nature and the universe." She had taken an early interest in Theosophy but found the followers she encountered "puritanical and uninteresting." Watts was certainly neither of those, and her interest in Asian thought bloomed.

When Gidlow had arrived in San Francisco, she felt that the city "felt fresh, young, expectant, confirming my similar mood. It faced not Europe but China." She and her longtime partner lived on the edge of Chinatown, which further engaged her in Asian culture. While volunteering at KPFA, she was impressed by one of Watts's programs, which sent her to the American Academy of Asian Studies (AAAS) to study Chinese and calligraphy. Gazing at the waves breaking on Stinson Beach below Druid Heights, she probably concurred with Watts's thought, that the waves were "timeless time...the breathing of eternity."

Over the years, Gidlow wrote, their land went from a "rural slum" to "beauty where there was waste, wildness, or squalor. We have fruit and an ample variety of vegetables free of poisons." Druid Heights was a creative place. James Broughton's *The Bed* was filmed there, with Watts, the photographer Imogen Cunningham, various dancers, and Somers playing music in a tree. Somers then offered his workshop to Gerd Stern to build the mixed media kinetic sculpture "Contact Is the Only Love."

Back in San Francisco, AAAS had given up the ghost, morphing into the California Institute of Integral Studies (CIIS), a respected graduate school in psychology. A number of the AAAS's students followed Watts's student Claude Dalenberg into a communal living situation, the East-West House, at 2273 California Street. Dalenberg had met Watts at Northwestern as an engineering student, but soon changed his major to philosophy. Following his teacher to San Francisco, Dalenberg also studied Zen with Watts's friend Nyogen Senzaki (of the "floating zendo" in Los Angeles) and with Hodo Tobase at Sokoji, which was San Francisco's Japantown community temple, located in an old Orthodox Jewish synagogue at 1881 Bush Street.

Seekers started filling up the East-West House. Snyder's friend Philip Whalen took refuge there, as well as another member of their Reed circle,

122 **The Last Great Dream**

Lew Welch. A young North Beach poet named Joanne Kyger joined them, as well as Michael McClure's friend from Wichita, Dave Haselwood, then establishing the Auerhahn Press. One student of Senzaki's, Albert Saijo, would live in a kindred place, Hyphen House, not far away in the middle of Japantown.

Jack Kerouac passed through East-West and loved the place. "You can rush into any room and find the expert, like say [Philip Whalen]'s room and ask, 'Hey what did Bodhidharma say to the Second Patriarch?'—'He said go fuck yourself, make your mind like a wall, dont pant after outside activities and dont bug me with your outside plans.'" Originally, the residents had planned to be a formal extension of AAAS, with classes and rules, but the idea of rules slipped away and only a general attentiveness to Asian thought remained.

Joanne Kyger had more specific plans. She had met Gary Snyder during one of his visits back to San Francisco, and romance had blossomed. "I was living at the East-West House and was getting ready to go to Japan (by now it's 1959) so I thought I should learn how to sit [*to sit* Zazen is to meditate]. The EW House, on California Street, was very social at that time. Maybe because I had moved in." She was probably right; charming and attractive and in a minority as a woman, she was the recipient of a fair amount of attention. "The only rule" at the house, she recalled, was "that you had to get along with everyone else. There was a very nice library of the Buddhist books that were then available in English."

Kyger traveled to Japan in 1960. Ruth Fuller Sasaki, the abbess of the First Zen Institute at Daitoku-ji in Kyoto, insisted that Kyger and Snyder marry—there was to be no shacking up at the institute. Before she departed, Kyger had indeed learned how to sit Zazen at what would become the primary institutional birthplace of Zen in America, Sokoji Temple on Bush Street. Hodo Tobase had returned to Japan, and the Soto Zen organization in Japan had sent a truly exceptional replacement, an elfin, charismatic Zen priest who'd learned English as a teen and had long harbored the ambition of spreading Zen outside Japan (and even more ambitiously, hoping that it would reinvigorate Zen within Japan). His name was Shunryu Shogaku Suzuki.

Commonly called Suzuki Roshi (a term of respect, meaning "elder"), he arrived in San Francisco on May 23, 1959, and was expected to minister to

Asian Thought and America

the Issei (first-generation immigrants) and Nisei (their children) people of the congregation. It was not long before Suzuki Roshi had two congregations—the regular members of Sokoji, and an increasing number of guests.

Within a week of Suzuki's arrival, he'd accepted an invitation to speak at AAAS. Three women—Betty Warren, Della Goertz, and Jean Ross—attended the class and responded immediately to him. Goertz recalled, "The first night we met Suzuki we wanted to be his students. We liked his gentle manner and we liked that he was willing to be so practical with us. We got down on the floor and faced the wall that night doing meditation. He talked a little bit about Zazen but before the night was over we meditated and we all wanted to join him at Sokoji."

Bill McNeill, an artist from Black Mountain College, was one of the other first Anglo sitters and Suzuki's first formal student. Another of the earliest arrivals was Don Allen, the editor of *The New American Poetry*. In line with contemporary practice in Japan, almost none of the Japanese Americans were interested in Zazen, but more and more Anglos came through the door.

Their essential ignorance of Buddhism was an advantage, thought Suzuki: "In the beginners' mind, there are many possibilities; in the expert's mind, there are few." He believed in that premise so deeply that when the sitting group at Sokoji established itself in 1962 as the San Francisco Zen Center and then in 1969 was able to move into a former boardinghouse for young Jewish immigrant women at 300 Page Street, he named it Hosshin-ji, Beginner's Mind Temple.

Suzuki was a remarkable man. Quite small, and at the beginning of his residence in America of limited fluency in English, he deeply impressed those who met him simply by his presence. One of his most senior students, the North Beach painter and trumpet player Mel Weitsman, came to Sokoji in 1964 and metaphorically never left, eventually becoming abbot of the Berkeley Zen Center and then the San Francisco Zen Center. Mel recalled, "We just observed the way he was. The way he sat down and stood up; it was all very easy, very smooth, and he was always right in time. He would never get ahead of himself or behind. He was always right present, in time. And that was pretty remarkable [to observe] because he didn't have anything that was driving him, and he didn't have anything that was holding him back."

Kyger spoke of a seemingly silly but telling moment with Suzuki. She was in New York, and Suzuki and his student Dick Baker were on a fundraising trip there. "Robert Duncan was there, having done a reading at the Guggenheim. I remember Suzuki sitting at the table and all of a sudden he put his napkin on top of his head and sat there with it. It was such a tension breaker. We were wondering how to act around this teacher. So we all put our napkins on top of our heads." She added, "I was always watching to see if people were going to be 'human' in the roles they were taking at the Zen Center, which was getting more hierarchical. But I never saw that in Suzuki Roshi. He wasn't carrying a lot of baggage, that's what was so appealing."

Diane di Prima was about to marry, and her friend Don Allen suggested she meet Suzuki Roshi. An archetypally tough, cynical New Yorker, she met the priest and on first sight felt "total trust" in him, the likes of which she'd never had for another human being.

Baker would prove to be a brilliant fundraiser, and in 1967, the Zen Center would open the first Zen monastery outside of Asia at Tassajara, fifteen miles east of Big Sur in the Ventana Wilderness. Students came and went, and in the next half century, some would go back to their hometowns and establish temples of their own, varying in size from miniscule to imposing. Along with other sources, Suzuki Roshi's Zen Center took an essential part in the establishment of Zen in America and of what is now called Western Buddhism.

16

Four Freshmen, the Rise of Student Activism, and New Options for Women

As the new decade began, elements of the younger, "silent" student generation began to speak up, injecting a critical new energy into the civil rights and social justice movements, not only in the Deep South but across the North and especially in San Francisco Bay Area colleges. The impulse would be an important part of what happened to a significant portion of white youth, including in the Haight-Ashbury. The bohemians might not always be activists, but their sympathies toward fellow youth were clear.

President Eisenhower had not been interested in civil rights; his intercession in the desegregation of Little Rock's Central High School was forced on him and accomplished little. Something strikingly different happened three years later, when four freshmen at the Agricultural and Technical College of North Carolina documented that moral purpose does not require exalted credentials. Ezell Blair Jr., David Richmond, Franklin McCain, and Joseph McNeill were talking about the segregation in their lives when McNeill said, "Let's do something."

126 **The Last Great Dream**

The next day, Sunday, January 31, 1960, they went to their local Woolworth, bought a tube of toothpaste, and sat down at the segregated lunch counter and asked for a cup of coffee. Refused service, they stayed until closing. The next day, sixteen students joined them, along with a television crew. By Wednesday, there were fifty students, along with high school students and white co-eds from the Woman's College of the University of North Carolina.

By the next week, there were sit-ins all over the state, then South Carolina, then Nashville, where seventy-six were jailed. As they sat, they read the Bible or the Constitution, and when they were punched off the stool, they quietly got up and sat back down.

Sit-in leaders gathered at Shaw University in Raleigh, declined pressure from the "adult" civil rights organizations to become junior members, and stayed independent; SNCC ("snick," the Student Nonviolent Coordinating Committee) was born. Within days of the first sit-in, sympathy picket lines popped up at Bay Area Woolworth stores, and fifteen to sixty people marched twice a week in Oakland for the next year. On April 1, Thomas Gaither from Claflin University in South Carolina spoke to an overflow crowd at UC Berkeley ("Cal") and described demonstrators being assaulted by fire hoses and hostile police. Within weeks, the Cal students would experience that treatment firsthand.

Before that, a significant number of Cal and other Bay Area college students would come together to stand against state-supported executions. Caryl Chessman had been convicted of robberies and sexual assault (forced fellatio) in 1948. The perpetrator having moved his victims out of their cars, he was additionally charged with kidnapping, which enabled the prosecution to pursue the death penalty. Although the court transcript was essentially unreadable, he was convicted and sent to death row.

In 1954, Chessman published *Cell 2455, Death Row*, which persuaded many observers of his innocence, or at least of his rehabilitation. The "expert" criminologists could not believe that a man capable of writing so well could fool them; to execute him was to deny the possibility of rehabilitation itself. Because Chessman failed to display contrition, the previously anti–death penalty governor Pat Brown refused to intervene, and on May 2, 1960, Chessman was executed at San Quentin Prison, visible across the bay from the Cal campus.

Four Freshmen, the Rise of Student Activism 127

The day before, Herb Caen had devoted a column to Chessman, wondering aloud why, if the state needed to kill someone, it did not do so plainly in public rather than in a gloomy room behind walls "as though the act itself, the final demonstration of the majesty of the law, were some dark and dreadful thing. And a dark and dreadful thing it is." Students had been morally engaged by their attempt to save a life, and their failure left them feeling betrayed by the forces of law. One of those students, Michael Rossman, wrote, "Our eyes were opening, a mystification was breaking, we were beginning to see the acts of Official America as ugly."

That year, the writer Joan Didion (Cal '52) described Cal students as "America's lushest growth of passive nihilism." In fact, a Cal student named Fred Moore had demonstrated against compulsory ROTC the previous year with a hunger strike, and a thousand students had supported him. A movement based on moral and spiritual qualities with enormous political consequences had begun to step into the light.

The rising student left at Cal was never especially ideological. The ideologue Michael Harrington observed that they were "courageous, dedicated, and existential in a way that sometimes borders on the anti-intellectual." As the highly political Jack Newfield observed, the "mysticism, anarchy, anti-intellectualism, sexual and drug experimentation, hostility to middle-class values, and idealization of the Negro and voluntary poverty" of the Beat scene and thereafter "all have clear parallels in the New Left." A new consciousness was arising, what Newfield called "an Awakening in white America, touched off by psychic contagion from the black Awakening."

The students were electrified when their idea of Satan, the House Un-American Activities Committee, brought its traveling circus/witch hunt to San Francisco's city hall in May 1960. The committee had attempted such a spectacle in 1959, subpoenaing one hundred teachers and making sure that a copy of each subpoena was passed to their local school board. Several of those teachers had been summarily fired, entirely without due process. The ensuing public furor led the HUAC to cancel that visit.

Then the HUAC's primary partner, the FBI, learned that one of the essay questions for 1959 applicants to the University of California was "What are the dangers to a democracy of a national police organization, like the FBI, which operates secretly and is unresponsive to criticism?" J. Edgar Hoover

128 **The Last Great Dream**

swore vengeance. His de facto chief publicist (as well as chief of PR for the American Legion), Cartha DeLoach, initiated a covert campaign against UC using the American Legion and Hearst newspapers—it was no accident that the HUAC's next big stop would be San Francisco, home of the Hearst flagship *Examiner*. Nor was it surprising that the committee chose city hall rather than the more appropriate Federal Building as the location. Given that their goal was intimidation and fearmongering, the more public the site, the better.

The Cal students organized, creating an ad hoc Students for Civil Liberties (SCL) group. By the time of the hearings, they had collected over 1,600 signatures at a petition table in the traditional free speech area off Bancroft Way on the edge of campus. More than fifty subpoenas went out from the HUAC, targeting students, teachers, longshoremen, and public commentators. The hearings began on schedule on Thursday, May 12, 1960, as more than a thousand silent, disciplined picketers organized by the SCL marched around city hall supported by a rally in Union Square downtown addressed by state assemblyman (and, later that year, Congressman) Phillip Burton.

William Wheeler, the HUAC's chief investigator, distributed entrance tickets to the hearing room almost exclusively to a group of older women, many of them members of the patriotic Daughters of the American Revolution (DAR). None went to students, and some two hundred of them who'd been left in the hallway outside began to sing the "Battle Hymn of the Republic." Inside, Archie Brown, a Communist Party (CP) official and a subpoenaed witness, was ejected, which dominated Friday morning's headlines. The atmosphere intensified exponentially. Four thousand picketers surrounded city hall on Friday, with one hundred police, fifteen on horseback, keeping order. The ticket system remained in place, with students who'd waited for hours ignored as a select few were welcomed in. Student leaders met with the sheriff, who promised to ask the committee to reconsider and admit all on a first-come, first-served basis.

That afternoon, only a tiny group of students was admitted. The crowd of the excluded, which extended down city hall's grand marble staircase, first pressed forward and then sat down. At the door to the hearing room, Inspector Michael Maguire of the SFPD Intelligence Unit became aware that

Four Freshmen, the Rise of Student Activism

at least a few students had gotten past him. He scuffled with one student, grew offended, and ordered fire hoses turned on the crowd, which had begun to sing "We Shall Not Be Moved." The singing turned into a prolonged scream.

As city hall workers stared down in horror from the floors above, the hoses stopped and the police charged, swinging their nightsticks and dragging students, often feetfirst, down the steps, their heads bouncing off each tread. Sixty-four people, thirty-one of them students, were arrested on charges of disturbing the peace, inciting to riot, and resisting arrest.

Back in the hearing room, William Mandel, a CP member and popular KPFA commentator, testified. Addressing the committee as "Honorable beaters of children and sadists," he continued. "If you think that I'm going to cooperate with this collection of Judases, of men who sit there in violation of the United States Constitution, if you think I will cooperate with you in any way, you are insane."

Press coverage was predictably pro-police, excepting Herb Caen, who remarked that a "mature" police department should be able to prevent demonstrations from becoming riots. When an SF politico dismissed the demonstrators as a "bunch of Beatniks," Herb suggested that the "well-dressed British" probably said something similar about the Yankee farmers on Breed's Hill. The SF Fire Department pointedly issued a statement noting that they had not operated the hoses.

Eventually, all but one of those arrested submitted their case to a judge, who dismissed all charges in June, by which time the *Chronicle* applauded his discretion. The one student remaining, a former marine named Robert Meisenbach, had been charged with stealing an officer's nightstick and clubbing him with it as he supposedly leaped over the barricade to break into the hearing room. His trial would come a year later. Meantime, on Saturday, May 14, five thousand students, joined by a large contingent of burly longshoremen, converged on the city hall picket line.

In the days after the hearing, the HUAC subpoenaed television coverage and hastily put together a film, *Operation Abolition*, that asserted the students were communist dupes. They then began to sell the film for a hundred dollars a copy to TV stations and private organizations for viewing; the Department of Defense used the film as mandatory training for five hundred thousand soldiers. The navy bought 150 copies to show sailors. Standard Oil, Pacific Gas

& Electric, Pacific Telephone & Telegraph, Lockheed, and Boeing screened it for employees. It was shown in high schools, colleges, and churches.

The FBI produced a report, *Communist Target—Youth*, which parroted the same line—and lies, because their scenario of the riot was revealed as an empty fraud when Meisenbach was tried and quickly acquitted. Photographs clearly showed him throughout the period of conflict on the other side of the rotunda, nowhere near the barricade.

Astonishingly, the students had won. The HUAC would attempt one more showy attack, this time on Women Strike for Peace (WSP) in December 1962. Along with the new president, John Kennedy, WSP supported a treaty to ban nuclear testing in the atmosphere. The hearing room was filled with women, many with babies. As each witness approached to testify, their supporters handed them bouquets of flowers, and the committee looked simply absurd; it was flower power before the phrase was invented. The HUAC was dead, and Hoover would have to turn to his internal program, COINTELPRO, to attack and disrupt the various social and political movements of the '60s.

His program would have a great deal on its hands. That summer, a philosophy student and journalist from the University of Michigan who identified his heroes as *Mad* magazine's iconic wiseass Alfred E. Neuman, James Dean, and Holden Caulfield, read *On the Road* and hitchhiked to Berkeley before going on to Los Angeles to cover the Democratic convention. His name was Tom Hayden, and he would exemplify the nonideological, personalist concerns of the emerging New Left. When he came to write the "Port Huron Statement" that established the Students for a Democratic Society in 1962, he cited as a primary value the desire to end the "depersonalization that reduces human beings to the status of things....[W]e regard men as infinitely precious and possessed of unfulfilled capacities for reason, freedom, and love."

In later years, one might assume that he would have chosen *people* or *human beings* as being infinitely precious, but African Americans weren't the only group of Americans with substandard civil rights. Women had a very great deal to consider. At one option in their lives, San Francisco had been the birthplace of the first American lesbian rights organization, the Daughters of Bilitis (one of Sappho's lovers). In September 1955, Rosalie "Rose" Bamberger suggested to Del Martin and Phyllis Lyon and two other couples that they begin a secret social club that would allow them to dance together without

Four Freshmen, the Rise of Student Activism   131

fear of the police. They began to publish the *Ladder* in 1956, wrote stacks of letters to legislators, and in 1960 held their first national convention, with two hundred attending. So did the police, who were led inside by Martin to observe women wearing dresses, stockings, and heels. The attendees heard a debate about the morality of gay bars, a presentation by the ACLU, and a diatribe from an Episcopal priest that denounced them as sinners.

For the plurality of women who were heterosexual, the 1960 FDA approval of Enovid for use as a birth control pill was even more significant. After decades of activism, Margaret Sanger had located funding from an heir to the International Harvester fortune, Katherine McCormick, and a researcher, Gregory Pincus of the Worcester Foundation for Experimental Biology. For a front man, she had Dr. John Rock, the chief of gynecology and obstetrics at Harvard Medical School. At first, Enovid was marketed as a treatment for menstrual disorders, but the FDA's decision gave Sanger the triumph of a lifetime. Women could now control their own reproduction and by extension their own sexual lives. The resulting social fallout would be immense.

Not coincidentally, two years later, Betty Friedan published *The Feminine Mystique*. After graduating from Smith College in 1942, Friedan had worked for a labor newspaper. When she gave birth to her second child, she was fired, and her union, the American Newspaper Guild, would not defend her; the concept of women's rights did not exist. Years later, she was assigned to write a piece on what had happened to her college class. She sent out a questionnaire and found "a deep pool of doubt, frustration, anxiety and resentment." At her fifteenth reunion, she spoke to members of the about-to-graduate Smith class of '57 and was generally told that they were going to get married and make babies.

Her article was rejected as being "too angry," but she pushed on and spent long hours in research at the New York Public Library, where she came to see advertising and women's magazines as the proximate causes leading women down a rabbit hole of consumption, competition, and delusion. Her work was powerful, part of what would become a tidal wave of analysis and understanding. Increasingly and for the foreseeable future, issues of gender and sexual orientation would join class and race as essential elements in every serious consideration of the meaning of liberation.

The rising alternative culture allowed some room for the freer expression of sexual activity for women, although it largely fell short of any clear understanding of women's concerns; it would be up to women to take up those issues. One example of Beat women might be taken as reasonably representative. Kathy Mason was a young woman who'd finished high school in the San Fernando Valley of Los Angeles late in the '50s. She'd never felt comfortable there. "I was different from everybody else. I was not conservative. We didn't have a family church. My mother was an astrologer. My father had married late, so he was an older father. He was also a gambler at the track who lost all his money, so we were poor, and I didn't fit in."

The siren song of the Beat generation lured her to Berkeley in 1961 to visit a friend, but Mason wasn't allowed to stay in the dormitory. Naturally, she headed to North Beach to look for a place. As she scouted Grant Avenue, a threatening stranger began to follow her, and she ducked into a jewelry store, which turned out to be owned by a well-known bohemian named S. Paul "Sam" Gee. "So I went home with him, and eventually apprenticed myself to him and learned to make jewelry."

Miles Davis and Cannonball Adderley were among his customers—the Jazz Workshop was right around the corner on Broadway—both for his art and also for pot. Sam was also an enthusiastic psychedelicist, handing out Sandoz LSD to those he judged worthy. "I wore lots of black and went to the Trieste every day," Mason recalled. She'd failed seventh grade art, but in more harmonious surroundings, she blossomed, eventually attending SFAI. "Finally, I fit in."

17

The Folk Scare

Folk music would be the next major element in the creation of the early-'60s youth culture; many of the later San Francisco rock musicians got their start playing folk music. It had been associated with the political Left at least since the Industrial Workers of the World published *The Little Red Songbook* in 1909, then through the union movement of the '30s and Woody Guthrie and his friends in the Almanac Singers of the '40s. Renamed the Weavers, they even scored a national hit in 1950 with Lead Belly's "Goodnight, Irene" before being redbaited out of the music business.

Harry Belafonte, who would come to be a significant figure in the civil rights movement, put West Indian calypso folk songs like "Day-O" and "Matilda" on the charts in the mid-'50s, but through much of the decade, the flame of folk music was largely kept alive by Weavers member Pete Seeger, working a circuit of liberal college campuses (Oberlin, Bennington, Antioch), churches, and camps.

Then in 1958, folk's audience grew exponentially when the Kingston Trio, three apolitical, shiningly clean-cut young men in matching striped shirts, homogenized the harmonies of a song called "Tom Dooley."

133

134 **The Last Great Dream**

Young men of privilege, they came together around Menlo College in the early 1950s. Emulating the Weavers and Gabby Pahinui, the brilliant Hawaiian slack-key guitarist, they sang in the bars around Stanford and Menlo Park. In November 1956, they auditioned at the Purple Onion in San Francisco, the second-tier club after the hungry i in what was becoming a show business mecca.

Harry Charles "Enrico" Banducci was the driving force in the district, having bought the original hungry i from North Beach character Eric "Big Daddy" Nord. At first a poet and actor hangout, the hungry i had moved in 1954 to 599 Jackson Street, with a club upstairs and a four-hundred-seat showroom downstairs. Banducci's place would change American stand-up comedy, presenting material that was dark, skeptical of conventional values, and clearly hip. Tom Lehrer, Dick Gregory, Woody Allen, Mort Sahl, Jonathan Winters, Nichols and May, Richard Pryor, Lenny Bruce, and many more played the room.

Just before the Kingston Trio began at the Purple Onion, Frank Werber saw them at another North Beach club. An escapee from a Vichy concentration camp, he'd wandered through many jobs before he became a photo stringer for UPI, where he learned how publicity worked. Then he went to work for Banducci and learned something about the stage part of the entertainment business.

Werber was a North Beach guy who lived on a Sausalito houseboat, and the three young men were mightily impressed. He would be an equal partner and more. He was their Professor Henry Higgins, instituting fines for lateness, dictating their stage costumes, and editing their patter. They spent 1957 rehearsing, either in his office above the barber shop next to the Onion, or onstage at the Onion. Hired as temporary replacements in May, they would stay for seven months.

Their eponymous first album, released in June 1958, included "Scotch and Soda," "Sloop John B," and an Appalachian song about a murderer named Tom Dula. Led by "Tom Dooley," the album would be number one by November 1958 and would stay on the charts for four years. On August 3, 1959, they were celebrated on the cover of *Life* magazine. Attractive and funny, working colleges across the country, they and "Tom Dooley" made folk music an appealing alternative to the pop Brill Building material that had supplanted '50s rock as young people's music.

The Folk Scare 135

* * *

There was one significant counterweight in the folk world to the pop trio, a collection of music assembled by a curious and important figure, Harry Smith. A cosmic visionary and serious anthropologist from the age of fifteen, a true bohemian and psychedelic pioneer, Smith's physical growth had been stunted in his childhood by rickets, and he was small, hunched, and not infrequently difficult, a penurious, maddening, cranky, and belligerently opinionated alcoholic mooch. But his record collection accomplished something very important.

He began his artistic career with surrealist visual art and then what the critic Jonas Mekas described as "magic, cabalistic space cinema." In 1951, he found himself in New York with an enormous collection of 78 rpm records made in the beginning of the electronic (as opposed to acoustic) recording era, from around 1927 to 1932, when the record business by and large went belly-up. Desperate for money as always, he tried to sell the collection to Moe Asch, the boss of Folkways Records. Moe countered by suggesting they release a selection on the newly invented LP records, which would be called *The Anthology of American Folk Music*. Packaged with alchemical symbols—the cover came from the legendary Robert Fludd—the *Anthology* also included Smith's imaginary headlines in a quirky *Variety* style that described each song, which featured deaths, catastrophe, violence, and hatred.

It was not an act of nostalgia but an attempt to preserve a passing culture, a reimagining of cultural continuity and a part of Smith's lifelong attempt to find a unified field theory of culture. It was also entirely illegal, since they obtained no permissions from the original record companies. Somehow, that was largely ignored. Not the least significant thing about it was that he did not generally identify the race of the performers, which made the entirely accurate point that Black and white musicians had been exchanging influences at least since the Great Awakening of the 1740s.

The collection, which sold only fifty copies the first year, somehow found its way to young musicians all over the US who would be the backbone of the folk revival. "It was our Talmud, it was our Bible," said Dave Van Ronk. Bob Dylan, Jerry Garcia, and John Cohen of the New Lost City Ramblers all claimed Smith's work as an essential source. When Allen Ginsberg tired of Smith's lengthy residence on his couch, he went to Jerry Garcia and asked him to support Smith with a grant from the Grateful Dead's Rex Foundation. Garcia replied, "Of course. I owe him a lot for that collection."

A collegiate scene that was looking for more authentic American roots music was already in place in Cambridge, Massachusetts. Paula Kelley and Joyce Kalina, both Brandeis University class of '57 graduates, opened a jazz-centered coffeehouse at 47 Mount Auburn Street in Harvard Square on January 6, 1958. It bumped along at first, but in the spring of 1959, a man named Peter Robinson suggested they hire a woman folk singer. When they rebuffed him, he rented the club for the night and introduced a Boston University freshman named Joan Baez to Cambridge. She was noticeably beautiful, but it was her voice that was utterly staggering. By that summer, the Club 47 poster listed her for Tuesday nights, with jazz Thursday to Saturday.

The different pieces—musicians, promoters, audiences—of an active music scene were at hand. In Boston, Manny Greenhill's Folklore Productions was where Pete Seeger played when he came to town. Greenhill was a New York trade unionist who'd taken guitar lessons from the blues/folk singer Josh White, then learned theater by putting on Spanish Civil War benefits. He'd established the Foreign Language Press in Boston, and once it was well on its way, he began Folklore Productions to present shows.

The yeast in the musical loaf was a quartet of Harvard students who would become the Charles River Valley Boys (CRVB). One of the Boys was Eric Sackheim, a young graduate student in Japanese who would become their primary source for old-time music. Sackheim loved Appalachian country music like Uncle Dave Macon, Charlie Poole, and Gid Tanner. Not poor, he had an enormous record collection, knew about Harry Smith's *Anthology*, and was, his friends thought, "a one-man folk revival."

Fueled by the great songs he kept bringing around, Clay Jackson of Texas, Bob Siggins of Nebraska, and Ethan Signer, an MIT graduate student in biophysics, joined Sackheim to play old-time music with great skill but no burning desire for commercial success. All in all, Cambridge was a benign and healthy place. Bob Neuwirth, who came to Boston to attend the School of the Museum of Fine Arts, would later contrast Cambridge with New York City: "You could be loose in Cambridge and not have your head kicked in."

As 1959 passed, the scene thrived. Two more clubs, Café Yana and the Golden Vanity, opened in Boston. George Wein, who had a jazz club in Boston called

The Folk Scare

137

Storyville and since 1954 had been the impresario of the Newport Jazz Festival, noticed all the action and began booking Odetta into Storyville. He decided to add an afternoon of folk to the jazz festival, then realized the level of interest dictated that folk have a festival of its own. Working with Pete Seeger and Odetta's manager Albert Grossman, he booked a first festival in 1959 that featured Seeger, bluegrass banjo player Earl Scruggs, Odetta, Sonny Terry and Brownie McGhee, Bob Gibson, and the New Lost City Ramblers. The star of the festival was an unbilled special guest; Gibson had heard Joan Baez in Cambridge and invited her to join him for two songs. She walked off the stage barefoot and a star.

The year before, three thousand miles away in Berkeley, a kindred folk music scene took root when a left-wing guitar picker and martial arts teacher named Rolf Cahn, in partnership with his new wife, the blues/folk/jazz singer Barbara Dane, opened a club called the Blind Lemon, with Odetta taking the stage on opening night.

Barry Olivier's Berkeley Folk Music Festival, held on the Cal campus, began that year. KPFA's *Midnight Special* kept folk music coming on Saturday nights. And the next year, 1959, recent Berkeley High graduates and *Midnight Special* regulars Neil Rosenberg, Mayne Smith, and Scott Hambly formed the Bay Area's first native bluegrass band, the Redwood Canyon Ramblers. Finally, the pioneering musicologist and producer Chris Strachwitz had just begun the long and outstanding history of El Cerrito's own Arhoolie Records, recording people like Mance Lipscomb and later Clifton Chenier, among hundreds of others.

In 1963, Cahn joined with Debbie Green, a BU classmate of Joan Baez's and the source of many of her early arrangements, and Chandler Laughlin, more commonly known as Travis T. Hipp, to open a much larger and more influential club, the Cabale. The name a tribute to the Kabbalah, the Cabale came with a satellite bed-and-breakfast for touring musicians, the home of Midge and Phil Huffman. (The Cambridge version was the home of Nancy Sweezy and her daughters.) Truly hospitable, the Huffmans might put up Sonny Terry and Brownie McGhee for a couple of weeks. Since Brownie had a tendency to stay up all night, and since Midge and Phil's bed was in the living room, she would simply vanish, put on her pajamas, come back, and crawl into bed…and go to sleep, no matter the volume of the gathering.

In terms of spread and activity, folk was at a peak. There was by now a booking circuit connecting Club 47 and the Cabale, elegantly depicted in picker and artist Rick Shubb's poster, *Humbead's Revised Map of the World*, which depicted a single Pangaea-style continent that was largely Cambridge, Berkeley, San Francisco, and New York City. Ann Arbor had the Canterbury House, Chicago had Albert Grossman's Gate of Horn, Denver the Exodus.

Los Angeles was big enough to have two important clubs: Ed Pearl's Ash Grove, which was a roots-oriented place that presented Bill Monroe, Son House, Muddy Waters, and Doc Watson, and the Troubadour, not far from the Ferus Gallery, which was somewhat more commercially oriented. San Francisco had the Drinking Gourd on Union Street and the Coffee Gallery on Grant Avenue, which was the natural habitat for what fellow musician Dan Hicks called "a rough, tough beatnik" from Texas named Janis Joplin.

Always a singer, Joplin heard Elvis Presley sing "Hound Dog" when she was in her early teens and then managed to find the original version by Big Mama Thornton. A story about *On the Road* in *Time* sent her to the actual book, and she was a beatnik for life. Odetta and then Bessie Smith became her singing role models. Her taste in music and her circle's attempt to integrate their local lunch counter made her a pariah in her hometown of Port Arthur, a hellish sinkhole of oil refinery effluvia.

After a brief foray to the West Coast, she chose Austin and the University of Texas as the most reasonable way to get out of Port Arthur, and found a kind mentor in Ken Threadgill, who ran a honky-tonk in an old gas station. She also fell into a social scene at "the ghetto," an old army barracks then used as student housing. College was a joke, and she hit the road to San Francisco.

It did not go well. She sang at Coffee and Confusion and then the much larger Coffee Gallery, where the bartender, Howard Hesseman, treated her well. She'd long recognized her own bisexuality, but her relationship with Jae Whitaker was erratic, and Janis began to abuse methedrine.

Her best encounter in the period was at another stop on the circuit, the Folk Theater in San Jose. She stuck her head into the dressing room and asked the assembled players if someone would care to play some blues behind her. Jerry—birth name Jorma—Kaukonen allowed as he wouldn't mind, and it was a musical highlight of her life; he loved Bessie, too. The two were booked for a show in April at the Tangent in Palo Alto, but by now, her love affair with shooting speed was taking over her life. At length, she crashed hard enough to force a return to Port Arthur.

The Folk Scare   139

*   *   *

Ultimately, the folk circuit ended in New York City, the media capital of America. Home to Woody Guthrie, Pete Seeger, and Lead Belly in the 1940s, the Village's Washington Square was a public home for folk music on Sunday afternoons from then on. One visitor recalled being startled that one unassuming group in the corner of the square one day was in fact the well-known Greenbriar Boys—John Herald, Ralph Rinzler, and Bob Yellin.

South of Washington Square, Israel Young's Folklore Center sold instruments and acted as a community center, while along Bleecker and MacDougal Streets, "basket houses"—so named because the musicians passed a hat/basket for donations—like the Café Wha? came and went. Alongside the well-known and upscale Bitter End, the Gaslight Café was ruled by Dave Van Ronk, known as the "Mayor of MacDougal Street," and would present Woody Guthrie's friend Ramblin' Jack Elliott, Mississippi Fred McDowell, the Reverend Gary Davis, and oh so many more.

Folk music covered a wide span of music, from the Reverend Gary Davis to the New Lost City Ramblers (NLCR), who performed scrupulously authentic versions of '20s- and '30s-era country string band music, to Village-born Maria D'Amato, part of the Even Dozen Jug Band, and Colorado import Judy Collins, who made her New York debut in February 1961 at Gerde's Folk City before going on to a brilliant career as a vocalist rather than a folk singer per se.

The next month, another outlander, Minnesotan Bob Dylan, debuted at Gerde's. He played, as he put it in his memoir, "hard-lipped folk songs with fire and brimstone servings." A deeply serious student of the music, he presented songs from both Black and white sources. He was also considerably influenced by his reading. Dismissing what he heard on the radio as "milk and sugar," he wrote, "The *On the Road*, *Howl* and *Gasoline* street ideologies that were signaling a new type of human existence weren't there, but how could you have expected it to be?" Folk songs were his "preceptor and guide into some altered consciousness of reality, some different republic, some liberated republic." He had "no ambitions to stir things up. I just thought of mainstream culture as lame as hell and a big trick."

Dylan would sit in the Kettle of Fish, the bar above the Gaslight, and watch people like Kerouac's musical cohort David Amram, Beat poets Gregory Corso and Ted Joans, and Weaver Fred Hellerman go by while the jukebox played Bumble Bee Slim and Percy Mayfield. Though Dylan revered Woody Guthrie and would be associated with him for years, his ears were open to much more. Van Ronk showed him around the Village's jazz scene—the Vanguard, the Village Gate, the Blue Note. At one point, he introduced himself to Thelonious Monk and said that he played folk music. "We all play folk music," the sage replied. Over the next couple of years, Dylan would absorb Village culture and see LeRoi Jones's *Dutchman* at the Cherry Lane Theatre, the Living Theatre's *The Connection*, Brecht onstage, and Red Grooms in the museums.

Ten months after his arrival, he was in the studio being recorded by the famed producer John Hammond. Dazzled to the point of awe by the gifted playing of the NLCR's Mike Seeger, who "played these songs as good as it was possible to play them," he concluded that he would have to violate the folk canon and write his own songs. By spring 1962, he had written his first classic, the civil rights anthem "Blowin' in the Wind," and by the time his second album, *The Freewheelin' Bob Dylan*, was released in May 1963, he'd added the tender "Girl from the North Country," the caustic "Masters of War," and the prophetic "A Hard Rain's a-Gonna Fall"—on side one.

Dylan's impact was felt in many ways. His manager Albert Grossman played wizard by assembling a folk supergroup called Peter (Yarrow), Paul (Stookey) and Mary (Travers), which would be phenomenally successful on its own terms in the commercial side of folk and would also put some of Dylan's songs onto the radio, giving a gigantic boost to his career.

By 1963, a television program called *Hootenanny* presented the more pop-oriented folk acts to America on a weekly basis, although their continued blacklisting of Pete Seeger meant that Dylan and Baez would boycott it. The Newport Folk Festival that summer presented a radically different character, firmly aligning folk and the ongoing civil rights movement. Given the importance of singing to the movement, centrally the anthem "We Shall Overcome," the linkage was quite genuine. Dylan, Baez, Theodore Bikel, and the Freedom Singers, a quartet of student activists from Georgia, closed the festival with a heartfelt rendition of the song.

Newport also featured a man from the past. It had occurred to certain fans that some of the musicians who had recorded in the late 1920s might still be alive. Mississippi John Hurt had recorded thirteen tracks in 1928 and then returned to his farm in Avalon, Mississippi. Two of those tracks had been included in *The Anthology of American Folk Music*, and a pair of resourceful blues fans found Avalon on the map, and then Hurt himself. He came onstage at Newport and captured the festival.

Not all the rediscovered musicians would play as well nor enjoy their new exposure so much as Hurt. Bitter because he knew he wasn't playing his best but was lauded anyway by unsophisticated fans, Son House was one of them. The motivations of the young white searchers were complex as well. Dick Waterman, who had taken part in the search and later acted as an agent for many of the bluesmen, was widely accepted as a clear-eyed and ethical participant in the process. He would observe that "our motivation was a strange combination of ego, scholasticism, and power." But the impulse to search out and recover living fragments from an American past that was largely a mystery to the mainstream culture seems generally admirable.

18

The Tape Music Center and Its Cohorts

San Francisco's counterculture roots had begun with poets and painters. Popular music, from early rock to folk, would also have considerable influence on the young. The audience for avant-garde electronic music was somewhat more rarified, but in the early '60s, the art form in San Francisco would be incubated in an institution, the Tape Music Center (TMC), that would be an extraordinary locus of creative activity in the city, bringing together music, dance, and theater. In the spring of 1963, the three principals of the TMC, Ramón Sender, Pauline Oliveros, and Morton Subotnick, moved into 321 Divisadero Street (at Page Street), a former Masonic Lodge and then the California Labor School.

The ground floor had a hall with seating for a hundred and another room that held fifty. There was a large space upstairs that served as a production studio. They had two cotenants to help with the $175 rent; one was KPFA, which had a morning program of avant-garde music and wanted a San Francisco site. The station would build a soundproofed control room and help fit out the downstairs performance space. The other was Ann Halprin's Dancers' Workshop.

143

144   **The Last Great Dream**

The moment was pivotal, if unplanned, signaling the shift of the San Francisco experimental arts culture from North Beach, where tourists had driven up rents, to a site just one block from Haight Street. The TMC was unique as a workshop unassociated with a larger institution, but the presence of Halprin and KPFA made it clear that TMC's organizers saw it as a community center, with public access at the core of their mandate. Their ongoing drive to collaborate with other art forms made the TMC the nucleus of a much larger energy.

Born into the Spanish Civil War, Ramón Sender recalled his earliest memories were of gunfire. Sent to the US, he suffered from refugee trauma as a child and took refuge in music and playing the piano. In 1956, he attended a New York concert that included Karlheinz Stockhausen's just-completed *Gesang der Jünglinge*. "It just knocked me out, I was just absolutely amazed by that piece of music....The minute the concert was over I went out and rented a wire recorder."

Visiting San Francisco in 1957, he walked into City Lights and saw Lawrence Ferlinghetti talking with Michael McClure. Sender introduced himself and asked, "What young composers should I be meeting?"

"Well," McClure replied, "there's a guy, Morton Subotnick, who's been doing a piece based on the tarot cards."

It would take a few years for them to connect, but the advice was excellent.

After a spell in a commune in Georgia, the Macedonia Cooperative Community (the future peace activist Staughton Lynd was also a member), and then with the pacifist small-*c* communist Society of Brothers, the Bruderhof, in upstate New York, Sender returned to California and began to study with Robert Erickson at the San Francisco Conservatory of Music.

Pauline Oliveros was the daughter and granddaughter of piano teachers, and from childhood, she practiced what she came to call "deep listening" to all sounds, in particular the insects and birds in the wetlands near her Houston home. By the age of sixteen, she knew she wanted to compose, and she enrolled at SF State, where she also studied with Erickson, who emphasized improvisation.

She also wanted to write songs to poetry and to know the poet first, so she went to SF State's Poetry Center and introduced herself to the director, Robert Duncan. He received her warmly, and she became part of his and his partner

Jess's social circle. Given her own lesbian orientation, she moved comfortably in Duncan's orbit. She also took a writing class from Duncan's friend Jack Spicer. And she improvised, both with Sender and also with her former SF State classmates Terry Riley and Loren Rush at KPFA, where they recorded the soundtrack for a film called *Polyester Moon*.

Morton Subotnick had come from his army service to graduate school at Mills College while also playing clarinet part-time in the San Francisco Symphony orchestra, and full-time in the ballet and opera orchestras. By 1961, he was composing for the Actor's Workshop production of *King Lear*, musique concrète that conveyed, he said, "a landscape of sound that created the sonic rage that was the storm of Lear's view of a world out of control."

In June 1961, he also took part in the first program of an Erickson-conceived Composers' Workshop series at the conservatory, which included student work but also performed material by John Cage, Lou Harrison, Harry Partch, Karlheinz Stockhausen, and Luciano Berio.

Terry Riley did not enjoy the academic atmosphere of the Cal music department graduate program, and his solace was his work as co–music director of Ann Halprin's Dancers' Workshop. His partner was another graduate student, La Monte Young. Young had been raised in a Mormon village in Idaho, and from his earliest years, he was entranced by sounds—the harmonics of a transformer, the wind through trees and telephone lines. While in college in Los Angeles, he played jazz with future legends of '60s free jazz Eric Dolphy, Billy Higgins, and Don Cherry. Deeply influenced by northern Indian classical music, he began using a sustained drone as a key element in his composing, in contrast to Riley, whose minimalism came from the repetition of short patterns.

The Cal music department was open enough to have a Noon Concert series in May 1959 that included Riley's "Concert for Two Pianos and Five Tape Recorders," and a Young piece that included "frying eggs, a game of marbles, a pianist playing Beethoven...students walking in the aisles reading from textbooks, Young shouting 'Green!' and Bruce Conner passing out literature."

Along with this startling surfeit of five gifted young electronic composers appearing in the same time and place, San Francisco was home to a woman busily engaged in reinventing movement by creating postmodern, "organic rather than representational" choreography, a dance that was "ordinary and extraordinary at the same time," said her biographer, that made the stage a place "where the self might unfold rather than [be] depicted."

Anna Schuman had grown up dancing but attended the University of Wisconsin rather than Bennington College, the center of dance in America, because Jews were not then accepted there. Adopting the name *Ann* after marriage, she followed her new husband, Lawrence, to Harvard, where he was to study landscape architecture and city planning in the Graduate School of Design, the now Ann Halprin audited design classes and absorbed the lessons of the Bauhaus faculty refugees who were just then arriving at Harvard, most notably Walter Gropius.

Settling in San Francisco and then in Marin County after World War II, she connected with the bohemian world through her friendship with James Broughton, and from him to Michael McClure and later Bruce Conner. She consciously strove to link her work to other art forms, so that one 1960 Dancers' Workshop show featured poetry by Richard Brautigan and art by Manuel Neri and Joan Brown as well as dance. It was a democratic impulse. Her rebellion, said the dance critic Rachel Howard, "was to declare that any movement, performed with presence and intention, could be a dance, and anybody could be a dancer."

Two elements set her work apart. Her vision was rooted in nature, as she said, from "being in nature and noticing that there'd be a foghorn in the distance and then the red berry would fall." She and her husband had built an extraordinary deck at their home in Marin as her classroom, a part of the landscape rather than an intrusion, with two trees forming a proscenium. It floated above the ground and reflected the change of the seasons as bark and flowers fell on it.

Secondly, she included improvisation in her choreography, for which the dance world excoriated her. Sometimes so did her audiences. Her 1961 *Four Legged Stool* flopped badly, in large part because the audience simply couldn't grasp it. As her archive described it, it had been "designed as a sensory experience without deliberate meaning or continuity, the purpose of the content was to be whatever the audience saw."

The Tape Music Center and Its Cohorts   147

*   *   *

The Tape Music Center had gestated in the attic of the conservatory, where Sender had created a studio that consisted of three tape recorders (one good one), some things to bang on, and an upright piano to serve as an echo chamber. He and Oliveros began a concert series called Sonics in December 1961. The first show included his *Traversals*, her *Time Perspectives*, and Terry Riley's *M…Mix*. Their equipment was primitive, but their vision was not.

Oliveros's piece was in four-track, made by using two stereo machines. They lined the tapes up by rolling the reels down the long halls of the conservatory and then synced them up by hand. Riley's piece started as a blues piano riff and the sound of "Laughing Sal," a feature at the local amusement park, before the tape was manipulated, he said, via a "thirty-five-foot tape loop that extended all the way around the studio, using several wine bottles as 'spindles.'" The night concluded with an improvisation they dubbed "Opera" and was topped off when Subotnick showed up and said to Sender, "Can I play, too?"

The event also introduced them to a studious high schooler named Michael Callahan, who would eventually become their technical director. He'd seen a picture of them posed in front of electronic equipment and came mostly to see the equipment. By the time they got to the new home at 321 Divisadero, he'd also be interested in the music. As he joined, Terry Riley and Pauline Oliveros departed for Europe—Riley played piano in servicemen's bars while Oliveros had won a prize that took her to Holland. Earlier that year, another new composer, Steve Reich, had joined the city's avant-garde scene.

In later Sonics performances, Halprin dancers John Graham and Lynn Palmer joined in on the Opera improvisation, on at least one occasion in tandem with a Maytag washing machine filled with spinning, tumbling rocks that served as the percussion instrument. The musicians, along with Terry Riley, also improvised to a Bruce Conner painting. The final Sonics included the *Tropical Fish Opera*, surely among the most hilarious examples of random choice in composition ever conceived.

As Sender recalled it, "I brought a bowl of tropical fish as a score to a concert and four of us, Morton Subotnick, Pauline Oliveros, Loren Rush, and myself, proceeded to block out certain areas on the glass sides of the tank—a staccato area, a low-pitch area, and so on. We sat down and played the fish as notes from the four sides of the tank, thus producing four simultaneous versions from different dimensions. This tickled the audience enormously." In a later performance, Sender recalled, there was no heater in the tank, which left the fish logy and the music "exceedingly low and slow."

Perhaps the fish were a bit much. When Sender asked the conservatory director to budget for their work and was rejected, he and Subotnick, Oliveros having departed for Holland, went off on their own. Callahan told them about a building at 1537 Jones Street that was due to be razed and was consequently rent free, and they took it over in June 1962.

They decided that every show should be a collaboration with other people, and so they put on Robert Duncan's play *Adam's Way*, which included the poets Robin Blaser and Helen Adam and paintings by Jess. Another production, directed by a young assistant director at the Actor's Workshop, Ronnie Davis, was dubbed *Event II*. The audience members were covered by a black cloth with holes cut for their heads, and they watched, wrote the TMC's historian, two naked "dancers sitting on toilets in a mirrored closet pondering the process of producing stool."

The year presented an exceptional coming together of arts collaboration. In June, the San Francisco Museum of Art hosted a poetry festival that featured Kenneth Rexroth and work by Michael McClure read by David Meltzer, as well as a Jordan Belson film, music by Pauline Oliveros, the Dancers' Workshop, collages by Robert LaVigne, mime from Ronnie Davis's troupe, and music by the Vince Guaraldi Trio. In December, the Actor's Workshop presented Brecht's *Galileo* with music by Subotnick, mime from Davis, and projections by a new artist named Elias Romero. (Later, Sender would note a practical reason for the mixing: "We said, 'We'll do music for your plays in return for an introduction to your best sponsor.'")

Their creative high point at Jones Street was unquestionably *City Scale*, which they brought off on March 9, 1963, in collaboration with Ken Dewey, another of the Actor's Workshop assistant directors, and Tony Martin, a new painter in town who had already created an exhibition for Ann Halprin at the SF Museum of Art—*Theater for Watchers, Walkers, Touchers*. It featured a touch piano in which different keys had different surfaces—"sandpaper, rubber bands, or liquid." Martin would become the TMC's visual composer.

The Tape Music Center and Its Cohorts 149

Their set for *City Scale* was a wide expanse of the city. Two rented trucks took the audience from TMC to Ina Coolbrith Park, which overlooked North Beach, where they witnessed an automotive ballet, cars with different-colored headlights moving through the neighborhood and then lining up in front of Coit Tower facing the audience just as firecrackers went off beneath them in the bushes below their overlook. There was a "book-returning ceremony" at City Lights, a trombone player in the Broadway Tunnel, and a woman singing Debussy while wearing a bathrobe in a storefront window. It was the audience's job, said Sender, "to look more carefully at everything and try to figure out if a particular event was staged or just happening."

At one point, the two trucks full of audience members arrived at a small park above the Mission District, where Sender had placed four seventeen-foot weather balloons. As they entered the park, they saw two street gangs apparently preparing to rumble. When the audience members began to chase balloons and one another around the park, the gangbangers seemingly concluded that the artistes and their fans were scarier than they were and departed.

Soon after *City Scale*, the building on Jones Street burned down, and TMC moved to the more substantial home at 321 Divisadero. The new facility welcomed a new flock of students. Lucy Lewis was a dancer from Los Angeles who'd transferred to SF State in 1962. After rejecting ballet as a child, she'd become so involved with modern dance that by the age of ten she already felt somewhat outside conventional society. The dance department at SF State was home, and when her teacher there, Halprin dancer John Graham, invited her to come take a class at 321, she jumped at the chance. Not long after, she asked Halprin for a scholarship and became a part of the Dancers' Workshop.

Lewis also choreographed, and she created her own avant-garde company, which she called 123 as a play on the TMC address. For music, she relied on her boyfriend, an embryonic architect by the name of George Hunter. They had met at San Fernando Valley State College, although Hunter had never registered there. When she moved to San Francisco, he followed, bringing with him "one of those old Ampex tape machines in the brown leatherette case. I would record lots of different tones on a tape, cut it up into little pieces, and then reassemble it to get all these weird sounds."

He set up shop in a closet opposite the studio at 321. "You'd go in there, and there'd be all these pieces of tape hanging in little loops," Lewis recalled.

Hunter produced one particularly exotic sound by replacing the needle in a phonograph cartridge with the end of a Slinky toy. "I used the cartridge like a contact mic—that's basically what it was. You could take the needle out and put anything in there to generate all different kinds of sounds."

Hunter also had a new friend, an SF State music student and reed player named Richie Olsen who'd come to San Francisco after the jazz magazine *DownBeat* had praised the local musical scene. At SF State, he began to smoke pot, possibly some of what Hunter was buying in Los Angeles to resell in San Francisco at twice the price. Olsen was playing in a rock club where his sax was drowned out by the electric guitars, and it was much more satisfying to work with George and Lucy in quieter circumstances. He also had more time, because his increasingly long hair had gotten him kicked out of the music department. Being at 321 introduced him to a swath of interesting people, including the young composers Steve Reich and Terry Riley, and the San Francisco Mime Troupe.

Lewis's primary focus was Ann Halprin and the Dancers' Workshop, especially when Subotnick introduced Halprin to Luciano Berio and the Dancers' Workshop received an invitation to perform at the Venice opera house, La Fenice, as part of the 1963 Biennale. Halprin's "laboratory," the dance deck, featured tree houses and ropes, and led to the remarkable set for *Esposizione*, a cargo net to dance on with music by Berio.

"At specific times," Lewis recalled, "the dancers had to be at specific places. But the most important thing was, at a specific time, we had to be at the top of the cargo net, because the music was going to absolutely explode at that moment, and we all were to fall down and roll down the net." After Venice, they moved on to Paris, where they were part of *The Gift*, a production directed by Ken Dewey, with music composed by Terry Riley. His music was a much-manipulated cut-up tape of Chet Baker playing "So What," although in Paris, the living Baker also took part.

The multiform chemistry of the San Francisco art scene seemed to be spreading wide.

19

The Church on Capp Street: A New Culture Blossoms

Just as the Tape Music Center found its new home near the Haight in spring 1963, Ronnie Davis's San Francisco Mime Troupe established its own base at an abandoned church at Twentieth and Capp Streets in the Mission District. Both places would see arts collaboration and fusion at the highest possible level.

After a Fulbright year in Paris studying mime, Davis had arrived in San Francisco in 1958. He began working as an assistant director for the Actor's Workshop (AW), but late in 1959, he also premiered *Mime and Words* at the San Francisco Art Institute, and near the end of 1960 began a late-night series, the Eleventh Hour Mime Show, at the AW's Encore Theatre. The troupe included the visual artist William Wiley, the composer Steve Reich, and Ruth Maleczech and Lee Breuer, also members of the AW. The performances were improvised and without narrative, combining movement and music to create an environment.

In the first years of the new decade, the troupe moved from Beckett—*Act Without Words* and *Krapp's Last Tape*—to a happening, *Event I*, which

151

152 **The Last Great Dream**

Davis described as "a madman show for insane people who were struggling to present all of the world in one hour." One *Event* participant, Breuer, thought it was thirty years ahead of its time. In 1962, the three assistant directors at the Actor's Workshop, Ken Dewey, Lee Breuer, and Ronnie Davis, joined with Ann Halprin as the American Cooperative Theatre to stage Jean Genet's *The Maids* at the Mission Neighborhood Playhouse. That year, Davis's troupe embraced commedia dell'arte as its primary mode of presentation with a version of Carlo Goldoni's *The Dowry*, and in the summer, they initiated a long tradition by presenting it free in the park.

By 1963, they were the San Francisco Mime Troupe. Davis had left the Actor's Workshop over objections to their funding from the Ford Foundation. Highly political, he took his anti-capitalism seriously, although as a more doctrinaire but puzzled leftist pointed out, he also wanted to maintain his "individual prerogatives." He wanted the troupe "not merely to entertain, rather to educate, not merely to educate, to be an example; not merely to be an example, to create an opposition...." In that, he frequently succeeded. "Unencumbered by party, program or theory," Davis wrote, "we practiced escaping from the bourgeois doldrums. Inevitably, we drifted toward an alternative culture."

The old church became a crucible for a new American theater that combined the mime troupe's politicized commedia dell'arte with an emerging post-Beat cultural scene. This was reflected early on by the lineup for an October 20, 1963, benefit for Arthur Richer, a Wallace Berman–circle painter who'd been arrested for cannabis possession. It included an art show featuring Jay DeFeo, Wally Hedrick, Wallace Berman, and more, poetry from four of the five readers at the 6 Gallery, dance from the Halprin choreographer Fumi Spencer, and, as the invitation had it, "jazz in the afternoon / a magical auction / poems / oracles / a San Francisco sunset / films / lite and sound and dance / a festival of joy / Mr. Richer may appear / and / other spontaneous love actions / all day long." The show also included Elias Romero and Bill Ham, which signaled the beginning of yet another development in San Francisco arts, the light show.

Seymour Locks was a sculptor who'd begun teaching at SF State in 1947. By 1952, he'd discovered that an overhead projector could accommodate bowls filled with oils and pigments and beam hypnotically swirling shapes

The Church on Capp Street: A New Culture Blossoms   153

and colors onto the wall. It combined inexpensive military surplus equipment with bright new materials like Day-Glo paint and aniline dyes. Romero was an art student and friend of Berman who'd either taken a class from Locks or seen work done by some of Locks's students; in any case, he began working with the light show format, and by 1963, he was taking part in the Mission church events.

Ham described them: "Sunday nights, they'd have a collective whatever happened thing—Ronnie and some of his people would do things, the musicians included Bill Spencer, who was a composer of concrete sound and live music, Christopher [Tree] played there. So there was music and dance, and Elias Romero had come up from LA and was renting the downstairs with Ronnie, and he would do projections. So that was the first time that I saw Elias Romero do projections." A painter, Ham saw Romero's work as the next step in art by adding kinetic energy to abstract expressionism. It set him on his life's path.

Ham also influenced San Francisco culture in another way—by creating hip real estate. He had moved to the city in 1960 and taken up residence at 2111 Pine Street, which he described as "the first neighborhood to spill out of North Beach," not terribly far from the Ghost House of a decade before. It was a reasonable walk to jazz on Broadway, with a convenient stop for ten-cent pork buns in Chinatown on the way home. He became the building manager, which also included the flats at 2115 Pine and a rooming house at 1836 Pine.

Under his auspices, artists, actors of both genders, and musicians found a welcome, and a Pine Street arts community sprang up around a group of people who would become much better known in the very near future. Bob Cohen, a sound engineer, was one of the first. Then Lee Breuer, Ruth Maleczech, and Susan Darby from the Actor's Workshop. Elias Romero followed, which gave Ham someone to share a joint with on the odd morning. Later, Luria Castell, a leader in the W. E. B. Du Bois Club at SF State, and her friends Ellen Harmon, Jack Towle, and Alton Kelley came to Pine Street. Sokoji, the home of Suzuki Roshi, was close by, and lots of Zen people became familiar with Ham and his friends.

By now, Steve Reich had become the mime troupe's music director. He'd created a score for their December '63 production of *Ubu Roi*, which they dubbed *Ubu King*, which included clarinet, a strummed violin playing a

154   **The Last Great Dream**

single chord, and a kazoo amplified by a traffic cone. Reich had come to the Bay Area from the East Coast to study with Luciano Berio, although he spent at least as much time at the Jazz Workshop mesmerized by John Coltrane. He drove a cab, worked in the post office, and spent time with Terry Riley, who'd returned from Europe.

Riley's minimalism influenced Reich, and the result was *It's Gonna Rain*, or, as Reich described it, "Meet Brother Walter in Union Square after listening to Terry Riley." Brother Walter was a street preacher, and Reich began by recording him on a cheap tape recorder, which caused things to shift out of phase. The composition began with the original brief sound bite of Brother Walter's prophecy, then single-phrase pieces of it in endless repetition, and eventually returned to the original phrase, phasing in and out. It was stark and hypnotic.

His model was Riley's early tour de force, *In C*, which debuted at the TMC on November 4, 1964. Ramón Sender, Pauline Oliveros, and Morton Subotnick all performed, as well as Reich, his friend Jeannie Brechan, and a friend of Riley's, the seemingly omnipresent Mel Weitsman, who by now was increasingly involved with Zen but happy to take part on recorder. Reich introduced a pulse, and then the performers entered when they chose, moving from module to module (there were fifty-three, each one measure long, and all in C) as the spirit moved them. Modal and improvised, *In C*, along with *Rain*, would define the early phase of minimalist composition.

At Mills, Reich had met and taken a great shine to another Berio student, Phil Lesh, which led to their playing together at *Event III (Coffee Break)* at the mime troupe church in February 1964. Davis and Fumi Spencer added movement. Lesh was none too sure what they were up to: "Tell a story? Channel our aggressions? Epater les bourgeois? Nobody knew. Nobody cared....In retrospect, this event, the manifestation of a collective *unconscious*, served as the prototype" for gatherings he'd be part of later the next year.

Event III included what he called "broad swaths of colored light sweeping through space; chaotic but hypnotic music" played by Reich, Lesh, a friend of Lesh's named Tom Constanten, and a drummer from Oakland named Wahlee Williams, "Ronnie Davis in a cop uniform descending from a ladder in grotesque, disjointed moves as I rise from a trapdoor playing 'Twinkle, Twinkle, Little Star' on trumpet." Lesh dismissed his own composition "6

The Church on Capp Street: A New Culture Blossoms   155

7/8 for Bernardo Moreno" as "pretentious crap," but the center of the show was improvisation, and *that* he enjoyed. It turned out that he had a future in playing improvisational music.

The experimental arts reached a certain high point that year of 1964. Sender's signature *Desert Ambulance* was "a vehicle of mercy sent into the wasteland of [academic] modern music." Oliveros played it on accordion but received the score via instructions through headphones, which allowed her to play in the dark while Tony Martin projected images onto her for a visual score. Alfred Frankenstein called it "aural pop art."

For all-out strangeness, Lee Breuer's *The Run* was hard to beat. Breuer had followed his partner Ruth Maleczech into the mime troupe scene, and from that into the Actor's Workshop (prior to Davis's departure). The AW was a little too buttoned down for Breuer. It wasn't "avant-garde," he said later. "It approached French avant-garde through the eyes of academia."

Two years earlier, he had worked with the TMC on a Composition Series for Actors, in which he tried to distill pure theater—not movement or script or lights but a "formal sequence of emotions akin to a series of musical figures *performed* in 'characterizations'—personality presentations that were to some extent archetypical." He and his compatriots formed a chorus that sat in chairs and performed a set of emotions without words—tears, laughter, rage—which led him to a "post-Brechtian dialectical methodology."

The Run went beyond *that*. Breuer had become friends with Oliveros, and she invited them to present it at the TMC, whose looseness appealed greatly to Breuer. Opening in May 1964, *The Run* featured light projections by Elias Romero, Halprin dancers Fumi Spencer and Norma Leistiko, music by William Spencer (prepared piano) and Warner Jepson, and a sculpture of a dog by Bill Ham. Originally, they'd planned on Bill Ham's actual dog, but as he put it later, "rehearsal time was short." Inspired by Kafka, it was densely abstract. Breuer was pleased with the results, commenting that the ensemble "was decades ahead of its time. Elaborating the ideas that first surfaced in these pieces has been my work for forty years." He would carry the work out primarily with the Mabou Mines company, which he, Ruth, and Philip Glass would establish in New York City.

After the play, Romero moved across the street from Ham, who had been deeply impressed with his projections. Having no room for it, Romero lent

Ham an overhead projector. Romero, Ham thought, worked in a "controlled, minimal, almost poetic manner." Ham wanted to be totally spontaneous and full screen, and in the next couple of years, he would get his chance.

Strange as *The Run* might have appeared, something perhaps at least as odd took place the same night. Next door to the TMC, a man named Michael Ferguson opened the Magic Theater for Madmen Only, a shop selling antiques, clothing, books, and junk. The name was of course taken from Hermann Hesse's *Steppenwolf.* In the back, there was a table with tea and a Pine Streeter named Ellen Harmon. If she approved, one could go through the shop into an apartment behind it, where there was a large bowl of marijuana, which went with the rolling papers that were also for sale. It was in fact America's first head shop, if partly undercover.

On the Magic Theater's opening night, various people, among them the dancer Lucy Lewis, posed as mannequins in the store window. Ham smiled at the confusion; having just come from a very strange theater piece, the audience now found itself wondering who (or what) was real in the window.

Drugs were becoming ever more au courant. About then, Reich introduced Ramón Sender to peyote, and on his first experience, Sender "lived my life backwards, all the way to the moment of conception....The tectonic plates of my reality had just shifted." When he came down, Sender called Reich and asked if he could buy the remainder of his stock.

The TMC even sprouted a film affiliate by acting as host for screenings from the Canyon Cinema collective, a group that included Bruce Conner, Robert Nelson, Ben Van Meter, and Jerry Abrams, the latter three joining Conner in rising to prominence in the next couple of years. As filmmakers, they pursued synesthesia, where all the sense perceptions were simultaneously triggered, what the Bauhaus painter László Moholy-Nagy called a "theater of totality." Founded in the early '60s by Bruce Baillie in the town of Canyon, behind the Berkeley Hills, it began with Baillie screening unusual films in his backyard. By 1962, he had connected with Jordan Belson, Jonas Mekas in New York, and Stan Brakhage.

The TMC was about to morph radically. Early in 1965, the Actor's Workshop moved to Lincoln Center and took Morton Subotnick with them.

The Church on Capp Street: A New Culture Blossoms   157

The TMC was offered a substantial grant by the Ford Foundation, subject to their affiliating with a college, and Pauline Oliveros voted yes. Ramón, always an idealist and now more than ever a purist, argued that they should live communally and thus not need to get large grants, but did not object when Pauline supervised the center's move to Mills College. He would find other adventures.

The Dancers' Workshop had already established its home on Ann Halprin's dance deck in Kentfield. In September 1965, the Dancers' Workshop premiered a Swedish commission, *Parades and Changes*, with music by Subotnick. By now, Halprin's choreography was dominated by task performance, "a parade of changes," said her biographer, "in which the task of theater becomes the creation, rather than the *depiction* of a life situation." One of the tasks was dressing and undressing while locking eyes with an audience member. There were six sections to the piece; Halprin had six index cards, as did the conductor. Very much in the spirit of John Cage, both of them proceeded to shuffle their cards. The nudity, of course, brought a great deal of attention. In Sweden, a critic saw it appropriately as a "ceremony of trust." Others exhibited less equanimity.

TMC's move to 321 Divisadero had unintentionally signaled a geo-cultural shift from North Beach to the Haight for the bohemian community. The Haight was already marginalized as an increasingly Black neighborhood, the city planners having destroyed the adjacent Fillmore District's business center in the name of urban renewal. A convenient streetcar commute to SF State, the Haight was also a student neighborhood.

Shortly before the TMC arrived, a man named Bob Stubbs decided to open a coffeehouse called the Blue Unicorn on Frederick Street near Stanyan in the Haight. After a while, he moved to 1927 Hayes Street, just north of the Panhandle. Legend has it that he later sold the business for $2,500 and a kilo of pot. It was that sort of place.

A series of *Chronicle* articles by Michael Fallon portrayed Stubbs as amiable, bearded, and philosophical about the Unicorn: "A coffeehouse is a creation that must harmonize within itself rather than being run as a business to make money. I think of it as an art form." The place was clearly a community center for local bohemians. Fallon called them *hippies*, although the term would not become widely used for at least a year. It was, he wrote, "a forum for causes from pacifist to planned parenthood, a shelter for sketchers and doodlers, a mailing address for the dispossessed, a clearing house for the lost."

Charles Perry, who would later chronicle the Haight, added that the prevailing philosophy of the Unicorn centered on "a revolution of individuality and diversity that can only be private....It is essentially a striving for *realization* of one's *relationship* to life and other people." Since Fallon had opened his first article with a customer who'd just come from an all-day meditation session at the San Francisco Zen Center, that seemed about right.

Home to folk music and poetry readings, it was also the primary hangout for a circle of poets and writers that included the playwright Ed Bullins, the teacher Stephen Gaskin, and the poet Michael McClure. It was also the local headquarters for both the Sexual Freedom League and for LeMar, the first and perhaps most idiosyncratic of cannabis-legalization efforts.

Lowell Eggemeier objected to marijuana laws and acted on his beliefs by walking into the San Francisco Hall of Justice, firing up a joint, and politely announcing, "I am starting a campaign to legalize marijuana smoking. I wish to be arrested." He spent a year in prison and then retired from activism. But his attorney, James R. White, although highly conservative, started LeMar with four briefs that cited the LaGuardia Committee report, which had found marijuana less harmful than alcohol and had then predictably been ignored by Federal Bureau of Narcotics chief Harry Anslinger. A demonstration in San Francisco's Union Square followed. It included Allen Ginsberg, who returned to New York and, with a local poet and bookstore owner named Ed Sanders and others, founded a Greenwich Village branch.

One of Eggemeier's friends was named Chet Helms, and he can be credited with bringing LeMar to the Blue Unicorn. Helms would be a significant participant in the events of the next few years. Raised primarily by his grandfather, a Baptist minister, he acquired Grandpa's missionary impulse, if not his disapproval of dancing and popular music. His uncle was a printer, and from the age of twelve, Helms learned about posters and promotion. At the University of Texas, he became a civil rights activist, floating around the local folk music scene and then joining the Young People's Socialist League.

He also discovered peyote, omnipresent in Austin, and headed to San Francisco in 1962, hoping to catch the tail end of the Beat poetry scene. He found it unwelcoming and eventually fell to abusing methedrine. After an experience with psychedelics convinced Helms that speed was the path to hell, he and his partner in drug abuse submitted to the kind ministrations of their friend Luria Castell, who fed them, massaged them, and would not allow them to leave her apartment until they were clean and sober. It worked. He began to organize poetry sessions at the Blue Unicorn for fun, while diving for the antiques that could be found in the Haight's attics. But the emerging Haight music scene had his attention, and before long, he found a path into it.

20

The Arc of the Moral Universe—Civil Rights in the South, San Francisco, and Berkeley

The spontaneous act of the four Greensboro freshmen set in motion the youth activism that crystallized in SNCC (Student Nonviolent Coordinating Committee), whose members manifested an almost unimaginable bravery as they joined with James Farmer of the Congress of Racial Equality (CORE) on the Freedom Rides that challenged segregation on interstate buses, already ruled illegal twice over by the US Supreme Court. A former ministerial student named John Lewis represented the Nashville SNCC group.

The riders left Washington, DC, on May 4, 1961. In Anniston, Alabama, members of the Ku Klux Klan stopped their bus and tried to burn them alive, and only the presence of an armed undercover police officer saved them. Once in Birmingham, the city's commissioner of public safety, Eugene "Bull" Connor, turned the Klan loose on the riders, clubs and all.

Nashville sent a second contingent to carry on. Acting to protect the administration, attorney general (AG) Robert Kennedy dispatched a Department of Justice (DOJ) official, John Seigenthaler, to negotiate with the governor of Alabama. When he learned of the second Nashville group, Seigenthaler told Diane Nash, coordinating things from the home base at Fisk University, that "people are going to die." "Then others will take their place," she replied.

In Montgomery, the state police protection the governor had promised melted away, and the Klan went to work; Seigenthaler was one of those attacked. When the AG asked James Farmer for a cooling-off period, he replied, "We've been cooling off for 350 years, and if we cooled off anymore, we'd be in a deep freeze." On May 30, the AG filed with the Interstate Commerce Commission to end segregation. The Freedom Rides continued through the summer. SNCC moved on to step two, sending people like Robert Parris Moses to register voters in McComb, Mississippi.

Inspired and challenged by SNCC's example, Northern white youth came together in Port Huron, Michigan, in June 1962 to form Students for a Democratic Society (SDS). Tom Hayden, who would draft their manifesto, had attended an SNCC meeting the previous fall and had seen what a participatory, decentralized leadership could do. It became their model. In stark contrast, he also covered the ongoing Freedom Rider trials in Jackson, Mississippi. There, he wrote, the words "race, freedom rider, white, Negro and CORE," were banned from the courtroom as irrelevant to the charge of breach of peace. The legal system seemed revealed as a sham. There was no protection, either from the state of Mississippi or the federal government, since J. Edgar Hoover asserted without evidence that Martin Luther King Jr. and the civil rights movement was a Communist-inspired plot and refused to allow the FBI to protect civil rights activists.

Hayden's primary intellectual sources were Albert Camus and C. Wright Mills, the Columbia sociologist who had developed a post-Marxist social critique that identified alienation generated not by capitalism and class oppression but by oppressive affluence and corporate gigantism. In turn, Hayden advanced the hope "that politics has the function of bringing people out of isolation and into community." Born in comfort, SDS members were more than a little naïve in not anticipating that the oppressed would want to

The Arc of the Moral Universe

have the privileges of the middle class, nor could they anticipate the nihilism that frustration would induce in them by the end of the decade. But at this stage, Hayden wrote, they "were having a transcendent experience."

The cause began to spread. Three months after SDS began, César Chávez and Dolores Huerta founded what would become the United Farm Workers.

The privileged do not easily relinquish their advantages. An air force veteran named James Meredith attempted to enroll at the University of Mississippi on September 30, 1962, two years after he had filed suit and twenty days after Supreme Court justice Hugo Black had ordered his admission. In response, a white mob rampaged over the campus, killing two as they attacked federal marshals with stones and small-arms fire. Once again forced to respond by the inaction of an overtly racist state government, the president sent in federal troops and the Mississippi National Guard. Enduring unthinkable harassment and isolation, Meredith would go on to graduate in 1963.

The movement's focus moved to Birmingham, Alabama, where on May 2, 1963, leaders went all in and permitted children to march. Commissioner of public safety Bull Connor set cattle prods, dogs, and fire hoses on them, and AP photographer Bill Hudson's pictures went around the world.

The impact of the savagery visited upon the children of Birmingham came to San Francisco, and twenty thousand rallied at city hall against Connor. On May 18, students from SF State marched through the Fillmore District and the student neighborhood of the Haight-Ashbury with banners denouncing segregation.

A thoughtful white SF State student, Stephen Vincent, wrote in his journal, "Until I in some way work to oppose Connor's position, my color now makes me both responsible and guilty for his atrocious actions." Black students began to demonstrate separately on campus, and Vincent acknowledged that their actions had "to take place apart, or divorced from a white involvement. I imagine the question is how to get on the bandwagon without wrecking it." One answer was the left-wing W. E. B. Du Bois Club, which would take a leadership role for Black and white youth alongside CORE and the NAACP. Among the Du Bois activists were future important Haight-Ashbury community figures Luria Castell and Rock Scully.

The coalition brought the civil rights movement to San Francisco. In August 1963, they began to picket the Select (apartment/home) Rental

164 **The Last Great Dream**

Agency in the Mission District. In mid-September, the owner, Samuel Peitchel, had eleven picketers arrested, including Terry Francois, former head of the SF NAACP, and Terence Hallinan, leader of the SF State W. E. B. Du Bois Club. Hallinan was one of six sons of Vincent, a militant atheist and an attorney who'd represented the left-wing labor leader Harry Bridges and then run for president in 1952 on the Progressive Party ticket. Vincent was a legendary and beloved all-around San Francisco shit-disturber.

Floating on the majesty of Martin Luther King Jr.'s "I Have a Dream" speech at the March on Washington just two weeks before, and then devastated by the murder by bombing of four children—Addie Mae Collins, Cynthia Wesley, Carole Robertson, and Denise McNair—at the Birmingham Baptist Church the day after the San Francisco arrests, the demonstrators were not deterred. The pickets continued for several months, and Peitchel eventually agreed to cease discriminating.

The coalition added another student organization, the Direct Action Group, and turned to a popular local diner chain, Mel's Drive-In, which investigation had revealed to be discriminatory in hiring. The scale of arrests soared, eventually reaching ninety-three, and on November 9, a few days after John Shelley became the city's first Democrat mayor in fifty-five years, Mel's owner settled and signed an agreement that committed him to nondiscriminatory hiring and the establishment of training schools. It was a major win.

The wind at their backs, the activists chose the Lucky supermarket chain as their next target and unveiled a new tactic, the "shop-in." Participants would gather up items, go to the counter, and concede that they had no money. Full shopping carts began to accumulate near the checkout area as students would then resume shopping. In March 1964, Lucky signed an agreement, with the new mayor aiding in the negotiations.

Even before that victory, they'd begun picketing the swank, highly visible Sheraton-Palace Hotel. On a rainy March 2, 1964, police arrested 81 "hymn chanting demonstrators," among them the comedian and activist Dick Gregory, in front of the hotel, loading them into three paddy wagons. The city asked for $110 bail, but the judge released them on their own recognizance except for one of the six Hallinan brothers, Matthew, who was accused of assault on a police officer. Arrests continued, eventually totaling nearly 200,

The Arc of the Moral Universe

almost all of them white students. On March 7, as 1,500 picketed outside and against the advice of their partners in the NAACP, 500 activists invaded the Sheraton-Palace's lobby and sat down.

The newspaper coverage of the hotel demonstrations was surprisingly positive. The *Chronicle* observed that the pickets were 60 percent white, half women, and ranged from bearded youth to men in suits. Even the *Examiner* reported that children and families were a prominent part of the action. After twenty-two hours on the floor, and with the mayor engaged in negotiations that included the chief of the state's Fair Employment Practices Commission as well as a representative of the Culinary Workers Union, the demonstrators were rewarded when Tracy Sims of the Ad Hoc Committee announced a signed pact guaranteeing the hiring of minority workers in a variety of positions. It was an unconditional victory.

One of those arrested—it was his first—was a Cal philosophy major named Mario Savio. He'd started his activism by working with the Maryknoll Society in Mexico, then took up politics at Mel's Diner. He would spend the summer of 1964 as a civil rights volunteer in Mississippi.

After the Sheraton-Palace victory, even larger crowds showed up in March and April actions along Auto Row, the auto salesroom district that ran down San Francisco's Van Ness Avenue. The pattern continued—pickets outside, sit-ins on the showroom floors, hundreds of arrests, and finally signed agreements to diversify hiring.

There was yet another blow for freedom that summer, although in a different realm. Ron Boise was a welder who'd become a sculptor working with sheet metal recovered from scrapped cars. In 1964, he had a show of eleven small—the tallest was a foot high—sculptures depicting sexual positions from the *Kama Sutra* at the Vorpal Gallery, located in an alley behind the Vesuvio Café in North Beach. A police captain visited the gallery and praised the sculptures for their delicacy. Keeping *Howl* in mind, the gallery owner, Muldoon Elder, called Channel 7, whose reporter Roger Grimsby was on hand when five police cars and three paddy wagons arrived the next morning to arrest Elder. He'd sensibly also called the ACLU, and he would be found innocent. During the trial, the sculptures became a focal point for the Bay Area's nascent counterculture. Various bookstores, including the Hip Pocket in Santa Cruz, sold calendars and postcards featuring the sculptures.

166 **The Last Great Dream**

As the trial proceeded, Davey Rosenberg, the publicist for the Condor Club, a strip bar on Broadway, saw a TV clip about the sensational new Rudi Gernreich topless swimsuit and suggested to his boss that they have the club's dancer Carol Doda wear it. His idea ignited a topless craze in the bars on Broadway that did wonders for business. Eventually, the (Roman Catholic) Salesian Boys' Club, the Chinatown Y, and the *Examiner* persuaded the mayor to arrest Doda. The *Chronicle* editorialized in her favor, and with a defense team that included Patrick Hallinan and the "King of Torts," Melvin Belli, she was acquitted.

On a somewhat more idealistic level, the summer of 1964 was Freedom Summer in Mississippi, and some thirty Cal students participated, teaching classes in Black history, citizenship, and the meaning of freedom. Most of the teachers were from elite Northern colleges and undoubtedly learned more than their students. SNCC organizer Robert Moses had warned them, "Don't come to Mississippi to save the Mississippi Negro. Only come if you understand, really understand, that his freedom and yours are one."

On their second day of orientation in June, they learned that three SNCC volunteers—James Chaney, Andrew Goodman, and Mickey Schwerner—had disappeared. Their bodies would not be found until August. What the volunteers experienced, a historian observed, was a teaching model dependent on "dialogue and open-ended inquiry; upon the belief that education must be rooted in the lived experiences of students; and upon the faith in the intellectual capacities of all individuals."

They saw the federal government abdicate any responsibility for their safety as they endured eighty beatings, thirty-five church burnings, one thousand arrests, thirty bombings, and thirty-five shooting incidents that summer. Then they saw the Democratic Party dismiss the claims of Black people ("the Mississippi Freedom Democratic Party") at their nominating convention in August. As they returned to Berkeley at summer's end, they were more radical than ever, now armed with both a new approach to learning and the moral authority to challenge the top-down style of the megaversity that was Cal.

On September 14, dean of students (and former marine corps colonel) Katherine Towle announced a ban on posters, easels, and tables at Sproul

The Arc of the Moral Universe 167

Plaza, traditionally a free speech expanse of concrete on the edge of the UC campus, "because of interference with flow of traffic." Three days later, a coalition that included the left-wing SLATE, CORE, Youth for Goldwater, Campus Women for Peace, and the University Friends of SNCC announced a United Front in opposition to the new policy. They set up tables and advocated, the administration took names, and five people were summoned by the dean. Four hundred students signed statements that they, too, had worked at the tables and demanded disciplinary hearings of their own. Students sat in at the campus administration headquarters, Sproul Hall, and by the end of the day were told that those five students plus three more had been indefinitely suspended.

"It was the common supposition," wrote Michael Rossman, one of the students, that these changes were the result of pressure from the *Oakland Tribune*, which students had been picketing on Fridays from 5:00 to 7:00 p.m. for much of the year. "Only students sitting at tables sponsored by groups particularly active in Civil Rights were singled out for discipline by the Administration, and all eight suspended students were active in Civil Rights work." If they could not recruit or raise funds among students, the civil rights movement in Berkeley was entirely hamstrung.

The next day, October 1, a recent graduate named Jack Weinberg sat at the CORE table. When ordered to identify himself, he refused and was arrested, then bundled into a police car that had most unusually driven onto Sproul Plaza. Within minutes, hundreds of students had surrounded the car and sat down. The police car's roof became a podium, with a three-minute limit on speeches and a sign-up list. First came Mario Savio, who set precedent by carefully removing his shoes so as not to scratch the car's finish before eloquently making clear that his protest was not only on behalf of the civil rights movement but also the students of Cal themselves.

The United Front became the Free Speech Movement (FSM), and over the course of the fall, they negotiated with an administration that did not acknowledge their right to do so and thus operated in bad faith. Earlier in his career, UC president Clark Kerr had defended free speech, even winning a civil liberties award from the Association of University Professors, and thought of himself as a liberal. But his concept of the university as "the knowledge industry" was based on a technocratic understanding of society in which managers managed and everyone else obeyed. "There is no place for anarchy," he wrote, "in the logic of industrialism."

Savio would later say that Kerr was the manager, the faculty were employees...and students were "raw material." Students were there to study, not advocate. Giving up on the administration, the students resumed tabling and waited for the other shoe to drop, which happened on November 28, when the administration began disciplinary proceedings against FSM leaders. The students argued that the proceedings were a matter for the courts and set a deadline of December 2 for the administration to respond.

Five thousand students filled Sproul Plaza that day in protest, and Mario Savio gave one of the decade's defining political speeches: "There's a time when the operation of the machine becomes so odious, makes one so sick at heart that you can't take part, you can't even tacitly take part, and you have to put your body upon the gears and the wheels, upon all the apparatus, and you've got to stop it. You've got to indicate to the people who run it, the people who own it, that unless you're free the machine will be prevented from working."

Alice Waters would later change the way Americans dined, but on December 2, she was another student onlooker listening to Savio. She was moved by his idealism, she later wrote, with his idea that "we can live differently, we can be peacefully united...we could create an entirely new sort of society."

Joan Baez sang, and 1,000 students entered Sproul Hall and sat down. At 3:30 a.m., police from all over the Bay Area converged on Sproul and began the process of arresting 773 people. The campus shut down with a general strike. On December 7, Kerr called a campus meeting at the Greek Theatre, where he offered a settlement that promised no disciplinary action but no guarantee of free speech. Savio rose to reply and in front of an audience of 10,000 was manhandled by campus police. Kerr allowed him back to speak, and he invited the meeting to the plaza to talk. The next day, the appalled faculty senate met in a meeting broadcast on loudspeakers to students outside. It voted 824–115 to support the FSM, then exited the auditorium through a crowd of cheering students.

Trailed by the FBI, which had observed the campus events from the time Weinberg had been hustled into the police car, the FSM leaders hit the road to raise money for their legal defense. A week later, James Farmer of CORE spoke to three thousand at the disputed free speech area and remarked, "Freedom is

The Arc of the Moral Universe 169

indivisible, whether it is the freedom to eat a hot dog in Mississippi or freedom of speech on the Berkeley campus." The next day, James Baldwin lectured in San Francisco at a benefit for the legal defense fund.

The regents had fired the chancellor who'd encouraged the arrests, and it was a new, acting chancellor, Martin Meyerson, who on January 3, 1965, announced a new policy: Political activity on campus was no longer forbidden. The students had won. No longer needed, the FSM voted to disband later in the semester.

In years to come, observers would portray the politicized students at Berkeley, both in the FSM and in later anti-war activities, as entirely different from the hedonists of the Haight-Ashbury. It was a false dichotomy. As one historian later observed, "For sixties activists, the quest for social justice was in many ways a direct extension of the search for personal authenticity. They were as much concerned with questions of psychic liberation as with economic and political issues."

At least initially, drug taking, either in Berkeley or San Francisco, was as much an act of rebellion as of indulgence. FSM activist Michael Rossman later argued, "When a young person took his first puff of psychoactive smoke, he also drew in the psychoactive culture as a whole, the entire matrix of law and association surrounding the drug, its induction and transaction. One inhaled a certain way of dressing, talking, acting, certain attitudes. One became a youth criminal against the State."

Later, Rossman would conclude that the entire experience of the FSM, of "facing, alone and then together, an unsought and terrifyingly wild field of choice of actions and ways of being, in a universe in which somehow anything had become possible," was in itself a mystic altered state.

The Free Speech Movement came with many consequences, almost none of them anticipated. Along with the Watts Rebellion of 1965, it helped elect Ronald Reagan governor in 1966...and president in 1980. It fed the power of the FBI, which established the COINTELPRO program to investigate even the most peaceful of protesters.

And for a campus that had once been notorious for frequent panty raids, it left a legacy of honorable defense of free speech, with the corollary that freedom of speech was pointless if the right of nonviolent action in support of that speech was not upheld.

21

London, No Longer Dull

id-'60s London would give birth to two parallel phenomena, one visual—Swinging London, a matter of style—and one aural—the British Invasion.

The cultural process that would end up with the label of "Swinging London" came first. By 1961, the photographer David Bailey had found his Eliza Doolittle, Jean Shrimpton, who was neither debutante nor aristocrat but an ambitious farm-raised convent school graduate who'd attended a secretarial college. Tall and strikingly beautiful, her look, he said, was "not beatnik and not classical exactly—but more beatnik than classical." As a model, she attended to her own hair and makeup, and their shoots consisted of the two of them putting a pile of clothes into his car and going to the country. Somehow, it worked.

Swinging London was based on a sense of style that had begun with the Chelsea fashionista queen Mary Quant, was amplified by Shrimpton and Bailey, and then moved to a hairdressing salon owned by yet another working-class Cockney, Jewish to boot, Vidal Sassoon. A refugee from an orphanage, he apprenticed himself to a hairdresser and found he had a gift. In 1963, he cut Mary Quant's hair into a short, elegant mode that freed

171

the recipient from gels, permanents, and upkeep, and she loved it. His Bond Street salon's business rocketed. Sassoon was enthusiastically heterosexual and a manly Israeli army veteran, so men like Peter Sellers, Peter O'Toole, and Terence Stamp were comfortable crowding into the shop.

The crowning glory of English fashion erupted on an undistinguished lane in Soho called Carnaby Street, where fashion and style would seize a portion of the British imagination. John Stephen was a grocer's son from Glasgow who'd come to London in the mid-'50s to start a clothing business. He began with a job at Vince Man's Shop on Newburg Street, one block east of Carnaby. It was the first store in London where men could buy clothing with color, a reflection of Chelsea upper-class bohemians' trips to Morocco and Asia combined with art students hungering to be distinctive.

Initially, it catered to a gay clientele, supported by the presence of a popular public bathhouse just around the corner. Himself gay, Stephen had a sure grasp of city taste, and the store prospered. Working nights as a waiter in a coffee bar, he saved his money, opened his own shop, His Clothes, and soon moved to 5 Carnaby Street. Painting the exterior chrome yellow and filling the place with loud pop music, he made shopping exciting, and his customer base expanded to a larger group of young actors and adventurous Chelsea dressers eager to dandify. Soon he had filled a good portion of the storefronts on the block with his clothes. By the mid-'60s, Carnaby Street was a phenomenon.

Music followed fashion, and rock and roll conquered Albion. As ever, London was the home of British ambition as well as its recording industry, and in 1962, four talented and ambitious young men from Liverpool came to the city: John Lennon, Paul McCartney, George Harrison, and Ringo Starr. Liverpool was an entirely logical starting point for fresh music; not only did sailors return there from American voyages with the latest in R & B music, among other things, but an enormous US air base sprawled just outside the city and exerted an influence.

Elvis Presley's music had utterly seized John Lennon's imagination and led him to form the Quarrymen, a skiffle group, which soon added McCartney and Harrison as members. Britain's Education Act of 1944 had designated art

London, No Longer Dull

173

schools—along with trade, business, and academic education—as recipients of support. Like many of the brightest minds of his musical generation, Lennon nurtured his talent in just such a place, keeping his ears wide open.

Chuck Berry came to England, and Lennon and McCartney's music became rock 'n' roll. They had become the Silver Beetles by the time they backed up a British Beat poet named Royston Ellis, who allegedly suggested a change in spelling as homage to all Beats. Since Lennon had created a newspaper in high school called *The Daily Howl*, it clearly appealed to him. Now they were the Beatles.

They acquired a manager named Brian Epstein, who eventually took an acetate of their music to a producer at Parlophone, George Martin. At the time he met the Beatles, Martin was best known for producing comedy albums for *The Goon Show* and *Beyond the Fringe*, which gave him massive credibility with the musicians despite the aristocratic manner he'd acquired through serving in the navy and working at the BBC. He recognized that they were a group and not a star and backups, and he immediately heard the unique harmony that Lennon and McCartney had developed.

In January 1963, Parlophone released their second single, "Please Please Me," which proceeded to zoom straight to the top of the charts and remain there. They worked very hard to sustain their success, and that year, they performed 229 live shows in three countries, 53 radio shows, 37 television shows, put out 2 albums, and performed twice on *Sunday Night at the London Palladium*, Britain's top television program.

By the end of the year, they were not only pop sensations but saviors of the national mood. John Profumo, the secretary of state for war, had an extramarital affair with Christine Keeler. Bad form. Worse form was lying to the House of Commons about it. By the time the Profumo affair was over, British politics was in serious disarray. Alongside the Great Train Robbery, the scandal poked a giant hole in the façade of British stability and moral rectitude, and the national newspapers, collectively known as Fleet Street, determined to find something happy as a substitute. Few institutions on the planet were as capable of finding what they were looking for.

On October 13, the *Daily Mirror*'s coverage of the Beatles' performance at the Palladium conjured up images of rioting in the streets, though nothing like that had happened. But the Beatles were clean, sharp, working-class wits who made a pleasant contrast to the upper-class morass of lies that was the government, and the rest of Fleet Street followed suit. By spring 1964, as the opening images of their movie *A Hard Day's Night* made vividly clear, the near riots and frenzied fandom were quite real; in the *Mirror*'s splendid phrase, it was "Beatlemania."

Their style was now widely imitated in youth fashion, and in their wake came the Mods, so termed because their taste in clothing and music was modern: bebop and cool jazz like Chet Baker, Miles Davis, Gerry Mulligan, and Thelonious Monk. The Mods were carrying out their perception of the Beat rebellion, but only if it came with a quality wardrobe.

Ready Steady Go!, the Friday-night music program that featured bands lip-synching their hits, had debuted in the summer of 1963, and by the time the Beatles appeared on it in March 1964, it was the focal point of British youth culture. From then until 1966, it included not only every significant British act but the best Black American acts—all the Motown groups, Otis Redding, Nina Simone, Wilson Pickett, and more. Visually, the show helped introduce pop art to England, said Pearce Marchbank, the designer of the London entertainment magazine *Time Out*: "targets, chevrons, bright colours, crisp hard edges."

Stratospherically on top of things, the Beatles needed a foil for longevity's sake, even if they didn't realize it. In September 1963, a rather tipsy John and Paul, fresh from a Variety Club luncheon celebrating the Beatles, ran into Andrew Loog Oldham, then nineteen years old, who'd done some promotional work for Mary Quant and then Brian Epstein and was now the manager of a band called the Rolling Stones. The Stones had emerged from the blues (versus the Beatles' rock) end of the British music spectrum that had progressed from the trad scene at the Ealing Club in 1962 with the band Blues Incorporated (Cyril Davies, Alexis Korner, and Long John Baldry). It would lead to bands like the Yardbirds, John Mayall's various groups, and the Who.

The Stones thought of themselves as blues purists; in Keith Richards's words, "We were missionaries, disciples, Jesuits [of the blues tradition]." As such, they were slow to write original material. Songwriting was what the Beatles did best, and they were happy to teach the Stones their latest effort, "I Wanna Be Your Man," which brought the Stones immediate record sales.

Working from that, Oldham constructed a Stones persona that would make them the opposite of the amusing, stylishly suited Beatles. One industry insider

London, No Longer Dull

175

put it this way: "The Beatles were thugs who were put across as nice blokes, and the Rolling Stones were gentlemen (the lead singer was a London School of Economics dropout) who were made into thugs by Andrew." They became, as Oldham put it, "the group parents loved to hate." Or, as a teenage girl in the hinterlands of Maine, simultaneously thrilled, intrigued, and revolted, informed the author when the Stones first came to the US, "They don't even take baths!"

More to the point, observed one of Oldham's employees, Andrew was keenly aware of being illegitimate and "used them as a conduit for his angst, and thus created the first group with a seriously antisocial stance." The Beatles were clearly part of showbiz media; the Stones came with a number of contradictions. Mick Jagger would spend the next twenty years and more as a walking challenge to conventional masculinity, an eyeliner-wearing borderline drag queen who was among the chief cocksmen of rock and roll at its most openly lustful. Socially, he was a rampant hedonist who dreamed of consorting with the upper classes and would eventually embrace a knighthood.

Though primarily associated with music in general and Beatlemania in particular, it should be noted that the British Invasion had actually begun in 1962, when the film *Dr. No* initiated a craze for 007, Bond...James Bond. Having been endorsed the previous year by President Kennedy, a genuine fan, the books became movies, and Sean Connery and Ursula Andress made Bond an essential element in American pop culture. Late in 1963, after the president's devastating assassination, the US was another nation that was distinctly ready for some fun.

"I Want to Hold Your Hand" was released in America in December 1963 and by February 1 was the number one song in the land. After a publicity avalanche that swept the country, the Beatles arrived in New York to a frenzied mass of adulation that didn't quit during their stay, most notably when they played to seventy million people, 60 percent of all American television viewers, on *The Ed Sullivan Show*. It was reliably reported that the New York City crime rate that evening was the lowest in fifty years. Even hubcaps were safe. After seven weeks, "Hand" was supplanted at number one by "She Loves You." By April, the Beatles held down the top five spots on *Billboard*'s chart. It was the most all-encompassing pop-culture sensation in the life of the baby boomer generation.

They brought more than music. Their haircuts started young men growing their hair out. That March in *Vogue*, the Paris designer Courrèges

176   **The Last Great Dream**

blessed Mary Quant's latest creation, the miniskirt, which she said was named after her favorite make of auto, the Mini Cooper; both were "optimistic, exuberant, young, flirty." American girls rushed to join their English sisters. *Fab* and *gear* entered the American lexicon, as well as a growing realization for both genders of the attractions of an English accent.

The band returned to England and began work on what proved to be a superb film, *A Hard Day's Night*. It captured more than a pop sensation; it caught them in a moment of remarkable growth. In January, a disc jockey in Paris had given them a copy of Bob Dylan's second album, *The Freewheelin' Bob Dylan*, and it resonated; after all, their roots were in skiffle, very much part of the folk canon. Dylan was also part of the Beat tradition, thought Paul: "We liked him because he was a poet, far out, a friend of Ginsberg, on the same road as Jack Kerouac." Later that summer, they would meet Dylan, who would turn them on to pot, a further gift to their creativity. It was proof of their brilliance that success did not confine them to love songs.

Shot documentary-style with handheld cameras, from a script that brilliantly recognized that Beatlemania itself was all the subject they needed, *A Hard Day's Night* was, in the words of one critic, "maybe the only pure instance of pop art in the cinema, a film part documentary, part slapstick comedy, part avant-garde technical spree, part musical—and only one of the greatest movies ever made."

The British Invasion was by no means spent. The Beatles and the Stones were followed by a dozen bands, many of them from the pop fluff end of the spectrum, but at least one, the Who, built to last. Pete Townshend was another of those art school rebels who grasped the visual aspects of pop art and Mod. The victim of considerable abuse, both personally from his grandmother and as a member of a generation abused by World War II, Townshend joined screaming feedback to his frequently brilliant lyrics. Driven by the powerful Marshall amplifiers Townshend had persuaded London music shop owner Jim Marshall to build, the Who released their iconic "My Generation" in October 1965.

By then, Swinging London had defined itself as a visual phenomenon par excellence, summed up with genius in the film *Blow-Up* and the television series *The Avengers*. The television series had been running for four years

London, No Longer Dull 177

when, in 1965, John Steed's (Patrick Macnee) new partner became the inimitable Mrs. Emma Peel (Diana Rigg). Now shot in color on 35 mm film and therefore viewable in America, the series mixed humor, wit, understated sexiness, and science fiction/fantasy elements to spoof and transcend the James Bond secret-agent genre.

Blow-Up went further. Michelangelo Antonioni had grown curious about the East End photographers who now dominated British fashion. After considerable research, he began filming in April 1966. It was by no means a realistic portrait; rather, the film posed a challenge to conventional reality. As one critic noted, he changed the colors of things, so that "streets were painted true black and pigeons were dyed; fire hydrants and doorways and the fronts of houses were repainted into bold primary hues." The visual impact of the photographer shooting in his studio combined with the cryptic clues suggesting a murder and the final mimed tennis game brought enormous power to a truly beautiful mystery film.

By mid-1965, Swinging London was a genuine phenomenon. In June, the Beatles were awarded the MBE (Member of the Most Excellent Order of the British Empire). That summer, said one historian, their second movie, *Help!*, was "Swinging London personified—part music, part color supplement travelogue, part Pop Art strip cartoon." London was not only swinging, but for a time, it was the focal point of the Western world's youth culture.

That May, Bob Dylan checked into London's Savoy Hotel to play two sold-out concerts at the Royal Albert Hall. D. A. Pennebaker's remarkable cinema verité documentary *Dont Look Back* depicts an otherworldly virtuoso onstage whose songs had completely transcended the already exceptional political work of "Blowin' in the Wind," "Only a Pawn in Their Game," and "Masters of War" with surrealist masterworks like "It's Alright, Ma (I'm Only Bleeding)," "Gates of Eden," and "Love Minus Zero / No Limit."

Remarkably, Dylan also permitted Pennebaker to capture him offstage at his worst back at the Savoy, mocking the singer Donovan and throwing a tantrum when his advances were refused by the beautiful folk singer Marianne Faithfull, then all of eighteen, pregnant, and about to be married. The reason, at least in part, was drugs. Faithfull wrote, "They were all so hip, so devastatingly hip. (They were also all so fucking high.) Every five minutes or so someone would go into the bathroom and come out speaking in tongues. Sparks were flying off them....I was scared to death."

The one person around with whom she could speak was Allen Ginsberg, so cordial and curious about other people that he did not qualify as cool, even though he had just been deported by the Czech government for his sexual orientation after the city's youth had celebrated him as King of the May, the two events not unconnected.

London was so happening that Ginsberg stayed on and helped put together the peak event of the summer, the Royal Albert Hall International Poetry Incarnation on June 11, just a month after Dylan's shows. The event would seal the influence of Beat attitudes on English youth culture. The surrealists had argued that by changing the aesthetic (representational painting, conventional harmonics in music), one could change society. Mix in a rejection of conventional politics and the omnipresent British class system and, wrote the poet Jeff Nuttall, "you effect a sort of non-specific revolution, which was not programmed, which was not dictated....It erupted, I would say, with Allen Ginsberg's *Howl*."

Already publishing a mimeographed literary magazine called *Tree*, a budding young literati named Barry Miles connected with Beat poetry in 1960 by writing off to City Lights for a catalog. He bought *Howl* by mail and was as entranced as Nuttall. Lawrence Ferlinghetti also wrote and gave him permission to reprint freely from the City Lights oeuvre. In 1965, about to open the quintessentially hip Indica Books, Miles was a prominent part of the Royal Albert reading. He wrote that it "really started the scene. That was when people looked around and thought, and said, 'Wow, there's thousands of us!'"

The Clash's Joe Strummer thought so, too: "You can mark the beginning of the British underground scene of the 1960s to that particular night." It seemingly rekindled the performance aspects of poetry for the British public. The decade-old vibrations of the 6 Gallery had resurfaced, and selling out the Royal Albert Hall with poetry amply documented the power of the rising youth culture.

Six weeks before the Royal Albert event, the Rolling Stones were touring America. Early in May, Keith Richards heard a riff in his dreams and

London, No Longer Dull

awakened enough to turn on a tape recorder, repeat the riff, mumble the words, "I can't get no satisfaction," and resume snoring. The first version was a Dylan-esque folk song, but they rerecorded it in Los Angeles on May 12 and 13. With a cracking beat from Charlie Watts and a fuzz tone effect adding snap and snarl to Keith's guitar, "Satisfaction" became the touchstone of future Stones songwriting, a mixture of R & B, Motown beat, rock, and sexual aggression/longing. It would define the Rolling Stones and be a key part of the soundtrack of the summer of 1965.

22

Transformation via LSD

The various elements that would combine to create the community that would be the Haight-Ashbury in 1966, 1967, and after had floated up into a social solution that awaited a catalyst. A new vision of freedom, a more open sexuality, a refusal to bow down to the implicit portions of the American identity—all this was in place. One thing was left.

Among all the cultural elements that combined to create the Haight-Ashbury and the national and international counterculture, no experience had a greater impact than ingesting LSD.

For two thousand years and more, alchemists had pursued the mythical philosopher's stone, the magical element that could transmute all substances, take one through the veil to a higher reality, transform lives, and confer immortality. If anything could at least metaphorically assume that role in modern times, it was LSD.

In the spring of 1965, Owsley "Bear" Stanley, an air force veteran and student of alchemy who was obsessed with the pursuit of quality, was deeply immersed in *The Kybalion: A Study of the Hermetic Philosophy of Ancient Egypt and Greece*, a twentieth-century tract that proclaimed itself as the teachings of Hermes Trismegistus, the Greek god of communication. Owsley was

The Last Great Dream

also interested in making psychedelics. He purchased what proved to be four hundred grams of the raw material lysergic monohydrate from the Cyclo Chemical Corporation for $16,000, and by May, he'd synthesized quite a lot of lysergic acid diethylamide-25, also known as LSD, or simply acid.

He described the experience:

> You perform a process which within a matter of milli-seconds converts this totally inert material into something which will affect your consciousness at 25 millionths of a gram. So you have something that is hundred times 40,000. So that's 4,000,000. Four million minds can be changed in a perceptible way by these hundred grams of material that came into existence in a very, very tiny space in a very, very tiny amount of time. And I believed in those days that holding your hands around the flask was important, and concentrating on the reaction was important. I also believed that at that moment that those chemicals came together that you had altered the universal mind in some significant fashion to suddenly produce something that was extremely powerful and you had produced a lot of it. I still believe that is true.

It was not surprising that Bear's acid was generally acknowledged as the purest and most powerful psychedelic known to mankind.

Largely controlled by the CIA's MK-ULTRA program, LSD received considerable press coverage through the 1950s and early '60s in significant part because the CEO of *Time* and *Life*, Henry Luce, and his wife, the distinguished conservative political figure and ambassador Clare Booth Luce, had experienced it ("tripped"), Henry only once, Clare a number of times. The loss of her only child had challenged her ambition and success, and she had turned to Roman Catholicism and psychotherapy. In the process, Aldous Huxley's friend Gerald Heard became her adviser, and he introduced her and her husband to psychedelics.

Heard also recruited Dr. Oscar Janiger, a Los Angeles psychiatrist who with his partner Murray Korngold treated the actors Cary Grant, James Coburn, and Jack Nicholson with LSD. Heard also turned on Myron Stolaroff, an executive at the Ampex Corporation who would resign in 1961 to establish the International Foundation for Advanced Study, which offered LSD to the engineers of what would become known as Silicon Valley. Luce, of course, was the most influential person Heard would advise.

As America's foremost media mogul, Henry Luce made an effort to be knowledgeable about many things, including the avant-garde. One of his employees, Rosalind Constable, spent from 1948 to 1962 preparing a biweekly report on the cutting edge of the arts world by scanning some 160 publications, "the weirder the better," she said, "if there is reason to believe the author knows what he is doing…[they might be] inventing a new language which takes most people, including most critics, time to learn."

Even before Luce tripped, *Time* and *Life* featured positive coverage of LSD. The first, a 1954 *Time* article titled "Dream Stuff," noted the potential benefits of acid as an adjunct to therapy. In 1957, *Life* gave the banker/mycologist R. Gordon Wasson a substantial platform to talk positively about his experiences with hallucinogenic mushrooms in Mexico. "The Psyche in 3-D," a 1960 *Time* piece, touted the benefits of LSD therapy for alcoholism, in particular for Cary Grant.

Naturally, Allen Ginsberg was an early explorer of LSD. Invited to Stanford by Gregory Bateson in 1959, he saw the experience as "fantasy much like a Coleridge world of Kubla Khan…[an] identity common with everything—but a clear and coherent sight of it." The next year, he attended a writers' conference in Chile and then pursued wanderings in Bolivia and Peru, which included repeated ingestion of the psychedelic vine yage, or ayahuasca.

At one point, "the whole fucking Cosmos broke loose around me," but after confronting what seemed to be death/oblivion, later trips made him conclude that one should "widen the area of consciousness till it becomes so wide it includes its own death. That is the purpose of life." Later that year, he read some of his drug poems before the Group for the Advancement of Psychiatry. Impressed, Humphry Osmond suggested Ginsberg connect with a researcher at Harvard named Timothy Leary. A week after Ginsberg wrote to Leary, he opened his door to see the professor standing there. Ginsberg was surprised to discover that Leary had never smoked pot and knew nothing about Beat poets.

A troubled soul, Leary had been married twice, relationships plagued by alcoholism and infidelity, the first having ended with his wife's suicide on his thirty-fifth birthday. Though apparently successful, he was a bright but bored academic. Then he read about Wasson's mushrooms in *Life*, sampled them, and grew excited. At Harvard, he received approval from the Department of Social Relations to research the mushroom derivative psilocybin. He connected with another young psychologist, Richard Alpert, and they met with Aldous Huxley, then a visiting lecturer at MIT. Huxley then took Leary to meet with Osmond in November 1960.

Osmond advised discretion, offering it to a limited group of gifted artists and thinkers. Ginsberg, who'd accepted Leary's invitation to take psilocybin, argued that consciousness expansion was a universal right. Acting as a conduit, Ginsberg shared the drug with Thelonious Monk, who asked if he had anything stronger, Dizzy Gillespie, who enjoyed himself, Barney Rosset, who had a miserable experience, and the poet Robert Lowell, who loved it.

An early experiment with prisoners at Concord State Prison showed good results but gave birth to a number of confusing consequences. One was that many of the prisoners turned toward the spiritual, toward an applied mysticism, which neither penologists nor psychiatrists, who saw themselves as scientists, could entirely accept.

Leary and Alpert themselves started to seek answers in Asian spiritual thought, becoming attuned to the study of psychedelics as a matter of experience rather than as an object of analysis. The rest of the department started to hyperventilate as rumors began to spread around campus. Giddily soaring beyond all protocols, Leary gave psychedelics and lessons in how to offer them to a woman named Mary Pinchot, a Washington socialite formerly married to a high-level CIA staffer named Cord Meyer who also happened to move in President Kennedy's social circle. The CIA began to take notice of Leary's activities.

One day late in 1961, a man named Michael Hollingshead popped up in Cambridge with a mayonnaise jar full of LSD in his pocket. More powerful than psilocybin, LSD stunned Leary, and he began to follow Hollingshead as though he were the new messiah. Psilocybin had weakened Leary's academic orientation; LSD ended it. Now he, too, became a guru. The new drug also disturbed the ambience of the researchers, dividing them into those who had taken the drug and those who had not. At least one member of the community, Ralph Metzner, now concluded that psychedelics were not intrinsically "holy or wise," as he had previously thought.

Leary was developing signs of megalomania. He wrote, "We began to see ourselves as unwitting agents of a social process that was far too powerful for us to control or more than dimly understand. A historical movement that would inevitably change man at the very center of his nature, his consciousness." In time, he would coin slogans seemingly out of a Madison Avenue ad agency—"Turn on, tune in, drop out"—and do incalculable damage to anything resembling a thoughtful exploration of consciousness.

By 1962, the psychiatric profession, despite a clear record of positive results and only the rarest adverse reaction, began to worry aloud about LSD. In part, this was a turf war about controlling research traffic in the mental realm; they wanted to keep things in their own profession and out of the hands of countercultural pilgrims they labeled as "borderline personality types." That year, Congress passed a law giving the FDA control over all new drugs.

Inevitably, news of the program's excesses made its way into the *Harvard Crimson* and then to the Boston press. The project was shut down, and six months later, Alpert was terminated for having given psilocybin to an undergraduate. He and Leary would be rescued by Peggy Hitchcock, a wealthy young true believer in the cause of psychedelics. She and her brother Billy, heirs to the Mellon fortune, would offer Leary and his companions a refuge at their 2,300 acre estate in Millbrook, New York. It would become, said one historian, "a school, a commune, and a house party of unparalleled dimensions."

They chose for their working name the International Foundation for Internal Freedom (IFIF), which later became the Castalia Foundation (from Hesse's *Glass Bead Game*). Life at Millbrook could be bizarre, as when one Millbrook resident, Art Kleps, was slipped a thousand micrograms of LSD as a prank, which literally knocked him to the floor.

Somewhat more seriously, Leary worked on his book *The Psychedelic Experience*, a derivation of *The Tibetan Book of the Dead*. The notion that every psychedelic experience involves the death and presumed rebirth of the ego is questionable; establishing an explicit set of expectations and a format for something like an LSD trip seems dubious indeed. As Kleps later wrote, "Psychedelic visionary experience simply refuses to conform to anyone's particular structural system and will inevitably betray anyone who tries to use it as the justification for a neurotic fantasy or paranoid power grab....It's a language, that's all, without words—just the images themselves."

*   *   *

The other best-known advocate for LSD, Ken Kesey, had a different approach. A charismatic All-American success story from Oregon, he earned a Woodrow Wilson Fellowship and in the late '50s entered the Stegner writing program at Stanford, where Wallace Stegner and Malcolm Cowley were his teachers and his peers included Larry McMurtry, Ed McClanahan, Wendell Berry, Gurney Norman, and Robert Stone. Of this very impressive group, McMurtry thought, Kesey wanted to be the "stud duck," and succeeded; he was a "very winning man, and he won us."

In Palo Alto, he lived on Perry Lane (actually Avenue, but *Lane* sounded better), the bohemian cheap side of Stanford, alongside people like Chloe Scott, a free-spirited dancer who'd known Jackson Pollock in the Hamptons, and Vik Lovell, a psychiatrist who would introduce Kesey to the drug-testing program at the Menlo Park VA hospital. Kesey had already tried peyote, and now the CIA would give him LSD and several other psychedelics.

As a writer, he was a clear heir to the Beats, having read *On the Road* three times. It "opened up doors for us just the same way drugs did. It gave us a new way to look at America." The peyote he'd taken had given him an image of a Native American narrator named Bromden and a protagonist named Randle Patrick McMurphy, RPM, who would be the fulfillment of Kerouac's "The only people for me are the mad ones." McMurphy would lead the patients in a war of resistance to Nurse Ratched, the grinding, stifling establishment.

Presumably via Malcolm Cowley, he sold *One Flew over the Cuckoo's Nest* to Viking, which published it in July 1962 to great reviews and substantial sales that would eventually total in the multimillions. The houses on Perry Lane were razed, and with the money from *Cuckoo*, Kesey bought a home in La Honda, a forest village in the coastal range between Palo Alto and the ocean. Many friends followed, and a scene developed around acid and each other. Ed McClanahan, Robert Stone, Vik Lovell, Chloe Scott, and the artist Roy Seburn all visited. The circle around Kesey as a whole came to be called the Merry Pranksters.

"Suddenly people were stripped before one another," Kesey wrote, "and behold: we were beautiful. Naked and helpless and sensitive as a snake after skinning, but far more human than that shining nightmare that had stood creaking in previous parade rest. We were alive and life was us."

Their avatar wasn't only Ken but also a new friend, *On the Road*'s Dean

Transformation via LSD

Moriarty himself, Neal Cassady. A two-year sentence in San Quentin for possessing two joints had pushed him to "the yoga of a man driven to the cliff edge by the grassfire of an entire nation's burning material madness," wrote Kesey. "Rather than be consumed by this he jumped, choosing to sort things out in the fast-flying but smog free moments of a life with no retreat." The Prankster George Walker would reflect, "Kerouac drew the map, but it was Cassady who took us on the road and guided us through it."

Literally on the road. Neal's method of practice was driving a car, and riding in a car with Neal was...educational. Prankster Lee Quarnstrom would describe it:

> And Neal would *still* be carrying on separate romantic mumbles or arguments with each of his women and *still* having simultaneous conversation with the rest of his passengers. His multi-level, multi-layer chatter, punctuated by frequent puns, references to Greek myth, baroque music or Ottoman architecture or Shakespearean sonnets or you-name-it, was a work of verbal art that surpassed the complex mixes of rock, raga, symphonic and folk music on the Beatles' finest albums....Except that Neal's verbal symphony was composed on the fly...And if you were high enough and paid attention, it was all wise and funny and spectacularly erudite and it all made sense, to boot.

When Kesey's second novel, *Sometimes a Great Notion*, neared publication in the summer of 1964, he and the Pranksters conceived a psychedelic quest to free America from its robotic conditioning. They splashed a hallucinogenic paint job on a 1939 International Harvester school bus, decorated the rear with the sign "Caution: Weird Load," and with Neal at the wheel, rode it across America, making a movie of their journey. It was Hesse's *Journey to the East* on LSD. Somewhat later, the journalist Tom Wolfe would immortalize the trip in a masterwork of reportage, *The Electric Kool-Aid Acid Test*.

The slow trudge of writing fiction no longer appealed to Kesey. Now he wanted to conduct lightning into the body politic. His friend Walter Curtis said that he "wanted to go beyond novels to become a white knight and cosmic commentator." The Pranksters came home to La Honda from their bus ride and settled down to edit the movie. It was more difficult than they

188 **The Last Great Dream**

had anticipated; the technology of lenses and focus did not meld with cosmic eyes, and much of the footage was unusable.

Eventually, Kesey decided to share the experience directly. In November 1965, at his partner Ken Babbs's place near Santa Cruz, Kesey and the Merry Pranksters threw a party. Among the attendees were somewhat younger friends, including most of a musical group that had just changed its name from the Warlocks to the Grateful Dead. They all agreed to continue with the parties, which came to be called *acid tests*. On December 4, they threw one in San Jose, inviting the crowds leaving that evening's Rolling Stones show just down the block to join them. December 11's affair took place at a small community center in Muir Beach, a tiny coastal village just north of San Francisco.

Muir Beach was the first to include Owsley, already a local legend. He'd visited La Honda that summer, and although Kesey was not initially impressed with him—Owsley was rather short and myopic—he and the Pranksters were certainly taken with Bear's LSD. Bear was equally, if not altogether positively, struck by Kesey and his friends. Kesey, he said, "was the kind of guy that reached out, took your knobs, and tweaked them all the way to ten. All of them. And the whole scene was running at ten all the time. It was almost as sudden, and as different, as discovering psychedelics themselves for the first time, at another level." The combination of drugs and life as a mysterious ongoing therapy session was like "being strapped to a rocket sled."

Bear's first acid test was not a good time for him, but in early January, at the Fillmore Auditorium Acid Test in San Francisco, he connected with the Dead's bass player Phil Lesh over a shared love of science fiction, and Bear would become the Dead's sound mixer. Entirely aside from their enduring association with psychedelics, he would leave his mark on them by inculcating them with an extreme drive for quality that they might never have otherwise known.

Each of the band members came from a different musical background, and in the harnessing of that dissonance, they found their musical souls. Lead guitarist Jerry Garcia had been a bluegrass banjo player who'd adopted Jack Kerouac as his sociocultural role model while taking art classes from Wally Hedrick at CSFA. "I feel like I'm part of a continuous line of a certain thing in American culture, of a root....I can't imagine myself without that."

The drummer, Bill Kreutzmann, had come out of a James Brown–style R & B band. Rhythm guitarist Bob Weir was a folkie. Phil Lesh had played Stan Kenton big-band trumpet and then turned to avant-garde composition. Their front man, Ron "Pigpen" McKernan, was a hard-drinking, live-the-life blues man, a vocalist and harp player. Later, they would add a second drummer, Mickey Hart, who would share with them exotic time signatures from the Indian classical tradition.

Along with the LSD that they consumed both on- and offstage, their fundamental approach to performance was improvisation, which they learned from the great jazz players, particularly John Coltrane. Kesey thought that "they weren't just playing what was on the music sheets. They were playing what was in the air. When the Dead are at their best, the vibrations that are stirred up by the audience is the music that they play." They were, he added, "in touch with the invisible."

It was the acid tests that fully and permanently defined the Dead's approach to music. The tests generated an ambiance of exotic sorcery, said Garcia. "It always seemed as though the equipment was able to respond in its own way…there were always magical things happening. Voices coming out of things that weren't plugged in…it was just totally mind boggling to wander around that maze of wires and stuff like that. Sometimes they were like writhing and squirming. Truly amazing."

The fundamental point was that at the acid tests, the Dead were not the entertainment; everyone in the room was the entertainment. The band was there to supply a soundtrack—if they chose to play, which was not always the case. Instead of being artistes delivering music to passive listeners, they learned in the tests to see the audience as their partners in a quest, a mission that Gary Snyder would term "the real work of modern man: to uncover the inner structure and actual boundaries of the mind." As Weir said of meeting Cassady, "For one thing I had to abandon all my previous conceptions of space and time….There was a world of limitless possibilities….We were dealing with stuff like telepathy on a daily basis."

Both proponents and opponents of LSD thought that it would change the personality. Generally, this wasn't necessarily so, at least not dramatically. There *was* one seemingly universal reaction to LSD, which was to see the world as one, as interconnected, just as the most temperate Buddhist might.

What LSD ultimately did was challenge the rational materialist Western approach to life and suggest that there was far more going on than the authorities taught. It emphasized personal understanding versus societal demands, encouraged skepticism regarding authority, and suggested that process was more important than outcome.

It was the philosopher's stone for an entire generation and for many in succeeding generations. Having seen "heaven in a wildflower," few could avoid seeing a multitude of new possibilities in life.

23

The Village in the Mid-'60s

John Gruen was a savvy observer of Village life, tracking the new generation of bohemia that arose in the mid-'60s migration of energy east of Washington Square to what came to be called the East Village. In 1964, he wrote that "there are more beards and black sunglasses per square foot of the East Village than fish in a dime store aquarium. Blue jeans, sweaters, leather jackets and beat-up raincoats are the accepted mode of dress for both males and females. Hair grows long for both sexes." After all, if Allen Ginsberg lived there—he and his partner Peter Orlovsky had moved to 704 East Fifth Street near Avenue C, sixth floor, thirty-five dollars a month—it had to be hip.

Ed Sanders was perhaps the epitome of the young middle-American poets who had read Ginsberg and moved to New York, hitchhiking from Missouri in 1958 to attend New York University (NYU) and study Greek and Egyptian hieroglyphics. He haunted Ted and Eli Wilentz's Eighth Street Bookshop, the Village's poetry central, and attended every reading the Village had to offer. Art, jazz, happenings, civil rights and peace demonstrations—Ed was there. His special interest became Jonas Mekas's underground film scene, which, by 1962, had become the Film-Makers'

Cooperative at the Charles Theatre at Twelfth Street and Avenue B, not far from Stanley's, a bar full of poets, artists, and civil rights/peace activists. There the new generation of bohemia gestated. Ed lived across the street at 509 East Eleventh Street.

Inspired by a Mekas film, Sanders established *Fuck You/ A Magazine of the Arts* in February 1962; he solicited submissions by buttonholing the crowd at Stanley's. The magazine's basic slogan was a "Total assault on the culture." By issue five, he was "printing" (as with almost all these publications, it was mimeographed) Charles Olson, Joel Oppenheimer, and a young San Franciscan named Lenore Kandel. Remarkably, the post office regularly delivered the letters addressed to "Fuck You."

By that fall, Sanders was hanging around at the Living Theatre, where he took part in his first of many benefit poetry readings, this one organized by Bonnie Bremser for her poet/outlaw husband, Ray. The bill included LeRoi Jones, Philip Lamantia, John Wieners, Diane di Prima, and Herbert Huncke. Cecil Taylor played.

Sanders was finally able to meet his inspiration, Allen Ginsberg, in early 1965 when Ginsberg returned to New York from his world travels. Ginsberg had evolved considerably during his wanderings; the man searching for cosmic consciousness had, as he put it, come back to his body, a fundamental act of self-acceptance that he recorded in his poem "The Change." Perhaps because of this, and in the face of various acts of repression designed to suppress consciousness, including the censorship of *Naked Lunch* and the imprisonment of Neal Cassady for marijuana, Ginsberg took on a larger role as social activist. One of the year's causes célèbre in the Village was the arrest of not only the filmmaker but the audience attending a showing of Jack Smith's *Flaming Creatures*, a case that would eventually go to the US Supreme Court.

But it was the arrest of Lenny Bruce that most engaged Ginsberg and his new group, the Committee on Poetry. Two years before Lenny arrived in New York, an interfaith group of ministers with powerful political connections organized Operation Yorkville and demanded a crackdown on pornography in the Times Square area, which yielded 130 arrests there between April 1963 and August 1964. Before Lenny had even taken the stage at the Café Au Go Go on April 3, 1964, both he and the owner, Howard Solomon, had been arrested for obscenity. The arrests were repeated on April 7.

The Village in the Mid-'60s

Just before Lenny went on trial in June 1964, the influential Francis Spellman, archbishop of New York, called for a commission to stop the "powerhouse of perversion" from taking over the city. Bruce's neck was in the noose, and Allen mobilized a resistance. As a later expression had it, he was a natural-born networker. His partners at the Committee on Poetry were Helen Elliott, one of the local literati, who worked the celebrities, and a writer and ex-lover of Jack Kerouac, Helen Weaver, who handled the literary world. Together they placed a petition supporting Lenny in the *New York Times* signed by the cultural elite of the city: Woody Allen, James Baldwin, Bob Dylan, Susan Sontag, John Updike, and on and on.

In a trial lasting six months for a misdemeanor and aided by an increasingly delusional Bruce, the Manhattan DA's office set out to destroy Lenny. Vincent Cuccia, one of the assistant district attorneys on the case, later confessed: "I feel terrible about Bruce. We drove him into poverty and bankruptcy and then murdered him. I watched him gradually fall apart. It's the only thing I did in [Frank] Hogan's office that I really feel ashamed of. We all knew what we were doing. We used the law to kill him."

In the end, a nonrational Lenny became convinced that all would be well if he could do his act in front of the Supreme Court. That would never happen, but he succeeded in his first goal, that of liberating language from hypocrisy to make speech truly free. To a considerable extent, his sacrifice changed a great deal.

One result was that when Sanders opened the Peace Eye Bookstore in the East Village in March 1965 and was then raided by the NYPD, the subsequent obscenity trial was among the last such travesties. By then, Sanders had also heard the Beatles and added another art to his repertoire. He had met the poet Tuli Kupferberg in front of the Charles Theatre as Tuli hawked copies of his own mimeo magazine, *Birth*. They started a band. At first, they wanted to call themselves the Freaks, but then they took a word from Norman Mailer's *Naked and the Dead* and called themselves the Fugs. With song titles like "Jackoff Blues," "Coca Cola Douche," and "Kill for Peace," they were not destined for radio play or the pop charts.

Their swing to music was in perfect keeping with the zeitgeist of change that was the Village in 1965. Boundaries were falling everywhere. In the aftermath of abstract expressionism, visual art had morphed into multiple modes, from photorealism to earth art, pop art to process art.

For avant-garde music, New York was the home of Fluxus, a "hinge," said one scholar, between John Cage and later La Monte Young. Young had come to New York from Berkeley and become music director of a series of performances at the loft of Toshi Ichiyanagi and his wife, Yoko Ono. Working with Billy Linich (later "Billy Name" in the Warhol circle), drummer Angus MacLise, and John Cale, he created the Theatre of Eternal Music, the epitome of what would be called the "downtown" loft scene of New York music. Engaging with the minimalist experimental music au courant in the Village required considerable dedication, and it was destined to remain the interest of a small minority.

In close parallel to Fluxus, "happenings" had a brief vogue as a theatrical way of accommodating the lack of center that was fragmenting art. A Cage student, Allan Kaprow, identified a number of rules to guide the phenomenon: "1. The line between the Happening and daily life should be kept as fluid and perhaps indistinct as possible....6. Happenings should be unrehearsed and performed by nonprofessionals, also, once only....7. It follows that there should not be (and usually cannot be) an audience or audiences to watch a Happening." Absent audiences, it was inevitable that happenings would not last long as a phenomenon.

Gerd Stern, the former KPFA PR director, was part of another attempt to recast art, specifically in the light of technology. He had said farewell to the Bay Area with a major show at the San Francisco Museum of Art called *Contact Is the Only Love*, which included his enormous sculpture of that name, a seven-foot octagon that included a motor, flashing lights, and eight loudspeakers. It sat on a stage that held his slideshow of words found on street signs, *Verbal American Landscape*, alongside isolation booths in which celebrities read, with everything connected by closed-circuit television. It was, in sum, a giant clusterfuck of media designed to overwhelm the audience. Stern's partner in crime was the Tape Music Center's former technical director, Michael Callahan. Alfred Frankenstein reviewed the show in the *Chronicle* as a "Landmark of a Flop," a review Stern would cherish.

After the show, M. C. Richards gave Stern a copy of Marshall McLuhan's *Understanding Media*, and McLuhan's theories would guide Stern's art for the next decade and more. Both Stern and Callahan moved to the Hudson Valley and settled in a community of Black Mountain College veterans that included

The Village in the Mid-'60s

Richards, John Cage, and David Tudor. Stern and Callahan joined with the artist Steve Durkee and formed USCO, a deliberately anonymous group name that eschewed ego as "the company of us." Their goal was to fuse technology with multimedia art and psychedelics to produce sensory overload. As Stern put it, "My intentions in these works were to extend concepts of poetry into more elaborate modes of expression."

Their closest associate, a young man named Stewart Brand, would spend the next years weaving Zelig-like through a variety of highly creative groups and events. As a freshman at Stanford, he had written in his journal, "I will fight for individualism and personal liberty. If I must be a fool, I want to be my own particular brand of fool—utterly." His avenue into the creative and countercultural was Frederic Spiegelberg, who'd returned to Stanford after leaving AAAS and introduced Brand to Beat literature, something that the English department did not see fit to teach. Brand also spent considerable time in North Beach and then found his way to Jean Varda's floating salon and Druid Heights.

Brand had met Steve Durkee in the Bay Area and reconnected with him in New York City while serving in the army at Fort Dix in New Jersey. Although Brand had earned airborne wings, he declined Ranger training and found his way into photography and then multimedia, taking a photography class at SF State after the army—and also a poetry class from Kenneth Rexroth. Extensive time spent taking photographs on a number of Native American reservations led him to present *America Needs Indians*, a multimedia show that included two film projectors, sound, audiotape, and live action.

While working on that, he had read *One Flew over the Cuckoo's Nest* and found a way to meet Kesey, then experienced LSD for the first time at Myron Stolaroff's International Foundation for Advanced Study. Supporting USCO with his photographs introduced him to McLuhan, technology, and a sense of tribalism. The artists of USCO were effectively mysto-technologists.

There was yet another mystical artist in New York at this time, and late in 1964, he created one of the great works of Western religious music. His name was John Coltrane, and the album was *A Love Supreme*. Working from a simple four-note riff, "a-love-su-preme," he and his band—Elvin Jones on drums, Jimmy Garrison on bass, McCoy Tyner on piano—touched the heavens. The album was released in January. One wonders if Bob Dylan heard it that month, just as he went into the studio to change American pop music.

The Last Great Dream

When Allen Ginsberg had first returned to America, he recalled, his friend Charles Plymell had played Dylan's "Masters of War" for him, and "I actually burst into tears. It was a sense that the torch had been passed to another generation." Ginsberg would be enchanted by Dylan, and his impact on Dylan's language would be profound. Beginning in January 1965 with the album *Bringing It All Back Home* (*BIABH*), Dylan would transform American popular music.

LSD and Ginsberg had greatly expanded his range. His relatively simple early folk songs had morphed into gorgeous poetry, although "Chimes of Freedom" carried the same message as "Blowin' in the Wind"—only more subtly and evocatively. There were exquisite love songs like "Love Minus Zero / No Limit" and "She Belongs to Me." There were even two protest songs on the album, although the surreal "Subterranean Homesick Blues" concerned consciousness and alienation and was so laden with sardonic humor (it is based on Chuck Berry's "Too Much Monkey Business") that the serious core was not at all obvious.

The second protest song, "Maggie's Farm," rejected the role of protest singer assigned to him. The point was perhaps made even more effectively by the album cover photo, in which Dylan said goodbye to blue denim with an elegant jacket and french cuffs, the impossibly chic and soigné Sally Grossman, his manager's wife, posed behind him.

Although he recorded band versions of "Gates of Eden" and "It's Alright, Ma," he wisely chose solo acoustic ones for the album. The language is allusive, metaphorical, and dense. They are brilliant statements about personal identity, and they would be road maps for the seekers of an entire generation.

Perhaps there was something in the air. Two weeks after Dylan finished *BIABH*, James Brown recorded, in one hour, "Papa's Got a Brand New Bag," thereby inventing funk as a new genre.

After the spring tour in England that ended in triumph at the Royal Albert Hall, Dylan had reached the limits of what he could do as a solo musician and was almost entirely consumed by the experience. Overcome with disgust, he holed up and in June wrote what he said was a ten-page poem, "a rhythm thing on paper." "Like a Rolling Stone" was putatively aimed at a princess, a Miss Lonely, but Dylan would come to realize it was mostly self-directed.

Later that month, he walked into the studio with a bare, uncased Telecaster guitar on his shoulder still dripping from a rain shower. He dried it off, plugged it in, and said, "Let's go." The musicians recalled it as a chaotic session, with producer Tom Wilson not really in charge and Dylan still writing songs as they were being recorded. He told his special invitee Mike Bloomfield, a string-bending Chicago blues legend, to play more like folkie Jim McGuinn than B. B. King.

The session had an interloper named Al Kooper, who slid into the vacant organ seat although he'd never played the instrument. On the fourth take, they created one of the very greatest rock songs ever, a testament to the challenge of maintaining personal integrity and an enduring demand for honesty. Despite its unusual length at over six minutes, Columbia released "Like a Rolling Stone" on July 20, and it instantly evinced a visceral response among the young.

Five days later, Dylan played the Newport Folk Festival. A few weeks before, the Newport Jazz Festival had featured, on one night, Thelonious Monk, Miles Davis, and John Coltrane with truly great bands. Because of Dylan, the Folk Festival would garner even more attention.

According to Jonathan Taplin, who worked onstage at the festival, Dylan made a spontaneous decision to play electric after hearing Alan Lomax's condescending introduction to the electric Paul Butterfield Blues Band on Saturday. He put together a band of Kooper (whom he'd invited, so perhaps this was not quite so spontaneous as Taplin recalled), Bloomfield, and the Butterfield rhythm section to play on Sunday night. In between the traditional acts of Cousin Emmy preceding him and the Georgia Sea Island Singers following, he dropped a giant firecracker into folk music with ragged but incendiary electrified versions of "Maggie's Farm," "Like a Rolling Stone," and "It Takes a Lot to Laugh, It Takes a Train to Cry," then known as "Phantom Engineer."

There were cheers, there were boos. Joe Boyd, who'd worked for the producer George Wein on his American Folk Blues Festival tours in Europe and at Newport, would reflect that "the rebels were like children who had been looking for something to break and realized, as they looked at the pieces, what a beautiful thing it had been. The festival would never be the same, nor would popular music and nor would 'youth culture.' Anyone wishing to portray the history of the sixties as a journey from idealism to hedonism could place the hinge at around 9:30 on the night of 25 July, 1965."

24

Los Angeles and Folk-Rock

The American musical response to the so-called British Invasion of the Beatles and the Stones came in many forms, from Dylan to Motown to Stax/Volt. One of the major forms folded folk into rock and first used one of Dylan's songs to do so.

Folk-rock sprang up in Los Angeles, where the sheer spread of the place—sixty suburbs in search of a city—militates against community, especially for the young, who may not have a car. It's terribly hard to find a center. For youth and the emerging '60s culture, one of the earliest means of connection was the first of the so-called underground newspapers in America, the *Los Angeles Free Press* (universally known as the *Freep*).

Art Kunkin was a master machinist whose left-wing inclinations had led him to be the business manager of the Socialist Workers Party journal the *Militant*. The trial first issue of the *Freep* in May 1964 was part of a fundraising event for Los Angeles's KPFK, the Pacifica network sister station to Berkeley's KPFA, and the positive response led to regular publication beginning in July.

The *Freep*'s offices were in the basement of a Sunset Strip coffeehouse called the Fifth Estate, which had room for folk singing, an art gallery, and

199

a space for showing silent European films. The atmosphere was loose, with pets, children, and odd-duck wanderers off the street passing through, all set to a soundtrack of rock and roll. It was the definition of California casual.

Lawrence Lipton, the grand poo-bah of Venice Beach, would become an early columnist, and at first the paper was fleshed out by reprints from back east like the *Village Voice*'s John Wilcock (writing from Athens, Greece) and Jonas Mekas. In coming years, the *Freep* would also feature the cartoons of Ron Cobb, who worked for free because he wasn't censored, and a column by Charles Bukowski, Notes of a Dirty Old Man.

Censorship issues were the *Freep*'s early topic of choice, from the conviction of a theater manager for showing Kenneth Anger's *Scorpio Rising* to the obscenity arrest of a painter named Connor Evarts to the prosecution of John Haag, the proprietor of a coffeehouse called Venice West, for allowing a poet to read aloud ("entertainment without a permit"). That Haag was also the local ACLU chapter president and an advocate for a civilian police review board was noted. As usual, the case was later dismissed.

Visitors from San Francisco ranging from the mime troupe to fundraising members of the Free Speech Movement were made welcome. A Harry Partch concert received attention. In March 1965, the *Freep* reported that six thousand people had sat in at the local Federal Building to protest events in Alabama. In sum, the *Freep* connected its readers with the issues and events of concern to local youth.

Initially, the *Freep* covered only jazz and blues, but this changed when it was electrified by the eruption of local bands playing rock and roll, one of the varied American reactions to the British Invasion. Those responses, including Motown in Detroit and Stax/Volt in Memphis as well as folk-rock in Los Angeles, would be the central focus of youth culture for at least a decade.

Music on the radio that summer of '65 had never sounded better. An extraordinary Detroit entrepreneur named Berry Gordy had created Motown in 1959/'60 with his first hit, "Money (That's What I Want)," sung by Barrett Strong. Then he found a brilliant singer-songwriter named William "Smokey" Robinson, and together, they produced "Shop Around." Soon Gordy added the songwriting team of Lamont Dozier, Brian and Eddie Holland, and a studio band based on the world class rhythm section of bassist James Jamerson and drummer Benny Benjamin. Guided by his brilliant business sense and

Los Angeles and Folk-Rock

the principle of making Black music that white people would also like, they produced classics from Martha and the Vandellas' ode to summertime, "Dancing in the Street," to Smokey Robinson and the Miracles' epic "The Tracks of My Tears."

Memphis' Stax Records was just as good. White-owned but racially mixed in its staff, house band, and writing team, it had started as a country label until co-owner Jim Stewart (his partner was his sister, Estelle Axton, and the company name linked their last names) discovered R & B and then the local band the Royal Spades, which became, at Axton's urging, the Mar-Keys. Their 1961 hit "Last Night" would anchor the company. Booker T. Jones (keyboards), Steve Cropper (guitar), Duck Dunn (bass), and Al Jackson (drums) would become Booker T. and the MG's, but in shifting lineups would also be the Stax house band.

Stax also had Otis Redding, one of the great American voices, and de facto (he was signed with Atlantic), Wilson Pickett, who in 1965 would write the classic "In the Midnight Hour" with Cropper.

American Bandstand had moved to Los Angeles in 1964, signaling a geographic shift in the record industry from New York to the west. To that point, LA's keynote sound was the pop surf music of the Beach Boys, which enshrined the SoCal variant of the American dream—blue sky, beaches, surfboards, and beautiful blond girls. But in December 1964, their central fount of creativity, Brian Wilson, suffered a breakdown and left the road to stay home and compose dreamscapes.

The energy shifted to the Sunset Strip, a mile and a half of Sunset Boulevard that had been a mecca for nightclubs in the '30s and '40s and began to rebound in January 1964 with the opening of a discotheque complete with go-go dancers called the Whisky a Go Go. The Whisky also presented live music and instantly became popular.

The Strip was always a place to visit rather than a neighborhood where people lived, but its architecturally surreal/borderline psychedelic essence had young people high before they took any drugs. And even though the clubs that sprang up in the wake of the Whisky were small (Ciro's, for instance, held no more than three hundred), they had a powerful impact. With an increasingly large collection of recording industry decision-makers at close hand, the Strip was a magnet for ambitious musicians.

202 **The Last Great Dream**

Three of them were Jim McGuinn, Gene Clark, and David Crosby, veterans of commercial folk acts like the Chad Mitchell Trio and the New Christy Minstrels. In August 1964, the trio went to see *A Hard Day's Night*. "I can remember coming out of that movie so jazzed that I was swinging around stop-sign poles at arm's length," wrote Crosby. "I loved the attitude and the fun of it; there was sex, there was joy, there was everything I wanted out of life, right there. They were cool, and we said, 'Yeah, that's it. We have to be a band. Who can we get to play drums?'"

In homage to George Harrison, Jim marched out and bought a Rickenbacker twelve-string guitar. Over the next few months, they added bluegrass mandolin player Chris Hillman on bass and Michael Clarke on drums, the latter at least in part because he resembled Brian Jones. They connected with producer Jim Dickson, which gave them access to a serious recording studio so that they could actually hear their work, but they often rehearsed at Vito Paulekas's dance studio on Laurel Avenue near Beverly. Vito had a troupe of dancers with names like Carl "Captain Fuck" Franzoni, Karen Yum Yum, and Johnny Fuck Fuck, plus attendant teenagers who called themselves "freaks." Vito's wife, Szou, dressed in vintage clothing and owned a boutique that sold velvet dresses, '40s chemises, and other antique fashions, and would be at least as influential as her husband. Hers might not have been the first such store, but it was certainly memorable.

By November, Dickson's good friend Benny Shapiro, Miles Davis's manager, had gotten Miles to call Columbia, and they had a record deal. There was no question what their first single would be. Dickson had heard Dylan perform "Mr. Tambourine Man" at Newport that summer and located an unreleased version Dylan had recorded with Ramblin' Jack Elliott. He brought it to the band, which had adopted the name the Byrds, complete with Beatlesesque misspelling.

They recorded it on January 20, 1965, or rather their vocals and Jim McGuinn's twelve string were married to the work of the killer studio professionals Leon Russell (piano), Larry Knechtel (bass), Hal Blaine (drums), and Bill Pitman and Jerry Cole (guitars). The vocals, the bass, and McGuinn's highly compressed twelve string were what came through, and that "jingle jangle sound" carried a union of brilliant folk lyrics and rock 'n' roll. It was an instant hit.

Los Angeles and Folk-Rock   203

The Byrds opened at Ciro's Le Disc (later, simply Ciro's) on March 21, following Ike and Tina Turner and Little Richard. They brought with them Vito's kinky dance troupe. The dancers did not impress everyone—one observer caustically described them as an "ad hoc assemblage of assorted rag-tag hangers-on, jail bait, and other unfortunates without a serviceable full-length mirror or the self-awareness to avoid appearing in public in ill-fitting leotards"—but they clearly helped amp up the energy in the room to astronomic levels. With the help of their publicist, former Beatles spokesperson Derek Taylor, and a visit from Dylan himself, the Byrds' run at Ciro's immediately blew up into a phenomenon.

At the end of April, Paul Jay Robbins described it in the *Freep*:

The Byrds have gone through The Beatles and into a totally novel and fascinating place. They successfully united an audience of average teen-agers, Bach, Bartok, and Cage, aesthetics, folkniks, sophisticated middle-agers, r & r devotees, and serious hippies into one joyous commitment. The key words are "unite" and "commitment.".... They represent what's going on in the ranks of the Aware....What The Byrds evoke is an Enlightenment in the full psychedelic sense of the word....They all crossed over to find freedom and delight—and their discovery of it is ours....Dancing with The Byrds becomes a mystic loss of ego and tangibility; you become pure energy someplace between sound and motion and the involvement is total.

Though the psychedelic union of dancing and rock 'n' roll would become very familiar over the next few years three hundred miles north, it happened first in Los Angeles, at the very least in Robbins's clearly LSD-inspired mind. The look of the audience was also starting to morph. An *LA Times* writer passed by and noted that the dancers looked "like they had just struggled out of Sherwood Forest, wearing jerkins and tights and chains and robes and leather aprons." As the summer passed, more and more teens came to the Strip, in part because a recent ordinance amendment permitted minors to dance in public eating places without their parents.

The young lovelies of the Strip would become legendary in their pursuit of their rock star heroes, most famously Pamela Des Barres (née Miller),

204 **The Last Great Dream**

largely because of her highly entertaining memoir, *I'm with the Band*. Raised in the suburban San Fernando Valley, she was apparently obsessed with the opposite sex from early on, and an extreme infatuation with the Beatles quite naturally followed. She wrote that she "dreamed of what was between Paul's thighs"; the next year, she graduated to the Rolling Stones at the Long Beach Arena, where she was "a sticky, sweaty, teenage girl, squirming my way into womanhood....My heart was beating below my waist."

Naturally, she was at Ciro's for the Byrds, sufficiently falling for Chris Hillman to commence stalking him. When he gave her a ride in his Porsche, her feelings were so intense that she had to leave two pages of her journal blank.

Having commercialized folk and humanized rock, the genre was dubbed *folk-rock*, a merchandising term created to tell record sellers how to classify and sell product. It was an inherently limiting and reductionist branding, aptly first appearing in the music business trade journal *Billboard*, but it held sway for a good part of the year, frequently applied to musicians working in Los Angeles.

In New York, the Lovin' Spoonful had already thought of blending folk and rock and were a bit chagrined that they'd been beaten to the punch. Nonetheless, they put out "Do You Believe in Magic" in July and enjoyed its rise. Folk-rock even rescued a song, perhaps a career. Paul Simon and Art Garfunkel's album *Wednesday Morning, 3 A.M.* had flopped. But their producer, Tom Wilson, listened to the advice of his promo men and recut "The Sound of Silence" with some of the same session players who'd backed Dylan. Remixed, it was released in September and was number one in December.

Under the canopy of the genre, a canny music executive like Lou Adler of Dunhill Records could instruct a local songwriter, P. F. Sloan, to listen to *Bringing It All Back Home* because he knew Sloan to be "a great mimic." A week later, Sloan showed him a number of songs, one of which was called "Eve of Destruction." At Ciro's that week, Adler spotted an ecstatically dancing audience member and learned that he was Barry McGuire of the New Christy Minstrels. The next week, he brought in some studio aces and recorded the song with McGuire. They only completed a rough vocal track, but before they could finish, someone leaked the song to a disc jockey, and it was off and running; out in August, it was number one in September.

John Phillips was a veteran of commercial folk with a splendid ear for vocal harmony. Earlier in the '60s, he'd met a lissome and adventurous seventeen-year-old named Michelle Gilliam at his show at the hungry i in San Francisco. Divorcing his first wife, he married Gilliam the next year. Moving on to New York, they partnered with John Sebastian, Zal Yanovsky (both later part of the Lovin' Spoonful), Jim Hendricks, Cass Elliot (born Ellen Naomi Cohen), and Denny Doherty to form the Mugwumps. Running out of patience with the music business and New York City, John, Michelle, Cass, and Denny retreated to Saint Thomas in the Virgin Islands in 1965. When they heard "Tambourine Man" and "Do You Believe in Magic," John correctly saw folk-rock as their future.

They arrived in Los Angeles penniless but armed with at least two excellent songs, "California Dreamin'" and "I Saw Her Again." Crashing with their friend Barry McGuire, they met Lou Adler, who could do little wrong at this point. They dubbed themselves the Mamas & the Papas, went into the studio with the usual Los Angeles session sharks (later dubbed the Wrecking Crew), and in November recorded "California Dreamin'," which launched their career at high velocity.

The summer of 1965 had lots of folk-rock songs, but "I Got You Babe" stood out. Cherilyn ("Cher") Sarkisian LaPiere, sixteen in 1962, was a high school dropout who'd always wanted to sing. Needing a place to live, she moved in with a music business hanger-on named Sonny Bono, at first as housekeeper and cook. The next year, Bono landed a promo job with the producer Phil Spector, and she began to spend time with Sonny at Spector's Gold Star Studios, where they would both sing on the Righteous Brothers' "You've Lost That Loving Feeling."

From the day they'd met, Bono had worn his hair in a long Prince Valiant bob—truly a rarity in the pre-Beatles era. Given her striking beauty and long black hair, they dubbed their duo Caesar and Cleo. By 1965, they were Sonny and Cher, and that spring recorded "I Got You Babe." The lyrics were banal but captured an us-against-them, youth-against-old-people attitude, and the musical structure was complex. Sonny's limited voice vaguely resembled Dylan's, which suited the genre, and their careers were launched.

Their appearance had an even greater impact. Driving down La Cienega Boulevard one day, they saw a blond girl wearing bell-bottom pants in what Cher recalled was a "fabulous flower pattern with lots of bright colors—yellow, purple, orange, green—with the front tied up with grommets and rawhide

206 **The Last Great Dream**

lacing." "Stop the car!" Cher learned that her name was Colleen and that Colleen's friend Bridget was the seamstress and creator. Later, Colleen and Bridget would move into the apartment above Sonny and Cher's garage, and from then on, Cher and the girls designed the outfits and the girls sewed them. Where Bridget got her ideas, other than possibly the US Navy, is unknown, but soon bell-bottom jeans, which Cher wore on widely seen videos of "Babe," were one of three hallmarks of the coming wave of American youth fashion.

The second marker was the "granny dress," which had been designed by Mary Quant. That fall, *Time* wrote that "the muumuu has gone Mod."

Small, rectangular, tinted glasses were the third style token, made immensely popular by the Byrds' Jim McGuinn, who began wearing them as early as April that halcyon year of 1965. He'd learned about them from John Sebastian, who'd gotten them from the originator, Fritz Richmond, a prominent element of the Cambridge folk scene as a member of the Jim Kweskin Jug Band.

Fritz enjoyed his marijuana and concealed his reddened eyes with handmade tinted glasses, antique frames that he filled with stained glass. Steve Allen would compliment them one night on his program, and Fritz replied, "It's very nice, peaceful and quiet behind here." Allen had been around the block and got the implication, and every stoner in America understood.

As the decade passed, Los Angeles would consolidate its position as the film and recording industry's headquarters in America. In the next year, two more bands would storm out of the city to fame, fortune, and influence: Buffalo Springfield and the Doors.

In Hollywood scriptwriter jargon, to *meet cute* is to arrange a highly improbable encounter, usually boy meets girl. In the annals of meet cute, the origin legend of Buffalo Springfield is the gold standard. Musicians Stephen Stills and Richie Furay had been looking for their friend Neil Young in Los Angeles for some weeks and on April 6, 1966, had given up. They were on Sunset Boulevard, headed for the highway to San Francisco, when Furay spotted a hearse with Ontario, Canada, license plates. Nine days later, the new band, named after a company that made steamrollers, opened for the Byrds.

Los Angeles and Folk-Rock

Buffalo Springfield was destined not to last. Neil Young was a gifted songwriter and musician, but frail, sensitive, and given to what would eventually be diagnosed as epileptic episodes. Stills, nicknamed "the Sarge," was a military-school graduate who demanded deference. Both were driven, but Young's delicacy had taught him to be self-protective. By contrast, Stills was born with a self-destructive streak. After a productive residency at the Whisky, their subsequent experience was, in one rock historian's words, "one long parade of walkouts, drug busts, power plays and psychodramas." Buffalo Springfield was the archetypal example of enormous talent wasted by ego and lack of judgment and leadership.

The Doors lasted longer, perhaps because the shamanic if self-destructive brilliance of vocalist Jim Morrison was set against a more intellectually balanced personality in keyboardist Ray Manzarek. Born in Chicago, Manzarek had had the good fortune to see the real home of the Chicago blues, the ongoing festival that was the Maxwell Street Market. After a hitch in the army, where he was introduced to pot while serving in Laos, he'd met Morrison at the UCLA film school, where they took directing classes from Josef von Sternberg and idolized Marlene Dietrich.

Manzarek visited San Francisco in 1964 and found it "looser and freer" than Los Angeles, "more sophisticated. Much more *adult*." City Lights Bookstore took his breath away, particularly when he saw a notice for a reading by Gary Snyder, Philip Whalen, and Lew Welch. Having already consumed *On the Road*, which he found "wild and hip and cool and dangerous and sublime all at the same time," he followed it up by soaking in the complete Beat oeuvre.

After graduating from film school, he ran into his friend Morrison at the beach in May 1965, and Morrison announced that he'd been "writing some songs." Manzarek naturally asked him to sing one, which proved to be "Moonlight Drive"; there was an instant connection. They found a drummer who loved Elvin Jones named John Densmore and a bottleneck guitarist named Robby Krieger, and began to play. By May 1966, they were working at the Whisky and building an audience until Morrison included the Oedipal portion of their song "The End," "Mother...I want to fuck you," and they had to find another club. No matter. Krieger brought in the song "Light My Fire," and an edited version made it one of the anthems of the summer of 1967. They would remain brilliant and disturbing for the rest of their run.

Los Angeles would contribute another element to the legend of rock and roll, the Sunset Strip "riots." The Friday and Saturday night gridlock created by the influx of youth onto the twelve blocks of the Sunset Strip infuriated local business interests and their friends in government, and on November 3, 1966, two local merchants announced that they'd asked the West Hollywood sheriff's office to enforce "curfew and loitering laws." On November 8, the conservative icon Ronald Reagan was elected governor, emboldening the forces of law and order.

By Friday, November 11, the city had invoked an age curfew, sending platoons of helmeted police armed with batons to clear the Strip. They arrested eighty. Youth reacted with leaflets that read "Protest Police Mistreatment of Youth on Sunset Blvd—meet tonight at 9 at Pandora's Box."

By late Saturday the twelfth, at least a thousand jammed the street, many sitting down on the pavement, and more arrests followed. Lambasted for their handling of the previous year's Watts Rebellion, the police were determined to stay in control. Charles Crumb, the commander of the Hollywood district, made the police attitude clear: "There are over a thousand hoodlums living like bums in Hollywood, advocating such things as free love, legalized marijuana, and abortion." The men of the LAPD and sheriff's department had apparently decided to save Western values.

Demonstrations continued for two more weekends, and eventually, the city backed away from plans to close the clubs. Meantime, Byrds manager Jim Dickson, their publicist Derek Taylor, Elektra Records publicist Billy James, the co-owners of the Whisky, and other rock managers formed CAFF (Community Action for Facts and Freedom). Being a Los Angeles group, CAFF's board also included the actors Jill St. John, Sal Mineo, Peter Fonda, and Dennis Hopper. Naturally, they planned a benefit. On February 22, 1967, at the Valley Music Theater in Woodland Hills, Peter, Paul and Mary, the Byrds, Buffalo Springfield, the Doors, and Hugh Masekela played to benefit CAFF. The show was produced by William Morris agent Ben Shapiro and Alan Pariser, a music fan who happened to be heir to a significant fortune.

They thought of it as a dry run for a much bigger show to be held in June in Monterey.

25

More Changes: 1965 in San Francisco and Thereabouts

Every year has its portentous events, but in the context of the Haight-Ashbury counterculture, 1965 seems genuinely extraordinary. Incidents piled up on events like a multicar accident, all of them consequential although seemingly quite different.

The civil rights movement came to an apogee on "Bloody Sunday," March 7, 1965, on the Edmund Pettus Bridge in Selma, Alabama, when Alabama state troopers and their local citizens' goon squad attacked mostly elderly marchers in a nationally televised atrocity. On March 15, 1965, a white Southern president named Lyndon Johnson told Congress, "I speak tonight for the dignity of man and the destiny of democracy....At times, history and fate meet at a single time in a single place to shape a turning point in man's unending search for freedom. So it was at Lexington and Concord. So it was a century ago at Appomattox. So it was last week in Selma, Alabama...really it's all of us who must overcome the crippling legacy of bigotry and injustice. And we shall overcome."

A week before, on March 8, 3,500 marines, the first official American combat troops, had arrived in Vietnam. The ensuing war would effectively end the government's serious attention to civil rights after the Voting Rights Act was passed, leaving James Baldwin to comment that the abandonment was "an indictment of America and Americans, an enduring monument, which we will not outlive, to the breathtaking cowardice of this sovereign people."

With those events as a background, the energy of the Haight and its Bay Area kindred turned to creating bands, music being the unifying thread of the youth culture. That spring of 1965, George Hunter's new band was starting to coalesce. Inspired like so many others by the British Invasion, he had gone beyond his tape music experiments and begun recruiting. He would be the lead singer and bang on a tambourine. His partner Richie Olsen didn't want to be a reed player drowned out by an amplified band again and picked up the bass. Walking down Haight Street near his home, Hunter ran into Mike Wilhelm, an old pal from LA. Wilhelm had studied blues with Brownie McGhee before playing in coffeehouses, including the Blue Unicorn. He would play lead. Mike Ferguson, founder of the Magic Theater, became the keyboard player. A seller of antiques, Ferguson wore his merchandise, and in his Edwardian threads, said Hunter, looked "like he'd just stepped out of a saloon."

Truthfully, the band was more advanced sartorially than musically. "George's mother used to call him [a charlatan]," Olsen said. "Everybody thought it was a great name for the band." It was "a musical and visual concept," said their front man.

They played Chuck Berry songs, "Got My Mojo Working," "Wabash Cannonball," and "Alabama Bound" in a folk-rock style that was more rowdy honky-tonk than what was current in Los Angeles. But they looked *so* good. One day Wilhelm and Olsen were walking down Grant Avenue in North Beach, Wilhelm recalled, "and this car pulls over and a guy leans out and says, 'Hey, are you guys the Byrds?' And I said, 'No, we're the Charlatans.' And he's like, 'You're a band, then, right?' And I said, 'Oh yeah, we're a band.'"

The driver was Chandler "Chan" Laughlin, one of the managers of the Berkeley folk club the Cabale. He was now helping remodel a building in the old silver-mining town of Virginia City, Nevada, a near ghost town on the eastern slope of the Sierra Nevada that looked out over a vast expanse of Nevada desert. The place would become the Red Dog Saloon, and for the summer of 1965, it would serve as a vision of the future, mixing LSD, a light show, dancing, and rock and roll into a memorable experience.

For their audition, the owner gave them all LSD, and their resultant performance was...disastrous. But he found it hilarious, and they were hired. Lovingly redecorated with period drapes, with waitresses in saloon-maid bodices and net stockings, and a "Miss Kitty" named Lynne Hughes, the Red Dog looked right. As Chan described life there, "You're in a B movie. Play it!" And they did. Early on, the local sheriff paid a courtesy call. He offered his firearm to the bartender and said, "Check my gun?" Behind the bar, one of the owners checked the cylinders, fired two shots into the floor, and returned it. "Works fine, Sheriff."

This saloon also came equipped with an automated light show built by Bill Ham and his friend and fellow Pine Street resident Bob Cohen. It featured three mobiles that moved to create forms, a color translator, and circuits that responded to sound. It would lead to bigger things for both Ham and Cohen, as well as San Francisco dance halls.

While they were at it, the Charlatans created something else that would grow incredibly in the next couple of years, the psychedelic concert poster. Commonly called "The Seed," it featured layout and band caricatures by Michael Ferguson while the border and information were lettered in exotic style by Hunter. Modeled on a 1914 poster for the Great Kar-Mi Troupe, it included a phrase from the original, "Limit of the Marvelous," which pretty well captured that summer at the Red Dog.

Back in San Francisco, a folk singer named Marty Balin wanted to form a folk-rock band. He'd recorded in Los Angeles and had led a commercial folk quartet called the Town Criers that was good enough to play the hungry i, but he wanted more. When he saw Paul Kantner at a Union Street coffeehouse called the Drinking Gourd, what he focused on was Kantner's long hair, newsboy cap, and guitar; he was in. Kantner had been one of the regulars at the Offstage, a San Jose folk club, and he recommended his friend from there, a gifted blues guitarist named Jorma Kaukonen. They added a rhythm section, which wouldn't last very long, and a fine vocalist named Signe Toly, and on August 13, 1965, they opened at a new club in San Francisco's Marina District, the Matrix. Kaukonen contributed the band name, a shortened version of an absurdist nickname first bestowed on him—Jefferson Airplane.

Balin had a roommate named Bill Thompson who was a copy boy at the *Chronicle*, which gave them access to Ralph Gleason, the jazz critic. Gleason had always covered folk and pop and would continue to cover jazz, but hearing Balin's new band would seal Gleason's move to emphasize rock in his coverage, which would put him and the *Chron* light-years ahead of every other newspaper in America. Combined with his undogmatic sympathy for left politics—he declared that his three *B*s were Bridges (Harry), Beats, and Berkeley—he would exert a significant and overwhelmingly positive influence on San Francisco's rock scene.

Jefferson Airplane could have been just another band, vaguely similar to their contemporaries the We Five. But in October, they decided to upgrade their bass player, and Kaukonen put in a call to his old high school pal, Jack Casady. Jefferson Airplane was Kaukonen's first serious band; Casady had been in many, although at that moment he was working in a music store and hadn't played in a while.

He took the first airplane flight of his life to San Francisco, and Kaukonen greeted him with "You better be able to play or I'm gonna kill you." Not to worry. Jefferson Airplane was a folk-rock band with wonderful voices anchored by a guitar-and-bass backbone that gave it heft and drive and bite.

Casady later reflected, "I came from a world of where you had leader / side man, and it was brutal stuff, you know, people were hired and fired. And, you know, side men had side-men salaries and leaders took the major share. Here we had independent organizations of bands that shared all the profits equally. That set up quite a democratic way of doing things. Now, it took forever to get anything done. That's what democracy is." His new city, he discovered, was also different, "very open, per se...you're surrounded by water...the mental climate's much more creative, too."

Their new drummer the next year, Spencer Dryden, would be equally impressed. Having worked in Los Angeles burlesque houses, he saw in the San Francisco scene "that all these people were out of step together....You're out on the ocean. This is the frontier. It really is. I mean, this is where everything starts anyway."

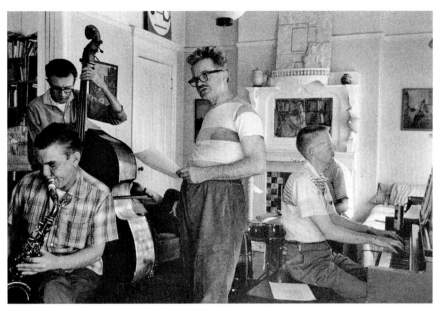

Kenneth Rexroth reads poetry to jazz. *Harry Redl*

Mel Weitsman blows his horn. A student of Clyfford Still's at California School of Fine Arts (CSFA), then a painter, player, and cabbie around North Beach. Became a serious student of Suzuki Roshi's, and eventually abbot of both the San Francisco Zen Center and Berkeley Zen Center. *Photographer unknown, courtesy of Elizabeth Weitsman*

Walter Hopps (left) and Irving Blum in the alley behind the Ferus Gallery. Hopps was an essential figure in bringing modern art to Los Angeles. *Photographer unknown, courtesy of Kristine McKenna and Ms. Lauren Graber of L.A. Louver (the Ed Kienholz Estate)*

The San Francisco Actor's Workshop brought real theater to San Francisco, not least when they brought *Waiting for Godot* (the second production in America, after Broadway) to San Quentin Prison. *Courtesy of Ms. Kathleen Woodward*

SAN QUENTIN AUDITORIUM

POINT SAN QUENTIN   SAN QUENTIN, CALIFORNIA

Tuesday Evening, November 19, 1957, 7 O'clock

The San Francisco Theatrical Federation
and
Actor's Equity Association

present

WAITING FOR GODOT

by

SAMUEL BECKETT

with

ROBERT SYMONDS   **EUGENE ROCHE**
ANTHONY MIKSAK   **JULES IRVING**   **JOSEPH MIKSAK**

Directed by Herbert Blau
Scene Design and Lighting by Robin Wagner
Costumes by Jean Parshall

CAST
ESTRAGON . . . . Robert Symonds
VLADIMIR . . . . Eugene Roche
LUCKY . . . . Jules Irving
POZZO . . . . Joseph Miksak
A BOY . . . . Anthony Miksak

SCENE—A COUNTRY ROAD
Act 1—Evening.
Act 2—Next Day. Same Time. Same Place.

The inimitable Alan Watts, who helped spread Asian thought and specifically Zen in America.
By Margo Moore, courtesy of Joseph Knedelhans

Harry Redl's brilliant composite picture of Allen Ginsberg pointing at his initial inspiration for "Howl," the top windows of the Sir Francis Drake Hotel.

A few months after the initial reading at the 6 Gallery, the young Beat poets did a second performance in Berkeley, on March 18, 1956. Allen Ginsberg, Phil Whalen, Michael McClure, Gary Snyder. *Photo by Walter Lehrman, courtesy of Daniel Davis at Utah State University*

Wallace Berman (self-portrait), the inspiration for so much that happened in Los Angele and San Francisco's art/poetry communities. *Courtesy of the Estate of Wallace Berman and Michael Kohn Gallery*

Wally Hedrick in his studio. Former CSFA student, then teacher, husband of Jay DeFeo, important assemblage artist. Teacher of Jerry Garcia. *Photo by Jerry Burchard, courtesy of Greg Burchard*

Jay DeFeo, at work on *The Rose*, the most important piece of visual art in San Francisco in the 1950s. *Photo by Jerry Burchard, courtesy of Greg Burchard*

A rare picture of Bruce Conner, the artist—at first assemblage, then film, then the light shows of the '60s—and resident gadfly of the bohemian visual art community of San Francisco. *Photo by Edmund Shea, courtesy of the Estate of Edmund Shea*

San Francisco Police charge demonstrators at City Hall on May 14, 1960. *San Francisco Call, courtesy of the San Francisco History Room, San Francisco Public Library*

Lenny Bruce, comedian and savage culture critic of American hypocrisy. *Photo by Edmund Shea. Courtesy of the Estate of Edmund Shea*

Jorma "Jerry" Kaukonen accompanies Janis Joplin in possibly her first Bay Area performance, 1963 at the Folk Theater in San Jose. *Photo by Marjorie Alette*

Tape Music Center group shot: Tony Martin, Michael Callahan, Ramón Sender, and Pauline Oliveros, with Morton Subotnick seated. *Courtesy of Ramón Sender*

Lucy Lewis at the Palace of Fine Arts, San Francisco. She was a dancer and one of the younger artists present at the Tape Music Center. *Photo by the late Gretchen Lambert, courtesy of Lucy Lewis*

Civil rights demonstrators at the Sheraton-Palace Hotel, San Francisco, March 1964. *San Francisco* Call, *courtesy of the San Francisco History Room, San Francisco Public Library*

Mario Savio helps kick off the UC Berkeley Free Speech Movement with a brief speech, October 3, 1964. Note the shoeless feet to not damage the police car. *Photo by Ron Enfield*

The torch is passed. On December 5, 1965, Bob Dylan posed with Michael McClure and Allen Ginsberg in the alley between Vesuvio and City Lights Bookstore. The shots were meant for his upcoming *Blonde on Blonde* album, although they went unused. *Photo by Dale Smith*

The high point of the acid tests, Saturday night at the Trips Festival on January 17, 1966, with Ramón Sender on top of the lights control structure. *Photo by Susan Hillyard*

Jay and Ron Thelin in front of the Psychedelic Shop on Haight Street, which opened January 3, 1966. *Photo by Herb Greene*

A superb evocation of the London psychedelic scene, "Sparklerman" was taken at the Roundhouse benefit for the *International Times* on October 15, 1966. *Photo by Adam Ritchie*

Digger street theater, circa 1966. *Photo by Chuck Gould*

Jerry Garcia, Phil Lesh, Ron "Pigpen" McKernan (partially obscured), and Bob Weir at the Love Pageant Rally, the Panhandle, October 6, 1966. *Photo by Susan Hillyard*

At the Be-In (January 14, 1967), Golden Gate Park. Allen Ginsberg dances with all his might.
Photo by Lisa Law

The crowd at the Be-In. *Photo by Jerry Burchard, courtesy of Greg Burchard*

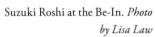Suzuki Roshi at the Be-In. *Photo by Lisa Law*

The pilgrims rush into the Haight in Spring 1967, although the young man in the poncho is in fact a local making the others welcome. *Photo by Herb Greene*

The Monterey Pop Festival, June 1966. A police officer exudes relaxation. *Photo by Elaine Mayes*

Jimi Hendrix at Monterey. *Photo by Elaine Mayes*

More Changes: 1965 in San Francisco and Thereabouts   213

Bill Thompson, who would soon be their manager, had previously worked in advertising, so even at their first gig, they had a catchy slogan, "Jefferson Airplane Loves You." Soon it was on a button and then a bumper sticker. From the first night, the Airplane suggested success, and in November 1965, they would sign with RCA for a then-staggering advance of $25,000. Unfortunately, they would begin by being seduced by a fraud of a manager, Matthew Katz, a dashing con man in velvet capes and a white Jaguar, and it would take considerable energy to extricate themselves from him.

Some bands take shape quickly, some take a bit longer. Big Brother and the Holding Company began in the basement of 1090 Page Street in the Haight that summer of '65. Peter and Rodney Albin were folk musicians attending SF State when their uncle purchased 1090 in 1964. Once a mansion, it had speaking tubes, more than twenty hardwood-paneled rooms, and a ballroom in the basement, complete with stage. They convinced him to make it a student boardinghouse, one of many Haight student co-ops along with, as a 1090 resident put it, "peacenik communes and folknik co-ops and drugnik flats. There were Wobbly communes and Trotskyite co-ops and grungy flats inhabited by people who liked to drink Coke laced with cherry-flavored codeine cough syrup."

A future SF rocker named Gary Duncan said of 1090 that there were "painters in one room talking to each other, musicians in another room. It was really cool, and to all outward appearances there was nothing happening. It was like a secret society....There was a while when the place [the Haight] was just totally free."

One night, a resident prepared to screen an experimental film he'd made, and Peter suggested musical accompaniment. He had a bass. Another resident, Chuck Jones, was a surf band drummer, and a guitarist named Sam Andrew lived down the block. They jammed to the movie, and it was a success. Yet another resident suggested making it a regular Wednesday night jam with a cover charge. At first it was a quarter, and then fifty cents.

Chet Helms, the LeMar activist at the Blue Unicorn, got involved. Having seen the Rolling Stones at the San Francisco Civic Auditorium that May, he had decided he wanted to be a manager—and his pot business introduced him to every musician in the Haight, of which there were plenty. The public jams at 1090 didn't last very long, but the core musicians, plus a second guitarist

Helms brought by in late December, Jim Gurley, kept playing. A stoned rap about "1984, monopoly capitalism, holding corporations, and holding in the sense of possessing drugs," said Sam Andrew, gave them their name: Big Brother and the Holding Company.

The mushrooming cultural scene was not limited to rock and roll. In Berkeley, Ben and Rain Jacopetti discovered what Ben, a theater major at Cal, called "the theater of LSD." Rain was a dancer, and they began to put on shows in their enormous attic. Under the influence of psychedelics, they began to work with slides and projections. When someone accidentally walked in front of the image wearing very little, they discovered that bare skin made a fine screen, and out of that evolved their show *Revelations*, presenting it at the Cabale and then a place on College Avenue under the name of Open Theater. They had mighty dreams: "A time has come, for man again to see Christ—to exalt in fellowship with men—we call it God, all-pervading spirit, state of enlightenment, what you will....Believe it, and it will exist."

The San Francisco Mime Troupe had not only continued but flourished. In June 1965, they presented *A Minstrel Show/or Civil Rights in a Cracker Barrel*, with music by Steve Reich and a film by Robert Nelson, *Oh Dem Watermelons*. A savage farce about American race relations in the form of a minstrel show, all the actors, white and Black, wore blackface. It was, wrote Peter Coyote, one of the actors, "a rare cultural epiphany perfectly in synch with the historical moment."

Their next piece, planned to run for the rest of the summer, was Giordano Bruno's *Il Candelaio*, adapted by a new member of the troupe, Peter Berg, with music by Pauline Oliveros. The city Recreation and Parks Department approved their application for forty-eight dates in the various parks, but after the first show, a commissioner complained that there was "far too much vulgarity," and their permit was revoked.

Delighted to confront censorship and having alerted the media by handing out leaflets downtown, they headed for their scheduled August 7 performance at Lafayette Park. Since they had no permit, they did not erect a stage, but Ronnie Davis made the usual announcement, "Ladieeeees and Gentlemen. Il Troupo di Mimo di San Francisco presents for your enjoyment this afternoon," executed a flying leap, and concluded, "AN ARREST!" And indeed, the police took him in hand. He was convicted in November, and the

More Changes: 1965 in San Francisco and Thereabouts 215

ACLU filed suit; inevitably, the judge found the arrest in violation of the First Amendment.

Eventually, the detention of Davis in Lafayette Park would have a great deal to do with the development of rock 'n' roll in San Francisco, although that was not obvious in August 1965. At that time, rock in San Francisco had more to do with a man named Tom Donahue and his partner Bobby Mitchell. Old-school East Coast disc jockeys, they had put a continent between themselves and emerging payola scandals to begin anew at KYA, San Francisco's leading Top 40 station.

In 1963, they began to promote concerts in the standard format of the era, with perhaps ten acts performing three songs each. Relentlessly entrepreneurial, they started Autumn Records, which had a few hits, including "Laugh, Laugh" by the Beau Brummels, but was most notable for their in-house producer, a talented young man from Vallejo named Sylvester Stewart, later Sly Stone.

Donahue's next move was to open Mother's, which he described as "the world's first psychedelic nightclub," among the topless joints on Broadway. Donahue had hired hip beatnik woodworkers from Big Sur to create walls covered with rippling sculptured wood and panels that pulsed with colored light in sync to the music, a décor Ralph Gleason likened to "a mural by Hieronymus Bosch." Since it was a nightclub meant for drinking, and since their target clientele was underage, it failed to prosper.

Mother's was precisely the sort of place that Luria Castell, Ellen Harmon, Jack Towle, and Alton Kelley wanted to avoid. They'd been in and around the Red Dog, and in their affinity for LSD, they harbored a certain contempt for alcohol (which was somehow okay in the saloon theater of the Red Dog but not otherwise). The four of them lived together at 1836 Pine Street, one of the four buildings that Bill Ham now managed, Kelley having discovered the place when he bought weed from a resident. Since everyone had a dog, it became known as the Dog House.

Kelley was a jack-of-all-trades and an extremely handy guy as well as a collagist and budding artist, a useful compliment to Castell's high-powered people-organizing skills left over from her W. E. B. Du Bois Club days. Collectively, they knew the scene and decided it would be fun to throw some dances. Castell knew about Longshoremen's Hall through her political connections and her North Beach roots and booked a date for October 16 under the name Family Dog. Jack set up the bank accounts, Harmon answered the phone, and Kelley worked on a handbill.

Built in 1959, Longshoremen's was a modern concrete building that had already hosted shows by Ray Charles, Louis Armstrong, and Count Basie, and also "Teens and Twenties" dances—old-fashioned compared to what they planned. Promotion was fairly simple; they visited Ralph Gleason. Castell explained, and Gleason agreed, that San Francisco was "a pleasure city…[it] can be the American Liverpool….Dancing is the thing…they've got to give people a place to dance. That's what's wrong with those Cow Palace shows. THE KIDS CAN'T DANCE THERE. There'll be no trouble when they can dance." She was quite right.

One of their best ideas was to give each show a name. They were all comic book fans, so the first was *A Tribute to Dr. Strange*, which suggested to Gleason a "feast day or saint's birthday and I thought at the time that a new religion was in the process of evolving." It would present the two biggest bands in town, the Charlatans and Jefferson Airplane, as well as the Great Society, a band so new it would debut only the night before *Dr. Strange* at the Coffee Gallery on Grant Avenue. The Dog purchased a modest set of ads on Russ "the Moose" Syracuse's popular KYA *All Night Flight* show, which brought him along as emcee. Marty Balin had also silk-screened three posters, which he posted at the Matrix and a couple of other cool places in town.

More than a thousand attended. They came in costumes—"velvet Lotta Crabtree to Mining Camp desperado, Jean Lafitte leotards, I. Magnin Beatnik, Riverboat Gambler, India Import Exotic"—wrote Gleason, decorated by lots of SNCC and peace buttons. The Charlatans were cowboys, and the Great Society's Grace Slick wore a stylish miniskirt with grape-colored stockings. The only woman wearing makeup was Lynne Hughes, the Red Dog's "Miss Kitty," who also sang with the Charlatans.

Chet Helms walked in and was swept by an "exhilarating sense of safety, sanctuary. The feeling was 'Well, they can't bust us all.' There was freedom and a moment of pure recognition. These were my people, my peers, all of a sudden together." They danced, as the saying later had it, as though no one was watching. Spiritually just as much participants as hosts, the four members of the Family Dog had as good a time as everyone else.

More Changes: 1965 in San Francisco and Thereabouts   217

The show also brought musicians together, which would inevitably lead to more music. John Cipollina was a rock guitarist from Marin County who came to *Dr. Strange* with his friend David Freiberg. They'd been in a band with a former coffeehouse folk singer named Dino Valenti (birth name Chester Powers), but Dino had been arrested for possession of pot not once but then a second time while awaiting trial. Consequently, he would be out of circulation for a while.

At the show, Cipollina and Freiberg, who both happened to be born under the sign Virgo, ruled by Mercury (also known as Quicksilver), met two more Virgos, Gary Duncan and Greg Elmore. Within days, they were all jamming at 1090, and Quicksilver Messenger Service came into being. Across the Bay in Berkeley, the mid-October anti-war Vietnam Day demonstrations gave birth to the Instant Action Jug Band, which would become Country Joe and the Fish.

A couple of weeks later, the Dog threw *A Tribute to Sparkle Plenty*. Thanks to good reviews from Gleason, the audience was even larger. The attendees included a band from Palo Alto then called the Warlocks, who in a few weeks would change their name to Grateful Dead. They'd spent the afternoon frolicking on Mount Tamalpais while enjoying some LSD and were still… elevated. When he saw the crowd—which was at least as high as he was—an extremely enthusiastic Phil Lesh braced Castell and said, "Lady, what this little séance needs is us." He never spoke more truly.

By the fourth show, *A Tribute to Ming the Merciless*, which featured a band from Los Angeles, Frank Zappa's Mothers of Invention, local and sometimes hostile teenagers began to come around. There were some fights and a glass door was broken, with Castell, not a small person, heroically chastising the hoods and serving as head of her own security. It was starting to be work.

On the same day as Ming, November 6, they had competition from a benefit for the San Francisco Mime Troupe's legal defense fund, *Appeal Party*, in a loft behind the *Chronicle* building south of Market Street. Bill Graham, an erstwhile actor who'd been working for a construction firm, had become the business manager for the mime troupe. After overdoing it on the talent end, with acts from John Handy to the improvisational comedy troupe the Committee, Sandy Bull, Allen Ginsberg, the Fugs, and Jefferson Airplane (who happened to rehearse at the loft), Graham improvised brilliantly when

218 **The Last Great Dream**

the police arrived because the room was majestically oversold. "Frank [Sinatra] is flying in from Vegas!" Hundreds were still there at dawn. Graham saw that the real draw was the Airplane and made plans to throw a second benefit, in December. For that, he'd need a bigger room.

Early December saw the Rolling Stones perform in San Jose, Ken Kesey and his friends the Grateful Dead throw their second acid test, and Bob Dylan play both acoustic and electric sets in Berkeley.

The day after his show, Dylan went over to City Lights Bookstore to pose for pictures for his next album, with Allen Ginsberg and Michael McClure. The pictures went unused, although the album, *Blonde on Blonde*, was memorable. The photo shoot was unmistakably a symbolic passing of the torch, from Beat to a new generation. The word *hippie* had been in use for some while, by Bobby Darin in 1960, by Kenneth Rexroth in 1961, in a 1963 pop song by the Orlons named "South Street," in *Time* in 1964, and soon, the meaning extremely unclear, by the *New York Times* in an article about an Omaha industrialist who owned racehorses.

In the near future, *hippie* would be set in stone; it was the people who listened to the newly electric music of Bob Dylan, the people now starting to fill the inexpensive flats of the Haight-Ashbury and the East Village. They largely called themselves *freaks*, from African American blues argot. But that was too edgy for the media, who wanted something softer, gentler. *Hippies*. It stuck. They were hippies.

26

The Trips Festival and What Followed

The expanding gestalt of hippie culture was revealed in the exponential growth of the acid tests, from fifty people at the first event in November to around five thousand two months later at the Trips Festival on Saturday, January 22, 1966. That the organizers got away with bringing together that many tripping people in a public place simply beggars the imagination.

Ken Kesey had coined the phrase *trips festival* in a conversation with Stewart Brand perhaps a year before. In December, Merry Prankster Mike Hagen had stopped by Brand's place after the Stinson Beach acid test and spoken of the need for a really big acid test, but nothing happened until Brand pulled out his address book and started connecting people.

Brand was certainly more organized and meticulous than the Pranksters and was totally comfortable with what he perceived as their direction. They had, his biographer would later write, "turned away from the politics of struggle and embraced the politics of consciousness."

220 **The Last Great Dream**

His first call was to Ramón Sender, who was by now so enthusiastic a psychedelicist that he left the Tape Music Center to work on the festival. Asked where he'd learned about Sender, Brand observed, "Most of the creative people in the Bay Area seemed to know each other then." Ben and Rain Jacopetti and their Open Theater followed. Brand's own America Needs Indians was a given, and Ann Halprin's Dancers' Workshop contributed *Parades and Changes*, complete with cargo net. San Francisco not being Sweden, they eschewed nudity. In sum, Brand and friends had gathered the cutting edge of the San Francisco performing avant-garde together to…do what they wanted.

Planning meetings were rare; as Brand recalled it, after one meeting became unpleasant, they simply didn't have any more. As plans grew more complex, Sender suggested that they bring in Bill Graham to be their designated organized person. Having produced a successful second and then third *Appeal* at the Fillmore Auditorium in December and early January, Graham's name was getting around town. On January 8, Kesey, the Pranksters, and the Grateful Dead tuned up for the festival with an acid test at the Fillmore, which ended comically when the police arrived to object to the post-closing hour and discovered that no one was drinking alcohol. Dead guitarist Bob Weir serenaded a cop who wanted him to come down from a tall ladder with "America the Beautiful," and the evening ended harmoniously.

The promotion of the Trips Festival by San Francisco's hippest adman, Jerry Mander, was superb. The *Chronicle* sent one of its newest reporters, the former bassist for the Limeliters, Lou Gottlieb. He sat down with Brand, Sender, and Ben Jacopetti, brought out a joint, and later wrote, "If I were to tell you that an event of major significance in the history of religion is going to take place in this City of Saint Francis this weekend, you would say, 'You stayed out of work too long.'…In His infinite wisdom the Almighty is vouchsafing visions on certain people in our midst alongside which the rapturous transports of old Saint Theresa are but early *Milton Berle Shows* on a ten-inch screen."

Two days before the festival, the front-page coverage of the arrest on marijuana charges of Ken Kesey and his Prankster friend Carolyn "Mountain Girl" Adams only added to the din.

Friday night led with Halprin and the Open Theater. Since the latter could not do *Revelations*, they settled for a comic anti-masturbation sermon

The Trips Festival and What Followed   221

from the 1920s evangelist Aimee Semple McPherson, and something they called "God Box." Looking back, Jacopetti felt that their material simply "didn't seem to fit. What [the audience] wanted was rock, and they got it." The Open Theater was followed by a rock band, the Loading Zone, which was better received.

Ann Halprin and her dancers opened on Saturday night, followed by Big Brother and the Holding Company in one of its earliest gigs, their sound also feeding the Tape Music Center's Buchla Box, an early synthesizer created by Don Buchla. Their rawness showed, and it wasn't long before Kesey edged them off the stage in favor of the Grateful Dead.

And the night took off. Jerry Mander's press release had promised a "drugless PSYCHEDELIC experience." The capitalization should have given it away. The place was awash with acid. Someone even laced some ice cream and offered it to the security guards, who soon drifted away from their posts. When some English tourists just off their flight from London wandered through the open doorway, they encountered Jerry Garcia's wife, Sara. They asked her what was going on, and as she later put it amid much laughter, she tried to tell them.

In her husband's words, it was

a tapestry, a mandala; it was whatever you made it. When it was moving right, you could dig that there was something that it was getting toward, something like ordered chaos. The test would start off and then there would be chaos. Everybody would be high and flashing and going through insane changes during which everything would be demolished, man, and spilled and broken and affected... just people being there, and being responsive. It wasn't a gig, it was the Acid Test where anything was okay. Thousands of people, man, all helplessly stoned, all finding themselves in a room full of other thousands of people, none of whom any of them were afraid of. It was magic, far out, beautiful magic.

Entirely sober, Ralph Gleason completely understood. "Dr. Lao would have been right at home. The variety of imagination, degree of exoticism and just plain freaky far-outness of the thousands who thronged to the Longshore [*sic*] Hall defies description." There were five movie screens on the walls, with projectors in the balcony splashing images from various Canyon Cinema experimental films. A platform in the middle of the room held Sender, engineers, and lighting people, including the TMC's Tony Martin. A pair of traffic lights blinked continuously. Strobes flickered, and what Gleason described as "lissome maidens danced under them for hours." Rock bands "produced the kind of sonic high that big bands used to, only the rock groups do it quicker and for more people." Evidently, Gleason not only didn't drink the Kool-Aid, he did not need to.

He pronounced that the "evening's success was directly related to the quality of the music." In fact, the sensory impact of rock, light shows, and LSD revealed some fundamental resonant affinity among electricity, high volume, and the psychedelic state. Those three things reduced, in the alchemical sense—that is to say, they synthesized, purified, reified—the previous twenty years of bohemian social and intellectual activity into an overwhelmingly physical and sensual experience that carried overtones of all that had preceded it. It was a shortcut to the harmonious, anticompetitive world that Kenneth Rexroth and Robert Duncan had intuited, even if it was something they'd never imagined.

One of the primary attractions of the Haight-Ashbury neighborhood was the cheapness of its rents. The large and frequently grand homes there had been carved into flats during the Depression, but the main reason for the low prices in 1966 was the federal government's interstate highway program, which had planned to extend a freeway up Fell Street along the Panhandle and through Golden Gate Park, allowing drivers to race through the city on their way to the Golden Gate Bridge. Neighborhood civil rights activists Sue Bierman and her husband, Arthur, along with a clutch of groups like the Haight-Ashbury Neighborhood Association, were having none of it.

In fact, the engineers and bureaucrats had planned to carve the city into boxes with nine freeways; by 1959, the board of supervisors had rejected seven. Progressive Democrats and the *Chronicle*'s Scott Newhall united to fight against centrist development Dems like Governor Pat Brown and Mayor John Shelley, who had the support of the Hearst-owned *Examiner*, labor,

The Trips Festival and What Followed

and business interests. As with a corresponding resistance to a nuclear power plant planned for seventy miles north at Bodega Head, citizens offered a morality-based environmentalism that would eventually become official city policy. Finally, on March 21, 1966, the board of supervisors voted against the two remaining planned freeways. The Haight neighborhood was free to become something different.

As the year passed, Haight Street, the main commercial corridor of the neighborhood, began to transform. Business after business catering to the students and other youth renting the flats opened their doors. The previous residents had fled to the suburbs during the 1950s; the newcomers were pursuing an explicitly anti-suburban impulse. The first store intended for them was Mnasidika, a Mod clothing shop at the corner of Haight and Ashbury owned by a woman named Peggy Caserta, which opened in April 1965.

Mnasidika was one of Sappho's lovers, and the name honored Caserta's orientation; when she'd first come to the city, she'd seen women wearing jeans arrested as cross-dressers. Louisiana-born, she worked for Delta Air Lines and sold jeans and sweatshirts and blazers her mother sewed back home and then shipped for free on Delta. The store had what Herb Caen said was a "coffeehouse atmosphere." Caserta was "energetic" and "innovative," and Caen approved.

By 1966, floating on LSD, she'd repainted her store with black-and-white stripes and purple swirls. The Grateful Dead would model clothes for her. The Airplane's stylish Marty Balin was her first really good customer. Bell-bottom pants were ever-more popular, and Caserta began to sell a version sewn by her friend Judy Dugan, who'd created them so her boyfriend could get his jeans over his boots. Finally, she visited the Levi Strauss factory and convinced an executive that bell-bottoms would sell, even though she could only afford to order ten dozen at a time. A very smart guy, he bought her pitch and let her have them exclusively for six months. In 1969, Levi's launched the 646 line of jeans, which would make the company a very large pile of money.

Ron and Jay Thelin would open the store that would come to represent the Haight for many, the Psychedelic Shop, at 1535 Haight Street, on January 3, 1966. Their father had managed the Haight Street Woolworth in the early 1950s, although they'd come of age in Yuba City, 125 miles north. Both of them had been Eagle Scout products of an all-American upbringing; Ron acknowledged that he'd voted for Nixon in the 1962 governor's race. But in the army, he'd read Thoreau and the Beats, then spent two years in Taiwan, where he learned some Mandarin and read Zen. He "found out that the people with the beards (beatniks) were the people who really dug Thoreau, who really dug the Declaration of Independence, who were artists."

For Jay, the turning point was reading an excerpt of James Baldwin's *The Fire Next Time* in the *New Yorker*, which "made the hair on the back of my neck stand up—it was so profound for me. I ended up weeping...white middle class Americans had no idea what Black kids were going through. We'd had a good education in the constitution and civil rights in junior high school, and I'm finding out that it isn't so."

In the first half of the '60s, the Thelin brothers attended SF State and spent their summers working at Lake Tahoe parking cars and renting out boats, working up to owning a profitable car concession. Their labors meant that in 1964 they were able to buy a substantial Victorian home at 848 Clayton Street. The two brothers and a friend each put up $333 toward a $1,000 down payment, and after their own rooms, they had five bedrooms to rent out at $50 each to cover a mortgage of that total, $250.

Civil rights and Vietnam were omnipresent issues on campus, and Jay took part in demonstrations that spring of 1965. The experience left him unsatisfied. "It didn't change consciousness," he thought. "What's going to do that?"

That fall, he attended a campus lecture by Timothy Leary's partner Richard Alpert. "I was transfixed about the possibilities of psychedelics in terms of human consciousness. It was amazing...he talked about imprinting [baby ducks imprinting on people]—with psychedelics, you could reprogram yourself and create a higher level of consciousness and see the world in terms of what the mystics and poets and Tibetans talked about." A neighborhood friend of his, Allen Cohen, got him some of Sandoz Pharmaceuticals' best LSD, and there on Clayton Street, he experienced a "rebirth." Jay had never even smoked pot.

Although Ron was married to his high school sweetheart, Marsha, and they had a daughter, Kira, the house was male-centric. Among the tenants were Marsha's high school classmate Herb Greene, a fashion photographer working downtown at the elegant I. Magnin, and Roger Hillyard, who was

The Trips Festival and What Followed   225

working with the San Francisco Mime Troupe, eventually becoming their stage manager. A responsible mother, Marsha was not drug oriented. "They were all guys, listening to Archie Shepp and Miles and all this dissonant jazz music; all of them were men, and here I was with a baby and all this pressure to take some drugs; talk about peer pressure."

All the same, Marsha was deeply aware that while their parents had given them everything, "something else was needed." And "the most amazing thing was it was happening to all of us at the same time...and that's unusual." It was, she said, "the change from the Age of Pisces (faith) to that of Aquarius (knowledge)." It was "an explosion of consciousness." As Ron put it to an academic studying the neighborhood, everyone in the Haight had been born at the same time, at the Trips Festival.

Ron continued, "There's a whole new symbolic reprogramming, and the programming is mankind. Planetary. Universal. It's one to one, it's joyous. I'm tempted to say it's wise. And it's moving, colorful, creative. And it's evolving."

Late in 1965, Jay was in Truckee painting a wall and suddenly flashed that "what the world needs is a place to go to find out what you need to have a good trip," tools to help do a better job of self-examination and reprogramming. It would be an information center with books and records that could help people fight what Ron had complained was "the tyranny of money, the fight for material things...[which] has become the American dream."

Jay called Ron and said, "Go down on Haight Street and see what's available." Ron did so and found a number of storefronts to choose from. Jay "quit [his] job and came down immediately. It was just before Thanksgiving. We started talking this over, and he really got into it, and it was $150 a month. We took 1535 because it was kind of in the middle, between Ashbury and Clayton. From Thanksgiving to January 3rd we were down there every day fixing it up. We glued burlap bags to the walls. Marsha made nice lampshades. We found out how to get books and records."

They stocked it with records by John Coltrane and Archie Shepp and Ravi Shankar and books about "mysticism, spiritual endeavors, Tibetan, Tao, Christian mystics. We got little porcelain statues of the Buddha, Shiva, all that stuff." And necklaces, posters, incense, and rolling papers. Jay recalled it as "pretty austere" at the beginning. They also listened to their clientele and followed suggestions, adding bells and Indian paisley fabrics.

One of their tenants, Lenny Silverberg, was an artist, and they hung his art. Another of their housemates, Susan Elting, was a photographer, and they showed her work. For "dessert," they sold the new and authorized edition (after a pirated version had earned enormous publicity) of J. R. R. Tolkien's *Lord of the Rings*, which would top that year's bestseller lists. In the end, the Psychedelic Shop was a community center; its most important commodity was the knowledge, conversation, and advice that came free.

The first of the many hip stores to join them on Haight Street was Tsvi and Hyla Strauch's In Gear, a jewelry store and clothing boutique. Hyla was an archetypal red-diaper baby from Los Angeles, and Tsvi had a master's from Harvard in the philosophy of language. They'd had a folk-art gallery in Pacific Heights called b'tzalel ("in the shadow of God") and then encountered LSD. Their minds blown by the Trips Festival, they moved to 706 Ashbury Street in March and opened In Gear in June 1966.

In Gear was actually preceded in late January by an interesting avant-garde art gallery, the UFO Gallery, at 1608 Haight. It was founded by Leonard Nathan, who was a bit older and not entirely part of the scene, but appreciated Haight Street as a comfortable place for unusual art. David Rothkop, a graduate student at SF State, passed by the Psychedelic Shop and thought an even more comfortable place to talk was needed, and opened the I and Thou coffee shop a little while later. A turn-of-the-century drugstore at Haight and Masonic, complete with vintage glass counters and glass medicine bottles, became the Drogstore Café.

In April, Jerry and Esther Seeland opened Far Fetched Foods at 1915 Page Street, near Stanyan Street (the end of the Haight neighborhood and the border to Golden Gate Park). Since they happened to be blind, the place was generally known as Blind Jerry's. He was a jazz bass player with an active side business in cannabis sales. In truth, marijuana was the economic base of the community, and the Haight was the central way station of pot between Mexico (American pot growing had not yet begun in any significant way) and the rest of Northern California.

The development of the Haight as a psychedelic alternative community was of course uneven, but for much of the year quite positive. A community health worker from the Langley Porter Psychiatric Hospital, Helen Swick Perry, moved to the Haight to observe things. No fan of LSD, she noted that some of

The Trips Festival and What Followed

the people who came looking for utopia were in obvious personal distress, but concluded that the "seekers in the H-A were not simply trying to escape from the sick values of the central society—they wanted to build a new world.... There was a contagion and joy in what was going on in the neighborhood, once one had tidily put away his rules and regulations for living." The local formal institutions, the churches, and the Haight-Ashbury Neighborhood Council, "gradually were won over to the meaning of the hippie culture...the immediate neighborhood became increasingly protective and sympathetic."

Along with psychedelics, the guiding inspiration of the Haight in 1966 was music, which required a venue, a home. Fortunately, San Francisco had not one but two of them.

Ten days after the Trips Festival, having concluded that presenting music was more enjoyable than being enmeshed in politics, Bill Graham furthered his path to becoming the Sol Hurok of rock by presenting Jefferson Airplane at the Fillmore on February 4, 1966. By then, the members of the Family Dog were on vacation in Mexico. Chet Helms, now managing Big Brother, and his partner John Carpenter, onetime house manager of Mother's, offered a partnership to Graham, who was not certain he could fill every weekend at the Fillmore. It was a union destined not to last. Taking the name Family Dog, Helms put on a *Tribal Stomp* on February 19 at the Fillmore, and then the *King Kong Dance* a week later. Graham capitalized on the popular camp television show *Batman* and put on the *Batman Dance*.

In late March, Graham and Helms together put on a weekend with the best band in America at that moment, the Paul Butterfield Blues Band, in which Michael Bloomfield channeled the genius of Chicago blues across race and generations. On Monday morning, Graham got up early and booked Butterfield's return to San Francisco for himself. That he only knew about the band because of his putative partners, Helms and Carpenter, never seemed to worry him. "I get up early" was his mantra.

Helms and the Family Dog sensibly parted ways with Graham and on April 22 opened their own place at the Avalon Ballroom, at Sutter Street and Van Ness Avenue. Bob Cohen did the sound and Bill Ham the lights; Pine Street was now part of the rock world.

To the Beat poet Michael McClure, "the Fillmore and the Avalon Ballroom were ongoing rebirthing organisms. Each night a new creature came into existence." The two rooms had significant differences. Graham was driven, creative, and open to advice, as when Lawrence Ferlinghetti suggested having Andrei Voznesensky open for Jefferson Airplane.

"Bill was the best promoter ever," said Marty Balin. "He just took care of every little detail. When you walked out onto his stage, it was ready for you. Everybody was calm, everybody was quiet. There was no rushing around. And Bill would be there, and he'd say, 'The stage is yours.' And you'd go out there and everything would be perfect. It was just the best stage you could ever play."

A distinguished sound engineer named Abe Jacob (nicknamed the "Godfather of Sound") said of Graham, "He would do anything he did for the band and for the artist as long as they gave a performance to the audience.… Bill said,] 'Everybody else has somebody representing them. I'm here to represent the audience.'" He was also a businessman who wanted to make a profit.

By contrast, Helms was a true believer. LSD had transformed the evangelical ethos of his childhood into an understanding of dancing to rock music as a religious ritual, an invocation of Dionysus in which the ballroom was a sacred space. He said of himself, "I suppose by nature I'm a zealot and so I attempted to apply what I knew and the skills that I had acquired to the circumstances of the dances. The manifestation of that for me was the ballroom, which in some sense was my church. The people who came to it were my congregation and I was the minister. They were the people I cared about and that I ministered to in many respects."

Dancing was central to the ballrooms. "Everybody was dancing," said Barbara Wohl, a San Francisco Mime Troupe member. "The world had a need to dance and everybody was a participant in it. You danced without clutching. Everyone was independent in their dancing, yet everybody danced together.…It was just this little instant of time when the dancer was equal to the musician on the stage and there was no difference between the performer and the performed upon."

One enormous difference between the venues was that there was no stage lighting at the Avalon. All light came from the light show, which gave the room

The Trips Festival and What Followed

an extraordinarily immersive power, making the venue what the journalist Ben Marks called a "glorious temple of psychedelic iniquity." The other difference was that Helms was not a particularly meticulous businessman and was not always entirely reliable about paying. Graham drove a hard bargain, but his checks never bounced.

Along with an increasingly appropriate presentation, rock music itself was growing more open to the psychedelic realm. Bloomfield had experienced LSD and created the modal "East-West," which was based on the drone of Indian music. The Byrds' "Eight Miles High," released in March, reflected David Crosby's intense love of both Ravi Shankar and John Coltrane (himself also by now influenced by Indian music). The month before, the Yardbirds had released "Shapes of Things," putting Jeff Beck's feedback into the center of the composition.

And in June, Bob Dylan reached an apotheosis of sorts with his masterpiece *Blonde on Blonde*, shimmering with what he would call "that wild mercury sound…metallic and bright gold, with whatever that conjures up."

27

Posters and Light Shows and Really Transitional Sexual Politics

Music would carry the San Francisco scene's message to the nation and the world, but the ballroom posters that came to embody the Haight's formal visual sense were very nearly as important. Given San Francisco's relatively small size and the centrality of Haight Street for the psychedelic community, posters were a supremely efficient way to communicate. It was some sort of cosmic good fortune that the San Francisco poster artists turned out to be gifted artists. From the beginning, the posters were cherished as art objects, torn down and carried off almost as soon as they were put up.

Wes Wilson had created a poster for Big Brother and the Holding Company at the Open Theater in January, and as Bill Graham began operations, he employed Wilson, sharing him with Chet Helms for a few months. By summer, Graham made it an exclusive arrangement. Consequently, when Helms moved to the Avalon, his first choice was the team of Stanley "Mouse" Miller and Alton Kelley.

231

232   **The Last Great Dream**

Those three, plus Rick Griffin and Victor Moscoso, would be tagged as the "Big Five" of the poster artists. They all shared art nouveau as an influence, but their primary source was the psychedelic experience itself. By July, Wilson had executed a brilliant poster that featured red lettering that became flames, establishing a pattern that most of the artists would use. (Ironically, the concert itself featured the most insipid pop bands Graham would ever promote.)

In this mode, the lettering, often somewhat difficult to read, was as much engaged in negative space as positive, a style Wilson had adapted from the Austrian secessionist Alfred Roller. Though promoters like Graham might grumble that they wanted the audience to get the information easily, the style demanded that the readers engage...and they were happy to do so. It was, said Moscoso, "a game" he played with his viewers. "I didn't letter the letters," he said. "I lettered the space in between the letters. It was quicker...and I liked the way it looked. It was more difficult to read."

Wilson had taken only a few months of figure drawing classes, but the other four had considerably more credentials. Moscoso had a degree from Yale and had attended SFAI. Mouse, whose father had worked for Disney on *Snow White*, had begun his career by airbrushing hot rods on T-shirts before following Big Brother's Jim Gurley from their homes in Detroit to San Francisco. His partnership with Kelley, unique among the poster artists, generally involved Kelley as the idea and layout man and image finder and Mouse as the designer. Among their most famous images was the skeleton and roses they permanently connected to the Grateful Dead, a design for the Avalon quite literally taken—Kelley absconded with the page cut from the SF Public Library's copy—from Edmund Sullivan's illustration of *The Rubaiyat of Omar Khayyám.*

The active visual aspect of the rock culture was of course the light shows. The Tape Music Center's Tony Martin had directed the lights at the Trips Festival, and the Thelins' housemate Roger Hillyard had been so impressed that he began to work with Martin at the Fillmore.

In May 1966, Graham put up screens for the Andy Warhol *Exploding Plastic Inevitable* show and left them up the following week. Hillyard reached out to his friend Ben Van Meter, a Canyon Cinema experimental filmmaker who'd been inspired by a Bruce Conner film he'd seen at a college film festival—"Crazy films. I'd like to make crazy films, too."

Posters and Light Shows and Transitional Sexual Politics   233

As a result, Ben had come to SF State to study photography, then acquired a Bolex motion picture camera. In his first film class. he was taught, "Never, never do a superimposition in the camera," which brought the reaction, "Oh, this is something I have to try." He would scratch his negatives and double and triple expose them, which made for fairly bizarre films. He described his documentary of the Trips Festival as coming from "the POV of a goldfish in the Kool-Aid bowl."

At the Fillmore, Hillyard and Van Meter filled up the screens with material from overhead and film projectors, and would eventually succeed Bill Ham at the Avalon, working as the North American Ibis Alchemical Company. Coming full circle, one of their partners in the enterprise was Bruce Conner, who among other contributions painted slides for them to use, a beautiful and logical expression of the psychedelic world he'd been visiting since 1958. He'd also contributed a pen-and-ink mandala drawing for a Trips Festival flyer. By now, he'd entirely sickened of the art business, finding the light shows more satisfying.

As they grew more sophisticated, they utilized two four-thousand-watt overhead projectors on dimmers so that they could cross-fade, twelve Kodak carousel slide projectors, and three film projectors, two 16 mm and one 8 mm. The pulsating colors of the overhead projectors remained central, and they mixed them with oil, alcohol, or propylene glycol; oil made the colors bubble and swirl, alcohol made things "open up and explode," Hillyard said, and the results with glycol were in between.

When they needed help, they brought in their friend and Hillyard's housemate, Lenny Silverberg, a painter who'd studied with Ad Reinhardt at Brooklyn College and was now working part-time at the Psychedelic Shop. Silverberg recalled various odd events about life at the Avalon, from the Hells Angel who had a silver papier-mâché whip and would dance and whip his girlfriend under the strobe lights, to Owsley Stanley, who would come up and ask them to be guinea pigs for his latest creation. "He gave us enough for three pills for everybody. Then I realized there were no clean dishes for the overhead, and I saw the two girls we'd hired to wash them huddled in a corner, mumbling to each other, 'I don't like it when I can't feel my body.'"

Haight Street proper had its own theater, the long-closed Haight Theater, which a group centered around Bill and Hillel Resner and Luther "Spike"

The Last Great Dream

Green renamed the Straight and tried to reopen. The Resners had grown up in the Haight, and Green had been around, having crewed for Ann Halprin in Venice (Italy), eaten mushrooms with Gordon Wasson's curandera Maria Sabina, and assisted Tony Martin at the Tape Music Center. The Dead played a benefit in May 1966 to support the future opening, but the organizers soon became enmeshed in the byzantine depths of the San Francisco permit process, which required fire and police department cooperation. Time passed...very slowly.

On May 2, 1966, Ronnie Davis and the San Francisco Mime Troupe crashed a lunch meeting of Mayor John Shelley's Arts Resources Development Committee. Since business leader Harold Zellerbach chaired the committee, it was held in his Crown Zellerbach Building. Ronnie was armed with a manifesto that defined the troupe as "guerilla theater" and that demanded city money for artists rather than for new buildings—a new culture center proposed by Zellerbach had been defeated at the polls the previous November—as well as increased support for the public library system. On May 4, the city's chief administrator announced the distribution of the Hotel Tax Fund, a levy created to support the arts community. Presumably because of their meeting crashing or perhaps their "bawdy" production of *Il Candelaio*, the mime troupe, which had received $1,000 in each of the previous two years, got nothing.

In response, the troupe organized the Artists Liberation Front (ALF), which the *Berkeley Barb* referred to as A POOR MAN'S ART COMMISSION WITH ARTISTS. The ALF's first meeting took place on May 10, with progressive assemblyman Willie Brown as chair. Davis and Peter Berg of the troupe, Bill Graham, Arthur Sheridan of City Lights, Yuri Toropov, manager of the band Sopwith Camel, and Carol Tinker, Kenneth Rexroth's secretary, were elected to the steering committee, to be chaired by Alan Meyerson of the popular satirical group the Committee.

At the first meeting of the steering committee on May 11, a draft policy statement encouraged supporting arts in neighborhoods, not just downtown, and placing power in the hands of artists rather than administrators. After a benefit at the Fillmore Auditorium headlined by Allen Ginsberg reading his new poem "Wichita Vortex Sutra," ALF stopped theorizing and planned

Posters and Light Shows and Transitional Sexual Politics   235

a series of Free Fairs, each in a different neighborhood (Hunters Point, the Haight, the Tenderloin, etc.), to take place in October.

Bands would play free outdoors while the fairs would also include kiosks with large rolls of paper and painting supplies so that kids of all ages could create their own art. On a good night at the Fillmore and Avalon, the line between performer and audience could blur, even be erased, as everyone in the room took part. That was the goal of the Free Fairs. It had a subtle but profound political element at its core.

The city's most important theatrical event that summer was the presentation of Michael McClure's *The Beard* at the Fillmore on July 24. The poet turned out to be a brilliant playwright, dismissing conventional plot and character to set free pure images—Billy the Kid and Jean Harlow—as archetypes that examine lust and sexual expression in a "Blue Velvet Eternity." One critic, Richard Cándida Smith, credited McClure's approach to a dictum of Nietzsche's: "To be a dramatist all one needs is the urge to transform oneself and speak out of strange bodies and souls." Mission accomplished.

As a film star, Harlow is always out of reach and is therefore the ideal object of lust. Billy is a standard testosterone-aggressive man. The sexuality is oral, in that it is words and actions united, so when the Kid mimes cunnilingus by pressing his face into Harlow's (clothed) groin, it is the consummation of a visionary poet's prophecy, one of a series of rituals designed to release repression in both McClure and his audience. For the playwright, Harlow and the Kid are divine because they are mammals.

The San Francisco Police Department did not appear to have any sophisticated theater critics on staff. When the play moved to the Committee Theater on Broadway in August, the two actors were arrested for "obscenity," "conspiracy to commit a felony," and "lewd or dissolute conduct in a public place." Once more, the ACLU came forward, and once more, there was a judge who'd read the Constitution. It was perhaps not a coincidence that the statewide Proposition 16, which would have prohibited "Obscene Materials and Conduct," was on that fall's ballot. Though Reagan would win the gubernatorial race, Prop 16 would fail. *The Beard* would go on to win two prestigious Obie Awards in New York.

Sexuality was at the center of another important event in San Francisco that summer of 1966. In 1955, control of bars in California had been moved out of the excise realm into a separate Department of Alcoholic Beverage Control, and police raids on gay bars increased, most notoriously at the Tay Bush (a bar at the corner of Taylor and Bush Streets) on August 14, 1961, when one hundred were jailed. Newspaper coverage mocked the police, and all charges were dropped.

Then the police screwed up so badly that the issue was resolved permanently on the side of gay rights. On January 1, 1965, the beyond-respectable Council on Religion and the Homosexual sponsored a Mardi Gras costume ball at California Hall on Polk Street. Despite negotiated promises of noninterference by the police, thirty-five uniformed and fifteen plainclothes police blocked off the street in front of the hall and had photographers shooting the arrested as they emerged. The ministers were irate, the city was furious, and the mayor seethed. Six years later, the city elected its first openly gay supervisor, Harvey Milk. By then, a majority of San Francisco residents were proud, as two sociologists wrote, that "deviance, like difference, is a civic resource."

The people at California Hall were employed and at the very least middle class. The people who gathered in August 1966 at Compton's Cafeteria at the corner of Taylor and Turk in the Tenderloin were distinctly not. It was still illegal to cross-dress in the city, but the clientele at Compton's was largely composed of trans sex workers who lived around the corner at the El Rosa Hotel on Turk. When not working their trade on the corner in front, they relaxed over coffee at Compton's, along with pimps and potential tricks, so that when the door opened, everyone looked up to assess business opportunities.

But hippies were challenging gender norms with boys in long hair and beads, and girls in pants. The civil rights movement had come to the Tenderloin with the appointment of Cecil Williams as senior pastor at Glide Memorial Church, a social gospel ministry that had established a night outreach for street youth, many of them hustlers. In July, a militant new gay organization for street hustlers and drag queens, Vanguard, began to hold meetings at Compton's.

One night in August, in a ritualized act of harassment and dominance, a police officer grabbed a woman sitting in a booth. She'd had enough, and so had all the others. She exploded, hurling coffee into his face, and the place erupted, with anything on the tables—salt, pepper, and sugar shakers, napkin dispensers—sailing at the cops and through windows. Heavy purses swung

Posters and Light Shows and Transitional Sexual Politics 237

by sixty queens smacked police heads, and they withdrew to the street; the queens followed them there and retaliated for years of humiliation, destroying a police car and setting a newsstand on fire. There was to be no more submission.

The city responded in a surprisingly civilized way by establishing social, mental, and medical support services in the Tenderloin. A beat cop named Elliot Blackstone became an advocate for transgender people. Cross-dressing laws were changed. The San Francisco Department of Public Health began to issue identity cards with altered genders, allowing trans people to get conventional jobs. The next public health director, Francis Curry, would be profoundly committed to ensuring access to treatment for street people. The hippie impulse for personal freedom and control of one's life had spread to the gritty streets of the Tenderloin, and there would be no going back.

The summer of '66 began and ended for the San Francisco rock world with the addition of women to two bands, front women who would take their groups high into the rock firmament.

For Big Brother, a new drummer came first. Dave Getz was teaching painting at the Art Institute and was also a member of the Studio 13 Jass Band. He had some doubts about playing with Big Brother...until he heard the new singer. To that point, Jim Gurley had been Big Brother's musical heart and soul, channeling John Coltrane's sheets of sound into feedback. Getz thought that their bond as a band was "a pact...[toward] a goal, and that was ecstasy."

But their manager, Chet Helms, thought the band could be greater, and he sent his friend Travis Rivers off to Texas to bring back the singer Helms had first met there, Janis Joplin. She came to their rehearsal space above Kelley and Mouse's studio at 80 Henry Street, and though she'd never really sung with a band, they knew they were onto something.

Then they brought her onstage at the Avalon, and they were certain. "She knocked us out, *instantaneously*," said Getz. As the weeks went by, the band stopped being entirely improvisational and began to do songs, which Joplin and not Peter Albin sang. Guided by Nancy Gurley, she began to replace her jeans and denim shirts with bracelets and feather boas. Life in hippie San

Francisco had given her the liberty to create music in her true persona, which included a raw, aching woman's sexuality that was new to rock music.

She was also an essential part of connecting Austin, one of the significant rock scenes that didn't happen to be on one of the coasts, with San Francisco. Over the next couple of years, Texans like Bob Simmons (who would work at the Avalon), broadcaster Dave McQueen, and the cartoonist Gilbert Shelton all headed west. Austinites had one advantage on the Bay Area: their access to psychedelics preceded LSD, because they had peyote.

Don Hyde was an Austinite peyote fan, and later the next year, 1967, he would be cofounder of Austin's own psychedelic dance hall, the Vulcan Gas Company, which was itself financed by the extraction of a kilo of mescaline from a mountain of peyote buds. Since he had a job at Hudson's Cactus, access was not a problem. As Don wrote, "A seed or roach could get you fifteen to twenty-five years in Huntsville [prison]...but there was PLENTY of PEYOTE and it was fucking LEGAL....In fact, at this time there was hardly a house or apt. that we could go to that didn't have a pot of peyote being boiled down on the kitchen stove. Most of the area around U.T. on the west side smelled like boiling peyote...and it was all legal as bubblegum."

As the summer of 1966 passed, the Haight scene expanded to include western Marin County. Big Brother moved to Lagunitas, Quicksilver Messenger Service to Olema, and the Grateful Dead to the Burdell Mansion at Olompali, near Novato, and then to Lagunitas. The Dead's residence at Olompali was brief, but it would be a hippie liberated zone for the next several years.

The Dead had rehearsed at the heliport in Sausalito, which was owned by a trust fund baby named Don McCoy. His wife, Paula, began a salon at 715 Ashbury Street in the summer, across the street from 710, where the Dead would move in September. Don stayed at Olompali with his daughters. When Noelle Barton, Jean Jensen, and her three daughters, Vicky, Rhonda, and Sherry, joined them, they became the Chosen Family, as they put it, because they chose one another. There would be a fire and other tragedies, but they would remain a family.

Another important rural hippie outpost popped up in April 1966, when Lou Gottlieb declared that the land he owned near Sebastopol north of San Francisco, Morning Star Ranch, was open to all. Ramón Sender took up

Posters and Light Shows and Transitional Sexual Politics 239

residence there after the Trips Festival, and the Open Theater's Ben and Rain Jacopetti followed, along with the filmmaker Bruce Baillie. Morning Star would become a rural counterpart to Haight Street.

San Francisco rock's summer of 1966 capped itself on October 16 at the Fillmore. Signe Toly had retired from performing to have a baby, and Jack Casady had invited Grace Slick of the Great Society to join the Airplane. It would be the final piece they needed. Their first album, *Jefferson Airplane Takes Off*, had been released in August. It had good songs, but the sound quality was poor—the RCA engineers would need to learn how to record rock and roll. Their next release would be a rock and roll classic.

In her memoir, Slick would identify her personality with a certain brand of postwar feminist comedy like Betty Grable's *The Beautiful Blonde from Bashful Bend*—sarcastic, independent, but not interested in feminist theorizing. She simply did as she chose. A childhood of fantasy and costumes sewn by her grandmother had prepared her to be an actress, except that she wouldn't speak someone else's lines. As she also put it, her entire life was "an exercise in counterprogramming. You say 'White,' I say 'Black.'"

She, her husband, Jerry, and his brother Darby saw Jefferson Airplane at the Matrix and immediately planned a band of their own. "My untrained voice was at least loud enough to compete with the amplifiers." Just a month later, in September, they debuted at the Coffee Gallery.

She joined the psychedelic world with peyote, she reported, which "made everything and everyone seem equally important. Suddenly I could see no isolation, no overabundance. It was all just energy, exhibiting itself in infinite dimensions." Life at the Fillmore, she told herself, was "*not* Kansas, Dorothy. But this is *Peter Pan, Alice in Wonderland, Oz...Stranger in a Strange Land, Naked Lunch*, and *Be Here Now*."

Grace Wing Slick was born for stories like that. After Casady invited her to join the band, she came to an Airplane show at the Fillmore to listen. But Signe was a no-show and Grace was thrown into the pool, emerging at the end of the night as one of the two queens of San Francisco rock.

28

London, Psychedelicized

The psychedelic culture crossed the ocean from America and found a warm reception in England as Timothy Leary's good friend Michael Hollingshead jetted off to London in September 1965 to spread the word. He brought with him copies of the *Psychedelic Review* and Leary's new book, the rewrite of *The Tibetan Book of the Dead* called *The Psychedelic Experience*, as well as five thousand hits of Czech acid.

Opening the impressively named World Psychedelic Centre in the chic King's Road area, he soon attracted attention from an associate of the radical therapist R. D. Laing named Joe Berke, Beat writer Alexander Trocchi, William Burroughs's associate Ian Sommerville, and film director Roman Polanski, as well as rock luminaries Donovan, Eric Clapton, and members of the Rolling Stones. All the Beatles but Paul had been ahead of the curve, taking LSD with the Byrds and Peter Fonda in Los Angeles in August. "Great," thought Marianne Faithfull as she felt it coming on. "It's something I'd always hoped I'd be granted: second sight."

It was a new England. The Labour win in 1964, followed by a second and enormous win on March 31, 1966, would lead to significant changes in laws affecting social issues like obscenity, divorce, abortion, and same-sex sexuality. It was also a happy England. On July 30, 1966, England won the World Cup at its own Wembley Stadium, soundly beating West Germany 4–2.

In this atmosphere, fresh alternative institutions like Indica Books, the Notting Hill Free School, the *International Times* newspaper, and the psychedelic band Pink Floyd and its home base club, UFO, gave the psychedelic world shelter and nurture.

As compared to Millbrook and the acid tests, the British reacted somewhat differently to LSD. One historian cited the Arthurian legend, William Blake, Lewis Carroll, and J. R. R. Tolkien to argue that psychedelics revealed the "Arcadian strain of English thought, the sense that decadence, foppishness, hedonism and even infantilism were part of a privileged, lost history of the island nation, a golden past that could best be apprehended by children, artistic geniuses, the mad, the sainted" and those on LSD. In England, he said, psychedelia was "precious, arcane, hermetic, linked more to the Epicurean than the apocalyptic." An influential subgroup of artists and musicians certainly grasped it with enthusiasm.

In January 1966, Robert Fraser opened his *Los Angeles Now* show at his eponymous gallery at 69 Duke Street, introducing Wallace Berman, Jess, Bruce Conner, and Ed Ruscha to England. Fraser was perhaps the most connected person in the emerging culture. His home at 32 Mount Street became a salon that welcomed both the rock aristocracy and young members of the actual nobility, along with drug dealers and outré intellectuals like William Burroughs and Terry Southern in a perfect blend of "Eton and Soho." Marianne Faithfull said of Fraser that he was a "serious conductor of lightning." Ruscha observed that "Robert wanted to break ground with his gallery and I don't think he had profit in mind."

The Rolling Stones embraced Fraser's air of aristocratic decadence—Mick Jagger would take it the furthest—but Paul McCartney was genuinely interested in modern art and aspects of the intellectual world not commonly available in Liverpool. This brought him to another nexus of the new in London, Indica Books. The name referenced a strain of cannabis, although when asked, the founder, Barry Miles, would vow that it meant "indicating."

Miles had come to London to work in a bookstore, Joseph Poole's, which was next door to *the* hip London bookstore, Better Books, where the newest Grove Press and City Lights books were first available. Before too long, he ran

London, Psychedelicized

243

the paperback department at Better Books. Miles was also deeply interested in happenings and the pop art scene of Andy Warhol, Claes Oldenburg, and Robert Rauschenberg. McCartney joined him in that world.

After the Royal Albert Hall poetry reading, Gregory Corso's friend Paolo Lionni had introduced Miles to Marianne Faithfull and her husband, John Dunbar, an art critic for a Scottish newspaper. Better Books was about to be sold, and there seemed a crying need for a bookstore that could change the world. With an investment from McCartney, Indica became a partnership of Miles, Dunbar, and Peter Asher, brother of McCartney's girlfriend Jane Asher.

"Indica," said Miles, "was the place where ideas could be promoted and experimental literature, poetry, ideas from the sixties could be discussed and pushed. It was a sort of editorial statement. It wasn't to make money. It stocked the small literary and mimeo-magazines from America and the underground newspapers, and we had a constituency of people who had an advanced, questioning view of life…everyone who felt disaffected from society was catered to." Derek Taylor, the Beatles' onetime publicist, said of the store that "it had absolutely rock solid 'street cred' and yet it was really good fun. There was no cynicism."

"I hung out with Miles a lot," said McCartney, "because I was interested in that kind of thing and I'd really only got a bit at school or as a student in the pubs." Miles would show him items in *Evergreen Review* and later brought him to Fraser's. "Miles was a great catalyst. He had the books." In return, Miles reported, McCartney helped build Indica, "put up the shelves and all the rest of it. He was very intimately involved with the whole beginnings" and even designed the first Indica wrapping paper, Miles's wife, Sue, recalled. "Lettered it all up, all by hand, and had it printed." Ian Sommerville, William Burroughs's lover and technical adviser, installed the lighting.

The impulse that begat Indica manifested itself in other ways. One of Miles's closest friends, John "Hoppy" Hopkins, was a Cambridge graduate who'd worked at the Harwell Atomic Energy Research Establishment even as he simultaneously pursued a path as a dope-smoking, pot-dealing anarchist. By 1960, he'd swapped physics for a camera, shooting musicians for *Melody Maker* while covering Campaign for Nuclear Disarmament antinuclear marches, poets, tattoo parlors, prostitutes, and fetishists. From the time he'd read *On the Road*, he'd been fascinated by America, and after a visit, he returned with two ideas: a free school and an underground newspaper.

Notting Hill was a racially mixed, low-rent neighborhood, the Haight-Ashbury of London. Late in 1965, Hopkins convened a meeting there of a potent group of bright minds. One was Peter Jenner, a Cambridge graduate who noted that "we'd won the lottery [by attending Cambridge], and yet it seemed terribly unsatisfactory." Then lecturing at the London School of Economics (LSE), Jenner found the idea of creating an alternative educational setup much more satisfying. John Michell had just attended a lecture that would engage him in the Earth mysteries movement, which argued that various landmarks and historic structures were connected by what were called *ley lines*. Joe Boyd, freshly arrived in London to be a producer for Elektra Records, came along to the meeting. Kate Heliczer, an actress and experimental filmmaker, sat in. The final grounding element was Michael de Freitas, better known as Michael X, a Trinidad-born neighborhood civil rights activist.

They contemplated classes in French, photography, and politics, to be offered to the poor and less educated of the neighborhood, who were mostly West Indian, Irish, and Polish immigrants. For a classroom, Michell offered his basement at 26 Powls Terrace, directly opposite David Hockney's studio. The building's other occupants, sex workers, perhaps better indicated the local demographics. In truth, the free school was more a concept than it ever was an actuality, although it clearly signaled the rise of an underground in England. It also generated a spin-off, a celebration of Trinidadian culture called the Notting Hill Carnival, which endures to this day.

Hopkins and his friends began with meetings directed at skeptical locals at All Saints Church as they planned a series of fundraising concerts at the church's hall with a new music group Jenner knew about.

Unlike the school, the band that Jenner and his partner Andrew King provided for the fundraisers would definitely have a future. Roger Waters, Rick Wright, and Nick Mason were students at Regent Street Polytechnic in London beginning in the fall of 1962; Wright and Mason were Londoners and Waters was from Cambridge, where he knew two other musicians, Syd Barrett and David Gilmour.

Mike Leonard was a teacher at Poly who was interested in building light machines; he also owned a London property and wanted tenants. Waters

London, Psychedelicized   245

helped him build the machines in Leonard's workshop, which was Mason and Waters's bedroom. In the fall of 1964, Barrett took a room there while he attended Camberwell College of Arts. By the spring of 1965, they were a band with a residency at the Countdown Club, where the long sets forced them to learn how to improvise to fill the time. They went through various names, and settled on Syd's idea, Pink (in tribute to the blues player Pink Anderson) Floyd (for Floyd Council) Sound.

Early in 1966, a series of Sunday afternoon happenings at London's home of the blues, the Marquee Club, mutated into the Spontaneous Underground, clearly a part of the new English rock subculture. Although they had a limited repertoire, Pink Floyd Sound got a slot. Barrett played feedback on his guitar, Wright made strange chords on his keyboard, and Mason used mallets on his drums. They were very avant-garde, Mason thought, and well suited to the show promotion: "Who will be there? Poets, pop singers, hoods, Americans, homosexuals (because they make up 10 percent of the population), 20 clowns, jazz musicians, one murderer, sculptors, politicians, and some girls who defy description."

The Underground might present a rock band, but the band wasn't entirely the focus. As Barry Miles recalled, "You had to pay money to get in, but there was nothing necessarily there. You had to make your own entertainment." On March 13, the Underground advertised the arrival of Pink Floyd Sound as "Trip/bring furniture toy prop paper rug paint balloon jumble costume mask robot candle incense ladder wheel light self all others march 13th 5 pm."

Since Notting Hill was the place to buy pot in London (at this time, by and large, Black people smoked pot, white people smoked hashish), the audience at the All Saints fundraisers tended to be stoned fans of improvisational music, which meant they welcomed Pink Floyd Sound. Peter Jenner decided that the music business would be more fun than LSE, and with his friend Andrew King formed Blackhill Enterprises to manage them. Taking their advice, the band trimmed their name and became Pink Floyd.

By now, stores were selling tourist guidebooks to Swinging London, so the April 1966 *Time* cover article on the phenomenon was only about nine months late. Andrea Adam, one of the editors who put the story together, and

246 **The Last Great Dream**

almost surely the only woman involved, suggested that the main attraction to the senior editors was the pictures of young women in miniskirts.

What was left of Swinging London gathered at Brian Jones and Anita Pallenberg's place on Courtfield Road in Kensington, what Marianne Faithfull called "a veritable witches coven of decadent illuminati, rock princelings, and hip aristos." "We were young, rich and beautiful," Faithfull declaimed, "and the tide was turning in our favour…we were going to change the rules. Unlike our parents, we would never have to renounce our youthful hedonism in favour of the insane world of adulthood."

Though Paul McCartney had no special problem with the upper classes, John Lennon tended to stick to his working-class roots, which was seemingly why the Beatles never became associated with the air of decadence that attached to the Stones. Instead, McCartney and Lennon and the gang smoked the pot that Bob Dylan had introduced them to the previous summer and created *Rubber Soul*, an album with considerable sonic debts to Stax and Dylan. By now, the musicians had creative control, and the gooey lyrics of "She Loves You" were replaced by adult songs like Lennon's "In My Life." "Nowhere Man" had no romance at all, and "Norwegian Wood" had shifting layers that were new to Beatles music. The album was a major marker of an ascending spiral of growth.

The next step was the album *Revolver*, released on August 5, 1966. The band had vetoed a third film planned by Brian Epstein and were happy to make magic at Abbey Road, writing material that could not be performed live. Using the studio as an instrument itself and with access to a wide array of instruments and sounds, they included Indian music on "Love You To," used a string octet to accompany their heartbreaking paean to loneliness, "Eleanor Rigby," and employed tape loops as part of Lennon's explicit hymn to LSD, "Tomorrow Never Knows."

Their longtime engineer, Norman Smith, had departed to produce Pink Floyd, and the new lad, Geoff Emerick, was challenged by John Lennon on his first day of work. "Make me sound like the Dalai Lama chanting from a mountaintop," Lennon demanded. Just twenty, Emerick earned his place in rock Valhalla by running the vocal for "Tomorrow Never Knows" through a Leslie (a speaker designed for organs), stuffing a sweater into the bass drum to dampen the sound, and then placing the drum mics close to the bass head, all very much against studio policy, but perfect for the Beatles.

London, Psychedelicized 247

There was apparently no preproduction; the singers brought in lyrics or a chord chart, and the songs grew in the recording. "Tomorrow Never Knows" took its lyrics from Leary's *The Psychedelic Experience*, but a tamboura created, George Martin said, a "silky, dreamy background sound, the musical equivalent of the joss-stick."

His time with Barry Miles had introduced McCartney not only to avant-garde visual art but also to John Cage and Karlheinz Stockhausen, and at home, he'd removed the erase head from a tape recorder and over-recorded tape loops of very dense notes. Martin chose sixteen six-second loops to work with. With tape recorders all over Abbey Road, each with someone using a pencil to hold the tape at tension, they mixed loops through the building sound-patching system, then mixed "Tomorrow Never Knows" with each band member manipulating the loops with a fader. The result was quite random and thus unique.

Hoppy Hopkins's other bright idea was an underground newspaper, which would embody the information and worldview of Indica. Miles and friends sat in a room tossing around names for a new paper until someone said, "Let's call it 'it,'" whereupon they figured out which two words would ideally fit "it."

On October 15, 1966, Pink Floyd and the Soft Machine played to benefit the *International Times* at the first show in a large new venue, the Roundhouse, an old railroad facility with standing room for three thousand, an event promoted as a "Pop / Op / Costume / Masque / Fantasy-Loon / Blowout / Drag Ball" featuring "steel bands, strips, trips, happening's." All those entering were given a (drug-free) sugar cube.

Sue Crane and Barry Miles had run away from their parents to Edinburgh to get married and had met American expat Jim Haynes, who'd begun the Paperback Bookshop there, Great Britain's first. Jim would become the editor of *IT*. Haynes was "everybody's friend," wrote Derek Taylor. "He was a comfortable reassuring figure, utterly fearless and very inventive." The *IT* offices settled in Indica's cellar, and London had a place where the people who'd been at the Royal Albert Hall poetry night or Dylan's show there could hang out, get stoned, and talk about turning on the world. It was an optimistic time, with the feeling that things could truly change.

The Roundhouse was a popular venue but enormous, and Hopkins and Joe Boyd plotted something more intimate. On December 23, 1966, they opened UFO, "a gloomy, low-ceilinged ballroom," said Boyd, "with a tiny stage and a smooth wooden dance floor." It was actually the basement of the Blarney Club, a Soho bar at 31 Tottenham Court Road. It was open from 10:30 p.m. to 6:00 a.m., when the subway resumed operations.

Since Indica sold Fillmore and Avalon posters, UFO decided to make their own and brought in Boyd's friend Nigel Waymouth, a partner in the year's hot King's Road psychedelic clothing boutique, Granny Takes a Trip. Waymouth and his friend Michael English would adopt the nom d'arte of Hapshash and the Coloured Coat. Pink Floyd was UFO's house band, and the Soft Machine played regularly. They showed films on the wall ranging from W. C. Fields to Akira Kurosawa, and it was all as true to the spirit of the Haight-Ashbury as possible.

What particularly distinguished Pink Floyd was their devotion to lights. Syd Barrett's roommate Peter Wynne-Willson was a professional theater lighting man, and he began to build a better setup than the primitive rig he'd started with. Mirrors vibrated to create curved Lissajous patterns. They added lights, and "worms of color" crawled about the stage. They affixed polarizers to the projector, then stretched condoms, which tended to be high-quality latex, over the lights for diffusion. Chet Helms would visit and decide it was a bit static by Avalon standards, but they were the hottest thing in England.

Ever-handsome Barrett stood front and center playing both lead and rhythm on songs like "Interstellar Overdrive," "Astronomy Domini," and "The Gnome." Taking his lyric ideas from fairy tales, the *I Ching*, Tolkien, folk ballads, and the blues, he was fearless, leading the band into atonal territory that was unique to them. Peter Jenner, their manager, argued that "the Floyd were the *only* psychedelic band...even the Grateful Dead, they had improvisations but they seemed a perfectly ordinary group, playing with chords and things. The Floyd didn't play with chords."

UFO would come to a premature end when the tabloid *News of the World* published "Hippie Vice Den," a particularly ripe story about topless girls there. The police leaned on their landlord, and the club soon shut down.

But it and Pink Floyd had manifested a truly psychedelic experience in England. Magic was alive in Albion.

29

The Diggers and the Love Pageant Rally

The primary reason for asserting San Francisco as the most influential source of countercultural ideas was the presence of the Diggers, whose critical thinking about freedom and materialism put a certain intellectual spine in the often-vague affect of the San Francisco scene. Emmett Grogan, their charismatic front man, got the attention of the street, and other thinkers like Peter Berg and Billy Murcott lent a sharp, if idealistic, intelligence to their message.

On September 27, 1966, a Black teenager named Matthew "Peanut" Johnson stole a car for a joyride, returned it, and was running away when a San Francisco police officer shot him in the back and killed him. Black neighborhoods from Hunters Point to the Fillmore exploded into rebellion. The National Guard was called out, and when members of the Progressive Labor Party and the Mission Rebels attempted to blockade the armory, troops with fixed bayonets broke through their lines.

The state imposed a curfew, and National Guard vehicles clanked down Haight Street. Michael Bowen, the art director of the new Haight Street newspaper the *Oracle*, put up signs urging hippies to stay indoors. Gazing down from a roof, Grogan and Murcott saw the Fillmore in flames and craved what Berg described as a "white equivalent of the black rebellion." LSD, Murcott thought, had made them free—free of prior assumptions and patterns. Now it was time to resist, not with suicidal rock-throwing but with alternative institutions like the Free Food that would pop up on the Panhandle in the coming days.

They took the name *Diggers* from the expression *to dig*, to understand. When told about the early British agricultural communist movement, they found it charming and accepted the Brits as pioneering ancestors. In the beginning, they spread their message with anonymous flyers tacked up on the street (and later published in the *Berkeley Barb*). Apparently, the first two came in August, before Hunters Point. The first was called "Time to Forget": "FORGET the war in vietnam [*sic*]. Flowers are lovely." It dismissed the Haight Street shops as "marketeers of expanded consciousness" as "a selfish hippy kissing the system's ass for the greater glory of the lonely dropout."

Their second effort, "Take a Cop to Dinner," noted the influence of racketeers who paid off cops and businesses that paid graft to police when on the job and further bribed them with corporate jobs on retirement. The essay concluded, "*regarding inquiries concerned with the identity and whereabouts of THE D I G G E R S: happy to report THE D I G G E R S are not that." The poetically savage humor and trenchant analysis was in part the work of Peter Berg, who had wanted to take the San Francisco Mime Troupe's political message into the street. That fall, he left the troupe and applied his talents to the Diggers.

Northern born, he'd grown up in Miami, Florida, and at the age of eleven or twelve saw what he decided was a mirage, a Seminole woman poling a canoe in the Everglades. He persuaded his parents to let him spend a night alone in the 'glades. Bug-chewed but happy, he came away from the night sure that there was more to reality than what school taught. It was a "baptism," he thought, into a different sort of life.

Arriving at the University of Florida in the fall of 1957, Berg was part of a small group of liberal students and was nearly expelled for putting up a poster that read "Integrate in '58." He heard *Howl* read aloud in a college bar and proceeded to read it for himself, keying on the phrase *peyote solidities of halls*.

The Diggers and the Love Pageant Rally

251

He found out about the garden supply stores of Texas where peyote could be purchased, and his search for experience proceeded apace. Hitting the road came soon after.

After a period of roaming, he arrived in San Francisco wanting to meet Henry Miller, Kenneth Rexroth, and Allen Ginsberg. When he heard about the SF Mime Troupe, he walked on, stretched the extent of his credentials, and told Ronnie Davis that he was a writer-director-actor. Ronnie handed him a copy of *Il Candelaio*, the work of Giordano Bruno. A Dominican friar, Hermetic occultist, and developer of post-Copernican cosmology who had been burned at the stake for heresy, Bruno was an ideal source for the troupe. Soon, they had a new script and a new assistant director.

Along with Grogan, Murcott, and Berg, two other mime troupers helped establish the Diggers—Kent Minault and Peter Coyote (born Cohon). They tended toward the self-righteous and purist, but their deep understanding of the consumerist exploitability of what was growing in the Haight was on point. Their grasp of political theater led them to ask the people who lined up for free food on the Panhandle to step through a twelve-foot-by-twelve-foot frame, the Free Frame of Reference, as part of the process. Subtle but not ineffective, it asked the recipient to consider their perspective as they ate. Free food was "not an act of charity," wrote one Digger, "but an act of responsibility to a personal vision" of a better world that would make food free.

The fact that the early broadsides and *Barb* articles were often signed by the "mad bomber" George Metevsky [*sic*; the proper spelling was Metesky] was a New York touch that suggested Grogan, but Murcott and Berg were equally influential, and they made excellent partners in a collective effort devoted to anonymity. They tried to stimulate a deeper political conversation about an America cleansed by the psychedelic experience. A broadside just after the Hunters Point rebellion told Haight Streeters that they were free, "free to be conditioned in school...to be a compulsory soldier....Free to pay sixty percent of your taxes to the military" and free to be protected from "obscenity" and drugs.

Soon they opened a free store, the Trip Without a Ticket. Ultimately, the store was a theater where people could "explore this notion of a free store." The Diggers were "life actors," they thought, conscious people trying to "create the condition you describe" with a theater that enlightened by demonstrating a path that could free everyone who chose to follow it. The phrases were taken from *Thespis*, a book by Theodor Gaster about myth, ritual, and drama in the ancient Near East. Free, they realized, was potent, because it could not be co-opted by the corporate world; there would be no profit in it.

Berg's essay "Trip Without a Ticket" was visionary. He described industrialization as "a battle with 19th century ecology to win breakfast at the cost of smog and insanity. Wars against ecology are suicidal....No children of White Western Progress will escape the dues of peoples forced to haul their raw materials....Millions of have-nots and drop-outs in the U.S. are living on an overflow of technologically produced fat....Our conflict begins with salaries and prices." And property.

Berg's cohort Peter Coyote understood the vision; they had, he wrote, "challenged ourselves to imagine a culture we wanted to live in and then to make it real, by acting it out." Such a culture would be liberated from normal roles and personalities by requiring both anonymity and Free, the absence of money. The highest value was, he wrote, "*authenticity*." They were trying to destroy the magic of property, of commodities. "Commodities are tools. They have no intrinsic value except in what they can do for you, but in this culture they are invested with all sorts of magical properties."

An heir of the Beat generation whose college bible had been Don Allen's *The New American Poetry*, Coyote had come to San Francisco State to be a poet but also joined the Actor's Workshop. A mystifying class with Robert Duncan persuaded him that he'd be a better actor, and he soon fell in with the mime troupe. When they began to collect money after their show in the Panhandle, using "ludicrous promises, obscene proposals, [and] scathing observations...as entertaining offstage as on," he was hooked. The troupe, he wrote, was "shock therapy and a crash course in a new curriculum."

The Diggers continued and extended the crash course. A circle swiftly formed around them, people mostly interested in action, working on things like the free food program or the free store, or new-era rituals conceived by Berg. The poet Lenore Kandel and her lover Bill "Sweet William" Fritsch of the Hells Angels were among them. Siena "Natural Suzanne" Carlton-Firestone, Grogan's lover, was another of the regulars who made the programs work.

So was Charlotte Todd. She recalled Berg inviting people interested in such rituals to stick around after the meeting. "Well, most everyone stuck

The Diggers and the Love Pageant Rally 253

around," said Todd. The idea was to change people from audience member to participants. And so Diggers, said Todd, would pass out "flowers, little mirrors, and whistles. There were specific things [actions] mentioned." Haight Street became, quite literally, a street theater.

"From our point of view," Coyote added, "freedom involved first liberating the imagination from economic assumptions of profit and property that demanded existence at the expense of personal truthfulness and honor, then living according to personal authenticity and fidelity to inner directives." If enough people woke up in such a fashion, society as a whole would simply be forced to accommodate them.

As the Diggers set to work, the Artists Liberation Front followed suit, producing Free Fairs in the course of October in different working-class San Francisco neighborhoods. In addition to engaging children with paper and art supplies, they also presented the Mocker (a joke in *A Hard Day's Night* in which Ringo is asked if he's a Mod or a Rocker and conflates them) Manor Blues Band, which included a then unknown young Mission District guitarist named Carlos Santana, as well as Dick Gregory, El Teatro Campesino, a children's dance troupe, a puppet theater, poets, and other bands, including Country Joe and the Fish.

In the Haight, the first weekend of October brought hot news: Ken Kesey had returned. At a Whatever It Is festival led by Stewart Brand at SF State on October 1, the entertainment included the Grateful Dead, Mimi Farina, the Congress of Wonders reading John Lennon pieces, a Bill Ham light show, a sensory awareness seminar run by a group called the Esalen Foundation, and a collaboration from the Perry Lane dancer Chloe Scott and the composer Lou Harrison. One sideshow featured Kesey, still a fugitive, broadcasting from a concealed location connected to the SF State radio station.

It was an easy commute to the show for the Grateful Dead, because on September 30, after a summer in Marin County, they'd moved into 710 Ashbury Street in the Haight. One of their comanagers, Danny Rifkin, had been the building's manager, and in fairly short order, he convinced the student tenants to give way to the musicians. The door was never locked, and 710 would become a central node in Haight-Ashbury society. It would be a very busy block, with Paula McCoy and various Hells Angels living across the street at 715, and at 743, the artist Frank Cieciorka, who would in the next few years create the stylized raised fist logo of student strikers.

The implicit violence of the fist was exactly what Allen Cohen and Michael Bowen of the soon-to-be-launched *Oracle* wanted to avoid. In mid-September, police had arrested a young man at 1090 Page Street for throwing a Coke bottle out of the window, and people paraded down Haight Street in protest. Watching them, Cohen thought, "They looked angry and vicious and violent as they circled the police station. We thought there had to be a better way to contend with the establishment without stooping to their level." As it happened, Allen and Michael had an issue at hand that called for a response.

On October 6, 1966, the possession and use of LSD would become illegal under California state law, and Cohen and Bowen decided to put on the Love Pageant Rally, a celebration instead of a demonstration, in the Golden Gate Park Panhandle, a narrow eight-block extension of the park on the northern boundary of the Haight in between Oak and Fell Streets. The Grateful Dead, Big Brother, and other bands agreed to play for free, and a couple of thousand people enjoyed themselves. "We wanted to create a celebration of innocence," said Cohen. "We were not guilty of using illegal substances. We were celebrating transcendental consciousness. The beauty of the universe. The beauty of being."

The Love Pageant Rally was a germinal event. It marked a certain maturity in the Haight scene, a sufficient critical mass of numbers and energy that demanded celebration. It initiated a tradition of free music in the Panhandle (and later in Golden Gate Park proper) for the Dead as well as other bands. In large part because it was intended not as promotion but as part of living in a community, "live in the park" would become a calling card for San Francisco music.

Cohen and Bowen were ecstatic with the turnout, Cohen commenting, "We saw the vitality of the event and the interest of the press and we knew we had captured the symbolic center of our movement. So we started to think how to make another event, even larger and more momentous....We knew we had the tiger by the tail. We knew that anything we did would attract the attention of the mass media."

Michael Bowen was at the center of the planning for a larger event. Born in Los Angeles, he'd shared studio space with Ed Kienholz and been part of the Wallace Berman and Ferus Gallery circles. Bowen's grandmother was a Theosophist, and he'd also studied esoteric metaphysics. His art would center on third eyes and occult symbols. One of his personal influences was a mysterious gentleman named John Starr Cooke, a designer of tarot decks, a practitioner of the Ouija board, and a student of Dianetics, the predecessor to Scientology. Cooke's sister was married to Sherman Kent, the head of the CIA's Board of National Estimates, and this connection would prove a fertile source of mystery and speculation ever after.

For the Love Pageant Rally, Bowen and his friends, fellow followers of Cooke called the Psychedelic Rangers, had drafted a riff on the Declaration of Independence that proclaimed, "We hold these experiences to be self-evident, that all is equal, that the creation endows us with certain inalienable rights. That among these are: the freedom of the body, the pursuit of joy, and the expansion of consciousness, and that to secure these rights, we the citizens of the earth declare our love and compassion for all conflicting hate-carrying men and women of the world."

That same day, the declaration and its appended list of suggested things to bring—"the color gold…photos of personal saints and gurus and heroes of the underground…children, flowers…flutes…drums…feathers"—was on a handbill for "LOVE / A Psychedelic Celebration" at Tompkins Square Park on the Lower East Side of Manhattan. The bicoastal hippie connection was flourishing.

30

The *Oracle* and Digger Ritual

However much influence the Diggers wielded, they were by no means the sole voice of the Haight. The *Oracle* newspaper was a softer, gentler expression of *hippie*, undoubtedly closer to what the mainstream assumed about the community.

Allen Cohen was a poet, an occasional distributor of Owsley Stanley's elixirs, and a clerk at the Psychedelic Shop. In the spring of 1966, he dreamed that he was flying around the world observing people in Paris, Moscow, New York, and China all reading a newspaper emblazoned with rainbows. He related the dream to his cohorts, and because the Haight in that time prized worthy dreams, Ron Thelin offered him start-up money.

The first expression of his idea was *PO Frisco*, which resembled the highly political *Berkeley Barb* and led with an article about government plans for concentration camps for dissidents and another on the joys of masturbation. Meetings ensued, Cohen recalled, with three groups emerging: One group wanted a traditional left-wing approach, one wanted the same politics but with a "more innovative McLuhanesque punch," and the third was a

257

258 **The Last Great Dream**

group of poets and artists who wanted something more visionary that would transcend "confrontational political dualisms." Groups one and two merged and, in the summer of '66, produced two issues of the *San Francisco Oracle*. Cohen thought it retained too much of the confrontational tone of the first incarnation…and it was still black and white.

There was another meeting, and the spiritual/psychedelic camp led by Cohen as editor and Michael Bowen as art director took over. On September 20, with a back page devoted to the upcoming Love Pageant Rally, they released the first issue of the *Oracle*. It was, Cohen said, "an attempt to break the lie of our linear habit. It was a contrast to regular papers, intended to show that most newspapers' objectivity was ugly and a lie…a judo on the newspaper formula.…Mostly we were interested in subjective reporting generating poetic, philosophic ideas in a newspaper format." The idea was "to provide guidance and archetypes for the journey through the states of mind that the LSD experience had opened up; and to invent and examine the new social and cultural forms and institutions that we needed to make the world align with our vision."

Along with coverage of the National Guard's occupation of Black San Francisco, and a Bruce Conner centerfold, the second issue also contained perhaps the most thoughtful single piece the *Oracle* ever ran—Gary Snyder's "Buddhism and the Coming Revolution." "Institutional Buddhism has been conspicuously ready to accept or ignore the inequalities and tyrannies of whatever political system it found itself under. This can be death to Buddhism, because it is death to any meaningful function of compassion. Wisdom without compassion feels no pain." In the West, "the national polities of the modern world maintain their existence by deliberately fostering craving and fear: monstrous protection rackets." In the end, each realm has something to offer: "The mercy of the West has been social revolution: the mercy of the East has been individual insight into the basic self/void. We need both."

The *Oracle*'s sixth issue, with its rainbow cover, brought it closer and closer to Cohen's goal, "the organic unity of the word and the image." His model was the Tibetan Buddhist thangka, in which the act of seeing the art was explicitly designed to induce a contemplative state of mind. By the seventh issue, they were selling 125,000 copies, many of them on the street for twenty-five cents (the street sellers kept a dime).

The *Oracle* and Digger Ritual

Their imaginative optimism could result in the risible, portraying Timothy Leary as a saint complete with glowing aura, and much speculation on flying saucers, astrology, and the coming of the next avatar. This was one of the passive threads of Haight life, in which, said one member, Shirly Wise, "you never interfere with anybody else's trip," even when the trip was patently damaging. There was also softheaded groupthink, for instance, about astrology. "Putting down astrology is definitely out," she said. It was one of the "massive in-things."

But the *Oracle*, at least, was also willing to listen to their sharpest critics, the Diggers. Grogan accused them of being "the *Time* magazine of the hippies," of "turning people on to selling," but also pointed out to Cohen that a proposed event on Hopi land was not only impractical but rife with "colonialist connotations," and Cohen came to agree.

The Diggers preferred the edgier, more political *Berkeley Barb*. The *Barb* had begun in August 1965, covering the continuing ripples of the Free Speech Movement, the Vietnam Day Committee, and the striking farmworkers led by César Chávez and Dolores Huerta. Although he managed to get it out each week, editor Max Scherr presided over one of the sloppiest, crudest-looking rags in publishing history. After anti-war politics and LSD, titillation rapidly became its third stock in trade, from an interview with "Rey Anthony," the author of *The Housewife's Handbook on Selective Promiscuity*, to in-depth reporting on the East Bay Sexual Freedom League's nude parties/orgies and close coverage of nude beaches.

In the fall of 1966, starting with the Love Pageant Rally, the *Barb* began to cover events in the Haight, with articles about the Artists Liberation Front Free Fairs on the Panhandle and then in the Tenderloin at Glide Memorial Church, where drag queens and hookers danced, poets read, a contortionist contorted, and the police kept an eagle eye out for the still-fugitive Kesey.

On October 21, the *Barb* became the outlet of choice for the Diggers with two articles, one a description of Digger origins that appeared to be written by a reporter, "Burocops Proboscis Probes Digger Bag." The second piece, "Delving the Diggers," was attributed to George Metevsky. The latter focused on the free food gatherings, with the classic reply, "It's free because it's yours."

Of course, somebody had to organize the food. Many at the wholesale markets contributed willingly. But the implications for those the Diggers regularly importuned, such as the Haight Street merchants making money off the young people on the street, were somewhat more complex.

260 **The Last Great Dream**

Phyllis Willner was an eighteen-year-old former Greenwich Village coffeehouse waitress who'd come to San Francisco on the back of a motorcycle, arriving with a black leather jacket and a purple dress to her name. After a quick visit to Tracy's Donuts, she spotted a notice about free food in the Panhandle, had some, and was soon part of the crew that included "Judy [Goldhaft] and Nina [Blasenheim] and Julie and Mona," who'd find food, cook it, and serve it. She was a Digger to the core, but she acknowledged the complications. "This is gonna sound awful, but we [the Diggers] were opportunistic in many ways." She referenced a card/image that circulated in the Haight with the image of an old-time Chinatown Tong warrior and the inscription "1% Free."

> So from the picture of the Tong and that history book on the hatchet men, the Diggers made the "1% Free" card. And the idea was to go to all the merchants that were making money off the hippie people and ask them for one percent of their earnings so that we could pay the rent on the Free Store and feed people. But in a way, that's menacing. And that's like gangsterism. And we were very much like Mafia. In our minds. Sometimes. [*laughs*] So, what's up with that? What were we doing, really? Are we threatening that we're going to harm them if they don't give us the one percent? Yes, that would imply that, in that card. Did anyone ever harm anyone? No. I don't think so.

By Halloween, Haight residents faced a gridlock of events. The FBI had apprehended Kesey on October 20. Word went out that he would hold an *Acid Test Graduation* at Winterland (a much larger venue not far from the Fillmore) on Halloween and talk about "going beyond acid." The show was to include the Grateful Dead (already booked to play California Hall) and was to be put on by Bill Graham. Amid fantastic rumors that after their graduation the Merry Pranksters were supposedly going to leave LSD on railings to dose (slip LSD into people without their knowledge) delegates at the California Democratic Party convention scheduled for the next week there, Graham and even Kesey's loyal friends the Grateful Dead concluded that they had other priorities. In the end, the *Acid Test Graduation* would be a low-key gathering of two hundred in a loft in the South of Market neighborhood.

The *Oracle* and Digger Ritual 261

Tom Wolfe's *The Electric Kool-Aid Acid Test* was truly brilliant reporting that would firmly establish Wolfe's reputation as a social observer and enshrine the legend of Ken Kesey even though he would not write another major novel, but it was skewed by Wolfe's effort to make the graduation an apocalyptic event. Finally able to witness in person the psychedelic community in action, Wolfe unsurprisingly chose to portray the Halloween "graduation" as a dramatic denouement. But LSD wasn't going away; the times simply called for discretion.

In the Haight, the happening event on Halloween was the Diggers' Intersection Game. On the twenty-ninth, they distributed fifteen hundred leaflets in the Haight and five hundred in Berkeley headlined PUBLIC NONSENSE NUISANCE PUBLIC ESSENCE NEWSENSE PUBLIC NEWS. The handbills invited participation in a game/dance contest at the corner of Haight and Masonic on the thirty-first.

On the appointed day, the Diggers put on a short play called *Any Fool on the Street* and then turned the action over to master puppet maker Robert LaMorticella and his two eight-foot-tall puppets, which moved back and forth through the Free Frame of Reference, the twelve-foot square that accompanied the food giveaways. The puppeteers encouraged bystanders to change their frame of reference as well.

The Diggers had also passed out hundreds of six-inch-square frames that people could hang around their necks. People "were looking at them and were talking to each other and the puppets were doing it," reflected Willner. "And was it better to be on the inside or the outside?" Then they moved on to the game, which involved seeing how many different polygons pedestrians could trace in crossing the intersection. Someone began playing music on a record player, which encouraged more graceful moves.

The game came to a halt when the police, unamused, arrested LaMorticella and four Diggers—Brooks Bucher, Emmett Grogan, Peter Berg, and Kent Minault—for blocking traffic. Released on their own recognizance, they came before the judge a month later to find that Artie Schaffer, the assistant district attorney in charge of their case, found it a ridiculous violation of freedom of expression and dropped all charges. A *Chronicle* photographer named Bob Campbell stopped them as they gleefully left the courtroom and got them to pose on the steps of city hall in one of the rare public pictures of the Diggers.

Earlier in November, the citizens of California had elected Ronald Reagan governor, which perhaps encouraged the SFPD to think that it was time to push back on the barbarian hordes of the Haight. On November 11, Ralph Gleason wrote of being exhilarated by the Digger example, even as he conceded that it was a feeling not resting on any logical system of thought. On November 15, the SFPD presented a different point of view, arresting the clerk at the Psychedelic Shop, Allen Cohen, for selling Lenore Kandel's erotic poem *The Love Book*. In the next few days, Psychedelic Shop co-owner Jay Thelin and City Lights Bookstore clerk Ronald Muszalski were also arrested. The jury convicted them, and it would take seven years for the court system to overturn the verdict.

The arrests were patently not about obscenity (the work certainly had "redeeming social value") but about resisting a rising tide of liberation flowing out of the Haight. Kandel had been a folk singer at the Coffee Gallery and a resident of East-West House who cherished her long-standing practice of Buddhism, so she'd quite naturally gravitated to the Haight, identifying with the tribal ideal and the spiritual search that followed the psychedelic experience. When sales of the book inevitably boomed, she stuck her tongue firmly in her cheek and promised 1 percent of the proceeds to the police. Six SF State professors announced a public reading the following week from *The Love Book* and from Michael McClure's play *The Beard*. No one was arrested.

"The Ideology of Failure" by George Metesky in the November 18 *Barb* was a culmination of Digger thought. It argued, cogently, that once you believe in success, you're locked into the American achievement game. Peter Berg told an interviewer around this time, "When I read *Howl*, I knew I didn't have anything to lose. That's what did it. That's what sent people out in search of experience." He wrote, "Hip and middle-class (as well as communist, fascist, socialist, and monarchist) values, goals, reactions and attitudes offer different styles, but amount to the same end: personal, national, or racial success. 'Rien ne reussi comme le sucès' ['Nothing succeeds like success']." The Diggers argued that there was only one way to treat success.

"And so, we stay dropped-out. We won't, simply won't play the game any longer. We return to the prosperous consumer society and refuse to consume. And refuse to consume. And we do our thing for nothing. In truth, we live our protest. Everything we do is free because we are failures. We've got nothing to lose, so we've got nothing to lose....To Show Love is to fail. To love to fail is the Ideology of Failure. Show Love. Do your thing. Do it for FREE. Do it for Love. We can't fail. And Mr. Jones will never know what's happening here, do you, Mr. Jones?"

The *Oracle* and Digger Ritual

The author packed a powerful critique into a brief essay. That most Americans would remain addicted to achievement and success made the manifesto no less accurate. A fourth essay a week later, "In Search of a Frame," added, "The street scene is the subliminal content of capitalism: egocentric, competitive, and material....Safety lies in the imagination, in harmony, in the resolution of contradictions between knowledge and action. We have lots of knowledge but it's useless unless it changes acts or frame of reference."

The Diggers did their best to change the frame, with large-scale rituals designed to enlarge perspectives to a "planetary frame of reference." On December 17 (after being rained out on the tenth), they presented their most elaborate street theater piece yet, a parade called *The Death and Rebirth of the Haight, the Death of Money.* Nymphlike young women in white robes handed out strips of paper that held a silk-screened message: "Now." The people gathering in the street divided into two groups between Ashbury and Clayton and began to chant. The north side said, "Oooooooh." The south side said, "Aaaaaaahhhh." The north, "Shhhhhhh." The south, "Be cool." A Muni bus stopped. The driver got out, did an elegant dance, and returned to his seat and job.

The parade kicked off led by a silver dollar sign on a stick, then a funeral cortege of black-clad women singing, "Get out my life why don't you babe," to the tune of Chopin's "Funeral March." Pallbearers carrying a coffin filled with "money" marched by, followed by marchers wearing enormous animal masks at least five feet high. At the rear, walkers gave away flutes, flowers, penny whistles, and lollipops so that everyone on the street was part of the show. Mirrors held by people on the rooftops angled the light of the setting sun into the street.

The event called for a close, for something loud. Phyllis Willner had crossed America on a motorcycle and felt a kinship with the Hells Angels—she'd been bold enough to remark to the Angel known as Gut, "Well, *I'm* a biker, y'know." She called Angels president Pete Knell, and the ceremony ended with Angel "Hairy" Henry Kot cruising down Haight Street with Phyllis behind him standing wrapped in a banner that read "Now" as she screamed, "Freeeeeeeeeeee!"

The police arrested Henry, and then his friend "Chocolate George" Hendricks. The coffin began to fill with (genuine) bail money, and a large group marched over to the Park Street police station. It was dark by then, and the marchers lit candles and surrounded the station with peace by singing "Silent Night." Tenderly bailed out, the two Angels had their charges dismissed a few weeks later.

The *Death of Money* ceremony was superb. The Diggers had taken LSD into a social context, in which Free was "social acid," an interactive drug that could destroy traditional social attitudes about social status, ethics, and above all, consumerism. Cloaked in anonymity, they had briefly touched Mystery.

Just two days after the ceremony, the first pebble of what would become a landslide of national media attention appeared on American newsstands. The December 19 *Newsweek* included a piece on the thriving bands of San Francisco, "The Nitty-Gritty Sound." If the editors had been wise enough to let their reporter, a young man named Hendrik Hertzberg, polish up his original notes, they might have published the best single article about the Haight ever written. For whatever reason, Hertzberg was not dazzled and distracted by the visual, verbal, sensual, and intellectual distinctiveness of the scene, which was what would happen to almost every other visiting reporter in the next months. The long hair, the argot, the sensory shock of light shows and loud music, the idealistic beliefs did not disturb him. His original piece is astonishingly free from "Ohmygod look at these oddballs."

He observed that, like the Beats, the hippies had dropped out of conventional status games, but the hippies "have created their own happy lifestyles to drop into." Their rejection of "prestige through money and job, and linear, cause-and-effect logical thinking" had led them to new "electric" and "tribal" values of total involvement. "On marijuana, he sees, hears, and feels colors and sounds more vividly. On LSD, his ego dissolves and is replaced by an abiding love and appreciation for all people and things. He becomes more existential than the existentialists, because his total immersion in the present is untainted by any sense of the absurdity of the future."

Alas, the editors produced something shorter and considerably less sensitive, down to declaring that the ubiquitous necklaces worn by both genders in the Haight were "the high sign of LSD initiation." That was merely silly, but indicative. The media's coverage was going to get much worse.

31

Hippie in New York

Across the continent, hippie came to Manhattan as well. The stylistic differences were the natural consequences of the atmospheric variations between the two cities.

On January 2, 1966, the NYPD celebrated the new year by raiding the Peace Eye Bookstore and arresting Ed Sanders for obscenity. They'd taken notice of the emerging East Village hippie culture signaled the previous October by the appearance of the *East Village Other* (*EVO*) and seemed determined to prevent things from escaping their control.

The Beat scene in the (West) Village had thrived on a diet of jazz and coffee, but the hippie culture of the East Village had a more difficult time. LSD encourages a natural setting, and Tompkins Square Park was all the East Village had to offer. San Francisco not only had Golden Gate Park as the Haight's front yard but easy access to beaches and the trails of Mount Tamalpais. The police of both cities shared less-than-generous notions of personal freedom, but the courts in San Francisco constantly reversed police excess. The overwhelming energy of New York, the physical sensation of being surrounded by many millions of people, was not conducive to serenity.

266 **The Last Great Dream**

In contrast to the *Oracle*'s largely pacific and spiritual outlook, much of *EVO*'s approach was grounded, in appropriate New York fashion, in competition. The first issue dismissed the "other" Village as "a sideshow of gnawing mediocrity and urban renewal," and over the next months reported on conflict between Jews and Puerto Ricans and the FBI's arrest of a member of the Catholic Workers. Then it presented an issue headlined AMERICA HATES HER CRAZIES / WANTED BY THE FBI formatted as a wanted poster including fingerprints of Leary, *Eros* publisher Ralph Ginzburg, and Allen Ginsberg.

In an unsigned editorial on August 1, 1966, *EVO* proclaimed, "We belong to a party that does not yet exist; civilization…It is the primary purpose of the *East Village Other* to…convince the young people of America and the world that they are not crazy or alone; that they are wiser than their elders who persist on a political and economic path which can only lead to total destruction." John Gruen published his book *The New Bohemia* that summer and in an excerpt for *EVO* used the phrase "Combine Generation" rather than hippie to describe the East Village newcomers, noting the many interracial couples and their practice of dancing as "an open war on self-consciousness and inhibition."

EVO was the collective effort of Walter Bowart, Ishmael Reed, Sherry Needham, Allen Katzman, and Dan Rattiner. Bowart had come from Oklahoma to be a painter, and perhaps that was why *EVO*, of all the so-called underground newspapers, would be the most creative and welcoming home to cartoonists like R. Crumb, Kim Deitch, Gilbert Shelton, Spain Rodriguez, Bill Beckman ("Captain High"), and Art Spiegelman.

In a couple of years, the first issue of *Zap Comix* would be published in San Francisco, and these artists would come to fame through it and kindred publications, known as *comix* rather than *comics* due to their edgy adult content. Even before the comix crowded in, *EVO*'s layout was a playground for absurdity and dadaist visuals. The Slum Goddess feature, which caricatured the posed women of *Playboy*, featured on one occasion a fully clothed eight-year-old East Village resident who opined that "Beatniks are nice people."

Recalling *EVO*'s founding, Ed Sanders wrote:

I first knew Walter Bowart around 1963 or '64 when he was a bartender at Stanley's Bar, located at 12th Street and Avenue B.

Hippie in New York

Bowart was an artist who did some design work in early 1965 for LeMar, the Committee to Legalize Marijuana, which operated out of my Peace Eye Bookstore located in a former Kosher meat store on East 10th Street between Avenues B and C.

Allen Katzman I had known since 1961 when he helped run open readings at various east-side coffeehouses, such as Les Deux Magots on East Seventh, and later the Cafe Le Metro on Second Avenue. Katzman was known at the time mainly as a poet. During the summer of 1965, Bowart, Katzman and others, including the artist Bill Beckman, Ishmael Reed, Jaakov Kohn, and Sherry Needham, decided to establish a newspaper. Poet Ted Berrigan, as I recall, came up with the name, *The East Village Other*, with "Other" coming, of course, from Rimbaud's famous line of 1871, "Je est un autre," I is an Other. Another account has Ishmael Reed coining the name. (The participants in the dada movement argued for fifty years over who first thought of the name "dada.")

The first issue cost fifteen cents and was, uniquely, a single large piece of newsprint folded into tabloid size. A Harvard Graduate School of Design dropout named Dan Rattiner, then publishing a small newspaper on the far reaches of Long Island, took one look and headed for Bowart's fourth-floor painter's loft at Second Street and Avenue B. As Dylan's "Ballad of a Thin Man" played behind them, they talked: "Walter...told me his philosophy. Radicalism. Anarchy. Legalize Marijuana. Free love, free drugs, free press. End the War in Vietnam."

"People don't know what's going on," said Bowart. "It's right here in the East Village. Listen to the song, man."

"Sounds good to me," Rattiner replied.

Soon they had a storefront on Avenue A between Ninth and Tenth Streets facing Tompkins Square Park. Bowart, recalled Rattiner, "brought in maniacs to answer the phone and type up stories. People with beards and rumpled clothes. Other people with capes and headbands. I hired salesmen in regular clothes and trained them by walking with them down St. Marks Place to sell space in the paper to bead shops, hip clothing stores and art supply houses. A disco called The Electric Circus was opening up. I sold it an ad....By January [1966] [*EVO*] was weekly. It was also supporting more pages and growing. It was a hit."

268 **The Last Great Dream**

Ishmael Reed was another regular at Stanley's Bar, where he became friendly with Bowart. He'd attended college in Buffalo and was planning to put out a community newspaper there. Knowing nothing about layout, he approached Bowart to design the community paper. "I went to his loft to see the result," Reed recalled.

> It was something unlike anything that I'd ever seen—suitable for an exhibit of Neo Conceptual art at the Whitney, but not for a community newspaper. He called the philosophy behind the paper pata-realist. But before I could utter my criticisms, he said, excitedly, "Hey, why don't we start a newspaper down here?"
>
> I was skeptical, but agreed to sit in on a series of meetings. During one meeting, there was a discussion of a name for the paper. Walter wanted to call it The Joint. I suggested The Other. I'd just read Carl Jung's introduction to Milton's "Paradise Lost," where he referred to Milton's Satan, the revolutionary Satan, as the "Other." And that's what we were: Cultural outsiders, who were not native New Yorkers; people who had ambivalent attitudes toward the city where we hoped to make our reputations as artists. We saw comic books as art, and now a newspaper that was a work of art. Walter took his painter's style to the newspaper.

Reed also wrote a couple of pieces for *EVO*, one of which was a denunciation of the owner of Le Metro Café, who had, he wrote, hired "thugs to monitor blacks who attended poetry readings there." Deprived of the venue, Reed and his friends in the Black poetry collective Umbra connected with the rector of Saint Mark's Church (131 East Tenth Street), which had already welcomed a program of free jazz on Sunday afternoons curated by the saxophonist Archie Shepp. Together they established what would be the long-running Saint Mark's Poetry Project, in which Reed ran a fiction workshop and his friend Joel Oppenheimer facilitated for the poets.

Given the city's enormous, densely packed population, New York institutions tended to develop protective layers of exclusivity—there wasn't enough room for democracy, much less anarchy. Consequently, the coolest room in Manhattan, Max's Kansas City, had a number of levels when it opened early in 1966. The upstairs dining room was for tourists, as was the bar. But the back room, lit in a hellish red by a Dan Flavin neon construction, was the very chic home to what one observer termed "artists, writers, film makers, underground eccentrics, pop intelligentsia and rich, beautiful people who then comprised the New York avant-garde." It was where one could find Robert Rauschenberg, Larry Rivers, Philip Glass, William Burroughs, and Willem de Kooning—also and most flamboyantly, Andy Warhol and his entourage.

Warhol had progressed from a career as a commercial artist to the pinnacle of pop art in multiple media, including painting, photography, film, and sculpture. From silk-screened Campbell's soup cans and a portrait of Marilyn Monroe to films like *Empire* that were legendary for their stupefying lack of action, Warhol became famous for a detached near nihilism and profound voyeurism that found S&M and intravenous methamphetamine abuse amusing. He also earned icon status for his tranquil acceptance of his gay sexual nature.

By 1966, Warhol had established a studio called the Factory on East Forty-Seventh Street filled with a clutch of drag queens, drug addicts, and the generally outré that he called his superstars. They helped him make his films and paintings and created the miasmic atmosphere that made him so celebrated. The true superstar was Edie Sedgwick, a beautiful, fragile, narcissistic flower of New England aristocracy raised on a California ranch that had its own oil wells. Repeatedly hospitalized for bulimia, she was shattered by the suicide death of her brother Francis ("Minty"). A second brother, Robert, died in a motorcycle accident.

Warhol's world at the Factory, where he worked surrounded by courtiers elbowing one another aside to be closer to him, became Sedgwick's second home. She was ideally suited for the Factory. In the words of her chauffeur, Tom Goodwin, she was "amoral, a facile liar. She would steal, rob, rip off." She was also exciting, full of energy, pushing "everything to the limit." Early in 1965, she met Warhol at the home of advertising maven and party-giver Lester Persky, whose television ads Andy greatly admired.

After nonspeaking roles in *Vinyl* and *Bitch* and a minor role in *Horse*, she starred in Warhol's *Poor Little Rich Girl*, sitting in her underwear talking about blowing through her inheritance. Half the film was out of focus, but perhaps it didn't matter. *Kitchen* in June, again with the underwear. *Beauty No. 2*, very skimpy underwear, and on July 26, the *Times* declared her Warhol's new star. Dyeing her hair platinum blond, she looked like Warhol's female twin, which not surprisingly delighted him. Per Truman Capote, Warhol wanted to *be* Edie: a "charming, well-born debutante from Boston." The rest of the Factory's crew members were less than pleased and initiated a campaign to subvert her.

Early in 1966, Bob Dylan visited the Factory for a screen test, which lasted all of two minutes and forty-five seconds. He quickly dismissed Warhol, and around that time, so did Edie. Though Dylan was newly married, he seemed to enjoy having Edie around. "Dylan liked Edie because she was one of the few people who could stand up against his weird little numbers: she was much stronger than the sycophants who were hanging around him at the time," recalled Dylan's onetime road manager Jonathan Taplin. More to the point, the association with Dylan, the popular assumption that his "Just Like a Woman" was at least partly inspired by her and that "Leopard-Skin Pill-Box Hat" was even more likely a portrait, made her more famous than Warhol ever could. Fame for its own sake seemed to be why Edie existed.

Musically, Warhol would forge a direct connection to another set of players. Lou Reed was a Long Island rock and roller who'd attended Syracuse University and studied with the poet Delmore Schwartz. One day in 1965, Reed sat down with John Cale, a member of La Monte Young's Theatre of Eternal Music, and played him two songs, "Heroin" and "Waiting for the Man." What astonished Cale was that he played them "on an acoustic guitar *as if they were folk songs*." They would not stay folk for long. Joined by Reed's old friend, guitarist Sterling Morrison, and Angus MacLise, Cale's housemate and fellow member of the Theatre, the quartet became the Velvet Underground.

An extreme purist, MacLise quit when they booked their first paid show, a high school gig opening for a Beatles-ish New Jersey garage band called the Myddle Class. It was December 11, 1965, and most of the high school kids there saw the band—all in black, two members wearing sunglasses—and then heard their discordant and very loud rendition of "Heroin" and backed away from the stage, although a small minority pressed forward. At a later show, a reporter overheard a young man say to his neighbor, "Maybe they're tuning up." "No, that's how it sounds," his friend replied.

A subsequent and more appropriate engagement at the Café Bizarre in the Village introduced them to Warhol, who became their manager and made them an essential part of his *Exploding Plastic Inevitable* show, which included lights and a leather-clad superstar named Gerard Malanga slashing the air around him with a bullwhip.

They played in front of the New York Society for Clinical Psychiatry, and one attendee described the Velvet's music as "a repetition of the concrete quite akin to the LSD experience." Seemingly, the majority of attendees were not enthralled. The next month, the Velvets would perform, as loudly as possible, in front of underground films at Jonas Mekas's Film-Makers' Cinematheque. There to review the films, Bosley Crowther enjoyed them no more than the shrinks had.

Put off by their sheer darkness, many of the early critics did not care for the Underground. Rock chronicler Lillian Roxon noted that "their concern was with death and violence....Oozing evil and lubricity, they made every other group look like kid stuff." In the *Los Angeles Free Press*, Paul Jay Robbins observed that Western culture has become "plastic: sterile, mechanistic, anti-human and transparent....The show proves it." It was "an intense spatter of nihilism—the peculiar brand of it so fashionable in New York circles....The only point Warhol has missed is that a new culture is queuing up backstage.... He says No to today—which is a good thing to say. However, he does not say Yes to tomorrow—which is a better thing to say."

It was certainly not commercial music. Their first album, *The Velvet Underground & Nico*, with a cover designed by Warhol, would do poorly, selling thirty thousand copies. In 1982, the musician Brian Eno would remark that every one of those thirty thousand customers went out and started a band. Later, *Rolling Stone* would place it as number thirteen on their list of the "500 Greatest Albums of All Time," describing it as "the most prophetic rock album ever made." Ellen Willis, one of the most perceptive of the early rock critics, explained why it wasn't commercial—and why over the long haul the critics would love it: "But the Velvets' music was too overtly intellectual, stylized, and distanced to be commercial. Like pop art, which was very much a part of the Velvets' world, it was anti-art art made by anti-elite elitists."

272   **The Last Great Dream**

*   *   *

In the course of 1966, several new personalities became prominent in the East Village cultural scene. Don McNeill had come to New York to attend NYU, dropped out, and was quickly revealed as a gifted young reporter for the *Village Voice*. From summer on, he covered the youth scene better than anyone. His October 8 piece, "Love, a Psychedelic Celebration," depicted flowers, incense, children, and chants of "Hare Krishna" in Tompkins Square Park, documenting people now called *hippies* celebrating the arrival of Swami Satchidananda in New York, his visit financed by the American heir to the Avon cosmetics fortune. The swami introduced himself with the remark, "America has everything, and it should have yoga too."

One of McNeill's best pieces detailed a conversation with Gary Snyder, in town to read at the Guggenheim Museum and arrange for publication of his book *The Back Country*. Snyder would quip that he wanted New York "leveled and made into a buffalo pasture," but said more seriously that "I think there's a real revolution going on. Somewhere below or outside the level of formal politics…God is dead and Western culture is on the way out. What's happening now, among other things, is the emergence of the vibrations, the music, the rhythms of all these nonwhite traditional cultures…peyote and LSD are really the American Indian's revenge." The drug "flips them out completely toward nature. It makes them feel at home in nature in a funny way."

Inevitably, McNeill also covered Timothy Leary, who in September '66 would announce the formation of the League for Spiritual Discovery at a formal press conference at the Advertising Club of New York. "Like every great religion of the past we seek to find the divinity within and to express this revelation in a life of glorification and the worship of God. These ancient goals we define in the metaphor of the present—turn on, tune in, drop out." Leary would say that he'd created the phrase as an act of homage to Marshall McLuhan. That the expression and the location he designed it for seemed to trivialize what was a potentially liberating spiritual experience clearly did not disturb him.

Abbie Hoffman also arrived in New York that year. A student of Herbert Marcuse, Max Lerner, and Abraham Maslow at Brandeis, he'd attended graduate school in psychology at UC Berkeley, taking part in the Caryl

Hippie in New York

273

Chessman and HUAC vigil/demonstrations. Working as a therapist at a state mental hospital did not suit him, and he became engaged with civil rights work, first with the NAACP and then with SNCC, working in the summer of 1965 in a freedom school in McComb, Mississippi. LSD sundered his marriage and life, and he headed to Manhattan. There he opened Liberty House, a store to sell Southern crafts—candles, quilts, dresses, dolls, hats—from Mississippi's Poor People's Corporation, on Bleecker Street in the Village. He also found an apartment at Avenue C and Eleventh Street.

As he would recall,

> We had no way of knowing that we had just taken a $101-a-month front-row seat to the cultural revolution. The local counter-cultural institutions were all in a ten-block radius: Paul Krassner's *The Realist*, Ed Sanders and his Peace Eye Bookstore, resident poet Allen Ginsberg....The *East Village Other* was a block away, the Psychedelicatessen, the country's first [sic] head shop, was around the corner at 10th St. and Avenue A, and Randy Wicker's Button Shop was right next door. Whatever cause people were pushing, they would go into Randy's and order a couple thousand buttons and get them for close to nothing. Buttons became a primary symbol of identity and expression.

What he called the "community meeting center," a corner store called Gem Spa, source of egg creams and Bambú rolling papers, was just around the corner.

Early in 1967, McNeill quoted Ginsberg, who was pondering how to hold a large spiritual gathering in New York City but was doubtful because he thought the East Village's music hall, the Dom, was not "a sacramental meeting place" on the order of San Francisco's Fillmore Auditorium. The best source of youthful music in New York was the Village's Café Au Go Go, on Bleecker Street.

But the music of the East Village would center on the Fugs, whom the *Times* critic Robert Shelton described as "the musical children of Lenny Bruce, the angry satirist. Their music, while growing in capability, is secondary to their lyrics, patter, and antics. Complete personal freedom, whether in sex

274   **The Last Great Dream**

or in drug experiences, seems to be one of the Fugs' ensigns." Writing in a December 1966 *New York Review of Books*, the critic Elizabeth Hardwick would predictably be more caustic. They were "neither art nor theater, but noise ('total assault') and Free Speech…dirty words, dirty feet, laughter. The Fugs are ideologues of some kind, not orgiasts; their ideas are few and simple, and all of them are pacific."

In other words, they were funny, but they couldn't really play.

32

The Be-In

At 1:00 p.m. on January 14, 1967, Gary Snyder blew into a conch shell to begin the Gathering of the Tribes, the Great Human Be-In, fulfilling what Kenneth Rexroth and Robert Duncan had begun twenty-five years before. It was a moment—in all senses—of high optimism and joy, an essentially spiritual event to celebrate life and community, not at all Western in its purposelessness.

It was also the beginning of the end of the Haight as a functional neighborhood. At least thirty thousand people sat in front of Snyder on the Polo Field in Golden Gate Park, and what had been only modestly noticed to that point would now pass into legend via an astonishing media scrum.

Although Michael Bowen was perhaps the first to talk it up, the notion of a large celebration was a complete natural for a neighborhood that was itself an ongoing celebration. The phrase "Be-In" came from the USCO artist Steve Durkee (or, one authority wrote, Gerd Stern), who passed it to Richard Alpert, who shared it with Bowen. To choose the day, someone approached one of the Haight's resident astrologers, Gavin Arthur, who'd been a socialist and New Ager since the 1930s, a friend of Robinson Jeffers and also of Edward Carpenter, thus linking him to Walt Whitman and

275

revealing a deep connection to American bohemianism. Roots. He chose wonderfully well; mid-January days in San Francisco are often miserably wet and raw, but this one was glorious.

Jay Thelin, whose appearance was relatively conventional—a low bar in his circle—went to the city's Recreation and Parks Department to get a permit and found a brand-new person in charge, assistant supervisor of recreation Peter Ashe, a bearded Haight Street sympathizer. The hippies got their papers.

On January 6, the *Barb* headlined THE BEGINNINGS OF THE HUMAN BE-IN...A GATHERING OF THE TRIBES. It would serve as a love feast that included both Berkeley and the Haight in a "new and strong harmony." Naturally, the *Oracle* went all out. The cover was literally purple: an Indian sadhu with three eyes designed by Bowen from a photo by Casey Sonnabend, a painter and sometime drummer for Ann Halprin, with decorations by Stanley "Mouse" Miller.

Allen Cohen agreed with the *Barb*: "We emphasized the unity of political and transcendental ideals, and we had a preference for non-violence." The roots, Cohen said—"Beats, LSD, anti-materialist, idealistic, anarchistic, surreal, Dionysian and transcendental"—were held in common. One of the most perceptive of the Berkeley radicals, Michael Rossman, termed the Haight "our Mark 1 ghetto community" and felt that "the Movement had expanded beyond all political bounds and recognition, and was on some verge—perhaps premature, but real enough—of carrying us through deep transformation into a new human culture."

On January 12, Snyder, Bowen, Jerry Rubin of Berkeley's Vietnam Day Committee, Cohen, and Jay Thelin held a press conference at the Print Mint poster shop on Haight Street to spread the word. "The days of fear and separation are over....All segments of the youthful revolutionary community will participate."

The night before the Be-In, the poets met at Michael McClure's home on Downey Street in the Upper Haight to plan the program. The main point of contention seemed to be identifying Timothy Leary as a poet (seven minutes) or a prophet (half an hour). It concluded when Ginsberg quipped, "If he starts to preach, Lenore can always belly-dance." The bulk of the day would be musical, but the recognition of the Haight's roots in Beat poetry was essential. Coupled with psychedelics and rock and roll, the day would

The Be-In

also stand for the shamanic and environmental vision represented by both McClure's biologically based mysticism and Snyder's profound connections to Indigenous culture and Buddhism.

Rumors of a Satanic curse on the event skittered around the Haight, so early on the morning of the fourteenth, Ginsberg, Snyder, and Alan Watts conducted a *pradakshina*, a Buddhist purification rite. The poets—Lawrence Ferlinghetti, McClure, Lenore Kandel, Ginsberg, Snyder—kicked off the day with readings, Kandel realizing that the day was about genuine community, about trust, because she was surrounded with people "that belonged to me and I belonged to them." Rubin raged against the war. Leary burbled his advertising slogan. The Diggers passed out thousands of hits of Owsley Stanley's finest and served turkey sandwiches, which Stanley had also contributed.

Strangely, the SFPD had apparently chosen to ignore the *Chronicle*, their entire presence that day consisting of two mounted policemen observing from a nearby hill. When a lady looking for a missing child approached them, they suggested she go to the stage and call for assistance; "We can't go down there, lady, they're smoking pot."

Ralph Gleason estimated the crowd at twenty thousand; other guesses ranged quite a bit higher. Every tribe that felt connected to the Haight had shown up, from Big Sur and Carmel in the south, to the gold country east of San Francisco, to Sonoma and much farther north. Persuaded by his students, the abbot of San Francisco Zen Center, Suzuki Roshi, attended and sat by the stage smiling and holding a flower. Dizzy Gillespie was there. Two unknown actors named Gerome Ragni and James Rado would channel the day into writing a play called *Hair*. The queen of groupies, a visiting Pamela Des Barres, was disturbed by the split ends of hair she saw around her but was able to see the obvious: "Everyone was smiling and glad to be alive on the planet... knowing the world could be saved if we loved one another."

There was trouble with the power source at some point, and the Hells Angels guarded the line and felt useful. Quicksilver Messenger Service played, and "Girl" Freiberg felt the same as Des Barres: "This is just like a really big family." The Grateful Dead kicked off their set, which would also include Charles Lloyd on flute, with "Dancing in the Streets," and Dizzy Gillespie pronounced them "swinging."

278 **The Last Great Dream**

A parachutist landed on the field. Sprawled out on blankets, people blew bubbles, shared oranges, lit incense, and gave one another small presents of bells and mirrors. They looked around astonished at the sheer number of people who were part of the gathered tribes. Ginsberg, who had whispered to Ferlinghetti when sitting on the stage, "What if we're all wrong?" ended the day by urging everyone to practice kitchen yoga and clean up—and they did so, leaving the field immaculate.

"No fights. No drunks. No troubles," reported Gleason. "An affirmation, not a protest. A statement of life, not of death, and a promise of good, not evil."

"My day was full," said the Dead's comanager Danny Rifkin, smiling.

Though the police had essentially ignored the gathering, they managed to make up for their kindliness by gratuitously arresting around one hundred youth on Haight Street for "blocking traffic" as they drifted home. The hip response would be HALO, the Haight-Ashbury Legal Organization formed by Brian Rohan and Michael Stepanian, young members of Vincent Hallinan's law firm, who would get all charges dropped.

McClure would declare that "the Be-in was a blossom. It was a flower. It was out in the weather. It didn't have all of its petals. There were worms in the rose. It was perfect in its imperfections. It was what it was—and there had never been anything like it before."

Even a black-belt cynic like the writer Hunter Thompson responded to the day. "There was a…sense of inevitable victory over the forces of Old and Evil. Not in any mean or military sense; we didn't need that. Our energy would simply *prevail*. There was no point in fighting—on our side or theirs. We had all the momentum. We were riding the crest of a high and beautiful wave." At least one Berkeley politico, ED Denson, would write that "nothing happened at the Be-In, and the opportunity to gather all of those people was wasted." Few attendees would have agreed.

By now, Allen Cohen noted, the *Oracle* was not a newspaper but a "journal of arts and letters for the expanded consciousness—a tribal messenger from the inner to the outer world." Most importantly, the *Oracle* had switched to a new printer, which allowed them, said Cohen, to "use the presses like a

The Be-In

paint brush" by splitting "the ink fountain of a web into three compartments with metal dividers and wooden blocks," with a different color ink in each compartment. Now Cohen really had his rainbows.

In something approaching formal journalism, the *Oracle* in February gathered Timothy Leary, Gary Snyder, Alan Watts, and Allen Ginsberg at Watts's home on the Sausalito waterfront, the SS *Vallejo*, for what was intended as a serious conversation about where the burgeoning alternative society might go. On the whole, the conversation came down to a sane, sober, and practical Snyder challenging Leary's airy platitudes, which began and effectively ended with "turn on, tune in, drop out."

A few years later, Snyder would offer the following quote to a speaker's bureau representing him: "As poet I hold the most archaic values on earth. They go back to the late Paleolithic: the fertility of the soil, the magic of animals, the power-vision in solitude, the terrifying initiation and rebirth, the love and ecstasy of the dance, the common work of the tribe. I try to hold history and wilderness in mind, that my poems may approach the true measure of things and stand against the unbalance and ignorance of our times."

Later still, in *Earth House Hold*, he summed up his stance as a faith in "the ancient shamanistic-yogic-gnostic-socioeconomic view, that mankind's other is Nature and Nature should be tenderly respected; that man's life and destiny is growth and enlightenment in self-disciplined freedom; that the divine has been made flesh and that flesh is divine; that we not only should but *do* love one another." Such views, suppressed by church and state, now seem "almost biologically essential to the survival of humanity."

Peering through a roseate fog, Leary predicted that, through LSD, groups of youth would "open one of those doors" and see "the garden of Eden, which is this planet," thus changing their consciousness. Snyder replied, "But that garden of Eden is full of old rubber tires and tin cans right now, you know?" What was important, he argued, was that "people learn the techniques which have been forgotten; that they learn new structures and new techniques. Like, you just can't go out and grow vegetables, man. You've got to learn *how* to do it."

If our culture was to change its relationship to the natural world, it had, he offered, a superb example at hand in Native American culture. Since the central problem of the exploitive modern capitalist society was consumption, Snyder also suggested group marriage as a way to lessen demand. His life had been an ongoing example of "cutting down on your desires and cutting down on your needs to an absolute minimum, and it also meant don't be a bit fussy about how you work or what you do for a living."

Leary suggested that we "dig a hole in the asphalt and plant a seed...do it on the highway so they then fix it and when they do we're getting to them. There'll be pictures in the paper"—publicity apparently being the solution to everything. He concluded, "All right. We'll change the slogan. I'm competing with Marshall McLuhan. Everything I say is just a probe."

About the same time as the conversation, Snyder and Ginsberg created and carried out a ritual that they offered as a way of both showing gratitude to the planet and clarifying one's own mind—namely, a circumambulation of Mount Tamalpais, the guardian mountain that looks down on the San Francisco Bay Area. The legend of Tamalpais had been romanticized and appropriated by Anglos as "the sleeping Indian maiden," most notably in a 1921 Mountain Play (there is an amphitheater near the summit that hosts an annual play) called *Tamalpa*.

The Beat response reclaimed the mountain as sacred. In 1965, Snyder and his friend Philip Whalen had designed a hike in the Japanese mountain monk (*yamabushi*) tradition that followed a route with stations where the pilgrims stopped to chant from various Zen and Tibetan Buddhist traditions, something not only Buddhist but shamanic. In the wake of the Be-In, they led their first public circumambulation on February 10, 1967.

Snyder's poem, "The Circumambulation of Mt. Tamalpais," would become the centerpiece of his late-life masterwork, the fruit of forty years of writing, *Mountains and Rivers Without End*. After taking tea with the artist Saburo Hasegawa at the American Academy of Asian Studies on April 8, 1956, he vowed to write a long and serious poem, and he completed it four decades later. It is a meditation on a classic Chinese landscape painting, something meant to be an invitation to mindfulness in Zen much as a thangka is in Tibetan Buddhism. The poem is a spiritual autobiography, a depiction of ecosystems, and a series of snapshots, all of which reflect one another.

It might well be one of the most important artistic consequences of the Be-In and the Haight-Ashbury scene.

33

After the Be-In

The aftermath of the Be-In and the attendant media onslaught led to a massive overwhelming of the ecosystem that was the small Haight-Ashbury neighborhood. The Diggers and local institutions tried to cope, but their efforts were inevitably limited.

In between exhorting the Haight Street merchants to go nonprofit—"That means if you're a store you take that money you make," Emmett Grogan said, "and share it with the people who make your beads and sandals. We want you to start living this love shit you're always talking about"—the Diggers proved they still had a sense of the absurd and the capacity to teach it. When some of the poets—Gary Snyder, Lew Welch, Lenore Kandel, Richard Brautigan, and others—held a fundraiser for them at the North Beach bar Dino and Carlo's, the Diggers demonstrated that they meant what they said about escaping money with Free by using the proceeds to buy drinks for all.

They also had one last major acte gratuit in store for San Francisco. On February 24, 1967, they put on the *Invisible Circus* at Glide Memorial Church in the Tenderloin district. Billed as a "72 Hour Environmental Community Happening," it became an orgy, which was appropriate for the neighborhood, if not for the venue.

282   **The Last Great Dream**

The prominent gay elements in the area had produced, as Digger Kent Minault put it, a "GENUINELY multi-ethnic and multi-sexual, multi-EVERYTHING. So that was really the melting pot of San Francisco." Minault recalled Grogan saying, "'We need to get together with the fags.' He put it just like that. 'The fags, man, that's where it's at.' And that's what really brought us to the Glide Church....He felt that that was a real source of kinship—that they got something that we needed to be involved with."

The *Invisible Circus* "just involved us actualizing our fantasies," said Peter Coyote. "What would you like to see in a room? No matter how improbable." In the planning stages, Lenore Kandel would respond to whoever expressed reservations, "Now wait a minute, that isn't liberating....Loosen up. You must liberate." It was a full-on Digger event, which is to say it turned into an anarchistic free-for-all.

A rock band, the Chamber Orkustra, played in the basement; next door was an orgy room filled with shredded plastic. The church's marriage preparation room became a seduction chamber decorated with K-Y jelly, candles, incense, silk, and satin. The main sanctuary saw a succession of activities, including Hindu chanting, candlelit processions, poetry readings, incense burning, a naked man roaming the room, African drumming, belly dancing, light shows, and lovemaking.

A film on satellites appeared on one wall, and then a troupe of belly dancers, some topless, burst into the room, attracting partners amid a mass of wriggling bodies. Michael McClure strolled around reciting poetry while playing the autoharp. His fellow poet Lenore Kandel, when not belly dancing or reading her own poetry, practiced divination not by reading palms but, at Coyote's suggestion, reading feet.

The Fellowship Room hosted a serious discussion of pornography and obscenity that included an ACLU attorney, a minister, a writer on sexuality, and a member of the SFPD's vice squad. As the very staid cop spoke, a door behind the speaking panel opened a crack, and the Digger behind the door displayed his wagging member. Apparently, the officer never understood why the audience was enjoying itself quite so much.

Then the minister arrived. Cecil Williams was a Black man from Texas who'd arrived at Glide, at the time still a traditional Methodist congregation, as director of community involvement in 1963. He'd become the minister in 1966. He was definitely not conventional; the cross over the altar had come down that September. He embraced a true Christian concern for those left behind but was ambivalent about the hippie "embrace of conditions I'd fought all my life to eradicate [that] angered and insulted me," since they could always return to their bourgeois origins. "Still, they realized the Dream had aborted....They were rebelling, and so was I. They were exiles, and so was I....Sons and daughters of white America who knew its emptiness and were daring enough to admit it."

The Artists Liberation Front event outside Glide had been successful. But what he saw in February when he arrived around 11:00 p.m. was...over the top. The church was bulging at the seams with what was estimated as five thousand people. The sanctuary was wall-to-wall bodies, with a woman in a G-string dancing on the church organ. He saw a crowd with "a boundless hunger and an ecstatic, desperate determination to have it fed. Their sense of raw vengeance, as if they had nothing left to lose but their appetites, left me uneasy....All limits had been broken down, afire, sending chaos throughout the sanctuary. Yet there was an eerie lack of tension."

One of the church's traditional Methodist ladies had been so disoriented by the chaos that she was importuning passing young men to take her home and have her. "Something had been ripped loose within her and she was drowning, another victim of the tidal wave that knocked down all in its path. Some of these things needed to be knocked down. I was aware of that. Maybe the woman needed to be touched, but it was all so indiscriminate, arrogantly disrespecting the border between liberation and destruction."

By dawn, the police had arrived, and Rev. Williams and the Diggers hammered out an arrangement that sent most of the celebrants to Ocean Beach, although quite a few returned Sunday morning. The church had been vandalized. In one bathroom, someone had scrawled, "Fuck the Church." Williams's response was not fury but revelation; "Fuck the Church and bring it life. Fuck the Church and make it feel. Fuck the Church and make it human, fully woman, fully man, fully child. Fuck the Church until it becomes *pregnant*, for its pregnancy is your pregnancy. Become pregnant with a new way of life."

That Sunday's congregation was hippies and street people, a basic part of Glide's future parishioners. The service included the singer Ann Weldon,

284   **The Last Great Dream**

whose primary venue was a gay bar called the Paper Doll, and Kandel. There was a reading from *Death of a Salesman*. The sermon was called "Born Free." The still-conventional choir members muttered of blasphemy under their breaths.

Williams knew that if the *Chronicle* printed the real story of Friday night, he and the church were dead. A reporter called him on Monday and said he'd been there, "one of the most profound experiences of my life, but if I print what actually happened, most people wouldn't understand it. So I'm not going to print it. Hell, I don't think anyone would believe it anyhow."

In the wake of the *Circus*, some of the Diggers began to scatter. Grogan headed back to New York while others went to Morning Star Ranch in Sonoma; on March 6, the Communications Company (more commonly known as Com/Co) leaflet service published a list of things needed for the farm, including "tools, lumber, tar paper, cement, tents, seed, rabbits, tractors," and so on.

It was probably a good time to step back. Even with Ralph Gleason's presence, the *Chronicle* began to compete with the *Examiner* for who could cover the Haight in the sleaziest way possible. As one SF State professor wrote, the press was "content to report what it saw: long hair, dirt, drugs, and sex." Any lingering spiritual aspects to the Haight were clearly invisible to the reporters who flooded the town after the Be-In.

Ironically, one of the worst offenders was *Ramparts*, a publication also intended to establish an alternative to the American mainstream. It had begun as a liberal, idealistic critic of the Roman Catholic Church, but as the decade passed, the editorial chair had passed to Warren Hinckle, who fused left politics with sophisticated notions of design and a wizardly grasp of public relations. Very much a part of Catholic San Francisco, from Saint Cecilia's parish to the (Jesuit) University of San Francisco, Hinckle was also a born gadfly and a rascal who'd managed as the editor of USF's college newspaper to arrange for the installation of a telephone extension in a nearby bar…and had gotten away with it.

Ramparts had moved leftward to break important stories about the CIA's highly illegal infiltration of the domestic National Student Association and Michigan State University's ethically dubious participation in the writing of Vietnam's constitution, brilliantly depicted by a cover featuring the president's wife, Madame Nhu, in an MSU cheerleading uniform.

When it became clear, post Be-In, that they simply had to cover the flowering Haight-Ashbury scene, Hinckle shoved the highly knowledgeable editor Gleason aside and wrote the story himself. Badly.

Hinckle's "The Social History of the Hippies," published in March 1967, was riddled with factual errors, from conflating the Trips Festival with the Love Pageant Rally to identifying the "Peyote Indians" as a Native American tribe to misspelling Jaime de Angulo's name (twice). Michael Bowen and Bill Graham would deny ever having been interviewed, Graham adding that he'd been quoted as using the word *cadre*, which was not a part of his vocabulary. All of this was consequent to Hinckle's general ignorance of the Haight.

The root problem came when he recycled Norman Podhoretz's equally false libel of Kerouac and the Beats and connected the Haight love of sensuality with "a distinctly fascist trend...which can be recognized by a totalitarian insistence on action and nihilism." He'd apparently never heard of the Haight emphasis on nonviolence and gentleness.

After blessing Emmett Grogan as the "conscience of the hippie community," he concluded, "if more and more youngsters begin to share the hippie political posture of unrelenting quietism, the future of activist, serious politics is bound to be affected." However pleasant dropping out was, "when that is done, you leave the driving to the Hell's [*sic*] Angels."

A serious consideration of the Haight's critique of American politics would have been welcome, especially considering that he acknowledged many "hippie" beliefs: "communal life, drastic restriction of private property, rejection of violence, creativity before consumption, freedom before authority, de-emphasis of government and traditional forms of leadership." It was not surprising that Gleason resigned in protest, nor that the magazine never granted a former editor the simple courtesy of printing his letter of resignation.

"The Social History" was simply one portion in a torrent of American media coverage of the Haight. The only expression of the scene that managed to evade distortion was *Surrealistic Pillow*, Jefferson Airplane's second album, released on February 1. Its first single, "Somebody to Love," rocked the world of American popular music and brought attention to San Francisco. But the second single, "White Rabbit," introduced every young American within listening range of the radio to the Wonderland of the Haight and its advocacy of the expansion of consciousness.

Grace Slick had seized upon Alice at least in part as a feminist avatar who needed no Prince Charming but pursued her own path of curiosity all the way to the last lyric, an open-ended invitation to learn and grow: "Feed your head." Drugs might be one thing to put in one's head, but so were books and the entire range of human experience.

The song's music was perfectly matched to the lyrics. Slick recalled that she'd written it after listening to Miles Davis's *Sketches of Spain* "50 times without stopping," and even the original version performed by the Great Society had a Spanish flavor.

But bassist Jack Casady and lead guitarist Jorma Kaukonen were gifted musicians on a different plane. Casady recalled that "the half-step movement within 'White Rabbit' was obviously of the Ravel *Bolero* nature. We had the triple drum rolls and I just applied it to the bass and did that as the intro as Jorma came in with the amazingly slinky and somewhat Middle Eastern sound of the scales." Soon after, Country Joe and the Fish brought out *Electric Music for Mind and Body*, which featured "Not So Sweet Martha Lorraine," and the message was clear: the Bay Area was the promised land.

A full span of media descended on the Haight. *Playboy* sent its roving artist/observer Shel Silverstein, who reported that soon after his arrival, "A long-haired girl takes my hand and leads me up a path through some trees, where we lie down. Afterward, she smiles and says, 'Welcome to Haight-Ashbury.' I think I'll wait and draw tomorrow." *Dragnet*, which that February returned to the air in color, opened with an episode called "The LSD Story," more commonly known as "Blue Boy," after a character with a painted face. Inspired by Merry Prankster Paul Foster's arrest the previous year at the Watts acid test, it was filled with misinformation and made surpassingly clear Jack Webb's take on mind expansion: Blue Boy dies.

Life weighed in on March 31 with Loudon Wainwright's major story, "The Strange New Love Land of the Hippies." Mostly sweet and concerned and certain that these children were going astray, Wainwright reported that "the hippies jarred me, but there is much about them that is distinctively appealing. Those I met use the word 'love' a lot....It is a weapon of astonishing power."

Much of the coverage was of the lowest-common-denominator sort, on the order of "Berkeley Coed, 19, on 'LSD' Plunges 3 Floors to Death." Or

Martin Arnold's *New York Times* screed, "Organized Hippies Emerge on Coast: San Francisco Haight-Ashbury Hippies Have It Made." New York's Greenwich "Villagers," Arnold assured his readers, "are for things. Hippies are for nothing." "Hippies like LSD, marijuana, nude parties, sex, drawing on walls and sidewalks, not paying their rent, making noises, and rock 'n' roll music." And, he added, their hair is dirty because they don't pay their water bills.

The *Times* also reached out to San Francisco writers for reports. The novelist Herb Gold surveyed local writing, mentioning *The Beard* and *The Love Book*. Unlike his old bête noire, the Beats, who wanted to disaffiliate from the world, the hippies, he thought, wanted to change it. "But they are still looking for their language."

Hunter Thompson's May contribution to the *New York Times Magazine*, "The 'Hashbury' Is the Capital of the Hippies," oozes contempt to an astonishing degree. To Thompson, the politicos of Berkeley had reacted to Reagan's election by moving to San Francisco and creating a "dope fortress" where they could withdraw and be stoned. While admiring Snyder and the Diggers for their practical tribalism, he saw nothing of value in the Haight culture, which was only the "orgiastic tip of a great psychedelic iceberg that is already drifting in the sea lanes of the Great Society."

New Yorkers celebrated Easter Sunday with a Be-In of their own in Central Park. Primarily organized by Jim Fouratt, a future gay rights activist, and Paul Williams, the editor of *Crawdaddy!*, the event was, reported the *Times*, "noisy, swarming, chaotic and utterly surrealistic."

Early in the day, a police car appeared; the first attendees pelted it with daffodils, and the cops wisely withdrew. There was no particular center of activity. Don McNeill reported that the main activity was giving—flowers, eggs, incense, and jelly beans. "Layers of inhibitions were peeled away and, for many, love and laughter became suddenly fresh." People joined hands to form huge circles, then hurtled to the center to form puppy piles. It was miraculous, he decided.

Among the revelers of the "hip Easter Parade" were the members of the English rock band Cream, then introducing themselves to America at the RKO theater on Fifty-Eighth Street in a package show that also included Smokey Robinson and the Miracles, Wilson Pickett, and the Who. Cream's guitarist, Eric Clapton, reported that the bass player, Jack Bruce, experienced his first acid trip by eating some "spiked popcorn." Another attendee, the mayor's wife, Mary Harrison Lindsay, pronounced the Be-In "fantastic!" There was also a smaller event at Elysian Park in Los Angeles.

Abbie Hoffman was one of the participants of the New York Be-In. In spring 1967, he had taken Stokely Carmichael's advice, handed Liberty House off to Black activists, and pursued anti-war organizing in the East Village. Just around that time, Grogan and other Diggers visited New York, and Hoffman grabbed on to the concept of Free with both hands, writing later in his memoir that "it is the only word, including *love, charity, equality, peace*, or any 'ism' that is incorruptible." Of course, he didn't mention the Diggers.

Nor was the Digger principle of anonymity in his lexicon. As E. L. Doctorow observed, with Abbie, one was never sure when he was "acting," "for real," or "acting for real." He was a true postmodern in whom there was no distinction between fiction and nonfiction; there was "only narrative." He was an adroit manipulator of the mass media because, he wrote in his memoir, he'd studied, practicing at home for talk shows and press conferences "just as singers and comedians practice their routines....You train to improvise....I trained for the one-liner, the retort jab, or sudden knock-out put-ons."

In the coming years, he would certainly stir things up, but much of his effect, wrote his partner Jerry Rubin, would be to trivialize their own principles, becoming "a parody of left-wing politics."

34

Pilgrims Overrun the Haight

The flood unleashed by the Be-In and the subsequent media coverage had come. For many in the Haight that spring, things seemed to be on the verge of coming entirely unglued. Their community had been created by adults who were generally engaged in some form of creativity. The new pilgrims were much younger and frequently bereft of resources, either material or emotional. More in sorrow than in criticism, one of the original settlers, Linda Gravenites, opined that before the Be-In, "people came because they were full to overflowing and were sharing their fullness. After that, it was the empties who came, wanting to be filled." Prankster Lee Quarnstrom agreed. Haight Street was filling up with "runaways...There wasn't room for everyone."

Runaways was the operative word. Pictures sent by distraught parents covered an entire wall at the nearby Park Street police station. As the crowds on Haight Street thickened, the police began to sweep the street, entering every store to check the identification of anyone who looked underage. Those lacking ID went to the waiting paddy wagons. Though the practice

290 · **The Last Great Dream**

was legally dubious, anyone who has ever dealt with anxious mothers and fathers concerned about missing children will probably spare a modicum of sympathy for whoever answered the telephone at Park Street.

As youth thronged Haight Street, one of the factors that ramped up the psychic intensity was Com/Co, the work of Chester Anderson, a Greenwich Village coffeehouse poet, editor of *Beatitude*, and novelist (*The Butterfly Kid*), and Claude Hayward, a staff person at *Ramparts*. Acquiring a Gestetner printing press and Gestefax stencil-cutting machine with the royalties to Anderson's novel, they set up as the neighborhood print shop, free to the Diggers and inexpensive to kindred organizations like the Artists Liberation Front, San Francisco Mime Troupe, and the Committee. They were able to distribute hundreds of bulletins up and down Haight Street in an extraordinarily speedy fashion, with varying results. When *Los Angeles Free Press* founder Art Kunkin visited the Haight in March, they told him that they'd put out five hundred leaflets totaling half a million copies.

Com/Co also told Kunkin that they claimed the right to be "outrageous pamphleteers who compete with the Establishment press for public opinion, to produce occasional incredibilities out of an unnatural fondness for either outrage or profit, to do what we damn well please, to supplement the *Oracle* with a more or less daily paper." Although they printed poems by Richard Brautigan and others, the bulk of their work was news and current events.

On one occasion, they identified a person as "the heat," received contradictory information, and retracted it. The next day, their original source was arrested, which they concluded was an act of retribution by actual informers. On March 16, they reported, "Pretty little 16-year-old middle-class chick comes to the Haight…(dealer shoots her full of speed, then 3,000 micrograms of LSD) & raffles off her temporarily unemployed body for the biggest Haight Street gang bang since the night before last."

True or not, the item resonated with the sense of impending doom now rife on Haight Street, the feeling that a tsunami of too many wanderers was headed their way. Kunkin would conclude in March that "San Francisco last weekend was a city that seemed on the verge of revolution. The streets of the

Pilgrims Overrun the Haight

Haight-Ashbury section were filled with hippies, patrolling police cars and bands of tourists, some of them crew cut types looking for trouble."

At the end of the month, the poet Lew Welch wrote in Com/Co that he expected two hundred thousand people by summer and advised people to gather into tribes and "disperse....Much of Cal is national forest. Work with the rangers. Take fire-fighting work....The haight-ashbury is not where it's at—it's in your head and hands. Take it anywhere."

Arthur Lisch was a latter-day Digger, an artist then receiving a stipend from the American Friends Service Committee for outreach in the Haight, and in February, he approached Father Leon Harris of All Saints Church, located a block off Haight and Ashbury on Waller Street, and asked if the Diggers could use the church kitchen to prepare free food. They also received the use of a room for administrative needs. Soon it was buzzing 24-7 with counselors, a doctor, and an attorney one afternoon each week, and a never-ending stream of volunteers bringing food, clothing, and offers of shelter.

That week, Father Harris, other clergy, and the president of the Haight-Ashbury Neighborhood Council held what the *Chronicle* dubbed a "squares for hippies press conference" in which they defended the new residents of the neighborhood. In an open letter, Harris told his parish that "residents of the Haight-Ashbury ought to be very pleased to be the center of a new movement of creativity and vitality which may well turn out to be historic." The day after the press conference, the *Examiner* quoted him saying, "I find myself becoming more and more proud of the community we are becoming."

Harris had been rector at All Saints since 1949, taking it into the Anglo-Catholic realm theologically, and practicing a true small-*c* catholicism in welcoming all races and classes, especially the Black people who had moved into the Haight after being urban-renewal-ed out of the Fillmore. When his parishioners grumbled about the presence of the hippies, he replied, "A congregation of members of Christ's Holy Church is not a private club which exists to make its members comfortable." Jay Thelin would pronounce him a "saint."

And any Christian would feel sympathy with this Digger message on Com/Co:

292 **The Last Great Dream**

Well, the time has come to share. Diggers are people who share… so be a Digger. There will be more and more and more and you will be more and more and more. The Diggers take part in the Invisible Government. God is on your side. Take part in the Invisible Government. Share food in the park every day at four. That's the Panhandle Park at the corner of Oak and Ashbury. Are you deeply religious? Share. Are you for peace? Share. Are you for freedom? Share. Are you overstuffed? Share. Are you just out for kicks? Share. Be responsible. Take part in the Invisible Government.

On March 21, Lisch and Roy Ballard of the Black People's Free Store warned the San Francisco Episcopal priest's organization of the impending influx of youth, many of whom would need care and feeding. The priests voted to condemn the city's Recreation and Parks Department, which had just passed a rule banning sleeping in the park.

The next day, chief of police Thomas Cahill announced he would do what he could "to discourage new arrivals to the hippie colony….Hippies are no asset to the community." On the twenty-third, the mayor chimed in, calling for a resolution from the board of supervisors "that such migration is unwelcome." The *Chronicle*'s headline was blunt: MAYOR WARNS HIPPIES TO STAY OUT OF TOWN.

The director of the city health department, Ellis D. Sox (really!), joined the chorus. Along with dire warnings about the potential for bubonic plague, he indicated that he would dispatch crack teams to inspect hippie crash pads in the Haight. Two days later, they reported inspecting nearly seven hundred buildings with eight teams (almost one hundred buildings per team per day seems quite astonishing), issuing abatement notices on thirty-nine buildings, one of which was 848 Clayton Street, a Digger crash pad. The *Chronicle* described it as a "raid" with the enticing headline INSIDE HIPPIE PADS.

The health inspectors were clearly ludicrous, but the police were not. On March 9, they arrested managers and/or employees at three different hippie stores for selling a poster that depicted Kama Sutra positions. One of the arresting officers was Arthur Gerrans, the Haight's least favorite cop. On Palm Sunday, the nineteenth, the city permitted chalking on sidewalks, even supplying 144 colored chalks at the Panhandle. That night, Gerrans busted four for chalking on Haight Street.

Pilgrims Overrun the Haight

On Easter Sunday, March 26, the hippies responded with a passive "Mill-In" on Haight Street, which brought traffic entirely to a halt for several hours. At length, the police arrived and closed off the street to cars, which caused hippies to pour into the empty street and sit down. The police began to move in, and at least apocryphally, a much larger confrontation was averted when Allen Cohen went to 710 Ashbury Street and pleaded with the Grateful Dead to go to the Panhandle and play; between twelve and twenty people were arrested, a very low figure given the possibilities. Police estimated the crowd at 2,500; UPI ran a piece that afternoon titled "Bay Area Officers Disperse Hippie Mob."

On April 5, the Gray Line bus company underlined the increasing absurdity of the situation by announcing the Haight-Ashbury Hippie Hop Tour, "the only foreign tour within the continental limits of the United States." Given the congestion on Haight Street, it lasted only a month.

Supposedly apolitical hippies were a large part of the crowd at the Mobilization Against the War March on April 15, as at least sixty thousand people, many of them young, marched from the Ferry Building to Kezar Stadium in Golden Gate Park to oppose the war and hear Coretta Scott King and Judy Collins. Mrs. King's husband, Martin, marched with Dr. Benjamin Spock, Stokely Carmichael, and Harry Belafonte in New York. The NAACP condemned his anti-war activism, as did the *New York Times*.

When the local Haight Ashbury Merchants Association refused to accept a Black man as a member, the younger store owners organized HIP, the Haight Independent Proprietors. One spin-off was their Council for the Summer of Love, initiated by Tsvi Strauch and his friend, a professor of philosophy at Sonoma State University named Stan McDaniel who had, as he put it, "fallen in love" with the Haight scene. They were both members of a psychedelic garage band called the Amplified Ohm, and under the aegis of the council, they began offering the newest Haight Streeters diversion and a way to avoid the police street sweeps in the shape of Saturday night shows at the All Saints recreation hall. Their April 23 press release also promised weekend afternoon Hatha Yoga lessons on Hippie Hill, just across Stanyan Street in Golden Gate Park. Stan also rented trucks to serve as stages in the Panhandle.

McDaniel and Strauch felt that the Diggers wanted "social chaos," and they did their best to block it, taking down Digger flyers and putting out missives of their own that suggested people emulate hobbits, who knew how to melt discreetly into the underbrush. Stan also persuaded the Thelin brothers to set up a meditation space inside the Psychedelic Shop as a refuge for the weary. One negative result, Jay thought, was that the meditation space substantially cut the area devoted to sales. Bedeviled by "inventory shrinkage" (i.e., shoplifting), the shop lost money that year and closed in October, with Ron giving away the remaining contents.

In the face of headlines like SAN FRANCISCO GIRDS FOR HIPPIE INVASION, the council's efforts were valiant but modest compared to the impending problem. The Diggers' response became ensnared in their own idealistic notions of anarchist purity. By mid-April, their office at All Saints was closed, because no one would take responsibility for enforcing the church's minimal rules about keeping the office and kitchen clean and not using the office as a crash pad. Anyone could claim to be a Digger, but no one wanted to claim the responsibility of scrubbing the kitchen.

Despite considerable strife within his congregation, Father Harris persevered in his expressed admiration for the youth of the Haight, telling *Life*'s Loudon Wainwright that "[the hippies] have some very fine ideas. They believe in sharing and they're against hypocrisy. They're for love and peace.... They may have washed their hands of the Establishment, but in many ways that is quite understandable. Our example has been far from good. These people are trying to find a way, and I admire them for that."

Things only got stranger in May. The *Barb* reported that in the previous month, fifteen storefronts on Haight Street "have either changed names or undergone drastic conversion in an all-out effort to get that tourist buck." A bar called Pall Mall now sold Love Burgers. The Golden Cask bar offered pizza under the logo of "Lee, Sam and Dick."

In Europe, the film *Blow-Up* was awarded the Palme d'Or at the Cannes Film Festival, recognizing that youth culture was at least momentarily regnant.

Los Angeles police announced that they expected seventy thousand people to invade the west side of the city come summer; they needed more men, more laws, and fewer lenient judges. According to Lieutenant Richard

Pilgrims Overrun the Haight

Rodriguez, LSD was the most dangerous drug of all and was likely to lead to violence.

In New York, reported Don McNeill, the Lower East Side's "pseudo-community center," the Dom, now called the Balloon Farm, was shuttered. On Memorial Day weekend, singing and chanting in Tompkins Square Park generated a noise complaint. When the police arrived, young people laughed. "They laughed at us. That's when the trouble started," said police officer John Rodd. Seventy members of the tactical squad arrived, forty hippies were arrested, and batons came down on at least one older person who protested the police behavior.

Once again soothing things, the Grateful Dead played their first East Coast show in Tompkins Square Park the next day, and all was briefly peaceful. In meetings the following week, McNeill reported, "many of the hippies…wished that Emmett Grogan, the Jesus of the Diggers, were back in town. Because he understood these things. He had landed in NY in March and rocked the East Side with a lot of lessons he had learned in San Francisco. He had said to turn on to the Puerto Ricans and fuck the leaders. But a lot of people forgot what he said."

Back in San Francisco, Peter Berg would argue

What…in fact happened, was that the police were the agency that closed down the Haight-Ashbury. You will read euphemisms, or excuses, for the demise of the hippie rebellion as being the introduction of hard drugs, or "the bloom was off the rose," or blahblah. The police closed down the Haight-Ashbury. They brought in mercury vapor lights that burned all night, bright orange. It looked like the Berlin Wall on Haight Street. They made the street one-way, so that traffic barreled through it. They put paddy wagons through it about every 15 minutes, picking up people from the street.

So they militarized Haight Street. And there was a reason for it. It was because we had withdrawn this neighborhood from the control of the city. [laughs]…People were walking DOWN Haight Street six and eight abreast; if you see footage from that period, it's unbelievable, it looks as though there's a parade in progress. And that was normal, daily activity.

296 **The Last Great Dream**

As the summer progressed, Haight Street and the Haight neighborhood became so overcrowded that life there seemed simply untenable. There were two last responses, both of which transferred the spirit of the Haight into new forms—the Haight Ashbury Free Medical Clinic and free-form radio, first at KMPX and then at KSAN.

The clinic was the brainchild of David Smith, among others. He'd been a Haight resident through medical school at UCSF, which loomed four steep blocks above Haight Street on Parnassus Avenue, and he'd observed the neighborhood evolve, as when the doughnut shop at the corner of Frederick and Stanyan began to sell LSD. After the Be-In, which he did not attend, he took LSD as a treatment for alcoholism, and in May, he concluded that "health care is a right, not a privilege."

A public health nurse, Flo Martin, told him about a neighborhood clinic in Watts, and then an LSD dealer he knew pointed out that the city could regulate a public health clinic, but a private practice open to the public was a way around the city's unwillingness to serve the Haight's population. On June 7, David E. Smith and Associates d/b/a the Free Clinic opened for business at 558 Clayton Street. They saw 250 patients the first day. As far as Smith knew, it was the first twenty-four-hour free clinic in the country. UCSF and Stanford doctors volunteered their services so that the only paid employee was a nurse.

One of his partners in medicine was Eugene (as in Debs) Leonard (originally Lenin, changed when the Rosenbergs were executed) Schoenfeld, a former volunteer with Albert Schweitzer. Having experienced LSD and pursued research on the impact of drugs on the brain, Schoenfeld was a trusted member of the community. People asked him for medical advice, and he gave it. Then Max Scherr at the *Barb* asked him to write a column, and a couple of years later when he refused to cross a picket line at the *Barb*, his column moved to the *Chronicle*: Dr. Hip Pocrates.

A second aftereffect to the Haight was "underground radio," which would create a community on the airwaves and spread across the country. In March 1967, Mills College hosted a conference on rock music that included speakers like Phil Spector, Ralph Gleason, and Tom Donahue. The latter mused aloud about why radio ignored everything but singles: "Why isn't rock and roll programmed on an aesthetic, artistic basis, rather than according to a

Pilgrims Overrun the Haight

playlist?" Afterward, Gleason told Donahue about Larry Miller's overnight show on the FM station KMPX, which mixed folk and classical music.

Beginning in 1965, the FCC had begun to limit the amount of programming that could be duplicated between co-owned AM and FM stations. Since FM sounded much better than AM, what had been the preserve of low-budget foreign-language programs began to invite development. Donahue found out that KMPX's phone had been disconnected, which suggested an opening.

By April, he was broadcasting a mélange of music in the afternoons, and by August, KMPX was a full-time rock station. Donahue found a pot dealer named Milan Melvin and hired him to sell advertising. Melvin went to hip businesses and got them to listen to the station, and after that, sales were rather easy—Mnasidika was one of the first customers. Members of the satirical troupe the Committee worked on commercials, as did the comedic group Congress of Wonders. The station also emphasized local musicians. The Committee's Howard Hesseman would sum up the ethos in his character Dr. Johnny Fever, who was much more than sitcom fodder, but rather a true believer in the first church of rock 'n' roll.

Turning on the radio was perhaps a limited substitute for the genuine if fleeting community in the Haight, but it certainly implied the same values and the same joy. For the next two decades, the incarnation later known as KSAN would be an essential part of San Francisco culture.

35

A New Guitar Hero in London—*Sgt. Pepper*

The highwater mark of what happened in the Haight would be the splendid June weekend of the Monterey International Pop Festival, which would connect music from Los Angeles, San Francisco, and London and come to an electric climax with the first American performance of the Jimi Hendrix Experience. Hendrix's journey to stardom was like a bolt of lightning—once it finally got started.

An obscure American guitarist named James Marshall "Jimi" Hendrix landed at London's Heathrow airport on September 24, 1966. On October 1, he sat in with Cream on the classic Howlin' Wolf tune "Killing Floor," his playing so dazzling Cream's Eric Clapton that afterward, the Englishman could barely light a cigarette. With Jeff Beck of the Yardbirds and Pink Floyd's Nick Mason in the audience, Hendrix was a legend among his new English peers in just one week.

He'd come a long way. The product of a dysfunctional childhood blighted by emotional and financial poverty and abandonment, he was shy, introverted, and silent. The guitar was his love and his vehicle for

299

self-expression, to such an extreme that he was fired from his first band after just one set because he was too flashy. It would not be the last time.

Offered the choice of military service or juvenile hall, he became a member of the 101st Airborne. A broken ankle—at least one biographer suggested that it was more a stratagem than an actual injury—set him free, and he found sideman work with the singer Solomon Burke, who found Hendrix's stage behavior so excessive that he supposedly traded him to Otis Redding for two horn players. Redding fired him after a week.

As the Beatles conquered America on *Ed Sullivan*, Hendrix joined the Isley Brothers. There was a tour with B. B. King, another with Little Richard, and yet another with King Curtis & the Kingpins; given Hendrix's penchant for missing shows for transparently flimsy excuses, no gig ever lasted very long. In 1966, he settled in Greenwich Village and began to find his footing, absorbing influences like Bob Dylan—he spent his last dime to buy *Highway 61 Revisited*—and also avant-garde jazz, opening his playing out of strict R & B changes.

By summer, he had a regular gig at Café Wha? with his own band, Jimmy James and the Blue Flames. For the first time, he was free to play what he wanted, and he seized the opportunity. Observing the example of Sun Ra drummer Jimhmi (and sometimes Jimmi) Johnson, he adopted a new spelling to celebrate his own evolution: Jimmy became Jimi.

About then, he met Keith Richards's longtime girlfriend, Linda Keith, a model and English rock scene insider who recognized his talent and set herself the task of promoting him. She invited him, along with others, to her place, asking him if he'd like to do some acid. The story goes that his reply was, "No, but I sure would like to try some of that LSD stuff." He spent his first trip of many listening to Dylan's *Blonde on Blonde*.

On July 2, after the Rolling Stones concert at Forest Hills, Linda brought the band to the Ondine to see Jimi. Bill Wyman and Charlie Watts were enthusiastic, and Brian Jones was enthralled. Mick Jagger and Keith Richards were more reserved, perhaps a bit jealous. Two days later, the Animals arrived in New York, and Linda brought the bass player, Chas Chandler, to Café Wha? Chandler wanted to be a producer. He heard the folk musician Tim Rose play a song called "Hey Joe," which he decided would be a hit as a rock song. To Chandler's considerable amazement, Hendrix pulled out a distinctly

A New Guitar Hero in London—*Sgt. Pepper* 301

rock version of "Hey Joe" at the Café Wha?, and wheels began to spin in Chandler's head.

When the Animals' tour ended two months later in Central Park, Chandler and the Animals' manager, Michael Jeffrey, reconnected with Hendrix. On September 23, the three of them flew first class to London. The British Invasion had reinvigorated rock and roll, and now the colonies would return the favor with a vengeance, sending London a giant of a blues player who could rock with the best. Chandler had a bass player (Noel Redding) and drummer (Mitch Mitchell) chosen and signed by the day of the Cream gig. By mid-December, the Jimi Hendrix Experience's first single, "Hey Joe," was in stores.

Songs came to him, and a young engineer named Eddie Kramer helped put the sounds in his head onto vinyl, using what one biographer described as "phase shifts, double-tracking, space sounds, wind sounds, even a more controlled feedback sound that could melt right into notes…white, pink, and blue noises—red noises." Their effort, an album called *Are You Experienced*, was released in May in England, but not until August in the US. Until then, the single "Hey Joe" had to do; the second single, "Purple Haze," would not be released until the day after the Experience's first American performance, although San Francisco's KMPX would play advance copies of the album extensively.

Propelled by psychedelics, music was the common currency, the essential bond of the youth culture. One album in particular would sum all that up, and naturally, it would come from the Beatles.

When they reassembled at Abbey Road studios in November 1966, several things were clear. One was that their San Francisco show in August had been their last live performance. Consequently, they were free to record anything. John Lennon noted with satisfaction that "if we don't have to tour, then we can record music that we won't ever have to play live, and that means we can create something that's never been heard before: a new kind of record with new kinds of sounds." The album would do their touring for them. After five years of nonstop lunacy, Abbey Road would give them peace, quiet, and privacy. The central inspiration for these new sounds and this new album was LSD.

The Last Great Dream

Late in 1966, Paul McCartney took LSD and found it liberating, both personally and musically. Suddenly, there were fresh possibilities in the world. McCartney described a trip with Lennon: "We had this fantastic thing. We had taken this stuff, incredible really, just looked into each other's eyes....Like just staring and then saying, 'I *know*, man,' and then laughing...and it was great, you know."

They began recording with a Lennon song called "Strawberry Fields Forever," written while he'd been in Spain that summer shooting the film *How I Won the War*. The song mixed mystery and nostalgia, the title taken from a Salvation Army home in Liverpool. Musically, the tone was set by John's new toy, a proto-synthesizer called the Mellotron, which he had brought in to the studio.

With George Harrison playing slide guitar and Ringo Starr's drums muffled by towels, McCartney came up with what their engineer, Geoff Emerick, recalled as a "stunning Mellotron line that opens the song. Paul's inspiration really set the stage. In many ways it was a harbinger of things to come over the next several months." The first version began with "Living is easy with eyes closed," which over the weekend would become the verse after Lennon came up with "Let me take you down" as the opening. After twenty takes, they had two versions with widely varying tempos, both of which Lennon liked. Producer George Martin thought of a frequency changer that could sync them up, and they had it.

After three days, they took up something much older, a ditty they'd played when something broke down mid-set in the Cavern back in Liverpool in another era in their lives, something McCartney had written before he'd even met Lennon, "When I'm Sixty-Four." A combined tribute and sweet satire on Paul's father Jim's style of music, they recorded it with two clarinets and a bass clarinet in a formal classical way that cut, Martin thought, "the lurking schmaltz factor."

"Penny Lane" was actually a bus transfer point between Lennon's and McCartney's childhood homes. As a song, it appears to have been Paul's response to "Strawberry Fields," a perfect portrait of the differing ways the two of them looked into the past—Lennon's version overtly psychedelic, where "nothing is real" and it's all a dream, and philosophical; "It doesn't matter much to me." McCartney's version is equally psychedelic, a kaleidoscope of

A New Guitar Hero in London—*Sgt. Pepper*

memory fragments from a neighborhood barber (the shop was called Bioletti's) to the poppies sold on (World War I) Remembrance Day, but sunnier, bouncy, rhythmic, and charming.

Brian Wilson's *Pet Sounds* was a clear influence; McCartney wanted what he called a "clean" American sound so that his piano comes through untouched. In fact, the track started with four different piano tracks (a conventional one, one with reverb, a prepared piano for a honky-tonk effect, and a harmonium for the high notes) mixed down to one.

"Good Morning Good Morning" was Lennon's dour ode to his life in Kenwood, the rather boring suburban mansion in a gated portion of the golfer/banker town of Weybridge, Surrey, that manager Brian Epstein had organized for him. Triggered by a breakfast cereal advertisement, it's a fine excoriation of anomie and the suburban rat race, where life is a half-asleep ruin, although Lennon would later reject it as filler.

Around Christmas 1966, Epstein, nervous about their lowered profile in the absence of touring, pleaded for a single. George Martin selected "Strawberry Fields" and "Penny Lane," which he later acknowledged as the single biggest mistake of his professional life. Both songs were entirely worthy of the A-side designation; consequently, due to the arcane rules of the *Billboard* charts, they competed against each other after the mid-February release. So when it only reached number two, the first Beatle single in thirteen tries not to reach the top, the music business whispered of failure.

Epstein grew ever-more nervous with their relatively slow progress as both their audience and the business became impatient. The Who's Pete Townshend told *Melody Maker* in mid-January that "I'm a bit disappointed they're not still making records. If they are, then I wish they'd hurry up. They are basically my main source of inspiration—and everybody else's for that matter."

By mid-January, Lennon would stop at McCartney's place in Saint John's Wood in the morning, where they'd get high and write before going into the studio. Since the album was largely determined by Paul and John, George and Ringo tended to sit around a lot, which led to Ringo learning how to play chess with their road manager, Mal Evans.

What they worked on next was a new song primarily by Lennon called "A Day in the Life." An inveterate newspaper reader, Lennon had been struck that December by the car-crash death of their friend Tara Browne, the handsome heir to the Guinness fortune and in general destiny's favored child. A meditation on fame and fate, the song took off from there, going so far that McCartney thought it was more about drugs than a car accident seemingly caused by alcohol. A bit in the *Daily Mail* gave Lennon the line about four thousand holes in Blackburn, Lancashire.

Briefly stuck, he turned it over to McCartney, who came up with the middle section, a brisk take on the working day that ends with a smoke and a dream, which was pretty much the way he and Lennon lived at the time of recording.

Just as they closed in on "A Day in the Life," McCartney conceived a major new song, "Sgt. Pepper's Lonely Hearts Club Band," a rocker with a stinging guitar lead that managed to have french horns dominate the sound at the instrumental break. In part a whimsical dalliance with Edwardian images, it established an alter ego that would perform the album for the Beatles. Later in the recording process, they realized that they could add the sounds of an audience with an orchestra tuning up so that this new band was performing a concert. McCartney's voice introduces the song, but it was important that Lennon's voice dominated the group singing; it was his band, too.

"Sgt. Pepper" now established, they returned to finish "A Day in the Life," which would require a full orchestra. Martin trimmed McCartney's request from ninety to forty musicians, but it would be a memorable night in the studio. For the penultimate crescendo, each instrument was to play a note from its lowest and quietest pitch and volume to highest and loudest over twenty-four bars, about forty seconds. Unusual, and only the beginning.

"Let's make the session more than just a session," said Paul. "Let's make it a happening." The finest symphonic musicians in London put on funny hats and clown noses. An assortment of friends, including Mick Jagger and Marianne Faithfull and Keith Richards, Pattie Harrison, Brian Jones, Graham Nash, and Mike Nesmith, were invited to sit on the floor and witness the festivities. The band wore what Martin described as "multicoloured flowing robes, stripy 'loon' flared pants, brilliant waistcoats, gaudy silk neckerchiefs, love beads, bangles, baubles, badges and bells."

The end-of-the-world piano chord that brings the record to a close had Paul, John, Ringo, Mal, and George Martin each at a piano, all of them hitting

A New Guitar Hero in London—*Sgt. Pepper*

the chord at once. It lasted forty-five seconds, with the engineer bringing the volume up as the notes decayed.

As the Beatles resumed work, McCartney effectively became producer, working until dawn and recording until his fingers bled. "Fixing a Hole," with George Martin on harpsichord, took only two days. It was in fact an homage to marijuana, which for McCartney let his mind wander in creative ways, liberated his art, and opened him to more possibilities.

"She's Leaving Home," another McCartney ballad, set his vocal against a string orchestra, with not a note played by a Beatle. A tender meditation on generations and the painfully common intra-family upsets of the '60s, it would resonate deeply with the youth culture in general and with all those runaways on Haight Street: "Home is the one thing that money can't buy."

"Getting Better" is another lovely example of the way Lennon and McCartney worked, with McCartney singing, "Getting better," and Lennon chiming, "Can't get no worse." Though McCartney is widely assumed to be the primary author, the business about beating "his woman" is actually from Lennon. Just to round it out as a full Beatles tune, there's a tamboura drone from George Harrison.

The last song primarily written by McCartney was "Lovely Rita," a humorous take seemingly sparked by the American expression *meter maid* (versus the British "traffic warden").

While shooting a promotional film for the "Strawberry"/"Penny" single in January, Lennon wandered into an antique shop and found a charming poster from 1843 advertising Pablo Fanque's Circus Royal. Inside Lennon's mind, the rather wordy poster rearranged itself into a jaunty song, "Being for the Benefit of Mr. Kite!" that he later described as a painting, "a pure watercolour." Musically complex, it included a harmonium, two different kinds of organs, and a bass harmonica played by Mal Evans. And when nothing else would do, Martin told Emerick to take some tape of the organs, cut it up, throw it in the air, and then splice it off the floor. If it sounded too literal, they ran it backward. Lennon had wanted an antique calliope sound that would make one smell the sawdust, and they succeeded.

Harrison finally had his moment in the sun with "Within You Without You," recorded with members of London's Asian Music Circle. It affirmed

The Last Great Dream

Harrison's philosophical devotion to anti-materialism and spiritual search; in truth, Harrison acknowledged, his heart was still in India, where he'd been studying sitar and Indian philosophy with Ravi Shankar. The fact that one portion of the album had music representing an entirely different and very spiritual culture seemed profoundly important to many listeners.

By the end of February, they were, thought Emerick, getting tired. Inspired by his three-year-old son Julian's picture of a schoolmate, Lennon's "Lucy in the Sky with Diamonds" was a marvelous composition and unquestionably psychedelic, even if he claimed that his source was primarily *Alice in Wonderland* (itself psychedelic even if Charles Dodgson never inhaled).

Nearing the end, Lennon and McCartney looked at each other and realized that they hadn't yet written a song for Ringo. Can't have that! Fortunately, they did not retain the original title, "Bad Finger Boogie." In its limited vocal range, simplicity, and universality, "With a Little Help from My Friends" is perfect; there's a reason that another musician, Joe Cocker, could make it a hit of his own.

Expressing solidarity and kindness to all, the song sets the tone for the entire album. They lived it, as well. They finished recording at nearly 6:00 a.m., and Starr was ready for bed. They cajoled him into staying to do the lead vocal. Then the three of them surrounded Starr in what Emerick called a "touching show of unity." The track was done.

Neil Aspinall, their personal assistant, pointed out, "You've given a concert," an illusion they'd created with audience sounds and studio effects. "Why don't you wrap up the concert with another version of 'Sgt. Pepper'?" On April 1, they came into Abbey Road to record the reprise. They were in the wrong studio, number one, which was an enormous barn built for hundred-piece orchestras, but Emerick built a hut of baffles in the middle, and they played "Sgt. Pepper" again.

They had not forgotten how to be a live band. The reprise was warm and beautifully energetic, capturing the feeling of a band at the end of a tour. Between takes, they looked at contact sheets of photos for the cover. Art-directed by Robert Fraser, it was created by London artists Jann Haworth and Peter Blake, who worked on the conceit that the Sgt. Pepper band had just played a concert and was posing with a cluster of fans behind them. Their fans were in fact their heroes; John put in a list, as did Paul. George asked for Indian gurus. Ringo left it to the others.

Blake and Haworth created an assemblage rather in the tradition of Bruce Conner and Wally Hedrick: Lenny Bruce, Bob Dylan, Terry Southern, Aldous Huxley, Marlon Brando, Shirley Temple, Laurel and Hardy, four gurus for George, Carl Jung, Aleister Crowley, Dylan Thomas, Edgar Allan Poe, Lewis Carroll, Albert Einstein, Karlheinz Stockhausen. And at Fraser's suggestion, Wallace Berman. It was, said one observer, "utopian, ironic, dreamlike, sophisticated but also cartoony—a pop art shrine, screaming with color," and very possibly the most effective album cover in rock history.

Released on June 1 in both England and the United States, the response was almost universally ecstatic. In one historian's words, it was "a revelation, a message from on high" to Western youth. Abbie Hoffman told Derek Taylor, "It was Beethoven coming to the supermarket! It allowed someone like myself to see the vehicle, the style, the modality in which we could put across counterculture politics—anti-war, anti-racist, anti-bomb—and the rest is history."

Early that June, John Barlow, a Wesleyan University student and Millbrook regular who also happened to be a close friend of the Grateful Dead's rhythm guitarist Bob Weir, brought the Dead to Millbrook. He also brought along a copy of *Sgt. Pepper*. After the record ended, Barlow later wrote, "Tim Leary stood up and in this incredibly pretentious, sententious mystical voice, said, 'My work is finished. Now it's out.' In a funny way, he was right. Because from that point forward, it was all going to take care of itself."

36

Monterey Pop

Responding to the Sunset Strip police riots in the fall of 1966, Byrds manager Jim Dickson and other music business figures organized CAFF (Community Action for Facts and Freedom). Benny Shapiro and Alan Pariser put on a benefit for them in February 1967, and then in March announced a larger show, to be held in Monterey in June. They soon had ex-Beatles and current Byrds publicist Derek Taylor on board. In March, Pariser and Taylor paid a visit to the royal couple of the LA music scene, John and Michelle Phillips, at their mansion on 783 Bel Air Road, once the home of Jeanette MacDonald.

John and Michelle, instantly joined by their producer and record company head Lou Adler, seized the idea and ran with it. They paid off Pariser's partner Shapiro and turned it into a nonprofit, and with Taylor's help soon had Paul McCartney, Donovan, Mick Jagger, Smokey Robinson, Johnny Rivers, Paul Simon, and Terry Melcher on the board. They set up an office in an empty club at 8428 Sunset Boulevard, and John and Michelle began to keep office hours. Shapiro and Pariser had signed Ravi Shankar to his regular fee, but he would be the only paid musician.

310 **The Last Great Dream**

On April 9, Paul McCartney took a brief holiday after recording *Sgt. Pepper* and visited Taylor in Los Angeles, hanging out with John and Michelle and David Crosby and Jim McGuinn, telling them all about Jimi Hendrix. The London end of psychedelia—and early in the process, it became quite clear that the Monterey International Pop Festival would be a celebration of hippie and psychedelic music—now had its first representative.

Paul Simon became a central figure in the development of the festival and the recruitment of San Francisco bands for the best and yet oddest of reasons, a song he had written. "The 59th Street Bridge Song (Feelin' Groovy)," recorded with Dave Brubeck's rhythm section of Joe Morello on drums and Eugene Wright on bass, had been part of Simon & Garfunkel's *Parsley, Sage, Rosemary and Thyme* album, released the previous October. The liner notes were written by the sage of San Francisco music, Ralph Gleason, who anointed the pair as paragons of "the philosophy of New Youth which is that of creativity AGAINST the machine and, thus, FOR humanity."

Groovy was a favorite hippie expression, taken from '40s jazz slang. Recording with Gene Krupa in 1941, Anita O'Day told her co-vocalist Roy Eldridge to "come here Roy and get groovy." Mezz Mezzrow used the expression. One of Dizzy Gillespie's masterpieces was "Groovin' High." Simon's song made him simpatico and graced him with a deep well of credibility, so that San Francisco's hippies trusted him, just as they did not trust Angelenos Adler and Phillips, who were assumed to be conventional denizens of the music business, which bands like the Grateful Dead, Big Brother and the Holding Company, and the Quicksilver Messenger Service did not entirely wish to be part of.

Somewhere in there, show publicist Taylor decided to fill a slow news day with an entirely spurious press release suggesting that one of the recipients of the festival's proceeds would be the Diggers, who were not pleased at having their name so appropriated. Peter Coyote, Peter Berg, Emmett Grogan, and Hells Angel Bill "Sweet William" Fritsch went to Los Angeles to meet with the promoters. Their message was simple: don't use our name to make your event hip.

As Coyote put it, "I said it nicely, Berg said it coldly, and Bill made it dangerous." Taylor understood and split. "That's it, I'm out of here. These guys have always been the hippest. If they say it's not happening, it's not happening. So I'm not playing. Why waste time?" While in Los Angeles, an undisclosed someone

Monterey Pop

offered them $2,500 "to help your work." Grogan picked up the phone, Coyote wrote, called Huey Newton, and donated the money to the Black Panthers.

Released May 13, "San Francisco (Be Sure to Wear Flowers in Your Hair)" served to market Monterey Pop perfectly, although Adler, who produced it with songwriter John Phillips, later denied it was so intended. No one in the San Francisco bands would have believed him. Phillips went to San Francisco to recruit bands, and he did not impress. The Dead's comanager Rock Scully would recall, "The hip malapropisms, the music-biz clichés, the fake sincerity. We are soon to discover that once you get beyond the fur hat and the beads he is just like a goddamn LA slicko."

Paul Simon would save things. Visiting the Dead at 710 Ashbury Street, he impressed Scully, who would recall that "Paul Simon is the spiritual leader of the festival and most of us get involved because of him. He rises above all the scaly maneuvering and makes us see it from the audience's point of view. The combination of Paul Simon's vision and Derek Taylor's acidic poise convinces us in the end. We do it for the fans and fuck the rest of it."

A further meeting with Ralph Gleason that ended with his blessing sealed the deal. Once he was on board, he pushed the promoters to add more San Francisco bands to the obvious choice of Jefferson Airplane, which had already been signed. By May 19, the *Barb* would headline, NO SHUCK!! / MONTEREY POP FESTIVAL LOOKS LIKE TRUE LOVE.

It was the pivotal moment of the festival. The promoters needed the credibility the San Francisco groups offered; after all, the promoters were selling it as a hippie festival: "Be free; wear flowers, bring bells." The extremely pro-LA writer Domenic Priore would argue that the energy and fire of the Los Angeles scene would channel into Monterey, which he concluded was simply "an outgrowth of Sunset Strip rebellion." The media would focus on San Francisco, he wrote, "whose elitist attitudes brought rock music to unheard-of levels of pretension....Self-absorbed, self-indulgent excess."

Well, no. The Los Angeles bands, which included the Association, Johnny Rivers, and the Mamas & the Papas, tended toward middle-of-the-road pop. The Byrds and Buffalo Springfield had been the real thing, but both were now riven by internal stresses. Neither would triumph at Monterey.

There was one further major point of contention. Late in the game, Phillips and Adler decided to bring in the documentary film director D. A.

Pennebaker, whose portrait of Bob Dylan, *Dont Look Back*, had just opened. Adler then made a deal with ABC television to broadcast the resulting film. All of which sounded like money, and with the exception of Jefferson Airplane, now managed by the wily Bill Graham, the ever-skeptical San Francisco bands said no to being filmed. The arguments would continue up until each band's showtime—and, in one important example, after.

As the kickoff approached and the success of the festival seemed ever-more assured, Scully, his partner Danny Rifkin, and Chet Helms fought for a free stage to be set up at the local junior college. "Virtually everyone who played on the main stage played in some configuration on the free stage," said Helms. "One jam involved Jimi Hendrix on guitar and David Freiberg on bass, and they played for several hours. We were totally out of our minds on acid and it was wonderful." Given his state of mind, the time estimate might reasonably be assumed to be mythic.

By Friday, June 16, the city of Monterey was overflowing with hippies, and they would turn out to be the first stars of the festival. The concert seating area of 7,500 was full, each seat decorated with an orchid flown in from Hawaii.

The surrounding fairgrounds featured forty shops and booths, which a young visitor recalled as a "county fair for the counterculture, with booths selling Fillmore posters and god's eye weavings." John Cooke, a veteran of the Cambridge folk scene who was there to work for Pennebaker, described it as a "tent-alley bazaar outside the arena, where the incenses and oils give off Middle Eastern aromas. The kaleidoscopic array of tie-dye and batik and beads and face painters is dazzling." There was a meditation room in the Seminar Building, a colloquium with Ralph Gleason, and a guitar workshop with Jim McGuinn and Michael Bloomfield. The simple knowledge of the free stage made things feel like preinvasion Haight Street.

Which was very good news, because there were many tens of thousands of fans above concert capacity roaming the fairgrounds, enough to bring on panic attacks in the most sanguine police official. *And nothing bad happened.*

The enduring image of Haight-Ashbury is of beautiful, beatifically high young people, flowers in their hair, listening to wonderful music while positively

Monterey Pop 313

exuding peace and tranquility. For four days at Monterey, it was reality, and it colored the next decade and more of the youth culture.

All the values that the avant-garde had represented, from the pacifism and mystic exploration of Kenneth Rexroth and Robert Duncan, the anti-racism, the joyful exploration of sensuality, all of it, would attach to the label "sex, drugs, and rock and roll." The label was perhaps reductionist, but the reality was far more complex and nuanced than has been commonly understood.

Things were so good that Rifkin, though a purist almost-Digger about Adler and Phillips, called his friend Jay Thelin and said, "You gotta get down here."

The music the first night was soft rock—the Association, the Paupers, Lou Rawls, Beverley Martyn, and Johnny Rivers—until Eric Burdon and the Animals. Simon & Garfunkel closed. The *Village Voice's* Robert Christgau would describe Simon & Garfunkel as "rock 'n' roll for people who don't like rock 'n' roll." In terms of radio play, they were certainly the biggest group in America at the time. Seeing his chance and wrapped in hippie love, Simon decided to debut his stoner anthem "Punky's Dilemma" at Monterey, knowing this audience would get it.

Saturday afternoon brought more edge, more volume, more rock. Canned Heat was from Los Angeles, but their commitment to blues gave them a great deal more weight than, say, the Association. They were followed by the first musical explosion of the festival, Big Brother and the Holding Company with Janis Joplin. The previous December, she'd been in the front row to see Otis Redding at the Fillmore, accidentally dosing herself on the first night, which was perhaps an ideal catalyst to further her transformation from plain folkie to rock queen. A few weeks before that pivotal night, she and other band members had gone to see Big Mama Thornton at the Both/And club. Joplin went backstage and asked Big Mama for permission to sing her song "Ball and Chain." The answer was a qualified yes: "Don't fuck it up," Big Mama said.

Joplin looked out at the audience and saw her people, later telling her sister, "Those were real flower children. They really were beautiful and gentle and completely open, man." Every bit of her remarkable capacity for emotional

314 **The Last Great Dream**

extravagance flashed into overdrive; Nat Hentoff said seeing her was like "being in contact with an overwhelming life force." In showbiz parlance, she flat-out killed.

Which began an argument. Big Brother's manager was Julius Karpen, a onetime Prankster and full-bore countercultural anti-materialist. His distrust of the LA music business duo of Adler and Phillips meant that the cameras had been off during the set. Staggered by her performance, Pennebaker was wild to have her in his film, and said so to Albert Grossman, who was there because his client Mike Bloomfield's new band, the Electric Flag, would close the afternoon. Big Brother turned to Grossman—after all, he was *Bob Dylan's manager*—and Grossman told them to do it. They were hastily scheduled to play a second set on Sunday.

Country Joe and the Fish. Al Kooper. The Paul Butterfield Blues Band, in its *Resurrection of Pigboy Crabshaw* incarnation. Quicksilver Messenger Service. Steve Miller. The Electric Flag, which wasn't ready for its first show. Bloomfield had been nervous and felt they weren't very good, especially after superb sets by Miller and Butterfield. The audience loved Flag anyway, which actually disturbed Bloomfield even more than his own performance.

The aura of "peace, love, flowers" had taken firm hold, and police chief Frank Marinello began sending some of his men home. One of the quintessential photographs of the festival featured a police motorcycle decorated with orchids threaded on its antenna by its smiling, pleasantly unbusy officer. It really was like that.

Backstage, Owsley Stanley handed out free samples of his latest batch, which he'd dubbed Monterey Purple, and hobnobbed with Brian Jones of the Stones, who'd come just to hang out. Stanley had just come from Denver, where he and his friends were tabbing up one hundred thousand doses, 270 micrograms to the pill, which was half the size of an aspirin, and colored purple. In the course of the weekend, he would stuff a camera lens case full of those tabs for delivery to John Lennon, which greatly pleased both of them. Judy Collins chatted up Janis Joplin, and Candice Bergen made the rounds.

Moving between backstage and their special row in the dress circle was a gaggle of record company executives that included, most prominently, Mo Ostin (Warner Bros.), Jerry Wexler (Atlantic), Jerry Moss (A&M), and Clive Davis (Columbia), all of whom would take cues for the next decade from what

Monterey Pop

315

they saw that weekend. Monterey, wrote musician/author Ben Sidran, would also be "a celebration of an industry about to explode....It was the beginning of the end of innocence." In the next ten years, rock would effectively take over the music business, and an enormous percentage of the idiosyncrasy and personality of the business would be washed away by a tidal wave of money. Two decades later, the corporatization would be complete.

Saturday night: Moby Grape had already been struck by lightning twice that month. In an ill-conceived promotional stunt, their record company had simultaneously released five singles, which seemed to almost everyone an act of extreme hubris. Hours after the launch party, three band members were arrested for canoodling with seventeen-year-olds and thus contributing to the delinquency of a minor. Ensnared in the machinations of their manager Matthew Katz, their set would not be in the movie.

Hugh Masekela. The Byrds. Laura Nyro.

With the Head Lights light show throbbing and shimmering on a screen behind them, Jefferson Airplane created the second epic moment of the weekend. Radio and their record had made them somewhat familiar, so it was not quite the shock that Big Brother's set had brought, but the Airplane delivered in a huge way, and the normally self-critical Grace Slick would cherish the day as "perfect...excellent in every way." The trees broke up the sun into "soft beams, making everything look like a Disney version of Sherwood Forest."

She continued: "We were all shamans of equal power. Channeling an unknown energy, seeking fluidity, I felt like a princess in a benign court—one without thrones or crowns....The audience was just more of 'us.'...It was shades of Huxley, Leary, the surrealists, Gertrude Stein, Kafka—the inexhaustible list of artists who'd encouraged multiple levels of observation. It was our turn."

Booker T. and the MG's. And then the third boom, Otis Redding.

Not too far from the stage, a soldier at the Defense Language Institute in the Presidio of Monterey named Mike Hochanadel heard the roar from the fairgrounds through his barracks window on Friday night. On Saturday, he hitched over.

When I got to the Fairgrounds, I realized I didn't have the four or six bucks it cost to get in. So I went around back to the end of the arena opposite the stage. And I climbed a tree, high enough that I could see in. Some climbers jumped out of the trees into the place, but security people chased them down in a sort of sport thing. As it got dark, I could see Brian Jones walking by himself at the back of the place.

Otis had the MGs and Mar-Keys behind him but he could have killed us backed up by chumps. Of course they weren't chumps, and they double killed us. What a great grooving soul machine!

One of the great voices in all American musical history, Redding represented the triumph of soul music, standing in for all of Stax, James Brown, and Aretha Franklin, who'd finally found the right record company in Atlantic and that March had put out the first of many great albums, *I Never Loved a Man the Way I Love You*. Her song "Respect" was number one that June. No singer was ever better equipped than Otis to close a show, and he did it up royally with "Try a Little Tenderness."

Sunday afternoon was devoted solely to Ravi Shankar and his equally brilliant partner, tabla player Allarakha. Shankar might not have approved of the use of psychedelics, but the rosy glow in which he was watched certainly seemed to aid the rapt concentration of the audience on classical Indian music, a performance that was one of the pivotal moments in the history of Indian culture and the Western world.

Sunday night: the Blues Project.

Big Brother and the Holding Company, redux. They cut to the chase, playing "Combination of the Two" and then "Ball and Chain," and Joplin made sure the performance was movie-worthy. In fact, it was the fourth boom.

The Group with No Name, which was led by Cyrus Faryar of the Modern Folk Quartet. Buffalo Springfield, with David Crosby substituting for Neil Young. Band members recall Crosby as rushing his parts, to which they attributed the decision to leave Buffalo Springfield out of the movie.

The Who's first American shows had been a nine-day run with Cream at the 58th Street Theatre in New York, having released two singles in America without much of a stir. They'd come to Monterey after playing Friday night at the Fillmore Auditorium. Backstage at Monterey, Townshend took notice of who was on the bill and declined to try to follow Hendrix. A coin toss ensued, and Pete got his wish. They would precede.

They were great. Introduced by Eric Burdon as "a group that will destroy you in more ways than one," they charged into "Substitute." Flailing magnificently away on the drums, Keith Moon generated enough energy to power Manhattan. Townshend looked foppish in a brocade jacket complete with lace stock at his throat, but he played like a buzz saw. Closing with "My Generation," they finished off something under half an hour of music with a memorable destructo-orgy of instrument demolition. Townshend smashed his Fender, then stabbed his amp with the neck as the festival sound crew scurried to rescue precious microphones. It was among the most memorable debuts ever.

The Grateful Dead. In his review, the *Voice*'s Robert Christgau would describe their performance of "Viola Lee Blues" as "the best guitar-playing of the festival." Perhaps, but the Dead didn't have a trace of theatrics in their stage presence, and it seems highly unlikely that anyone would particularly remember their set once the next act finished.

Bob Seidemann, a photographer and Haight Street regular, was backstage and remembered Jimi Hendrix performing a truly heroic metamorphosis. "I saw him take, literally, a handful of Owsley tabs. At least four, maybe six... And then he crumpled up in the corner....And he looked like a bag of laundry in the corner of the room, and people were taking bets if he could even stand, much less get onstage...guys came and picked him up, and sort of walked him to the stage. And as soon as he got onstage, he transformed into Jimi Hendrix, from a crumpled bunch of laundry into the greatest rock-and-roll guitar player in history."

His first album, *Are You Experienced*, would not be released in the US until August. His first American single, "Purple Haze," would come out on the day after the festival. Although KMPX was playing much of the first album already, a large part of his set would be material that would be brand-new to the audience. It didn't matter.

"Killing Floor." "Foxy Lady." Dylan's "Like a Rolling Stone," complete with a quotation from "Strangers in the Night." "Rock Me Baby," associated with B. B. King. "Hey Joe." "The Wind Cries Mary." "Purple Haze." And then what he called "the English and American combined anthem," "Wild Thing."

Hendrix had taken blues guitar into the twenty-first century, filling it with explorations of psychedelic space that suggested what might have happened if

Robert Johnson had been able to experience LSD and play an electric guitar. Allen Ginsberg's message from his time doing psychedelics in South America was "Widen the area of consciousness." Hendrix represented that notion as manifested in music.

Then he turned showman. "I just want to grab you, man, and just umm kiss you, but dig, I just can't do that…so what I want to do, I'm going to sacrifice something right here that I really love.…Don't get mad, don't get mad, no." With that, he squirted lighter fluid on his Stratocaster and set it afire. It wasn't the first time, and only possibly the last. But it was a great way to end a set.

The Grateful Dead's Bob Weir and his friend, actor and lyricist Gerrit Graham, gave some thought to the Haight-Ashbury scene in a song called "Two Djinn," working from the premise that a dream captured is already falsified, that only the act of dreaming is authentic. I think they were quite right. It is the story of the '60s. The dream died, but the dreaming continues.

> *A short while back, the door flung wide*
> *We all saw good luck on the other side*
> *The door blew shut, but here's the deal*
> *Dreams are lies, it's the dreaming that's real*
> *Dreams are lies, it's the dreaming that's real…*
> *It's the dreaming that's real…*

AFTERWORD

The combination of civic intransigence and sheer population overload served to make the Haight a dysfunctional place for years to come. But the creativity that had manifested there would change American culture in an enormous variety of ways from 1967 to the present and on into the future.

The impact of the Haight on American culture would be profound, although limited to realms of lifestyle and consciousness rather than politics and power. "The new consciousness itself, with its definitely Buddhist foundations, was also eventually ingested into middle-class culture," wrote Lawrence Ferlinghetti. It was a revolution, but the middle-class culture "was thus able to abort any true political revolution."

The remarkable ability of capitalism to absorb and turn a profit on criticism, making anything into a consumer product, does not make the Haight's collective vision of the world wrong, merely insufficient.

Instead of supplanting the power structure, the Haight and its kin affected sexuality. The image of the gentle hippie challenged the reigning paradigm. The questions raised would clear space for feminism (however benighted the average sexual relationship in the Haight might have been) and eventually lead to increasing freedom for all those who did not fit the heterosexual template.

Afterword

Post–Rachel Carson, Peter Berg was an early and significant environmental thinker, later grousing that "it's a pain in the ass being 30 years forward." A major proponent of bioregionalism, he would argue that the "ecological identity of a human being has to become the center" of human identity, that the economic and social impact of ecological changes, not "birds and bunnies," needed to be considered to "redefine the purpose, aim, activities, and objectives of human lives." At the time of this writing, the crisis in the planet's climate makes these issues impossible to miss. But Berg and the Diggers were highlighting them nearly sixty years ago.

The children of the Haight had grown up in the '50s on a diet deeply influenced by World War II that featured prepared and frozen foods grown on fields treated by one or more of the sixty-five approved pesticides—DDT foremost—that were the side effects of wartime nerve gas research. In the next decade, scientists would develop four hundred additives for the harvested food.

The psychedelic experience encouraged sensitivity to everything, and this frequently manifested itself in dietary issues. The hippies turned to what the historian Jonathan Kauffman called the "preindustrial roots of food," drawing on sources from "health food faddists, rogue nutritionists, mystical German farmers, [and] Japanese dietary prophets" like the macrobiotic theorist George Ohsawa, among others. Eating brown rice became a sociopolitical statement. Sugar was regarded with the deepest suspicion. Since Americans preferred bread to rice, the Diggers added whole-grain bread made in coffee cans to their cuisine. More sophisticated versions came from the Zen Center's Tassajara monastery; *The Tassajara Bread Book* would be a bestseller.

Haight residents had Far Fetched Foods close by on Page Street, and a few blocks away in the inner Sunset, Fred Rohé's New Age Natural Foods. Rohé was a New Yorker who'd been lured to San Francisco in 1959 by reading *On the Road*. In 1965, he bought a vitamin shop near the Haight and turned it into New Age, a store stocking whole grains in bulk along with tamari and miso, the staples of the macrobiotic diet. Spread by San Franciscans like Paul Hawken (later founder of Smith & Hawken) and former light show artist Roger Hillyard at Erewhon in Boston, natural food would develop into a $40 billion annual business.

The word *organic*, as applied to food, became an essential selling point. At the highest end, Alice Waters opened Chez Panisse to sell locally sourced organic food that was appropriate to the region and season. Having been

Afterword

moved by Mario Savio while a student at UC Berkeley, she was definitely ready to change things. Her taste embraced what she described as "formality and beauty and deliberation." Chez Panisse delivered that, splendidly.

The psychedelic experience encouraged the feel of natural fibers in clothing as well. After getting a graduate degree in marine biology, Jeanne Rose came to the Bay Area and took LSD, which brought her a personal belief system combining the Goddess of Nature, the *I Ching*, and Buddhism. She began sewing for her daughter, and after friends of hers in the music scene admired the results, she became the seamstress to many bands, most notably Jefferson Airplane. Her supple, organic creations and simple word of mouth put her into the pages of the *Village Voice* and *Women's Wear Daily*.

After a car accident and subsequent health problems, she went one day to the UC San Francisco medical library high above the Haight and found a seventeenth-century book by Sir Kenelm Digby, a natural philosopher. After studying distillation with a cognac maker and later with herbalists, she began preparing various formulations, starting with what she called *Bruise Juice*, which won friends for what seemed to be effective healing properties. One thing led to another, and she became active with preparations for aromatherapy. In the fifty years after, she has advocated for natural skin care, cosmetics, and health products in twenty-five books that began with the first American book of herbalism, *Herbs & Things*.

The skeptic might dismiss these phenomena as soft dreams of the hippie, although they have clearly had a substantial economic impact. But no sober person would suggest that the personal computer industry is a trivial aspect of contemporary life. A few years after the Trips Festival, Stewart Brand joined with the Portola Institute, birthplace of his *Whole Earth Catalog*, which facilitated access to the tools necessary for the communal movement of the '70s. Philosophically, it posed the idea that a new way of thinking about tools could lead to other alterations in consciousness. The tool they perhaps most affected was the computer.

One of the other people at Portola was a man named Bob Albrecht, who was a key player in the Homebrew Computer Club, which included two young men named Steve Wozniak and Steve Jobs, founders of Apple. Fred Moore, who had staged a hunger strike against required ROTC service at Cal, was the cofounder of Homebrew; peace values were another essential element.

Afterword

Early in the decade, Myron Stolaroff had offered psychedelics to engineers and others, including Brand, from all over the then nascent Silicon Valley. One result was the idea of the personal computer, a vision that would fuel the Homebrewers. There was a very basic reason why the personal computer was developed near Stanford rather than MIT; the atmosphere of the Haight and LSD imparted a vision of computers that served individuals rather than the original model, of computers the size of entire rooms served by Lilliputian attendants.

However much these manifestations changed or will change things at the very heart of life is open to much challenge. As we hurtle toward what clearly already appears to be environmental apocalypse, it may all be moot. What happened in the Haight was, as with all things, subject to Samuel Beckett's exhortation in the novella *Worstward Ho*: "Try again. Fail again. Fail better."

ACKNOWLEDGMENTS

This book is the fourth and last installment of what has turned out to be my life's work, telling the story of the postwar counterculture in (mostly) America. As such, I'm going to note people, some long gone, who contributed to the first three, as well.

For *Desolate Angel:* John Clellon Holmes, Lucien Carr, Tony Sampas, Stephen B. Oates, Jules Chametzky, Eileen Geoghegan, Jeff Briss, Maggie McNally, and Mary Driscoll.

For *A Long Strange Trip:* Jerry Garcia, Robert Hunter, Eileen Law, Janet Soto-Mayor Knudsen, Sue Stephens, Dick Latvala, Lawrence "Ram Rod" Shurtliff, Lou Tambakos, Barbara Lewit, Sandy Rosen, Nick Meriwether.

For *On Highway 61:* Dennis Alpert, Madeline Dames, Dick Waterman, Charlie Winton, Kelly Winton.

This volume began when Anthea Hartig (then of the San Francisco Historical Society, now at the Smithsonian) invited me to curate a photo show documenting and celebrating the fiftieth anniversary of the Summer of Love. It was a wonderful treasure hunt, and the best treasure was realizing that this was an ideal project for me. Alisa Leslie was my partner in crime for the show and helped greatly with the photographs for the book.

Joel Selvin lent books and encouragement. Tsvi Strauch, still living on Ashbury Street, shared his memories. Ramón Sender was supremely helpful.

323

Acknowledgments

John Lyon, a wonderful collector of ephemera from the era, shared his holdings with me. One of my readers was a Zen friend, Diane Miller. My first reader was my friend Pamela Hamilton. Jim Scriba shared interesting information about the art scene in Sausalito. Lisa Dunseth and Christina Moretta of the SF Public Library were—as seemingly all librarians are—remarkably kind. My wonderful agent Sarah Lazin took care of business and brought me to my editor Ben Schafer.

Special thanks to my family, Season, Jono, Julian, and Elias Korchin.

GLOSSARY OF NAMES

Ackerman, Gerald. At UC Berkeley in the late 1940s, he was briefly a lover of Robert Duncan's before going on to a career as an art historian.

Adam, Helen. A San Francisco poet from Scotland heavily influenced by the supernatural. Her poetry added mysticism to the San Francisco Renaissance.

Agee, James. Author of *Let Us Now Praise Famous Men* and *A Death in the Family*. Influential film critic for *Time* magazine and author of the scripts for *The African Queen* and *The Night of the Hunter*.

Albin, Peter. Folk musician, student at SF State, resident at 1090 Page Street, bass player for Big Brother and the Holding Company.

Albright, Thomas. *San Francisco Chronicle* art critic. A major supporter of the avant-garde painters in San Francisco in the 1950s and '60s.

Allen, Don. Editor at Grove Press who was responsible for *Evergreen #2*, the groundbreaking Beat issue. He then expanded it into *The New American Poetry*, the standard tome of the era. Allen was also an early student of Zen.

Anderson, Margaret. Founder and editor of *The Little Review*, one of the first modernist poetry journals, which published T. S. Eliot, Ezra Pound, and the first chapters of Joyce's *Ulysses* in America.

325

Glossary of Names

Anger, Kenneth. Experimental filmmaker who concerned himself with surrealism, homoeroticism, and the occult, especially Aleister Crowley. His gay-themed *Fireworks* was prosecuted for obscenity, but he was exonerated. He also produced the magnificently trashy gossip tome *Hollywood Babylon*.

Anslinger, Harry. Longtime head of the Federal Bureau of Narcotics, a racist who explicitly targeted African American jazz musicians. Joe McCarthy's source for morphine.

Arensberg, Walter and Louise. Legendary art collectors. They became close to Marcel Duchamp while living in New York City, then settled in Los Angeles in the 1920s. Their presence ensured the city's prominent place in modern art in America. Among the people they influenced were John Cage and Walter Hopps.

Asawa, Ruth. An artist interned as a child during World War II. She attended Black Mountain College and rose to prominence with wire sculptures and other art in San Francisco.

Ashbery, John. Much-awarded poet, member of the New York School. Frank O'Hara's Harvard roommate. Art critic, and later editor of the *Partisan Review*.

Baez, Joan. Folk singer and civil rights and anti-war activist.

Banducci, Harry Charles "Enrico." Owner of the hungry i (for id), later Vanessi's, a café. The club presented the majority of the new comedians of the era—Woody Allen, Mort Sahl, Richard Pryor, Lenny Bruce, and more.

Barlow, John. Lyricist songwriting partner of Bob Weir of the Grateful Dead.

Beck, Julian. Actor, director, painter, and cofounder of the Living Theatre. A major figure in the postwar Greenwich Village bohemian culture.

Belson, Jordan. A surrealist/mystic visual artist who presented nonspecific art in film. Partnered with Henry "Sandy" Jacobs in producing the Vortex series at the California Academy of Science's Morrison Planetarium in Golden Gate Park.

Berg, Peter. A member of the Diggers, and apparently the source of much of the intellectual critique of consumer culture that they represented. His early sense of environmental justice was unique—and critical. He later

Glossary of Names

founded the Planet Drum Foundation and advanced the concept of bioregionalism.

Berkson, Bill. Poet, protégé of Kenneth Koch, a younger member of the New York School. Also an art critic. In the 1970s, he moved to San Francisco and worked with local artists and at the SF Art Institute.

Berman, Wallace. Primarily Los Angeles–based artist and poet, he was hugely influential among the young avant-garde poets in the 1950s and early '60s. A friend to many painters, his periodic publication *Semina* was at the intersection of painting and poetry in its time.

Berry, Charles Edward Anderson "Chuck." The father of rock and roll guitar; he combined Bob Wills–style western swing with a Chess Records backbeat and a cheeky celebration of teenage life.

Besant, Annie. English social activist, she began as a Fabian socialist and atheist; she supported women's rights and home rule for Ireland and India. She then became a Theosophist, rising to be president of the Theosophical Society, whose headquarters were in India. In 1925, she traveled to the United States with her adopted son, Jiddu Krishnamurti, whom she celebrated as the new Messiah.

Bischoff, Elmer. Primarily figurative painter after an abstract expressionist start, he taught at the California School of Fine Arts.

Blaser, Robin. Poet, a member of the Berkeley Renaissance that included Robert Duncan and Jack Spicer. He went on to write plays and teach at Simon Fraser University in Vancouver.

Caen, Herb. Beloved San Francisco newspaper item columnist who wrote, in effect, a daily love letter to the city for close to sixty years.

Cage, John. The most influential avant-garde composer in twentieth-century America. From Los Angeles, he settled in New York City, where he studied Zen with D. T. Suzuki. Having come to include silence in his conception of music, he eventually composed "4'33"" in which the music was in fact the sound of the room.

Callahan, Michael. Technical wizard who worked with the Tape Music Center in SF and later with USCO in the New York area.

Campbell, Joseph. Eminent art historian, author of *The Hero's Journey*, culture critic, resident of Greenwich Village, and husband of the dancer/choreographer Jean Erdman.

Glossary of Names

Cassady, Neal. Inspired hustler, he served as the model for Dean Moriarity in *On the Road* and later served as the driver of Ken Kesey and the Merry Pranksters' bus and mentor to the members of the Grateful Dead.

Castell, Luria. Civil rights activist with the W. E. B. Du Bois Club at San Francisco State. One of the hip residents on Pine Street. Cofounder of the Family Dog, which put on four shows at the Longshoremen's Hall in the fall of 1965.

Cohen, Allen. Poet, founder and editor of the *Oracle*. Clerk at the Psychedelic Shop.

Cohen, Bob. A sound engineer, he was one of the arts people who lived on Pine Street. He and Bill Ham created a light show for the Red Dog Saloon, and both went on to work with the Family Dog at the Avalon.

Colyer, Ken. Postwar English "trad" ("Dixieland") trumpet player, a member of the Crane River Jazz Band. At intermissions, members of the band played "breakdown" music, which came to be called *skiffle*. Partnering with Chris Barber and Lonnie Donegan as Ken Colyer's Jazzmen, they were a success. Barber and Donegan eventually released a single under Lonnie's name, "Rock Island Line," that was such a hit it triggered a fad for skiffle in England.

Conner, Bruce. Brilliant assemblage artist from Kansas, founder of the Rat Bastard Protective Association. Later part of the North American Ibis Alchemical Company light show at the Avalon Ballroom.

Cowell, Henry. Early avant-garde composer who influenced John Cage and Lou Harrison. From the age of five, he was raised in San Francisco's Chinatown, and his writing was affected by Chinese and other Asian music.

Coyote, Peter. (Born Cohon) A member of the San Francisco Mime Troupe, he became part of the Diggers with Peter Berg and Emmett Grogan, among others.

CSFA. California School of Fine Arts, on Russian Hill in San Francisco. In 1961, it changed its name to the San Francisco Art Institute.

Glossary of Names

Cullen, Countee. Poet of African American themes, a major part of the Harlem Renaissance, and a public school teacher in New York. One of his students was James Baldwin.

Cunningham, Imogen. Celebrated postwar San Francisco photographer. In association with Ansel Adams and Edward Weston, she cofounded the Group f/64, which was devoted to sharp-focus portraits of real people.

Cunningham, Merce. Modern dancer, partner of John Cage. After coming to fame as the lead dancer in Martha Graham's company, he led his own dance company. He worked with many painters, including Robert Rauschenberg, Jasper Johns, and Roy Lichtenstein. His impact on the arts went far beyond that of dance alone.

Dalenberg, Claude. Student of Alan Watts at the American Academy of Asian Studies. A founder of the East-West House and later an early member of the San Francisco Zen Center.

Davis, Ronald G. "Ronnie." Assistant director for the San Francisco Actor's Workshop, founder of the San Francisco Mime Troupe, advocate for a liberating theater.

Day, Dorothy. Initially a socialist, she converted to Roman Catholicism. Meeting the peasant-intellectual Peter Maurin, they founded the Catholic Worker Movement, a small-c communist group of anarchist social activists who lived in voluntary poverty in hospitality houses in order to be social activists. Their best-known action was a refusal to cooperate with civilian defense air raid drills, for which she was repeatedly arrested.

de Angulo, Jaime. A founder of bohemian culture in California, an early settler on Partington Ridge in Big Sur, a linguistic anthropologist and student of Indigenous cultures, a novelist and friend of Robinson Jeffers, Robert Duncan, and other poets.

DeFeo, Jay. Painter, student at California School of Fine Arts (later, the San Francisco Art Institute). Created *The Rose*, the masterpiece of 1950s San Francisco art.

de Kooning, Willem. With Jackson Pollock, the leading figure of the abstract expressionist artists in New York.

DeLoach, Cartha. Deputy director of the FBI.

330 **Glossary of Names**

Desnos, Robert. Key early surrealist poet, member of the French resistance during World War II, he died in a German concentration camp in 1945.

Dewey, Ken. Assistant director at the San Francisco Actor's Workshop, he later worked with Ann Halprin in Paris.

Dick, Philip K. A student at UC Berkeley in the late 1940s who lived in the same boardinghouse as Robert Duncan, he went on to an influential and distinguished career in science fiction writing.

Diebenkorn, Richard. First a student and then a teacher at the California School of Fine Arts, he was an abstract expressionist painter who lived in Sausalito for a time and was one of the Sausalito Six group of CSFA students there.

di Prima, Diane. Poet, cofounder of the poetry newsletter *Floating Bear*, later an associate of the Diggers in San Francisco.

Donahue, Tom. Disc jockey who avoided a payola scandal and came to San Francisco's KYA rock station. An entrepreneur, he established Autumn Records and then a psychedelic nightclub called Mother's, but his great contribution was KMPX, later KSAN, a free-form station that allowed the DJ to play almost anything. It became the center of San Francisco's youth culture.

Donegan, Lonnie. See Ken Colyer.

Dreiser, Theodore. American naturalist novelist (*Sister Carrie*, *An American Tragedy*) and journalist, a leading figure of the Chicago Renaissance of the 1920s and '30s.

Duchamp, Marcel. Famed surrealist artist.

Duncan, Robert. Poet and anarchist/mystic. A leading figure of the late-1940s Berkeley Renaissance and '50s San Francisco Renaissance. An early "out" gay man.

Dylan, Bob. Folk musician from Minnesota who began recording in 1961. When he began to write originals, he became revealed as the poet of his generation, creating a surreal account of the decade.

Erdman, Jean. Dancer and choreographer, associate of John Cage, Lou Harrison, and other Greenwich Village figures, she was married to scholar Joseph Campbell.

Glossary of Names 331

Everson, William. Printer (at the conscientious objector Camp Angel) and mystical poet, a protégé of Kenneth Rexroth and later a Dominican friar before leaving the order to marry.

Ferguson, Michael. Founder of the "Magic Theater" shop, later keyboard player for the Charlatans.

Ferlinghetti, Lawrence. Poet, owner of City Lights Bookstore, founder of City Lights Press.

Ford, Gordon Onslow. Wealthy British surrealist painter, he settled in Mill Valley, California.

Frame, Pete. British music historian.

Frankenstein, Alfred. Music critic for the *San Francisco Chronicle* in the 1940s and '50s.

Freilicher, Jane. Representational painter and a leading figure of the New York School of poets and painters that included Frank O'Hara, Joan Mitchell, and Larry Rivers, whom she had inspired to paint when he first began.

Garcia, Jerry. A painting student of Wally Hedrick, later a folk guitarist, then bluegrass banjo player, then founding member of the Grateful Dead.

Getz, Dave. San Francisco Art Institute student and then teacher, drummer in the Studio 13 Jass Band, and later the drummer for Big Brother and the Holding Company.

Gidlow, Elsa. Born in the UK in 1898 and raised in Montreal, she was a poet, bohemian, and lesbian icon.

Gillespie, Dizzy. American jazz trumpeter and early bebop pioneer.

Ginsberg, Allen. New Jersey–born, a Columbia student whose social circle with Jack Kerouac, Lucien Carr, and William Burroughs would become known as "the Beats." Moved to San Francisco in 1954 and the next year wrote and presented the most famous poem of postwar America, "Howl." Later read onstage at the Be-In.

Gleason, Madeline. A San Francisco poet who financed her life working as a runner in the stock exchange, she was a founder of the San Francisco Poetry Guild (1947), which would become the Poetry Center at San Francisco State University.

Glossary of Names

Gleason, Ralph. San Francisco *Chronicle* music critic; the first full-time jazz critic for an American daily newspaper. A very positive influence on the evolution of the city's rock music scene in the '60s.

Goodman, Paul. Radical anarchist social critic deeply involved with the creation of Gestalt therapy, author of *Growing Up Absurd* (1960), influential Greenwich Village theater artist.

Gordon, Elizabeth. Editor of *House Beautiful* and conservative culture critic.

Gorky, Arshile. A painter, he was an escapee from Armenian genocide. In New York, he became a seminal early influence on the development of abstract expressionism in the 1950s.

Graham, Bill (Wolfgang Grajonka). Business manager of the San Francisco Mime Troupe, then concert promoter, first at the Fillmore Auditorium, then at venues across the Bay Area and the United States.

Graves, Morris. Painter from the Pacific Northwest, his style was described as mystic, based on Asian sources and a personal iconography of birds and flowers.

Gregory, Dick. Black comedian and civil rights activist.

Grogan, Emmett. Charismatic non-leader of the anarchist Diggers, he later wrote a memoir called *Ringolevio*. He came to the Diggers from the San Francisco Mime Troupe.

Gropius, Walter. Founder of the Bauhaus school and one of the essential creators of modernist architecture, he taught at Harvard after fleeing Europe and then taught at Black Mountain College.

Grossman, Albert. Owner of the Gate of Horn folk club in Chicago, manager of Odetta, he then began managing Bob Dylan and assembled the super trio Peter, Paul and Mary. He later managed Big Brother and the Holding Company and Janis Joplin.

Gruen, John. Publicist for Grove Press, composer of music set to poetry (e. e. cummings, Rilke), music critic under Virgil Thomson at the *New York Herald Tribune*, then chief art critic there. A knowledgeable Greenwich Village resident.

Guggenheim, Peggy. American heiress, bohemian, art collector, and owner of the influential gallery Art of This Century in New York City. An early supporter of the modern art of Picasso and beyond, including surrealism and abstract expressionism.

Glossary of Names

Hall, Manly P. Los Angeles–based mystic who claimed to explain alchemy, Hebrew number mysticism, the tarot, Rosicrucianism, and the esotericism of Shakespeare in his book *The Secret Teachings of All Ages.* He founded the Philosophical Research Society there in 1934.

Hallinan, Terence. Son of Vincent Hallinan, a leftist critic of American mores and the Roman Catholic Church. Nicknamed "Kayo," he was also an attorney and later district attorney of San Francisco.

Halprin, Ann. Dancer and choreographer, she was the epitome of the postwar San Francisco aesthetic, such that any movement enacted with intention could be a dance.

Hanrahan, William. Head of the San Francisco Juvenile Department squad and the cause of the *Howl* obscenity arrests.

Harris, Father Leon. Rector of the Haight-Ashbury's All Saints Church, a kindly supporter of the hippies.

Harrison, Lou. A San Francisco–based avant-garde composer first influenced by Henry Cowell, he moved from dissonance to integrating Asian music, particularly gamelan, into Western "classical." A friend of John Cage's in San Francisco and New York City, he returned to the Bay Area. Unusually in those times, he was "out"—open about his sexual orientation—from his teen years.

Hayden, Tom. One of the founders of Students for a Democratic Society, primary author of the "Port Huron Statement," which announced the organization.

Haywood, Bill. Founder of the Industrial Workers of the World and socialist, he led major strikes in Colorado; Lawrence, Massachusetts; and elsewhere. Post–World War I, he was targeted by the Red Scare and forced to flee to the Soviet Union.

Heard, Gerald. The "father of new age thinking," Heard was a historian and public intellectual who was English, gay, a pacifist, and a mentor to figures like Aldous Huxley, Henry and Clare Booth Luce, and Bill Wilson, "Bill W.," the founder of Alcoholics Anonymous. Along with Huxley, he moved to Los Angeles in 1937 and became involved with Vedanta. Later, he studied psychedelics and published his philosophical magnum opus, *The Five Ages of Humanity.*

Hedrick, Wally. Assemblage artist, student and then teacher at California

334 **Glossary of Names**

School of Fine Arts (later San Francisco Art Institute), one of the six founders of the 6 Gallery. Husband of Jay DeFeo and teacher of Jerry Garcia.

Helms, Chet. LeMar marijuana activist, he succeeded Luria Castell and Co. as leader of the Family Dog, which produced concerts at the Avalon Ballroom.

Hendrix, Jimi. American blues/rock guitarist, who developed a reputation in London and then returned and closed the Monterey International Pop Festival with an enormous bang.

Hennacy, Ammon. A pacifist, socialist, and member of the IWW, he came to New York City in the early 1950s, was baptized in the Roman Catholic faith, and joined Dorothy Day's Catholic Worker Movement.

Hill, Lewis Kimball. Pacifist, conscientious objector during World War II, and head of the ACLU's National Committee on COs. Founder of KPFA, "free speech radio," as an antidote to the repressive greater American culture.

Hoffman, Abbie. Political activist, first in the realm of civil rights, later in anti-war efforts. Hippie provocateur.

Hofmann, Albert. Swiss research chemist, he created a derivative of ergot fungus called LSD-25.

Hofmann, Hans. Greenwich Village's teacher of painting whose students included Jane Freilicher, Larry Rivers, Lee Krasner, and Joan Mitchell. He was also an important painter himself.

Hollingshead, Michael. Psychedelic advocate, associate of Timothy Leary's, he established the World Psychedelic Centre in London in September 1965.

Holmes, John Clellon. Author of *Horn*, a close associate of Jack Kerouac's, and a participant in the Beat circles of the 1940s.

Hoover, J. Edgar. Longtime head of the Federal Bureau of Investigation, legendary for having files on high-level government officials and civilians. Promoted anti-Communism and was against civil rights.

Hopper, Dennis. Hollywood actor, photographer, and collector of modern art.

Hopps, Walter. Influential art curator, he opened the Ferus Gallery in 1957,

Glossary of Names

establishing modern art in Los Angeles. Among his artists were Wallace Berman, Ed Ruscha, and Andy Warhol. He was also a major supporter of Jay DeFeo.

Hubbard, Al. A mysterious figure who was variously assumed to be an agent for the OSS, the CIA, the DOJ, and the ATF, he was a proselytizer for the use of LSD and introduced it to Aldous Huxley, who had already experienced mescaline.

Hughes, Langston. Poet, fiction writer, and columnist/social activist, the leader of the Harlem Renaissance in the 1920s and '30s that celebrated African American arts and life.

Huncke, Herbert. Times Square hustler and low-level drug dealer who acted as "Virgil" to Allen Ginsberg and Jack Kerouac, introducing them to the low-rent street bohemia of sex and drugs that was the neighborhood.

Hunter, Alberta. A Chicago-based jazz and blues singer between the 1920s and the '50s.

Hunter, George. One of the younger generation experimenting with tape music at the Tape Music Center, later a founder of the first of the best-known San Francisco 1960s rock bands, the Charlatans.

Huxley, Aldous. Celebrated English pacifist, social critic, and novelist, he settled in Los Angeles in the 1930s and in 1954 wrote *The Doors of Perception*, introducing the subject of psychedelic exploration to many Americans.

Isherwood, Christopher. The third (with Aldous Huxley and Gerald Heard) of three English pacifists who became involved with Vedanta and yogic religion in Los Angeles in the 1930s. His memoir of his time in Berlin would inspire the film and theater piece *Cabaret*. He would be an important contributor to the gay liberation movement.

Jacobs, Henry "Sandy." KPFA studio engineer who created musique concrète recordings, often with hipster humor ("Shorty Petterstein"). Partnered in the Vortex series at the Morrison Planetarium.

Jacopetti, Ben and Rain. Leaders of a theater group called the Open Theater. They performed at the Trips Festival.

Jeffers, Robinson. A poet focused on combining wild nature (he lived near Big Sur) and Greek myths; he settled in Carmel in 1914 and was a

336 **Glossary of Names**

spiritual forefather of the San Francisco bohemians of the 1940s and '50s, along with Jaime de Angulo.

Jefferson Airplane. The most prominent of the rock bands in San Francisco in the middle 1960s. Founded by Marty Balin (vocals), Paul Kantner (rhythm guitar), and Jorma Kaukonen (lead guitar), they added Jack Casady on bass and vocalist Grace Slick in 1966 and had the first major hit in the city with "Somebody to Love" and then "White Rabbit." They were stars at the Monterey International Pop Festival.

Jess (Burgess Collins). Assemblage artist, student at the California School of Fine Arts, partner of Robert Duncan's from 1951 until their deaths.

Joans, Ted. Surrealist poet and jazz trumpet player, he was an archetypal bohemian character of Greenwich Village and the Beat scene.

Johnson, Joyce. Novelist, feminist, editor, and briefly a romantic partner to Jack Kerouac.

Jones, Elvin. Outstanding jazz drummer, most notably with John Coltrane.

Jones, LeRoi (Amiri Baraka). Black poet and jazz critic, cofounder of *Floating Bear*, author of *Blues People*.

Joplin, Janis. Texas-born, she began as a folk singer. In 1966, she joined Big Brother and the Holding Company. She stole the show at the Monterey International Pop Festival and redefined women's vocals in rock.

Kael, Pauline. Came to prominence with a program on film on KPFA in the early 1950s and went on to fame as a film critic for the *New Yorker* in the '60s.

Kandel, Lenore. Poet, Buddhist, Digger. Her best-known work, *The Love Book*, was accused of obscenity, although she eventually won the case.

Kaufman, Bob "Bomkauf." Surrealist poet, denizen of Grant Avenue in San Francisco's North Beach neighborhood, the target of much abuse from the cop on the beat, William Bigarini.

Kaukonen, Jorma "Jerry." Folk blues guitarist, he began at the Folk Theater club in San Jose, working with Janis Joplin among others, and then picked up electric guitar to join the nascent Jefferson Airplane.

Kelley, Alton. Cofounder of the Family Dog, artistic partner with Stanley "Mouse" Miller in creating posters and album covers.

Glossary of Names

Kerouac, Jack. Author of *On the Road*, central figure in the development of Beat literature, a working-class child of Lowell, Massachusetts. He did not enjoy the fame of *Road*, which accelerated his alcoholism and hastened his death in 1969.

Kesey, Ken. A literary heir to the Beats, he was the author of *One Flew over the Cuckoo's Nest* and *Sometimes a Great Notion* and an advocate for the use of LSD. He and his friends, the Merry Pranksters and the Grateful Dead, organized a series of parties centered on consuming LSD. He was twice arrested on marijuana charges and fled the country before returning to serve time.

Krasner, Lee. Painter, wife of Jackson Pollock.

Krishnamurti, Jiddu. Indian spiritual teacher brought to the US by the Theosophist Annie Besant. In 1929, he renounced her claims of him as the new Messiah and taught purely as an independent seeker.

Kunkin, Art. Editor of the *Los Angeles Free Press*.

Lamantia, Philip. A visionary poet born and raised in San Francisco, then invited to join the surrealists around the magazine *View* during World War II. He returned home, where he remained prominent in the city's poetry scene, leading off the legendary reading at the 6 Gallery that introduced Allen Ginsberg's "Howl" to the world.

Laughlin, James. An heir to a steel fortune, Laughlin met Gertrude Stein and Ezra Pound in the 1930s in Europe and listened to Pound's comment that he would not be a great poet, and "Why don't you take up something useful?" like publishing. Returning to the US, he began New Directions Publishing, at first from his Harvard dormitory room, and eventually in New York City. NDP established modernist poetry in America with a list that included Stein, Pound, William Carlos Williams, Henry Miller, and e. e. cummings.

LaVigne, Robert. Beat painter, lover of Peter Orlovsky, who then took up with Allen Ginsberg. He made portraits of many Beat figures, including the wolf picture of Michael McClure as the cover of *Ghost Tantras*, and also designed sets for Herbert Blau and the Actor's Workshop.

Leary, Timothy. Harvard professor of psychology who would encounter psychedelics, test them as a scientist, and then become a slightly

Glossary of Names

megalomaniacal advocate. He would be forced to leave Harvard and took up residence at Millbrook. His Madison Avenue–esque slogan "Turn on, tune in, drop out," was representative of his thinking.

Leite, George. Berkeley-based bookstore owner, publisher of the anarchist/pacifist magazine *Circle*, and cabbie.

Lennon, John. Musician, first with a skiffle band, the Quarrymen, which evolved into a rock band called the Beatles. Their beyond-enormous success led to the import of British rock bands into America—the British Invasion.

Lesh, Phil. Musician and composer, he was part of the cutting edge at the San Francisco Mime Troupe's gatherings at their studio on Capp Street. He would be drafted by his friend Jerry Garcia into what would become the Grateful Dead.

Lewis, Lucy. Dancer and choreographer, member of Ann Halprin's Dancers' Workshop, partner of George Hunter, the founder of the first SF rock band, the Charlatans.

Lindsay, Vachel. Bardic poet, member of the Chicago Renaissance in the 1910s and '20s.

Lipton, Lawrence. Leader of the Beats of Venice Beach, depicted in his novel *The Holy Barbarians*.

Low, Jackson Mac. Greenwich Village resident, anarchist pacifist, poet, and performance artist particularly involved with the use of chance ("random") decisions in his art.

Luhan, Mabel Dodge. Early-twentieth-century bohemian, an associate of D. H. Lawrence in Taos.

MacAgy, Douglas. President of California School of Fine Arts (later, the SF Art Institute) from 1945 to 1950, during which time it went from near bankruptcy to an extraordinarily high level of quality and excitement, both in its students and faculty.

Mailer, Norman. American writer and culture critic, major contributor to the early years of the *Village Voice*, author of "The White Negro."

Malina, Judith. Actress and director, cofounder of the Living Theatre, devout bohemian, and anarchist/pacifist.

Martin, George. Producer for Parlophone Records who contributed greatly to the rise and astonishing success of the Beatles.

Glossary of Names

Martin, Tony. The visual component of the Tape Music Center, he worked with Ann Halprin's Dancers' Workshop as well.

McCartney, Paul. Musician, member of the Beatles, active participant in the poetry/hippie culture of London.

McClure, Michael. Poet and playwright. He was one of the six poets at the 6 Gallery and thus forever associated with the Beats. Later, his play *The Beard* attracted much attention. He was also one of the readers at the Human Be-In. His focus on the poet as mammal was essential to his work.

McCorkle, Locke. Student at American Academy of Asian Studies. A carpenter, "landlord" to Gary Snyder's cabin "Marin-An" in Mill Valley. Later, a Scientologist.

McKay, Claude. Jamaican-born African American poet and novelist (*Home to Harlem, Banjo*) and member of the Harlem Renaissance. A member of the IWW and a socialist, he became a member of the Catholic Workers late in life.

McNeill, Don. *Village Voice* reporter who covered the emerging counterculture, he died young in a boating accident in 1968.

Mekas, Jonas. The "Godfather of Avant-Garde Film," a poet, filmmaker, and film critic (*Village Voice*). Anti-censorship activist.

Meltzer, David. One of the young poets to emerge after the poem "Howl," Meltzer was included in *The New American Poetry*. He was also a musician; he and his wife, Tina, had a band in the 1960s called the Serpent Power.

Miles, Barry. English literary figure, an organizer of the Royal Albert Hall Poetry Incarnation, a founder of Indica Bookstore and the *International Times*, a leading participant in the culture of 1960s London.

Miles, Josephine. Academic poet who overcame great physical limits to teach at UC Berkeley, becoming the first tenured woman in that department. She was a founding scholar of using computational methods to analyze poetry and is considered a pioneer of "digital humanities."

Miller, Henry. Resolutely bohemian writer who explored sexuality (*Tropic of Cancer*) and social criticism (*The Air-Conditioned Nightmare, Big Sur*

340   **Glossary of Names**

and the Oranges of Hieronymus Bosch), he lived in the Big Sur area from 1944 until the early '60s and was a major influence on the culture of San Francisco in the postwar era.

Mills, C. Wright. Postwar American sociologist and leftist culture critic, arguing for a post-Marxist critique of capitalism that focused on consumerism and corporations rather than the class struggle.

Minton, Henry. Owner of Minton's, a jazz club at the Hotel Cecil in Harlem. Because of his status with the musicians' union, the American Federation of Musicians, his club escaped notice when musicians violated union rules with unpaid jam sessions. The result was the birth of the experimental new music, bebop (*bop* for short).

Monk, Thelonious. American pianist and among the very great American composers, he emerged in the creative laboratory that was Minton's during World War II, creating a new art music called *bop*.

Monroe, Harriet. Publisher and editor of *Poetry*, an influential figure in the introduction of modernism in twentieth-century American poetry and literature. Part of the Chicago Renaissance.

Morley, Grace McCann. Founder and executive director of the San Francisco Museum (later Museum of Modern Art) and a major influence nationally, welcoming shows to San Francisco from the New York Museum of Modern Art and Peggy Guggenheim's Art of This Century gallery. Her early support of the abstract expressionist painters was crucial to their discovery.

Morrell, Lady Ottoline. A socialite and active member of the Bloomsbury group of left-wing artistic intellectuals who frequented that neighborhood in London in the 1920s. It included Bertrand Russell, Virginia Woolf, John Maynard Keynes, and historian Lytton Strachey. Lady Morrell's country home, Garsington Manor, was one of the Bloomsbury group's country escapes from London.

Motherwell, Robert. New York–based abstract expressionist painter with several connections to the surrealist school.

Mullen, Frances. A pianist. With her husband, Peter Yates, she established in 1939 Evenings on the Roof, a series of avant-garde chamber music performances in Los Angeles.

Glossary of Names

Murao, Shigeyoshi. Clerk at City Lights Bookstore, arrested for selling *Howl*, declared not guilty by Judge Clayton Horn.

Neuwirth, Bob. Art student in Boston during the early folk days, he played as well. Eventually, he would be Bob Dylan's tour manager.

Nin, Anaïs. Diarist, author of erotic short stories, lover of Henry Miller among others, a profoundly important observer of bohemian mores.

Norse, Harold. A poet and member of W. H. Auden's inner circle (his former lover Chester Kallman became Auden's lifelong object of desire), his poetry was more inclined to common language on the order of William Carlos Williams. Later, Norse's memoirs of the gay scene in Manhattan brought much attention.

Nys, Maria. Aldous Huxley's wife.

Odetta. Important Black American folk singer known as the "Voice of the Civil Rights Movement" of the 1960s. She was both aesthetically and politically influential.

O'Hara, Frank. Poet, art critic, and tastemaker in the Village/gay/art scene of the 1950s. His "day job" was as a curator for the Museum of Modern Art. His poetry focused centrally on the arts, and he was the social nexus of many writers, painters, and musicians.

Oldham, Andrew Loog. Early and young (nineteen years old) manager of the Rolling Stones. He persuaded them to become the bad-boy alternative to the Beatles: "Would you let your daughter go out with one?"

Oliveros, Pauline. Composer of electronic music, she was cofounder with Ramón Sender and Morton Subotnick of the Tape Music Center.

Olsen, Richie. Clarinet and bass player for the Charlatans.

Olson, Charles. Modernist poet who linked the generations of Ezra Pound and T. S. Eliot and the younger poets of the New York and Black Mountain schools. Olson was the rector of Black Mountain College.

Osmond, Humphry. Canadian research psychologist who particularly advanced the idea of psychedelics being therapeutic for alcoholism. He is the man who introduced psychedelics to Aldous Huxley. He also coined the word *psychedelic*, "mind manifesting."

Park, David. Distinguished figurative painter, teacher at the California School of Fine Arts.

Glossary of Names

Parker, Charlie. Nicknamed "Yardbird," "Bird" for short, he was the essential element in the creation of modern jazz during and after World War II. A brilliant composer and player, he was personally handicapped by various addictions. He died in 1955.

Partch, Harry. Eccentric composer of avant-garde music, largely performed on self-created instruments. He rejected conventional "just" intonation and worked with multitone structures that sounded dissonant to Western ears.

Patchen, Kenneth. Poet and pacifist, a significant influence on the San Francisco poets, although ill health generally confined him to his home in Palo Alto.

Pennebaker, Donn Alan ("D. A."). American documentary filmmaker who pioneered the use of handheld cameras and cinema verité, first in his study of Bob Dylan in 1965, *Dont Look Back*, and then in the film *Monterey Pop*.

Phillips, John. Folk singer, leader of the Mamas & the Papas; later, the main organizer of the Monterey International Pop Festival.

Pollock, Jackson. The most famous abstract expressionist painter.

Porter, Bern. A scientist and poet with interests in Surrealism. Published Philip Lamantia's *Erotic Poems*, and *Circle* magazine, among other things. Also owned an art gallery in Sausalito.

Reagan, Ronald. Conservative governor of California elected in 1966 at least partly in reaction to the Free Speech Movement and Watts Rebellion; later, fortieth president of the United States.

Reich, Steve. Minimalist avant-garde composer best known for his *It's Gonna Rain*. He was music director for the Dancers' Workshop, an associate of the Tape Music Center, and created the soundtrack for experimental films, including Robert Nelson's *Oh Dem Watermelons*.

Rexroth, Kenneth. Poet, teacher, and anarchist thinker. Born in 1905, he was an essential element in the development of a vigorous poetry community in San Francisco by the 1940s and '50s. His politics and his interest in Asian poetry were highly influential.

Rexroth, Marie. Second wife of Kenneth Rexroth.

Richards, Keith. Guitarist and songwriter for the Rolling Stones.

Richards, M. C. Poet, teacher at Black Mountain College, and later a

Glossary of Names

343

student of Rudolf Steiner. An associate of John Cage and Merce Cunningham.

Riley, Terry. Avant-garde minimalist composer; student at SF State and then UC Berkeley graduate student, music director for Ann Halprin, and associate of the Tape Music Center. Composer of "In C."

Rivers, Larry. Saxophone player and artist who came to be called the "Godfather of Pop Art." A Village resident, he was primarily heterosexual but had an affair with the poet Frank O'Hara.

Romero, Elias. Early creator of liquid light shows, which he introduced in the Bay Area at San Francisco Mime Troupe gatherings in their church on Capp Street. A resident of the Pine Street homes managed by Bill Ham.

Rosset, Barney. Publisher of Grove Press, which brought *Waiting for Godot* to the US. It published the *Evergreen Review*, which was a major inflection point for Beat literary publications, and achieved important victories against censorship with various lawsuits, beginning with a defense of *Lady Chatterley's Lover*.

Rossman, Michael. Student at UC Berkeley and a leader in the Free Speech Movement, his *The Wedding Within the War* was an important work.

Rothko, Mark. Abstract expressionist painter and friend of Clyfford Still's, he taught for two summers at the California School of Fine Arts.

Rukeyser, Muriel. Poet and progressive whose most famous work was *The Book of the Dead*, about the deaths of West Virginia miners due to silicosis.

Russell, Sanders. Partner of Philip Lamantia in producing the single-issue poetry journal *Ark*.

Russell, Vickie. (Real name: Priscilla Arminger) Prostitute, friend of William Burroughs and Herbert Huncke, briefly a housemate of Allen Ginsberg's.

Ryan, John. Painter, Black Mountain College alumnus, bartender at San Francisco's bohemian bar the Place, one of the six who formed the 6 Gallery.

Sanders, Ed. Poet, protégé of Allen Ginsberg, Lower East Side advocate, founder of *Fuck You! A Magazine of the Arts* and the Peace Eye Bookstore. Also a founder of the Fugs, a rock band.

Glossary of Names

Sarria, José. Waiter and drag performer at the early gay institution the Black Cat bar, political activist and pioneer of gay rights in San Francisco. He was the first openly gay candidate for public office in the United States.

Sasaki, Ruth Fuller. As Ruth Fuller, she met D. T. Suzuki in 1930 and was a student of Zen for the rest of her life. Her daughter, Eleanor, was married to Alan Watts. During World War II, she moved to New York, where she met and married Shigetsu Sasaki. In the 1950s, she established an English-language group at the Rinzai Daitoku-ji monastery in Kyoto; Gary Snyder was her most prominent student there.

Savio, Mario. Cal student and a leader of the Free Speech Movement, he delivered one of the essential speeches of the 1960s.

Schafer, Andrée. An artist and first wife of Kenneth Rexroth.

Schoenberg, Arnold. Creator of the twelve-tone system of composition, which introduced dissonance into Western "classical" music. He was a refugee from Nazi Germany and settled in Los Angeles, where he taught at UCLA and composed.

Scully, Rock. A member of the W. E. B. Du Bois Club at SF State, he was comanager (with Danny Rifkin) of the Grateful Dead in its early days.

Sender, Ramón. Refugee from the Spanish Civil War, composer of electronic music, cofounder of the Tape Music Center in San Francisco, major participant of the Trips Festival, and a resident of Morning Star Ranch.

Senzaki, Nyogen. Japanese Zen monk who was among the first such to come to America (1905), teaching in what he called the "floating zendo" (wherever he happened to be) in Los Angeles. With the author Paul Reps, he translated Buddhist materials into an early English-language text, *Zen Flesh, Zen Bones*.

SFAI. San Francisco Art Institute, originally the California School of Fine Arts, it became SFAI in 1961.

Simon, Paul. Folk singer. With his partner Art Garfunkel, he recorded an album, *Wednesday Morning, 3 A.M.*, which flopped until the producer added rock instruments and made it folk-rock, and the song "Sound of Silence" became a hit. Later, he was an essential part of the organization of the Monterey International Pop Festival.

Glossary of Names

345

Smith, Harry. Cultural anthropologist and esoteric filmmaker, he was most famous for his collection of American genre music, *The Anthology of American Folk Music*, which would become a source of repertoire for the folkies of the 1960s.

Snyder, Gary. Poet, Buddhist, advocate for the natural order in his work. A graduate of Reed College, a student at the American Academy of Asian Studies, and a protégé of Kenneth Rexroth's, he was an influential voice in the bohemian community from the 1950s onward.

Spicer, Jack. A Berkeley student in the 1940s, he lived in the same house as Philip K. Dick and Robert Duncan. He, too, became a poet, although his contempt for publication limited his influence. He was a cofounder of the 6 Gallery, a founder of the Poetry as Magic workshop, and the host of Blabbermouth Night at the Place, the bohemian bar on Grant Avenue in North Beach, San Francisco.

Spiegelberg, Frederick. German-born scholar of religions who studied with Paul Tillich, Carl Jung, and Martin Heidegger. A refugee from Nazi Germany, he settled at Stanford University, where among his students was Stewart Brand. He helped set up the American Academy of Asian Studies.

Spohn, Clay. Faculty member at the California School of Fine Arts in the 1940s and '50s. A surrealist, his exhibit *Little Known and Unknown Objects* had a major impact on the students there.

Stanley, Owsley. A student of alchemy and creator of exceptionally pure and strong LSD, Stanley made the San Francisco scene possible by producing millions of doses of the drug. He also had a profound effect on the development of sound systems through his work as sound mixer for the Grateful Dead.

Stern, Gerd. Poet and visual cyber-artist, he was the early publicist for KPFA, worked with composer Harry Partch in Sausalito, and then moved to the Hudson Valley in New York and cofounded USCO (the company of us), a mixed-media psychedelic art collective.

Still, Clyfford. One of the first abstract expressionist painters, he came to the California School of Fine Arts in 1945 and helped make it a highly influential center of creativity both social and aesthetic, preaching a purist vision of the artist in society.

346 **Glossary of Names**

Stockhausen, Karlheinz. German-born avant-garde composer. Essentially created the concept of electronic music. He also worked with elements of chance in his compositions.

Stolaroff, Myron. His International Foundation for Advanced Study introduced psychedelics to many engineers in what would become known as Silicon Valley and led to the creation of the home computer there.

Subotnick, Morton. Composer of electronic music, he was cofounder (with Ramón Sender and Pauline Oliveros) of the Tape Music Center in San Francisco. He was also a composer for the San Francisco Actor's Workshop.

Suzuki, D. T. Japanese scholar of Zen who first came to the US as part of the 1893 Parliament of the World's Religions. Toward the end of his career, he taught religion at Columbia University.

Suzuki, Shunryu Shogaku. Founder of the San Francisco Zen Center.

Taylor, Derek. Journalist, press officer for the Beatles and later for the Byrds. An essential part of the production of the Monterey International Pop Festival.

Thelin, Ron and Jay. Proprietors of the Psychedelic Shop on Haight Street, one of the central nodes of hippie.

Thomson, Virgil. Composer of *Four Saints in Three Acts* with Gertrude Stein, chief music critic of the *New York Herald Tribune*. His salon at his rooms in the Chelsea Hotel was a significant meeting point for the arts, generally involving gay men.

Townshend, Pete. English art student and musician, cofounder of the Who, notorious for instrument-smashing finales of their shows.

Tudor, David. Pianist, close associate of John Cage; he was the nonplaying performer in the premiere of Cage's "4"33'."

Tzara, Tristan. Romanian poet and all-around avant-garde artist, a founder of Dadaism who later split with André Breton.

Van Meter, Ben. SF State student, avant-garde filmmaker, and then partnered with Roger Hillyard as the North American Ibis Alchemical Company light show at the Avalon Ballroom.

Van Ronk, Dave. Folk musician, the "Mayor of MacDougal Street." A

Glossary of Names

specialist in old-timey blues, he had a significant following in the Village, as his nickname suggests.

Varda, Jean. Artist specializing in collage, he lived in Sausalito and shared the ship SS *Vallejo* with Gordon Onslow Ford. Having moved in circles that included Picasso and Braque, he brought a touch of European chic to the Bay Area arts scene of the 1940s and '50s. He was also a living incarnation of Bacchus, celebrating life, love, and wine.

Watts, Alan. English-born religious scholar who studied Buddhism while young, eventually became an Episcopal priest, then became head of the American Academy of Asian Studies in San Francisco. His KPFA radio program on religion would run for twenty years, from 1953 to his death in 1973, introducing many to Zen, as would his book *The Way of Zen.*

weiss, ruth. A poet, she was probably the first to read poetry to jazz. Though a friend of Jack Kerouac's, she was not aligned with the Beats except by an affinity for freedom in poetry.

Weitsman, Mel. Student at the California School of Fine Arts, horn player who helped premiere "In C," later a Zen monk and abbot of the San Francisco and Berkeley Zen Centers.

Werber, Frank. Manager of the Kingston Trio.

White, George. Federal Bureau of Narcotics agent who took part in LSD studies under the rubric of Operation Midnight Climax, in which he observed subjects unwittingly administered LSD by prostitutes in a San Francisco bordello.

Williams, Tennessee. Southern-born playwright who introduced serious sexual issues to the postwar Broadway stage in classic plays such as *The Glass Menagerie, Cat on a Hot Tin Roof,* and *A Streetcar Named Desire.*

Witt-Diamant, Ruth. A longtime teacher at San Francisco State and the first director of the Poetry Center there.

Wolfe, Tom. Writer, one of the creators of "New Journalism." A superb social reporter, his study of Ken Kesey, *The Electric Kool-Aid Acid Test,* was a masterpiece.

Wyckoff, Carrie Mead. (a.k.a. "Sister Lalita") An important figure in the establishment of Vedanta in Los Angeles during the 1930s and '40s.

Glossary of Names

Yancey, Jimmy. Pioneering boogie-woogie pianist.

Yates, Peter. With his wife, Frances, he founded Evenings on the Roof, an avant-garde music series in Los Angeles in 1939. He was a writer and also interested in Krishnamurti.

Young, La Monte. Avant-garde composer from Idaho who played free jazz with Don Cherry in Los Angeles during his college years, befriended Terry Riley at UC Berkeley in graduate school, and then departed for what came to be called the "downtown scene" of New York City. His Theatre of Eternal Music was a central piece in the city's culture.

Young, Lester. Great jazz saxophonist from the generation before the bebop revolution, he was one of the few older players who admired and was admired by the boppers.

BIBLIOGRAPHY

INTERVIEWS

Michael Aldrich, April 25, 2020

Bill Belmont, January 20, 2021

Janice Belmont, January 21, 2021

Peter Berg, August 9, 2019 (a film interview by Cheryll Glotfelty and Eve
Quesnel, courtesy of Judy Goldhaft)

Tosh Berman, January 31, 2019, at City Lights

Tosh Berman, January 31, 2019, via telephone

Lee Breuer, October 3, 2018

Julia "Girl Freiberg" Dreyer Brigden, July 9, 2019

Bruce and Jean Brugmann, August 2, 2019

Jack Casady, February 6, 2017

Peggy Caserta, July 22, 2018

Ronnie Davis, August 2, 2016

Lawrence Ferlinghetti, February 12, 2003

Steve Fowler, April 3, 2017

Jerry Garcia, May 17, 1982

Dave Getz, September 6, 2016, and June 29, 2019 (public event at Art
House, Berkeley)

350   **Bibliography**

Judy Goldhaft, September 1, 2016
Bill Graham, January 12, 1980
Luther "Spike" Green, July 24, 2019
Jeff Gunderson, October 7, 2016
Annie Hallatt, January 9, 2020
Bill Ham, August 30, 2016
Paul Hawken, July 17, 2019, email query
Dennis Hearne, March 4, 2020
Roger Hillyard, October 10, 2018, and November 5, 2018
Susan Hillyard, August 29, 2019
Mike Hochanadel, February 11, 2020, via email
Alexandra Jacopetti, March 12, 2017
Roland Jacopetti, March 19, 2017
Denise Kaufman, October 4, 2016
Jim Kweskin, September 18, 2019
Chandler Laughlin, September 12, 1982
Kathy Mason Lerner, May 20, 2019
Lucy Lewis, January 9, 2020
John Lyon, June 25, 2021
Stan McDaniel, January 14, 2021
Barry Melton, August 8, 2019
Geoff Muldaur, September 18, 2019
Richie Olsen, November 5, 2019
Lee Quarnstrom, November 30, 2017
Travis Rivers, October 31, 2019
Jeanne Rose, January 15, 2021
Ron Schaeffer, November 7, 2021
Eugene "Dr. Hip" Schoenfeld, January 8, 2020
Pete Sears, April 17, 1982
Ramón Sender, December 17, 2019
Lenny Silverberg, February 7, 2020
Dr. David Smith, November 12, 2019
Gerd Stern, December 2, 2018
Tsvi Strauch, January 11, 2021
Jay Thelin, November 18, 2017

Marsha Thelin, December 7, 2017
Ben Van Meter, November 18, 2018
George Walker, July 2, 2018
Erik Weber, September 12, 2020, via email
ruth weiss, November 19, 2018
Mel Weitsman, January 30, 2020
Mike Wilhelm, November 3, 2017
Phyllis Willner, October 23, 2019
Tom Wolfe, September 10, 1973
Frank Zamacona, February 17, 2020

Adams, Ansel. "Conversations with Ansel Adams: Oral History Transcript / 1972–1975." UCB Oral History Project. Internet Archive. Accessed January 18, 2021. https://archive.org/details /convanseladams00adamrich/page/n11/mode/2up.

Albright, Thomas. *Art in the San Francisco Bay Area 1945–1980: An Illustrated History*. Berkeley: University of California Press, 1985.

Allen, Don. "Interview with Donald Allen." 1995. Cuke. Accessed April 21, 2020. http://www.cuke.com/Cucumber%20Project /interviews/allen.html.

Allen, Don, and Warren Tallman. *The Poetics of the New American Poetry*. New York: Grove Press, 1974.

Alves, Bill, and Brett Campbell. *Lou Harrison: American Musical Maverick*. Bloomington: Indiana University Press, 2017.

Andersen, Christopher. *Mick: The Wild Life and Mad Genius of Jagger*. New York: Gallery Books, 2012.

Anderson, Albert T., and Bernice Prince Biggs. *A Focus on Rebellion*. San Francisco, CA: Chandler Publishing, 1962.

Angelou, Maya. *Singin' and Swingin' and Gettin' Merry Like Christmas*. New York: Random House, 1976.

Anthony, Gene. *The Summer of Love: Haight-Ashbury at Its Highest*. San Francisco: Last Gasp, 1995.

Aukeman, Anastasia. *Welcome to Painterland: Bruce Conner and the Rat Bastard Protective Association*. Berkeley: University of California Press, 2016.

Babcock, Jay. "'The Do Was the Thing': A Lengthy Chat with Chuck Gould of the San Francisco Diggers." *Digger Docs* (blog), February 9, 2019. Accessed July 16, 2019. https://diggersdocs.home.blog/2019/02/09/we-wanted-to-lead-by-example-an-in-depth-conversation-with-chuck-gould-of-the-san-francisco-diggers/.

Babcock, Jay. "Fast Learner: Siena Carlton-Firestone (aka Natural Suzanne) Testifies on Her San Francisco Diggers Days." *Digger Docs* (blog), May 18, 2020. Accessed January 5, 2021, https://diggersdocs.home.blog/2020/05/18/fast-learner-siena-riffia-aka-natural-suzanne-testifies-on-her-san-francisco-diggers-days/.

Babcock, Jay. "'For the Duration of Our Parallel Flow': An Epic Interview with Phyllis Willner of the San Francisco Diggers." *Digger Docs* (blog), December 30, 2018. Accessed July 16, 2019. https://diggersdocs.home.blog/2018/12/30/for-the-duration-of-our-parallel-flow-an-epic-interview-with-phyllis-willner-of-the-san-francisco-diggers/.

Babcock, Jay. "A Guiding Vision: A Conversation with Peter Berg of the San Francisco Diggers." *Digger Docs* (blog), September 16, 2020. https://diggersdocs.home.blog/2020/09/16/peter-berg-of-the-san-francisco-diggers/.

Babcock, Jay. "'I Lucked Out So Many Times': Claude Hayward on His Life Before, During and After His Time with the San Francisco Diggers." *Digger Docs* (blog), October 2, 2021. Accessed December 15, 2021. https://diggersdocs.home.blog/2021/10/02/i-lucked-out-so-many-times-man-claude-hayward-on-his-life-before-during-and-after-his-time-with-the-san-francisco-diggers/.

Babcock, Jay. "'We're Gonna Do Economic Activity—Without Money!': Inside the Criminal Glamour of the San Francisco Diggers with Kent Minault." *Digger Docs* (blog), February 26, 2020. Accessed January 5, 2021. https://diggersdocs.home.blog/2020/02/26/were-gonna-do-economic-activity-without-money-inside-the-criminal-glamour-of-the-san-francisco-diggers-with-kent-minault/.

Bajko, Matthew. "Film Recalls Pivotal 1965 Gay Rights Episode." *Bay Area Reporter*, June 19, 2013. Accessed April 3, 2020. https://www.ebar.com/news///243634.

Barlow, John Perry, and Robert Greenfield. *Mother American Night: My Life in Crazy Times*. New York: Crown Archetype, 2018.

Barton, Noelle. *Love, Mom and Dad*. Sonoma County, CA: No-L Publishing, 2017.

Baxter, John. *De Niro: A Biography*. London: HarperCollins, 2003.

Beckett, Samuel. *Waiting for Godot*. New York: Grove Press, 1954.

Bell, Crystal. "The Rolling Stones, '(I Can't Get No) Satisfaction': The Story Behind the Music." HuffPost, August 6, 2012. Accessed April 24, 2020. https://www.huffpost.com/entry/the-rolling-stones-i-cant-get-no-satisfaction_n_1573493.

Berman, Tosh. *Tosh: Growing Up in Wallace Berman's World*. San Francisco: City Lights Books, 2018.

Bernstein, David W., ed. *The San Francisco Tape Music Center*. Berkeley: University of California Press, 2008.

Blake, William. *The Portable Blake*. New York: Viking Press, 1967.

Blau, Herbert. *As If: An Autobiography*, vol. 1. Ann Arbor: University of Michigan Press, 2012.

Blau, Herbert. *The Impossible Theater: A Manifesto*. New York: Macmillan, 1964.

Blau, Herbert. *Programming Theater History: The Actor's Workshop of San Francisco*. London: Routledge, 2013.

Bloch, Jesse. *KSAN Jive 95 FM: The Movie*. Prerelease edit.

Bogzaran, Fariba. "Vision Beyond Surrealism: Wolfgang Paalen and Gordon Onslow Ford." In *Surrealism: Dreams on Canvas*. Roslyn Harbor, NY: Nassau County Museum of Art, 2007. Accessed January 12, 2020. https://static1.squarespace.com/static/54401f44e4b089215d 5525ef/t/56ba4c0eab48de3ef4e83f0e/1455049761819/Vision +Beyond+Surrealism+copy.pdf.

Boone, Steve, with Tony Moss. *Hotter Than a Match Head: Life on the Run with the Lovin' Spoonful*. Toronto: ECW Press, 2014.

Booth, Stanley. *Keith: Standing in the Shadows*. New York: St. Martin's Press, 1995.

Bosworth, Patricia. *Marlon Brando: A Biography*. E-book version. New York: Open Road Media, 2012.

Boulware, Jack. "The Electric Clearlight Acid Mess." *San Francisco Weekly*, August 21, 1996. Accessed July 7, 2019. https://archives .sfweekly.com/sanfrancisco/the-electric-clearlight-acid-mess /Content?oid=2133344.

Boyd, Joe. *White Bicycles: Making Music in the 1960s*. London: Serpent's Tail, 2006.

Boyd, Nan Alamilla. *Wide-Open Town: A History of Queer San Francisco to 1965*. Berkeley: University of California Press, 2003.

Boyer, Paul. *By the Bomb's Early Light: American Thought and Culture at the Dawn of the Atomic Age*. New York: Pantheon, 1985.

Brady, Mildred Edie. "The New Cult of Sex and Anarchy." *Harper's*, April 1947.

Brand, Stewart. "Notes on the Trips Festival for Ralph Gleason." Unpublished manuscript, January 29, 1969. Courtesy of Ramón Sender.

Breuer, Lee. "When Performance Art Was Performance Poetry." In *The San Francisco Tape Music Center*, edited by Robert Bernstein. Berkeley: University of California Press, 2008.

Brigden, Julia Dreyer. *Girl: An Untethered Life*. Santa Rosa, CA: Personal History Productions, 2019.

Bright, Kimberly. "Sexy and Scandalous Scrap Metal: Ron Boise's Legendary Kama Sutra Sculptures." *Dangerous Minds*, August 6, 2013. http:// dangerousminds.net/comments/sexy_and_scandalous_scrap_metal _ron_boises_legendary_kamasutra_sculptures.

Brilliant, Larry. *Sometimes Brilliant: The Impossible Adventure of a Spiritual Seeker and Visionary Physician Who Helped Conquer the Worst Disease in History*. New York: Harper One, 2016.

Brode, Douglas. *From Walt to Woodstock: How Disney Created the Counterculture*. Austin: University of Texas Press, 2004.

Broughton, James. *Coming Unbuttoned: A Memoir*. San Francisco: City Lights Books, 1993.

Broyard, Anatole. *Kafka Was the Rage: A Greenwich Village Memoir*. New York: Carol Southern Books, 1993.

Bruno, Lee. *Misfits, Merchants & Mayhem: Tales from San Francisco's Historic Waterfront, 1849–1934*. Petaluma, CA: Cameron & Company, 2018.

Bibliography

Burroughs, William. *Naked Lunch*. New York: Grove Press, 1962.

Bush, William J. *Greenback Dollar: The Incredible Rise of the Kingston Trio*. Lanham, MD: Scarecrow Press, 2013.

Cabral, Ron. *Country Joe and Me*. Bloomington, IN: First Books Library, 2006.

Cage, John. *Silence: Lectures and Writings*. Middletown, CT: Wesleyan University Press, 1961.

Cain, Abigail. "An L.A. Gallerist Bought Out Warhol's First Show for $1,000—and Ended Up with $15 Million." Artsy, June 27, 2017. Accessed June 7, 2021. https://www.artsy.net/article/artsy-editorial -la-gallerist-bought-warhols-first-painting-1-000-ended-15-million.

Callahan, Mat. *The Explosion of Deferred Dreams: Musical Renaissance and Social Revolution in San Francisco, 1965–1975*. Oakland, CA: PM Press, 2007.

Cándida Smith, Richard. *Utopia and Dissent: Art, Poetry, and Politics in California*. Berkeley: University of California Press, 1995.

Carlin, Peter Ames. *Homeward Bound: The Life of Paul Simon*. New York: Henry Holt, 2016.

Carpenter, Don. "Poetry at the Old Longshoreman's Hall." Literary Kicks, September 20, 1996. Accessed July 16, 2019. https://www.litkicks .com/Longshoreman.

Caserta, Peggy, and Maggie Falcon. *I Ran into Some Trouble*. Deadwood, OR: Wyatt-MacKenzie, 2018.

Chadwick, David. *Crooked Cucumber: The Life and Zen Teaching of Shunryu Suzuki*. New York: Broadway Books, 1999.

Chase, Marilyn. *Everything She Touched: A Life of Ruth Asawa*. San Francisco: Chronicle Books, 2020.

Cher, as told to Jeff Coplon. *The First Time*. New York: Simon & Schuster, 1998.

Choy, Philip P. *The Architecture of San Francisco Chinatown*. San Francisco: Chinese Historical Society of America, 2008.

Choy, Philip. *San Francisco Chinatown: A Guide to Its History and Architecture*. San Francisco: City Lights Books, 2012.

Christensen, Mark. *Acid Christ: Ken Kesey, LSD, and the Politics of Ecstasy*. Tucson, AZ: Schaffner Press, 2010.

Christgau, Robert. *Any Old Way You Choose It*. Baltimore: Penguin Books, 1973.

Clapton, Eric. *Clapton: The Autobiography*. New York: Broadway Books, 2007.

Cohen, Allen. "The *San Francisco Oracle*: A Brief History." In *Voices from the Underground, Volume 1: Insider Histories of the Vietnam Era Underground Press*, edited by Ken Wachsberger. Tempe, AZ: Mica's Press, 1993.

Cohen, Lisa. *All We Know: Three Lives*. New York: Farrar, Straus and Giroux, 2012.

Cohn, Norman. *The Pursuit of the Millennium: Revolutionary Millenarians and Mystical Anarchists of the Middle Ages*. New York: Oxford University Press, 1970.

Collins, Judy. *Sweet Judy Blue Eyes: My Life in Music*. New York: Crown, 2001.

Collins, Ronald K. L., and David M. Skover. *The Trials of Lenny Bruce: The Fall and Rise of an American Icon*. Naperville, IL: Sourcebooks MediaFusion, 2002.

Conrad, Barnaby, ed. *The World of Herb Caen: San Francisco 1938–1997*. San Francisco: Chronicle Books, 1997.

Cooke, John Byrne. *On the Road with Janis Joplin*. New York: Berkley Books, 2014.

Corber, Robert. *In the Name of National Security: Hitchcock, Homophobia, and Political Construction of Gender Identity*. Durham, NC: Duke University Press, 1993.

Coyote, Peter. *The Rainman's Third Cure: An Irregular Education*. Berkeley, CA: Counterpoint Press, 2015.

Coyote, Peter. *Sleeping Where I Fall*. Washington, DC: Counterpoint Press, 1998.

Cross, Charles. *Room Full of Mirrors: A Biography of Jimi Hendrix*. New York: Hyperion, 2005.

Crow, Thomas. *The Artist in the Counterculture: Bruce Conner to Mike Kelley and Other Tales from the Edge*. Princeton, NJ: Princeton University Press, 2023.

Cunningham, Douglas. *The San Francisco of Alfred Hitchcock's Vertigo: Place, Pilgrimage, and Commemoration*. Lanham, MD: Rowman & Littlefield, 2016.

Cushing, Lincoln. "A Brief History of the 'Clenched Fist' Image." Docs Populi. Last updated May 6, 2021. https://www.docspopuli.org/articles/Fist.html.

Cypher, Pat. "Interview of Janine Pommy Vega." Maria Rogers Oral History Program. June 23, 2009. Accessed July 17, 2019. https://oralhistory.boulderlibrary.org/transcript/oh1594t.pdf.

Dalenberg, Claude. "Interviews with Ananda (Claude) Dalenberg." 1994. Cuke. Accessed April 21, 2020. https://www.cuke.com/Cucumber%20Project/interviews/ananda.html.

Davidson, Michael. *The San Francisco Renaissance: Poetics and Community at Mid-Century*. Cambridge, England: Cambridge University Press, 1989.

Davis, Matthew, and Michael Farrell Scott. *Opening the Mountain: Circumambulating Mount Tamalpais, a Ritual Walk*. Emeryville, CA: Shoemaker & Hoard, 2006.

Davis, R. G. *The San Francisco Mime Troupe: The First Ten Years*. Palo Alto, CA: Ramparts Press, 1975.

de Angulo, Gui. *The Old Coyote of Big Sur*. Berkeley, CA: Stonegarden Press, 1995.

DeCoster, Miles, Mark Klett, Mike Mandel, Paul Metcalf, and Larry Sultan. *Headlands: The Marin Coast at the Golden Gate*. Albuquerque: University of New Mexico Press, 1989.

DeFeo, Jay. Collected Papers. Archives of American Art, Smithsonian Collection. Accessed December 29, 2020. https://www.aaa.si.edu/collections/jay-defeo-papers-7417.

Derogatis, Jim. "The Overlooked Influence of Creem Magazine." *New Yorker*, August 17, 2020. https://www.newyorker.com/culture/cultural-comment/the-overlooked-influence-of-creem-magazine.

Des Barres, Pamela. *I'm With the Band*. Chicago: Chicago Review Press, 2005.

Desmarais, Charles. "A Lifetime of Bringing Bold Creations to Light." *San Francisco Chronicle*, January 4, 2018.

Bibliography

Desmarais, Charles. "Too Much Is Just Right." *San Francisco Chronicle,* October 29, 2016.

Diller, Phyllis. *Like a Lampshade in a Whorehouse: My Life in Comedy.* New York: Penguin Books, 2005.

di Prima, Diane. "On Digger Days." Excerpt from 1999 interview with David Meltzer. In *San Francisco Beat / Talking with the Poets,* edited by David Meltzer. San Francisco: City Lights Books, 2001.

di Prima, Diane. *Memoirs of a Beatnik.* New York: Penguin Books, 1998.

di Prima, Diane. *Recollections of My Life as a Woman: The New York Years: A Memoir.* New York: Viking, 2001.

di Prima, Diane, Lawrence Ferlinghetti, and Herb Gold, "Keep the Beat: The Greatest Minds of a Generation." *Washington Post* video, June 30, 2017. Accessed May 8, 2020. https://www.washingtonpost.com /video/entertainment/keep-the-beat-the-greatest-minds-of-a -generation/2017/06/30/068d0694-5a6b-11e7-aa69-3964a7d55207 _video.html.

Dizikes, John. *Love Songs: The Lives, Loves, and Poetry of Nine American Women.* Amenia, NY: Animal Mitchell, 2018.

Dorman, Michael. *Witch Hunt: The Underside of American Democracy.* New York: Delacorte Press, 1976.

Douglas, Ann. "Strange Lives, Chosen Lives: The Beat Art of Joyce Johnson." Introduction to Joyce Johnson, *Minor Characters: A Young Woman's Coming-of-Age in the Beat Orbit of Jack Kerouac.* New York: Penguin Books, 1999.

Duncan, Michael, and Kristine McKenna. *Semina Culture: Wallace Berman & His Circle.* Santa Monica, CA: DAP / Santa Monica Museum of Art, 2005.

Duncan, Robert. *A Book of Resemblances.* New Haven, CT: Henry Wenning, 1966.

Dylan, Bob. *Chronicles,* vol. 1. New York: Simon & Schuster, 2004.

Eames, David B. *San Francisco Street Secrets: The Stories Behind San Francisco Street Names.* Baldwin Park, CA: Gem Guides, 1995.

Echols, Alice. *Scars of Sweet Paradise: The Life and Times of Janis Joplin.* New York: Henry Holt, 1999.

Bibliography

Edelstein, Andrew J. *The Pop Sixties: A Personal and Irreverent Guide.* New York: World Almanac, 1985.

Einarson, John, with Richie Furay. *There's Something Happening Here: The Story of Buffalo Springfield, for What It's Worth.* London: Rogan House, 1997.

Eisner, Bruce. "Interview with an Alchemist: Bear: Owsley, LSD Chemist Extraordinaire, In Conversation with Bruce Eisner." *Psychedelic Island Views,* May 17, 1998. Internet Archive. Accessed July 10, 2019. https://web.archive.org/web/20050924043224/http://www.bruceeisner.com/writings/2004/01/interview_with__2.html.

Elder, Muldoon. "Busted!" Empty Mirror. Accessed July 8, 2019. https://www.emptymirrorbooks.com/thirdpage/busted2.html.

Emerick, Geoff, and Howard Massey. *Here, There and Everywhere: My Life Recording the Music of THE BEATLES.* New York: Gotham, 2006.

English, Ilene. *Hippie Chick: Coming of Age in the '60s.* Berkeley, CA: She Writes Press, 2019.

Epstein, Joseph. "My 1950's." *Commentary,* September 1993. Accessed May 9, 2020. https://www.commentarymagazine.com/articles/joseph-epstein/my-1950s/.

Erlewine, Michael. *Classic Posters: The Interviews, Part One.* Big Rapids, MI: Heart Center Publications, 2011. http://www.astrologysoftware.com/download/classic_posters_1.pdf.

Everson, William. *Archetype West: The Pacific Coast as a Literary Region.* Berkeley, CA: Oyez, 1976.

Everson, William. "Brother Antoninus: Poet, Printer and Religious: Oral History Transcript / and Related Material, 1965–1966." UCB Oral History Project. Internet Archive. Accessed January 18, 2021. https://archive.org/details/brotherantoninus00everrich/page/n19/mode/2up.

Faas, Ekbert. *Young Robert Duncan: Portrait of the Poet as Homosexual in Society.* Santa Barbara, CA: Black Sparrow Press, 1983.

Faithfull, Marianne, with David Dalton. *Faithfull: An Autobiography.* London: Michael Joseph, 1994.

Fallon, Michael. "Bohemia's New Haven." *San Francisco Examiner.* September 7, 1965.

Bibliography

Fallon, Michael. "New Hip Hangout—Blue Unicorn." *San Francisco Examiner*, September 6, 1965.

Fariña, Richard. *Been Down So Long It Looks Like Up to Me*. New York: Penguin, 1993.

Farrell, James J. *The Spirit of the Sixties: The Making of Postwar Radicalism*. New York: Routledge, 1997.

Ferlinghetti, Lawrence. *A Coney Island of the Mind*. New York: New Directions, 2008.

Ferlinghetti, Lawrence, and Nancy Peters. *Literary San Francisco: A Pictorial History from the Beginnings to the Present Day*. San Francisco: City Lights Books, 1980.

Fields, Rick. *How the Swans Came to the Lake: A Narrative History of Buddhism in America*. Boston: Shambhala, 1986.

Finney, Brian. *Christopher Isherwood: A Critical Biography*. New York: Oxford University Press, 1979.

Fleming, Thomas. "Segregation and the Civil Rights Movement in San Francisco." Interview by Chris Carlsson, January 9, 1999. FoundSF. http://www.foundsf.org/index.php?title=Segregation_and_the_Civil _Rights_Movement_in_San_Francisco.

Foley, Jack. "*O Her Blackness Sparkles!*": The Life and Times of the Batman Art Gallery, San Francisco 1960–1965*. San Francisco: 3300 Press, 1995.

Folsom, Tom. *Hopper: A Journey into the American Dream*. New York: It Books, 2013.

Foreman, Katya. "Short but Sweet: The Miniskirt." BBC, October 21, 2014. Accessed September 24, 2021. https://www.bbc.com/culture /article/20140523-short-but-sweet-the-miniskirt.

Foster, Mo. *Play Like Elvis!: How British Musicians Bought the American Dream*. London: Sanctuary, 2000.

Fowler, Gene. *Minutes of the Last Meeting*. New York: Viking Press, 1954.

Frame, Pete. *The Restless Generation: How Rock Music Changed the Face of 1950s Britain*. London: Rogan House, 2007.

Franger, Wilhelm. *The Millennium of Hieronymus Bosch*. New York: Hacker Art Books, 1976.

Frankenstein, Alfred. "New Music—Wacky and Interesting." *San Francisco Chronicle*, June 15, 1961.

Bibliography

Frankfort, Ellen. *The Voice: Life at the Village Voice.* New York: William Morrow, 1976.

Freeman, Jo. "Freedom Now! to Free Speech: How the 1963–4 Bay Area Civil Rights Demonstrations Paved the Way to Campus Protest." FoundSF. https://www.foundsf.org/index.php?title=Freedom_Now!_to_Free_Speech:_How_the_1963-64_Bay_Area_Civil_Rights_Demonstrations_Paved_the_Way_to_Campus_Protest.

Furlong, Monica. *Zen Effects: The Life of Alan Watts.* Boston: Houghton Mifflin, 1986.

Gagosian Gallery. *Ferus.* New York: Rizzoli International Editions, 2009.

Gans, David. *Conversations with the Dead.* New York: Citadel Press, 1991.

George-Warren, Holly. *Janis: Her Life and Music.* New York: Simon & Schuster, 2019.

Geselowitz, Gabriela. "The House on Middaugh Street." Bklynr, September 25, 2014. Accessed May 9, 2019. https://www.bklynr.com/the-house-on-middagh-street/.

Gidlow, Elsa. *Elsa: I Come with My Songs: The Autobiography of Elsa Gidlow.* San Francisco: Booklegger Press, 1986.

Gilmore, Bob. *Harry Partch: A Biography.* New Haven, CT: Yale University Press, 1998.

Ginsberg, Allen. *Howl: Original Draft Facsimile, Transcript, and Variant Versions...*Edited by Barry Miles. New York: Harper Perennial Modern Classics, 2006.

Ginsberg, Allen. "Poetry, Violence, and the Trembling Lambs." *San Francisco Chronicle: This World,* July 26, 1959.

Glancey, Jonathan. "Fender Stratocaster: A Design Icon at 60." BBC, October 21, 2014. Accessed June 4, 2020. https://www.bbc.com/culture/article/20140904-fender-stratocaster-guitar-hero.

Glaude, Eddie S., Jr. *Begin Again: James Baldwin's America and Its Urgent Lessons for Our Own.* New York: Crown, 2020.

Gleason, Ralph J. *The Jefferson Airplane and the San Francisco Sound.* New York: Ballantine, 1969.

Glotfelty, Cheryll, and Eve Quesnel, eds. *The Biosphere and the Bioregion: Essential Writings of Peter Berg.* London: Routledge, 2015. (Includes interview with Berg from 2011, just months before his death.)

Bibliography

Glueck, Grace. "Syndromes Pop at Delmonico's: Andy Warhol and His Gang Meet the Psychiatrist." *New York Times*, January 14, 1966.

Goertz, Della. "Interview with Della Goertz." Cuke. https://www.cuke.com /Cucumber%20Project/interviews/della.html.

Gold, Herbert. "When San Francisco Was Cool." *San Francisco Examiner Image* (Sunday magazine), June 2, 1991.

Goldberg, Danny. *In Search of the Lost Chord: 1967 and the Hippie Idea*. Brooklyn: Akashic Books, 2017.

Gonnerman, Mark, ed. *A Sense of the Whole: Reading Gary Snyder's Mountains and Rivers Without End*. Berkeley, CA: Counterpoint Press, 2015.

Gooch, Brad. *City Poet: The Life and Times of Frank O'Hara*. New York: Harper Perennial, 1993.

Goodman, Paul. *Growing Up Absurd: Problems of Youth in the Organized System*. New York: Random House, 1960.

Gordon, Lorraine, as told to Barry Singer. *Alive at the Village Vanguard: My Life In and Out of Jazz Time*. Milwaukee: Hal Leonard, 2006.

Gordon, Max. *Live at the Village Vanguard*. New York: Da Capo Press, 1980.

Grace, Nancy M., and Ronna C. Johnson. *Breaking the Rule of Cool: Interviewing and Reading Women Beat Writers*. Jackson: University Press of Mississippi, 2004.

Gravy, Wavy. *Something Good for a Change: Random Notes on Peace Through Living*. New York: St. Martin's Press, 1992.

Gray, Timothy. *Gary Snyder and the Pacific Rim: Creating Countercultural Community*. Iowa City: University of Iowa Press, 2006.

Green, Jane, and Leah Levy, eds. *Jay DeFeo and the Rose*. Berkeley: University of California Press, 2003.

Green, Jonathon. *Days in the Life: Voices from the English Underground 1961– 1971*. London: William Heinemann, 1988.

Green, Matthew. "Coffee in a Coffin." *Daily Telegraph*, March 9, 2017. Accessed June 12, 2020. https://www.telegraph.co.uk/travel /destinations/europe/united-kingdom/england/london/articles/the -amazing-story-of-soho-1950s-espresso-revolution/.

Greenfield, Robert. *Bear: The Life and Times of Augustus Owsley Stanley III*. New York: Thomas Dunne, 2016.

Bibliography

Gregory, Dick, with Robert Lipsyte. *Nigger: An Autobiography*. New York: Pocket Books, 1964.

Gruen, John. *The Party's Over Now: Reminiscences of the Fifties—New York's Artists, Writers, Musicians, and Their Friends*. New York: Viking Press, 1967.

Halberstam, David. *The Children*. New York: Ballantine, 1998.

Halberstam, David. *The Fifties*. New York: Random House, 1993.

Hamalian, Linda. *A Life of Kenneth Rexroth*. New York: W. W. Norton, 1991.

Hamm, Theodore. *Rebel and a Cause: Caryl Chessman and the Politics of the Death Penalty in Postwar California, 1948–1974*. Berkeley: University of California Press, 2001.

Handy, John. "John Handy: Visionary Jazz Saxophonist, Bandleader and Composer." UCB Oral History Project. Accessed January 22, 2021. https://digitalassets.lib.berkeley.edu/roho/ucb/text/handy_john.pdf.

Harding, Luke. "Life in the 'Hairy Underground': The Lost History of Soviet Hippies." *Guardian*, October 23, 2019. Accessed October 25, 2019. https://amp.theguardian.com/film/2019/oct/23/lost-history-of -soviet-hippies-documentary-communism.

Hart, Dakin, and Mark Dean Johnson. *Changing and Unchanging Things: Noguchi and Hasegawa in Postwar Japan*. New York: Isamu Noguchi Foundation, 2019.

Harvey, Matt. "Senator Joe McCarthy's Startling Morphine Source." Fix, May 3, 2013. Accessed May 17, 2020. https://www.thefix.com /content/mccarthy-aslinger-secret-morphine-addiction-source8203. (Site discontinued.)

Hassett, Brian. *The Hitchhiker's Guide to Jack Kerouac*. CA: Gets Things Done Publishing, 2015.

Hassett, Brian. *How the Beats Begat The Pranksters & Other Adventure Tales*. CA: Get Things Done Publishing, 2017.

Hathaway, Norman. "Type Confusion & Color Aggression: Interview of Victor Moscoso." March 5, 2015, at Cooper Union, New York City. Vimeo video, 1:41:29. Posted by Type@Cooper, March 21, 2015. https://vimeo.com/122859594.

Hayden, Tom. *Reunion: A Memoir*. New York: Random House, 1988.

Healey, Greg. "The Fugitive Truth." Interview with Moanna Wright. *Shindig!*, December 5, 2015. https://www.shindig-magazine.com/?p=874.

Heckman, Don. "Live: Celebrating the Ash Grove Years." *Notes from the Left* (blog), April 21, 2008. Accessed July 7, 2019. http://notes romtheleftcoast.blogspot.com/2008/04/live-celebrating-ash-grove -years.html.

Henderson, David. *'Scuse Me While I Kiss the Sky: Jimi Hendrix: Voodoo Child*. New York: Atria, 2008.

Herron, Don. *The Dashiell Hammett Tour: Thirtieth Anniversary Guidebook*. San Francisco: Vince Emery, 2009.

Hertzberg, Hendrik. *Politics: Observations & Arguments, 1966–2004*. New York: Penguin Press, 2004.

Heylin, Clinton, ed. *All Yesterdays' Parties: The Velvet Underground in Print: 1966–1971*. New York: Da Capo Press, 2005.

Hicks, Dan. *I Scare Myself: A Memoir*. London: Jawbone Press, 2017.

Hinckle, Warren. "A Social History of the Hippies." *Ramparts*, March 1967. Accessed January 28, 2021. https://www.unz.com/print/Ramparts -1967mar-00005.

Hinckle, Warren. "Warren Hinckle: Journalist, Editor, Publisher, Iconoclast." UCB Oral History Project. Accessed January 23, 2021. https:// digitalassets.lib.berkeley.edu/roho/ucb/text/hinckle _warren_2013.pdf.

Hinman-Smith, Daniel Peter. "'Does the Word Freedom Have a Meaning?': The Mississippi Freedom Schools, the Berkeley Free Speech Movement, and the Search for Freedom Through Education." Ph.D. diss, University of North Carolina, Chapel Hill, 1993.

Hjort, Christopher. *So You Want to Be a Rock 'n' Roll Star: The Byrds Day-by-Day 1965–1973*. London: Jawbone Press, 2008.

Hoffman, Abbie. *Soon to Be a Major Motion Picture*. New York: G. P. Putnam's Sons, 1980.

Holben, Lawrence R. *For All the Saints: The First Hundred Years of All Saints' Episcopal Church, San Francisco*. IN: XLibris Corporation, 2010.

Holmes, John Clellon. *Go*. New York: Thunder's Mouth Press, 1988.

Holmes, John Clellon. *Nothing More to Declare*. New York: E. P. Dutton, 1967.

Bibliography

Hopps, Walter, with Deborah Treisman and Anne Doran. *The Dream Colony: A Life in Art*. New York: Bloomsbury, 2017.

Horowitz, Mitch. *Occult America: The Secret History of How Mysticism Shaped Our Nation*. New York: Bantam, 2009.

Horowitz, Steven P. "An Investigation of Paul Goodman and Black Mountain." *American Poetry*, Fall 1989.

"Houseboat Summit Tape Transcript." Library of Consciousness. https://www.organism.earth/library/document/houseboat-summit.

Hutchinson, George. *Facing the Abyss: American Literature and Culture in the 1940s*. New York: Columbia University Press, 2018.

Hutchinson, Lydia. "The Rolling Stones' '(I Can't Get No) Satisfaction.'" Performing Songwriter. July 26, 2013. http://performingsongwriter .com/rolling-stones-satisfaction.

Huxley, Aldous. *The Doors of Perception*. CA: Otbebookpublishing, 2019.

Hyde, Don. "Notes." Unpublished notes for a memoir, courtesy of Don Hyde, 2020.

Illing, Sean. "A History of Happiness Explains Why Capitalism Makes Us Feel Empty Inside." Vox, October 31, 2018. Accessed July 19, 2019. https://www.vox.com/science-and-health/2018/9/4/17759590 /happiness-fantasy-capitalism-culture-carl-cederstrom.

Independent Voices Collection. Reveal Digital. JSTOR. http://revealdigital .com/independent-voices/. This collection of underground newspapers includes the *Los Angeles Free Press*, the *Berkeley Barb*, and the *East Village Other*.

Issel, William. "Land Values, Human Values, and the Preservation of the City's Treasured Appearance: Environmentalism, Politis, and the San Francisco Freeway Revolt." *Pacific Historical Review* 68, no. 4 (1999): 611–46. http://www.jstor.org.ezproxy.sfpl.org/stable/pdf/4492372.pdf.

Jackson, Andrew Grant. *1965: The Most Revolutionary Year in Music*. New York: Thomas Dunne, 2018.

Jackson, Blair. *Garcia: An American Life*. New York: Penguin Books, 2000.

Jacobs, Henry, and Jordan Belson. *Highlights of Vortex*. Record album. Liner notes. Smithsonian/Folkways FSS 6301.

Jarnot, Lisa. *Robert Duncan, the Ambassador from Venus: A Biography*. Berkeley: University of California Press, 2012.

Jarnow, Jesse. "Can Instagram & Colorful New Egg Cream Flavors Keep Gem Spa Afloat?" Gothamist, May 5, 2019. http://gothamist.com/2019/05/03/gem_spa_st_marks_2019.php.

Jarnow, Jesse. *Heads: A Biography of Psychedelic America*. New York: Da Capo Press, 2016.

Jenkins, Becky. "The House Un-American Activities Committee (HUAC) Hearing and Riot of 1960." FoundSF. Accessed July 7, 2019. http://www.foundsf.org/index.php?title=The_House_Un-American_Activities_Committee_(HUAC)_Hearing_and_Riot_of_1960.

Johnson, Joyce. *Minor Characters: A Young Woman's Coming-of-Age in the Beat Orbit of Jack Kerouac*. New York: Penguin, 1999.

Johnson, Wendy. *Gardening at the Dragon's Gate: At Work in the Wild and Cultivated World*. New York: Bantam, 2008.

Jones, Hettie. *How I Became Hettie Jones*. New York: E. P. Dutton, 1990.

Kamiya, Gary. "Protesters Made Sure Freeway Plan Skidded to a Halt." *SF Chronicle*, October 5, 2019.

Kaplan, Fred. "The Day Obscenity Became Art." *New York Times*, July 20, 2009.

Karlstrom, Paul. "Oral History Interview with Jay Defeo." Archives of American Art. Accessed May 13, 2020. https://www.aaa.si.edu/collections/interviews/oral-history-interview-jay-defeo-13246.

Karlstrom, Paul. "Oral History Interview with Wally Hedrick, June 10–24, 1974." Archives of American Art. Accessed May 12, 2020. https://www.aaa.si.edu/collections/interviews/oral-history-interview-wally-hedrick-12869.

Karlstrom, Paul, and Sergi Guilbault. "Oral History Interview with Bruce Conner." Archives of American Art. Accessed May 3, 2020. https://www.aaa.si.edu/collections/interviews/oral-history-interview-bruce-conner-12989.

Kato, Kazumitsu Wako. "Interview with Dr. Kazumitsu Wako Kato." August 27, 1995. Cuke. Accessed April 1, 2020. http://www.cuke.com/Cucumber%20Project/interviews/kato.html.

Kauffman, Jonathan. *Hippie Food: How Back-to-the-Landers, Longhairs, and Revolutionaries Changed the Way We Eat*. New York: William Morrow, 2018.

Bibliography

Kaukonen, Jorma. *Been So Long: My Life and Music*. New York: St. Martin's Press, 2018.

Keenan, Larry. "1960s & 1970s Counterculture Gallery." Empty Mirror. Accessed July 17, 2019. http://www.emptymirrorbooks.com/keenan/c1967-1.html.

Kent, Deborah. *Dorothy Day: Friend to the Forgotten*. Grand Rapids, MI: William B. Eerdmans, 1996.

Kerouac, Jack. *The Dharma Bums*. New York: Viking, 1959.

Kerouac, Jack. *On the Road*. New York: Viking, 1957.

Kerr, Mary, dir. *San Francisco's Wild History Groove*. Richmond, CA: CA Palm, 2011.

Kesey, Ken. *Kesey's Garage Sale*. New York: Viking, 1973.

Killion, Tom, and Gary Snyder. *Tamalpais Walking: Poetry, History, and Prints*. Berkeley, CA: Heyday Books, 2009.

Kiln, Richard. *Abstract Expressionism*. Danbury, CT: For Beginners Books, 2016.

Kirk, Kara. "Grace McCann Morley and the Modern Museum." SFMOMA, February 2017. Accessed April 17, 2020. https://www.sfmoma.org/essay/grace-mccann-morley-and-modern-museum/.

Klassen, Michael. *Hippie, Inc*. Boston: SixOneSeven Books, 2015.

Kleps, Art. *Millbrook: The True Story of the Early Years of the Psychedelic Revolution*. Oakland, CA: Bench Press, 1975.

Knight, Brenda. *Women of the Beat Generation: The Writers, Artists and Muses at the Heart of a Revolution*. Berkeley, CA: Conari Press, 1996.

Kraft, Jeff, and Aaron Leventhal. *Footsteps in the Fog: Alfred Hitchcock's San Francisco*. Santa Monica, CA: Santa Monica Press, 2002.

Kramer, Jane. *Allen Ginsberg in America*. New York: Fromm International, 1997.

Krassner, Paul. *Confessions of a Raving, Un-Confined Nut*. New York: Simon & Schuster, 1993.

Krieger, Susan. *Hip Capitalism*. Beverly Hills: Sage, 1979.

Kubernik, Harvey. *1967: A Complete Rock Music History of the Summer of Love*. New York: Sterling, 2017.

Kunkin, Art. "San Francisco Faces the Hippies: Communications Company, Diggers Organize." *Los Angeles Free Press*, March 21, 1967.

Kuo, Michelle. "Special Effects: Michelle Kuo Speaks with Michael Callahan About USCO." *Artforum*, May 2008.

Kyger, Joanne. "Interviews: Joanne Kyger—2." 1995. Cuke. Accessed April 21, 2020. http://www.cuke.com/Cucumber%20Project/interviews/kyger-2.htm.

Kyger, Joanne. *Strange Big Moon: The Japan and India Journals: 1960–1964.* Berkeley, CA: North Atlantic, 2000.

Lahr, John. "Panic Attack." *New Yorker*, May 18, 2009.

Lamott, Kenneth. "A Non-Hip View of a Human Be-In." *Los Angeles Times*, March 26, 1967.

Larsen, Stephen, and Robin Larsen. *A Fire in the Mind: The Life of Joseph Campbell.* New York: Doubleday, 1991.

Larson, Kay. *Where the Heart Beats: John Cage, Zen Buddhism, and the Inner Life of Artists.* New York: Penguin, 2012.

Lasar, Matthew. *Pacifica Radio: The Rise of an Alternative Network.* Philadelphia: Temple University Press, 1999.

Lattin, Don. *Distilled Spirits: Getting High, Then Sober, with a Famous Writer, a Forgotten Philosopher, and a Hopeless Drunk.* Berkeley: University of California Press, 2012.

Lattin, Don. *The Harvard Psychedelic Club: How Timothy Leary, Ram Dass, Huston Smith, and Andrew Weil Killed the Fifties and Ushered in a New Age for America.* New York: Harper One, 2010.

Lawlor, William T., ed. *Beat Culture: Icons, Lifestyles, and Impact.* Santa Barbara, CA: ABC CLIO, 2005.

Lee, Martin A., and Bruce Shlain. *Acid Dreams: The Complete Social History of LSD: The CIA, the Sixties, and Beyond.* New York: Grove Press, 1985.

Lemke-Santangelo, Gretchen. *Daughters of Aquarius: Women of the Sixties Counterculture.* Lawrence: University Press of Kansas, 2009.

Lenrow, Elbert. *Kerouac Ascending: Memorabilia of the Decade of On the Road.* Newcastle upon Tyne, England: Cambridge Scholars Publishing, 2010.

Lepore, Jill. *The Secret History of Wonder Woman.* New York: Alfred M. Knopf, 2014.

Lesh, Phil. *Searching for the Sound: My Life with the Grateful Dead.* New York: Little, Brown, 2005.

Bibliography

Levy, Shawn. *Ready, Steady, Go!: The Smashing Rise and Giddy Fall of Swinging London.* New York: Doubleday, 2002.

Lewis, Oscar. *San Francisco: Mission to Metropolis.* Berkeley, CA: Howell-North Books, 1966.

Lipton, Lawrence. *The Holy Barbarians.* New York: Messner, 1959.

Loeffler, Jack. "Interview with Stewart Brand, Gary Snyder, and Gen Snyder, April 22, 2008." Unpublished, courtesy of John Markoff.

Lotchin, Roger W. *The Bad City in the Good War.* Bloomington: Indiana University Press, 2003.

Lucky, Jerry. *The Family Dog Story: Life and Times of Chet Helms and the Avalon Ballroom.* Victoria, BC: 2008.

Lynch, David, and Kristine McKenna. *Room to Dream.* New York: Random House, 2018.

Lynskey, Drian. "Strange Fruit: The First Great Protest Song." *Guardian,* February 16, 2011. Accessed March 29, 2021. https://www .theguardian.com/music/2011/feb/16/protest-songs-billie-holiday -strange-fruit.

Lyon, John. Personal collection of 1960s-era civil rights, FSM, and counterculture ephemera. El Cerrito, CA.

Lyons, Jimmy, with Ira Kamin. *Dizzy, Duke, the Count and Me: The Story of the Monterey Jazz Festival.* San Francisco: A California Living Book, 1978.

Macker, John. "Stuart Z. Perkoff." OutlawPoetry, December 6, 2008. Accessed April 12, 2020. https://outlawpoetry.com/2008/john -macker-stuart-z-perkoff/.

Madison, Deborah. *An Onion in My Pocket: My Life with Vegetables.* New York: Alfred A. Knopf, 2020.

Malina, Judith. *The Diaries of Judith Malina: 1947–1957.* New York: Grove Press, 1984.

Manzarek, Ray. *Light My Fire: My Life with the Doors.* New York: Berkley Boulevard, 1998.

Markoff, John. *What the Dormouse Said: How the Sixties Counterculture Shaped the Personal Computer Industry.* New York: Viking, 2005.

Markoff, John. *Whole Earth: The Many Lives of Stewart Brand.* New York: Penguin, 2022.

Marks, Ben. "From Folk to Acid Rock, How Marty Balin Launched the San Francisco Music Scene." *Collectors Weekly*, October 16, 2017. Accessed October 31, 2017. https://www.collectorsweekly.com /articles/marty-balin/.

Marks, Ben. "Hippies, Guns, and LSD: The San Francisco Rock Band That Was Too Wild for the Sixties." *Collectors Weekly*, July 29, 2017. Accessed October 31, 2017. https://www.collectorsweekly.com /articles/hippies-guns-and-lsd/.

Marks, Ben. "Lightman Fantastic: This Artist Drenched '60s Music Lovers in a Psychedelic Dream." *Collector's Weekly*, June 21, 2016. Accessed December 27, 2019. https://www.collectorsweekly.com/articles /lightman-fantastic/.

Martenyi, Megan. "Wide Open Publics: Tracing Grace McCann Morley's San Francisco." SFMOMA, August 2017. Accessed April 17, 2020. https://www.sfmoma.org/essay/wide-open-publics-tracing-grace -mccann-morleys-san-francisco/.

Martin, George, with William Pearson. *Summer of Love: The Making of Sgt. Pepper*. London: Macmillan, 1994.

Martin, Linda, and Kerry Segrave. *Anti-Rock: The Opposition to Rock 'n' Roll*. Hamden, CT: Archon, 1988.

Mason, Nick. *Inside Out: A Personal History of Pink Floyd*. San Francisco: Chronicle, 2017.

Mason, Susan Vaneta, ed. *The San Francisco Mime Troupe Reader*. Ann Arbor, MI: University of Michigan Press, 2005.

May, Elaine Tyler. *Fortress America: How We Embraced Fear and Abandoned Democracy*. New York: Basic Books, 1988.

Mayes, Elaine. *It Happened in Monterey: Modern Rock's Defining Moment*. Culver City, CA: Britannia Press, n.d.

Maynard, John Arthur. *Venice West: The Beat Generation in Southern California*. New Brunswick, NJ: Rutgers University Press, 1991.

McChesney, Mary Fuller. *A Period of Exploration: San Francisco 1945–1950*. Oakland, CA: Oakland Museum Art Department, 1973.

McClanahan, Ed. *Famous People I Have Known*. New York: Farrar, Straus and Giroux, 1985.

McClure, Michael. *Meat Science Essays*. San Francisco: City Lights Books, 1963.

McClure, Michael. *Scratching the Beat Surface*. San Francisco: North Point Press, 1982.

McConville, David. "Cosmological Cinema: Pedagogy, Propaganda, and Perturbation in Early Dome Theaters." *Technoetic Arts* 5, no. 2 (2007): 69–85. https://www.researchgate.net/publication /233517719_Cosmological_Cinema_Pedagogy_Propaganda _and_Perturbation_in_Early_Dome_Theaters.

McCorkle, Locke. "An Evening with Locke McCorkle & Al Young." Interview by Al Young, Mill Valley Public Library, February 1, 2017. Vimeo video, 1:06:34. Posted by Gary Yost, February 4, 2017. Accessed July 16, 2019. https://vimeo.com/202559435.

McCorkle, Locke. "An Oral History Interview Conducted by Debra Schwartz in 2015." Mill Valley Oral History Program. http://ppolinks.com/mvpl39241/2016.023.001_McCorkleLocke _OralHistoryTranscript.pdf.

McCoy, Maura, prod. *The Olompali Movie: A Hippie Odyssey*. Screened on November 19, 2019. Lark Theater, Larkspur, CA.

McDonough, Jimmy. *Shakey: Neil Young's Biography*. New York: Random House, 2002.

McKenna, Kristine. *The Ferus Gallery: A Place to Begin*. Los Angeles: Steidl, 2009.

McKenna, Kristine, and David Hollander. *Notes from a Revolution: Com/Co, the Diggers & the Haight*. New York: Foggy Notion, 2012.

McKenna, Terence. *Food of the Gods: The Search for the Original Tree of Knowledge*. New York: Bantam, 1992.

McKenna, Terence. *True Hallucinations: Being an Account of the Author's Extraordinary Adventures in the Devil's Paradise*. San Francisco: HarperSanFrancisco, 1993.

McMurtry, Larry. "On the Road." *New York Review of Books*, December 5, 2002.

McNeill, Don. *Moving Through Here*. New York: Alfred A. Knopf, 1970.

McQuiddy, Steve. *Here on the Edge*. Corvallis, OR: Oregon State University Press, 2013.

Meltzer, David. *Beat Thing*. Albuquerque: La Alameda Press, 2004.

"A Message from the Hippie-Elders: The Houseboat Summit—1967." YouTube video, 1:07:12. Posted by "LucidMaul," December 16, 2011. Accessed April 8, 2020. https://www.youtube.com /watch?v=lKi4zoJPfFs.

Miles, Barry. *Call Me Burroughs: A Life*. New York: Twelve, 2013.

Miles, Josephine. "Poetry, Teaching, and Scholarship: Oral History Transcript / and Related Material, 1977–1980." UCB Oral History Project. Internet Archive. Accessed January 30, 2021. https://archive.org/details/poetryjosephine00milerich.

Miller, Douglas T., and Marion Nowak. *The Fifties: The Way We Really Were*. Garden City, NY: Doubleday, 1975.

Miller, Henry. *Big Sur and the Oranges of Hieronymus Bosch*. New York: New Directions, 1957.

Miller, Leta. "The Art of Noise: John Cage, Lou Harrison, and the West Coast Percussion Ensemble." In *Perspectives in American Music*, edited by Michael Saffle. New York: Routledge, 2000.

Miller, Melody C., dir. *ruth weiss: the beat goddess*. Screened on March 8, 2020, at Hammer Theater, San Jose, CA.

Mills, Marilyn Nathan. *Flashback: The Haight-Ashbury UFO Gallery*. Phoenix, AZ: UFO Press, 2007.

Minott, Berry, dir. *Harry Bridges: A Man and His Union*. San Francisco: MW Productions, 1992. Accessed July 21, 2020. https://www .youtube.com/watch?v=Kkbo7svtgp8&t=7s.

Montarelli, Lisa, and Ann Harrison. *Strange but True San Francisco: Tales of the City by the Bay*. London: PRC, 2005.

Morgan, Bill. *I Celebrate Myself: The Somewhat Private Life of Allen Ginsberg*. New York: Penguin, 2006.

Morgan, Bill, and Nancy J. Peters, eds. *Howl on Trial: The Battle for Free Expression*. San Francisco: City Lights Books, 2006.

Mungo, Raymond. *Famous Long Ago: My Life and Hard Times with Liberation News Service*. Boston: Beacon Press, 1970.

Bibliography

Mungo, Raymond. *Total Loss Farm: A Year in the Life*. New York: Bantam, 1971.

Murray, Nicholas. *Aldous Huxley: A Biography*. New York: Thomas Dunne, 2003.

Myers, Ronald L. "Urban Geomorphology and the Montgomery Block." Unpublished paper, San Francisco State University.

Needs, Kris. "Hendrix: The Gigs That Changed History—#3. Café Wha?" Louder Sound. Accessed May 7, 2020. https://www.loudersound.com/features/hendrix-the-gigs-that-changed-history-3-cafe-wha.

Needs, Kris. "Hendrix: The Gigs That Changed History—#4. Regent Polytechnic." Louder Sound. Accessed September 2, 2021. https://www.loudersound.com/features/hendrix-the-gigs-that-changed-history-4-regent-polytechnic.

Nelson, Steffie. "Brave New LA: Aldous Huxley in Los Angeles." *Los Angeles Review of Books*, November 22, 2013. Accessed April 1, 2020. https://lareviewofbooks.org/article/aldous-huxley-in-los-angeles/.

Newfield, Jack. *A Prophetic Minority*. New York: New American Library, 1966.

Newton, Christopher. *The Pondering Pig* (blog), February 14, 2014. Accessed February 22, 2018. https://ponderingpig.wordpress.com/2014/02/14/luminaries-of-the-haight-4-1090-page-street/.

Noakes, Tim. "Life Through a Lens: Jill Kennington." Fifth Sense, April 8, 2017. Accessed June 1, 2020. https://thefifthsense.i-d.co/en_gb/article/jill-kennington/.

Noble, Eric. "The Artists Liberation Front and the Formation of the Sixties Counterculture." Digger Archives. https://www.diggers.org/alf.htm.

Noble, Eric. "Highlights of the Digger Archives." Diggers Archives. https://diggers.org/highlights.htm.

Noble, Eric. "Sixties Date Machine." Diggers Archives. https://www.diggers.org/chrono_diggers_sql.asp.

Noble, Eric. "What's New at the Digger Archives." Diggers Archives. https://diggers.org/whats_new.htm.

Nolte, Carl. "William Mandel—Leftist Activist on KPFA Radio." Obituary. *San Francisco Chronicle*, December 8, 2016.

374 **Bibliography**

Norman, Philip. *SHOUT!: The Beatles in Their Generation*. New York: Fireside, 1981.

Norse, Harold. *Memoirs of a Bastard Angel*. New York: William Morrow, 1989.

Oakley, J. Ronald. *God's Country: America in the Fifties*. New York: Dembner, 1986.

Oldham, Andrew Loog. *Stoned: A Memoir of London in the 1960s*. New York: St. Martin's Press, 2000.

Oliveros, Pauline. "Pauline Oliveros: Improvisation, Deep Listening, and Flummoxing the Hierarchy." UCB Oral History Project. Accessed January 28, 2021. https://digitalassets.lib.berkeley.edu/roho/ucb/text/oliveros_pauline.pdf.

Ortenberg, Neil, and Daniel O'Connor, dirs. *Obscene: A Portrait of Barney Rosset and Grove Press*. New York: Arthouse Films, 2008.

Pagels, Elaine. *Why Religion: A Personal Story*. New York: Ecco, 2018.

Panek, Tracey. "How Haight St. Hippie Style Became a Levi's Sensation." Levi Strauss & Co. Accessed November 22, 2019. https://www.levistrauss.com/2019/11/22/how-haight-st-hippie-style-became-a-levis-sensation/.

Paulekas, Szou. "Vito and His Freaks: Interview." *Logos Media Podcast*, October 28, 2013. Accessed May 9, 2020. https://www.podomatic.com/podcasts/gnosticmedia/episodes/2013-10-28T00_13_44-07_00.

Pennebaker, D. A. *Monterey Pop*. New York: Leacock-Pennebaker, 1968.

Perry, Charles. *The Haight-Ashbury: A History*. New York: Wenner Books, 2005.

Perry, Helen Swick. *The Human Be-In*. New York: Basic Books, 1970.

Phillips, Lisa, ed. *Beat Culture and the New America: 1950–1965*. New York: Whitney Museum of American Art, 1996.

Phillips, Michelle. *California Dreamin': The True Story of the Mamas and the Papas*. New York: Warner, 1986.

Polte, Frank. Untitled, unpublished autobiographical fragment. Courtesy of Sally Robert (Ron Polte's widow).

"The Poster Boys." YouTube video. Posted by "telebob," December 26, 2019.

Bibliography

Accessed July 28, 2020. https://www.youtube.com/watch ?v=DDGaOq74cOc. (Video unavailable.)

Potter, Berit. "Grace McCann Morley: Defending and Diversifying Modern Art." SFMOMA, June 2017. Accessed April 17, 2020. https://www .sfmoma.org/essay/grace-mccann-morley-defending-and-diversifying -modern-art/.

Potter, Keith. *Four Musical Minimalists: La Monte Young, Terry Riley, Steve Reich, Philip Glass.* Cambridge, England: Cambridge University Press, 2000.

Priore, Domenic. *Riot on Sunset Strip: Rock 'n' Roll's Last Stand in Hollywood.* London: Jawbone Press, 2007.

Quarnstrom, Lee. *When I Was a Dynamiter, or How a Nice Catholic Boy Became a Merry Prankster, a Pornographer and a Bridegroom 7 Times.* Hollywood, CA: Punk Hostage Press, 2014.

Rabinovitch, Celia. *Duchamp's Pipe: A Chess Romance: Marcel Duchamp & George Koltanowski.* Berkeley, CA: North Atlantic Books, 2020.

Rabinovitch, Celia. *Surrealism and the Sacred: Power, Eros, and the Occult in Modern Art.* Boulder, CO: Westview Press, 2002.

Ramsey, Doug. *Take Five: The Public and Private Lives of Paul Desmond.* Seattle: Parkside Publications, 2005.

Raskin, Jonah. *For the Hell of It.* Berkeley: University of California Press, 1998.

Rattiner, Dan. "Founding of the East Village Other." *East Village Other.* Accessed May 7, 2020. http://eastvillageother.org/recollections /rattiner.

Reed, Ishmael. "Ishmael Reed on the Miltonian Origin of the Other." *East Village Other.* Accessed May 7, 2020. http://eastvillageother.org/ recollections/reed.

Reich, Charles, Jann Wenner, and Jerry Garcia. *Garcia: A Signpost to New Space.* San Francisco: Straight Arrow Press, 1972.

Reidel, James. *Vanished Act: The Life and Art of Weldon Kees.* Lincoln: University of Nebraska Press, 2003.

Reps, Paul. *6 Books in a Bag.* Honolulu: Unity Church of Hawaii, 1984.

Rexroth, Kenneth. *Collected Longer Poems.* New York: New Directions, 1968.

Bibliography

Rexroth, Kenneth. *One Hundred Poems from the Chinese*. New York: New Directions, 1971.

Richardson, Peter. *A Bomb in Every Issue: How the Short, Unruly Life of* Ramparts *Magazine Changed America*. New York: New Press, 2009.

Rivers, Larry, with Arnold Weinstein. *What Did I Do?: The Unauthorized Autobiography*. New York: Aaron Asher, 1992.

Robbins, Paul Jay. "Andy Warhol and the Night on Fire." *Los Angeles Free Press*, May 13, 1966.

Robbins, Tom. *Tibetan Peach Pie: A True Account of an Imaginative Life*. New York: Ecco, 2014.

Rolfe, Lionel. *Literary LA*. San Francisco: Chronicle, 1981.

Romano, Sally Mann. *The Band's with Me: TOUR 1964–1975*. Big Gorilla Books, 2018.

Ronstadt, Linda. *Simple Dreams: A Musical Memoir*. New York: Simon & Schuster, 2013.

Rose, Jeanne. "Jeanne Rose: Rock and Roll Couturière, Herbalist, Aromatherapist, Author, and Ecologist." UCB Oral History Project. Accessed January 11, 2021. https://digicoll.lib.berkeley.edu/record/219287?ln=en&v=pdf.

Rosemont, Franklin. "Rexroth's Chicago, Chicago's Rexroth: Wobblies, Dil Picklers, and Windy City Dada." *Chicago Review*, Autumn 2006.

Rosenbaum, Ron. "The Bob Dylan Interview." *Playboy*, March 1978.

Rosenfeld, Seth. *Subversives: The FBI's War on Student Radicals, and Reagan's Rise to Power*. New York: Farrar, Straus and Giroux, 2012.

Ross, Janice. *Anna Halprin: Experience as Dance*. Berkeley: University of California Press, 2007.

Rossman, Michael. *The Wedding Within the War*. Garden City, NY: Doubleday, 1971.

Roszak, Theodore. *The Making of a Counter Culture: Reflections on the Technocratic Society and Its Youthful Opposition*. Garden City, NY: Anchor Books, 1969.

Rothman, Sandy. "The Cabale Creamery." University of Oslo. Accessed July 7, 2019. http://folk.uio.no/alfs/cabale.htm.

Rubin, Jerry. *Growing (Up) at Thirty Seven*. Philadelphia: M. Evans, 1976.

Ryan, John Allen. "The '6' Gallery: Roots and Branches." Introduction to the catalog for *Lyrical Vision: The 6 Gallery, 1954–1957*. Exhibition at the Natsoulas/Novelozo Gallery, Davis, CA, January 12–February 28, 1990. Accessed February 17, 2020. https://communityofcreatives .com/hayward-king/.

Ryan, Paul William [Mike Quin, pseud.]. *The Big Strike*. New York: International Publishers, 1949.

Salinger, J. D. *Franny and Zooey*. Boston: Little, Brown, 1961.

Sanders, Ed. "Ed Sanders on EVO and 'The New Vision.'" *East Village Other*. Accessed May 8, 2020. http://eastvillageother.org /recollections/sanders.

Sanders, Ed. *Fug You: An Informal History of the Peace Eye Bookstore, the Fuck You Press, the Fugs, and Counterculture in the Lower East Side*. Philadelphia: Perseus, 2011.

Santana, Carlos. *The Universal Tone: Bringing My Story to Light*. New York: Little, Brown, 2014.

Schaffner, Nicholas. *Saucerful of Secrets: The Pink Floyd Odyssey*. New York: Harmony, 1991.

Schevill, James. *Where to Go, What to Do, When You Are Bern Porter: A Personal Biography*. Gardiner, ME: Tilbury House, 1992.

Schneider, David. *Crowded by Beauty: The Life and Zen of Poet Philip Whalen*. Berkeley: University of California Press, 2015.

Schumacher, Michael. *Dharma Lion: A Biography of Allen Ginsberg*. Minneapolis: University of Minnesota Press, 2016.

Schwartz, Mark, and Art Peterson. "The Place, Historical Essay." FoundSF. Accessed June 7, 2019. http://www.foundsf.org/index.php?title=The _Place.

Scriba, Jim. *"Sausalito Renaissance" & the Birth of Mid-Century Modern in Sausalito: The Artists, Poets & Impresarios of the Late 1940s*. Art exhibit. Bay Model, Sausalito, CA. December 2018.

Sculatti, Gene, and Davin Seay. *San Francisco Nights: The Psychedelic Music Trip, 1965–1968*. New York: St. Martin's Press, 1985.

Scully, Rock, with David Dalton. *Living with the Dead*. Boston: Little, Brown, 1996.

Selvin, Joel. *Hollywood Eden: Electric Guitars, Fast Cars, and the Myth of the California Paradise*. Prepublication manuscript, 2020.

378 **Bibliography**

Selvin, Joel. *Summer of Love: The Inside Story of LSD, Rock & Roll, Free Love and High Times in the Wild West*. New York: Dutton, 1994.

Sender, Ramón. "Desert Ambulance: Ramón Sender and the San Francisco Tape Music Center." English Transcription of Radio Broadcast, Museo Reina Sofia. Courtesy of Ramón Sender.

Sender, Ramón. *Home Free Home*. Unpublished manuscript. Courtesy of Ramón Sender.

Sender, Ramón. *An Idiot's Delight: My Life—The First 50 Years*. Unpublished manuscript. Courtesy of Ramón Sender.

Shafer, Jack. "The Time and Life Acid Trip." *Slate*, June 21, 2010. Accessed July 27, 2017. http://www.slate.com/articles/news_and_politics /press_box/2010/06/the_time_and_life_acid_trip.html.

Sheff, David. *All We Are Saying: The Last Major Interview with John Lennon and Yoko Ono*. New York: St. Martin's Press, 2000.

Shelton, Robert. *No Direction Home: The Life and Music of Bob Dylan*. New York: Da Capo, 1997.

Shteir, Rachel. "Everybody Slept Here." *New York Times*, November 20, 1996. https://www.nytimes.com/1996/11/10/books/everybody-slept -here.html.

Shurtleff, William, and Akiko Aoyagi, *History of Erewhon—Natural Foods Pioneer in the United States: 1966–2011*. Lafayette, CA: SoyInfo Center, 2011. https://www.google.com/books/edition/History_of _Erewhon_Natural_Foods_Pioneer/315vbOUinfEC?hl=en&gbpv =1&dq=William+Shurtleff+and+Akiko+Aoyagi,+History+of +Erewhon&printsec=frontcover.

Sidran, Ben. *The Ballad of Tommy Lipuma*. Madison, WI: Nardis Books, 2020.

Siegel, Jules. "Well, What Have We Here?" *Saturday Evening Post*, July 30, 1966.

Siff, Stephen. "Henry Luce's Strange Trip." *Journalism History* 34, no. 3 (2008): 126–34. https://doi.org/10.1080/00947679.2008.12062765.

Silverstein, Shel. *Playboy's Silverstein Around the World*. New York: Simon and Schuster, 2007.

Slick, Grace, with Andrea Cagan. *Somebody to Love?: A Rock-and-Roll Memoir*. New York: Warner, 1998.

Bibliography

Smith, David, and John Luce. *Love Needs Care: A History of San Francisco's Haight-Ashbury Free Medical Clinic and Its Pioneer Role in Treating Drug-Abuse Problems*. Boston: Little, Brown, 1971.

Smith, James R. *San Francisco's Lost Landmarks*. Sanger, CA: Word Dance Press, 2005.

Snow, Mat. *The Who: 50 Years of My Generation*. New York City: Race Point, 2015.

Snyder, Gary. *Earth House Hold: Technical Notes & Queries to Fellow Dharma Revolutionaries*. New York: New Directions, 1969.

Snyder, Gary. *Mountains and Rivers Without End*. Washington, DC: Counterpoint, 1996.

Snyder, Gary. *Passage Through India: An Expanded and Illustrated Edition*. Berkeley, CA: Shoemaker & Hoard, 2007.

Snyder, Gary. *The Real Work: Interviews & Talks, 1964–1979*. New York: New Directions, 1980.

Snyder, Gary. *Regarding Wave*. New York: New Directions, 1970.

Solnit, Rebecca. "Heretical Constellations: Notes on California, 1946–1961." In *Beat Culture and the New America: 1950–1965*, edited by Lisa Phillips. New York: Whitney Museum of American Art, 1996.

Solnit, Rebecca. *Secret Exhibition: Six California Artists of the Cold War Era*. San Francisco: City Lights Books, 1990.

Sounes, Howard. *Charles Bukowski: Locked in the Arms of a Crazy Life*. New York: Grove Press, 1998.

Sounes, Howard. *Down the Highway: The Life of Bob Dylan*. New York: Grove Press, 2001.

Southall, Brian. *Sgt. Pepper's Lonely Hearts Club Band: The Album, the Beatles, and the World in 1967*. Cambridge, MA: Carlton Books, 2017.

Starr, Kevin. *Golden Dreams: California in an Age of Abundance, 1950–1963*. Oxford, England: Oxford University Press, 2009.

Stein, Jean. *Edie: American Girl*. Edited with George Plimpton. New York: Grove Press, 1982.

Stein, Suzanne. "Cindy Keefer on Jordan Belson, Cosmic Cinema, and the San Francisco Museum of Art." SFMOMA, October 12, 2010. https://openspace.sfmoma.org/2010/10/jordan-belson/.

Stern, Gerd. "From Beat Scene Poet to Psychedelic Multimedia Artist in San Francisco and Beyond, 1948–1978." UCB Oral History Project. Accessed January 22, 2021. https://calisphere.org/item/ark:/13030 /kt409nb28g/.

Stevens, Jay. *Storming Heaven: LSD and the American Dream*. New York: Grove Press, 1987.

Stoll, Jerry, and Evan S. Connell Jr. *I Am a Lover*. Menlo Park, CA: Pacific Coast Publishers, 1961.

Stone, Robert. *Prime Green: Remembering the Sixties*. New York: Ecco, 2007.

Stroman, Elizabeth Leavy. *The Art and Life of Jean Varda*. Sausalito, CA: Purple Cottage Press, 2015.

Stryker, Susan, and Victor Silverman, dirs. *Screaming Queens: The Riot at Compton's Cafeteria*. San Francisco: KQED, 2005. https://www .youtube.com/watch?v=G-WASW9dRBU.

Subbiondo, Joe. "Cultural Integration Fellowship." Lecture, April 2, 2014, at CIF, San Francisco, CA.

Swed, Mark. "Some Enchanted Evenings." *Los Angeles Times*, April 11, 1999. Accessed April 1, 2020. https://www.latimes.com/archives /la-xpm-1999-apr-11-ca-26147-story.html.

Sweet, Charles, III. *Going Home: Coming of Age in the New Age*. Unpublished manuscript, 2019. Courtesy of Ramón Sender.

Szwed, John. *Cosmic Scholar: The Life and Times of Harry Smith*. New York: Macmillan, 2023.

Taylor, Derek. *It Was Twenty Years Ago Today*. New York: Fireside, 1987.

Thompson, Hunter. *Fear and Loathing in Las Vegas*. New York: Random House, 1972.

Torgoff, Martin. *Bop Apocalypse: Jazz, Race, the Beats, & Drugs*. Boston: Da Capo, 2016.

Townshend, Pete. *Who I Am*. New York: Harper, 2012.

Triest, Shirley Taschen. "A Life on the First Waves of Radical Bohemianism in San Francisco: Oral History Transcript / 1997." UCB Oral History Project. Internet Archive. Accessed February 6, 2021. https://archive .org/details/lifefirstwaves00trierich/page/180/mode/2up.

Trilling, Diana. *Claremont Essays*. New York: Harcourt, Brace & World, 1964.

Bibliography

Tritica, John. "Regarding Rexroth: Interviews with Thomas Parkinson and William Everson." *American Poetry*, Fall 1989.

Turner, Fred. *From Counterculture to Cyberculture: Stewart Brand, the Whole Earth Network, and the Rise of Digital Utopianism*. Chicago: University of Chicago Press, 2006.

Turner, Tammy L. *Dick Waterman: A Life in Blues*. Jackson: University Press of Mississippi, 2019.

Tytell, John. *The Living Theatre: Art, Exile and Outrage*. New York: Grove Press, 1995.

Unterberger, Richie. *Turn! Turn! Turn!: The '60s Folk-Rock Revolution*. San Francisco: Backbeat Books, 2002.

Van Buskirk, Jim, and Will Shank. *Celluloid San Francisco*. Chicago: Chicago Review Press, 2006.

Vanderknyff, Rick. "Vedanta Site Began as 'Clearinghouse for Religious Ideas.'" *Los Angeles Times*, September 8, 1989. Accessed April 5, 2020. https://www.latimes.com/archives/la-xpm-1989-09-08-li-2035 -story.html.

Van Meter, Ben, and John Lyons. *Rebirth of a Nation: The Story and Films and Art of Ben Van Meter and the North American Ibis Alchemical Company, and How the Sixties in San Francisco Weren't Just About Sex and Drugs and Rock and Roll*. CA: Edition One Books, 2018. Digital advance copy.

Van Ronk, Dave, and Elijah Wald. *The Mayor of MacDougal Street: A Memoir*. Cambridge, MA: Da Capo, 2005.

Varda, Agnès. *Uncle Yanco*. Paris: Ciné-Tamaris, 1967.

Vega, Janine Pommy. *Tracking the Serpent: Journeys to Four Continents*. San Francisco: City Lights Books, 1997.

Vincent, Stephen. "Poems in Street, Coffeehouse, and Print—The Mid-1960s." FoundSF. Accessed July 16, 2019. http://www.foundsf.org /index.php?title=Poems_in_Street,_Coffeehouse,_and_Print—The _Mid-1960s.

Vincent, Stephen. "Students Confront Race During Birmingham at San Francisco State College, 1963." FoundSF. http://www.foundsf.org /index.php?title=Students_Confront_Race_During_Birmingham_at _San_Francisco_State_College,_1963.

Bibliography

Vincent, Stephen. "Tracy Sims and the 1964 Civil Rights Protests." FoundSF. http://www.foundsf.org/index.php?title=Tracy_Sims_and _the_1964_Civil_Rights_Protests.

Von Schmidt, Eric, and Jim Rooney. *Baby, Let Me Follow You Down: The Illustrated Story of the Cambridge Folk Years.* Amherst: University of Massachusetts Press, 1994.

Wachsberger, Ken, ed. *Voices from the Underground, Volume 1: Insider Histories of the Vietnam Era Underground Press.* Tempe, AZ: Mica's Press, 1993.

Wainwright, Loudon. "The Strange New Love Land of the Hippies." *Life,* March 31, 1967.

Wakefield, Dan. *New York in the Fifties.* Boston: Houghton Mifflin, 1992.

Wakida, Patricia. "Through the Fire: Albert Saijo, Karmic Heart." *Rafu Shimpo: Los Angeles Japanese Daily News,* January 25, 2013. Accessed December 26, 2020. https://www.rafu.com/2013/01/through-the -fire-albert-saijo-karmic-heart/.

Walker, Franklin. *San Francisco's Literary Frontier.* Seattle: University of Washington Press, 1939.

Walker, Michael. *Laurel Canyon: The Inside Story of Rock-and-Roll's Legendary Neighborhood.* New York: Faber and Faber, 2006.

Walker, Michael. "Los Angeles: The True Home of the Summer of Love?" *Variety,* June 2, 2017. http://variety.com/2017/music/news/was -los-angeles-the-real-center-of-summer-of-love-1202451972/.

Wall, Rosalind Sharpe. *When the Coast Was Wild and Lonely: Early Settlers of the Sur.* Pacific Grove, CA: Boxwood Press, 1987.

Ward, Nathan. *The Lost Detective: Becoming Dashiell Hammett.* New York: Bloomsbury, 2015.

Wasserman, Abby. *Praise, Vilification & Sexual Innuendo; or, How to Be a Critic: The Selected Writings of John L. Wasserman, 1964–1979.* San Francisco: Chronicle, 1993.

Waters, Alice. *Coming to My Senses: The Making of a Counterculture Cook.* New York: Clarkson Potter, 2017.

Watts, Alan. *Cloud-Hidden, Whereabouts Unknown.* New York: Vintage, 1968.

Bibliography

Watts, Alan. *In My Own Way: An Autobiography, 1915–1965* [*IMOW*]. New York: Pantheon, 1972.

Watts, Alan. *The Way of Zen*. New York: Pantheon Books, 1957.

Weiss, Jeff. "Driving the Beat Road." *Washington Post*, June 30, 2017. https://www.washingtonpost.com/lifestyle/style/driving-the-beat -road/2017/07/03/99fc9860-5c53-11e7-9fc6-c7ef4bc58d13_story .html?utm_term=.4f51fbb53a7c.

weiss, ruth. *Can't Stop the Beat: The Life and Words of a Beat Poet*. Studio City, CA: DivineArtsMedia.com, 2011.

Wenger, Michael, and Kaz Tanahashi. "Creation in the Instant: An Interview with Painter Gordon Onslow Ford." *Wind Bell*, Fall 1991. Accessed November 16, 2019. http://cuke.com/pdf-2013/wind-bell/vol25 -no2-91.pdf.

Whitehead, Peter, dir. *Tonite Let's All Make Love in London*. London: Lorrimer Films, 1967.

Whitehead, Peter. "Wholly Communion 1." International Poetry Incarnation, Royal Albert Hall, June 11, 1965. YouTube video, 9:35. Posted by "actoto," September 10, 2010. https://www.youtube.com /watch?v=jWdYrd_UH9E.

Whiteside, Jonny. "What Were the 1966 Sunset Strip Riots Really Like? Eyewitnesses Look Back." *LA Weekly*, November 11, 2016. Accessed July 16, 2019. http://www.laweekly.com/music/what-were-the-1966 -sunset-strip-riots-really-like-eyewitnesses-look-back-7587386.

Whiting, Sam. "Anna Halprin—Modern Dance Innovator, Healer." *San Francisco Chronicle*, May 27, 2021.

Wieners, John. *The Journal of John Wieners Is to Be Called 707 Scott Street for Billie Holiday 1959*. Los Angeles: Sun & Moon Press, 1996.

Wilcock, John. "The Whither Eyes of *Time* Magazine." *Village Voice*, January 11, 1962.

Williams, Cecil. *I'm Alive!: An Autobiography*. San Francisco: Harper & Row, 1980.

Williams, Donnie, with Wayne Greenhaw. *The Thunder of Angels: The Montgomery Bus Boycott and the People Who Broke the Back of Jim Crow*. Chicago: Lawrence Hill, 2006.

Wilson, Adrian. "Adrian Wilson: Printing and Book Design." UCB Oral History Project. Accessed January 17, 2021. https://digicoll.lib.berkeley.edu/record/217166?ln=en&v=pdf.

Wilson, Elizabeth. *Bohemians: The Glamorous Outcasts*. New Brunswick, NJ: Rutgers University Press, 2000.

Wolf, Leonard, ed. *Voices from the Love Generation*. Boston: Little, Brown, 1968.

Wolfe, Tom. *The Electric Kool-Aid Acid Test*. New York: Bantam, 1968.

Wolfe, Tom. *The Kandy-Kolored Tangerine-Flake Streamline Baby*. New York: Picador, 2009.

Wolkin, Jan Mark, and Bill Keenom. *Michael Bloomfield: If You Love These Blues: An Oral History*. San Francisco: Miller Freeman, 2000.

Yenne, Bill. *San Francisco Then & Now*. San Diego: Thunder Bay Press, 1998.

Youngblood, Gene. *Expanded Cinema*. New York: E. P. Dutton, 1970.

Zack, Ian. *Odetta: A Life in Music and Protest*. New York: Random House, 2020.

NOTES

Introduction: "The great force": James Baldwin, a.q. Glaude, 82. "the westward edge": "Ode to Dick Brown" in Duncan; Jack Spicer, *An Ode and Arcadia* (Berkeley, CA: Ark Press, 1974), 25. SF and WWII: see Lotchin. "it was the Bomb": Meltzer, 45. "think of the mass murder": a.q, Boyer, 17. "a soupçon of pure": Barlow, 24.

Chapter 1: "crotchety": a.q. Jarnot, 84. Rexroth: Hamalian. "abandon formalist Trotskyite": a.q. Hamalian, 69. Personalism: see Farrell. "This is very": a.q. Jarnot, 19. "His conversation": Broughton, 64. "his true devotion": Faas, 109. "is to establish": a.q. Schevill, 74–75. CO camps: Lasar; A. Wilson; McQuiddy. "intellectual awakening…all in one": Everson, UCB OHP. "saw me as a sacramental": a.q. Cándida Smith, 82. "Strong meat": a.q. Cándida Smith, 46. "The State is the": Rexroth, "Phoenix," in *Collected Longer Poems*, 74. "When a technique": a.q. Schevill, 84. "brought up on": Duncan, a.q. Farrell, 55. "the integrity of the personality": a.q. Ferlinghetti, 155–56. "uncomfortably reminiscent": Brady, 320. "Their philosophy is": Brady, 320. Duncan and Josephine Miles: J. Miles, UCB OHP; Jarnot. "a poet who lived": a.q. Faas, 234. "a whirlpool": Broughton, 57. "I had always wanted": Broughton, 96. Helen Adam: see Knight. "lived to read": Broughton, 59. "a teacher lady…Virgin Mary…bookshops": Broughton, 59. Poetic voice: see Cándida Smith; Starr; Grace.

386   **Notes**

Chapter 2: Prewar: see Albright. Morley: see B. Potter; Kirk. "of the artist in": a.q. Lawlor, 221. "I held it imperative": a.q. McChesney, 50. "a guy unto": Weitsman interview. "Painting can blow": William Morehouse, a.q. McChesney, 42. "instilled in the": Karlstrom, "Hedrick." "art isn't what": Garcia interview. "a sense of urgency...his own way": Bischoff in AAA, a.q. Cándida Smith, 88. Photography: Adams, UCB OHP. SFAI in general: McChesney; Solnit; Cándida Smith; Aukeman; Albright. "a more earthy": a.q. McChesney, 75. Surrealism: see Rabinovitch. "His collages taught": a.q. Stroman, 40. Porter: Schevill. "bulwark against...indoctrination": a.q. May, 25. "Dupes and Fellow": *Life*, April 14, 1949.

Chapter 3: "blithe spirit of Californian...as a whole": a.q. Larsen, 162. "truth is a pathless": "Truth Is a Pathless Land," J. Krishnamurti Online, https:// jkrishnamurti.org/about-dissolution-speech. "floating zendo...monk": a.q. Fields. "ancient mathematics; alchemical": M. Horowitz, 32. Huxley: see Murray; Lattin, *Distilled*. "godfather": Lattin, *Distilled*, 6. Background of Vedanta: Lattin, *Distilled*, 127. Overview of Trabuco: Lattin, *Distilled*; Murray; Finney. "liberation from prevailing": from *Ends and Means*, a.q. Lattin, *Distilled*, 103, Kindle loc. 1881. "The concerts are for": Swed. Cage: L. Miller. "Germanic myth": Kauffman, 25. Huxley side pursuits: Murray, 387. "peculiar presentment": a.q. Stevens, 4. "remarkable but not": a.q. Stevens, xviii. "God's way of saving": a.q. Stevens, 313. MK-ULTRA: Lee and Shlain. "permitting the 'other'": a.q. Lattin, *Distilled*, 184, Kindle loc. 3126. "seeing what Adam": Huxley, 5. "If the doors": Blake. "what came through": a.q. Stevens, 56. "In a world...we have been born": Huxley, 37.

Chapter 4: "an experiment in...sex, society": a.q. Stevens, 9. "not merely expressive": Holmes, *Declare*, 105. "When the mode": Ginsberg, *Howl*, 145. Jazz and drugs: Torgoff. "the attempt to liberate": L. Miller, Kindle loc. 4474. Cage's development and prepared piano: Alves and Campbell, 67. Cage and Zen: Larson. "a sort of Village": Michael Harrington, "A San Remo Type," *Village Voice*, January 7, 1971. Cage and Lou Harrison: Alves and Campbell. "brake drums": a.q. L. Miller, 100, Kindle loc. 4894–903. "a respect for the autonomy": Tytell, 55. Origins of Living Theatre: Malina; Tytell. "We are

Notes   387

determined": Malina, 12/21/52, 259. "She is a beast": Malina, 10/21/47, 11. "reading L. Ron": Malina, 121. "Answer War": Malina, 8/18/50, 120. "Artists, in fact": E. de Kooning, a.q. Gruen, 214–15. Cage and Campbell: Larsen, 334. "Campbell's thought": Larsen, xix. "function instead of proportion": a.q. Larsen, 217. "The role of the artist": a.q. Larsen, 226. "What Campbell sought": Larsen, 258. "He is under": Malina, 12/11/56, 422.

Chapter 5: "Though white-skinned": Rivers, 22. "there was something": Rivers, a.q. Gruen, 133. "the 1950s exuberance": Rivers, 219–20. "Larry Rivers once said…in the bars across the street": Berkson, a.q. Gruen, 151. "the kind of hypersensitive": Gruen, 160. "disjointed chords": Ashbery, a.q. Gruen, 158. "Frank O'Hara was a": Denby, a.q. Gruen, 166. "G-spot": Rivers, 187. "At the club": Rivers, 282. "it was like belonging": Rivers, 282. "And when he worked": Lee Krasner, a.q. Gruen, 233. "no split between": a.q. Larsen. "like a seashell's…miraculous birds": Malina, 5/10/51, 162. "an affirmation of": Cage, *Silence*. "we were an artistic": a.q. Alves and Campbell, 156. "Feed her breakfast": a.q. Alves and Campbell. "a sort of frozen": Tytell, 78. "I freeze! I burn!": Malina, 222. Goodman: Tytell. "addled…own body": Malina, 11/20/52, 253; 10/11/52, 248. "militant insistence…revolutionary": Francine du Plessix Gray, a.q. Alves and Campbell, 166, "The Breaking (Making) of a Writer." "Theater Piece #1": Tytell, 88. *Desire Trapped* escapades: Tytell, 82. "unsettlingly handsome…He lies": Malina, 1/21/52, 207. "it was Thoreau's": Malina, 9/7/53, 293. Virgil Thomson circle: Alves and Campbell. "Jazz is my religion": Karen Newton, "Black Beat Surrealist," *Style Weekly*, July 23, 2024, https://www.styleweekly.com/black-beat-surrealist/.

Chapter 6: Gay bars: N. Boyd. "romantic, visionary": Frankenstein, a.q. Albright, 86. "for the life of the": Duncan, *Resemblances*, 10. Ghost House: Karlstrom, "Hedrick." "Thelonious Monk or Miles": Hedrick, a.q. Solnit, 34. "casual and artist": Brockway, a.q. Jarnot, 127. Interplayers: Wilson, UCB OHP; McQuiddy. "kitsch…How?…flower child": a.q. Lasar, 42. "agent of…storm": Lasar, 83. "beer-drinking": Lasar, 102. "thoroughly Indian": Snyder, *Earth House Hold*, 28. "a forgiving world": Lasar, 92. "an escape from the conventional": Snyder, a.q. Starr, *Golden*, 328. "Each…in his or

388 **Notes**

her": Lasar, 129. "Bloomsbury group": Lasar, 122. "My poetry is not": Stern, UCB OHP, 62. "gave us a whole...entertainer": McCorkle, "An Evening." Snyder on Watts: Furlong, xiii. "career as an": Furlong, 40. "unrepentant sensualist": Watts, *IMOW*, 47. "sincere, but not": Watts, *IMOW*, 156–57. "To be precise": Watts, *IMOW*, 177. AAAS: Subbiondo; Furlong; Watts, *IMOW*. "the practical transformation": Watts, *IMOW*, 247. "In retrospect...College of the Pacific": Watts, *IMOW*, 272–73. "kind of nuts": Snyder, a.q. Schneider, Kindle loc. 1509. "personal and philosophical": Snyder, *Tamalpais Walking*, a.q. Davidson, 103. "nourished each other": Snyder, *Regarding Wave*, 39. Also, Gary Snyder reading (with Jane Hirshfield) at Mill Valley Public Library, January 17, 2020.

Chapter 7: McCarthyism: see Rosenfeld. "absolute social": Dorman, 78. "alcoholism, drug addiction": a.q. Stevens, 91. Results of 10450: Oakley, 67. "Recognition of the Supreme": a.q. Miller and Nowak, 85. Norman Vincent Peale: Oakley, 326. Polls and atheism: Oakley, 185. "The young complacent": *The Causes of World War III*, a.q. Miller and Nowak, 64–65. "After all, this is a": Wolfe, *Kandy*, 170. Prosperity statistics: Oakley, 228. "TV and hi-fi": Oakley, 237. TV ownership: May, 28. "macho outsider": Bosworth, 56. "wild, sexy... rock and roll": Paglia, a.q. Bosworth, 83. "a counter-atmosphere...life giving": Blau, *Impossible*, 107. "fight the barbarians...outrage": Blau, *Impossible*, 65. "directs itself...society": Blau, *Impossible*, 121. "first minor step...to judge": Blau, *Impossible*, 168. "part of public": Elin Diamond, introduction to Blau's *Programming*, 2–3. "a more provocative...Brecht's": Blau, *As If*, 205, 203, 200. "that existential or absurdist": Blau, *Programming*, 68. "Nothing to be": Beckett, 13. "Not what you want": Yeats, a.q. Blau, *As If*, 149.

Chapter 8: Ferlinghetti: see Starr; Schumacher. "anarchism, pacifism": Ferlinghetti, a.q. Morgan and Peters, xi. Pocket Poets design: McQuiddy. Lenoir selling poetry: Hamalian. "It was as if...North Beach": McClure, a.q. Albright, 86, from Tim Holt, "North Beach," *San Francisco Magazine*, December 1972, p. 27. The Place: see J. Ryan. Bulletin board: J. Johnson, 156. "instead of listening...preening": weiss, a.q. Grace and Johnson, 70–71. weiss: weiss interview. "indifferent to reward...a privilege to live here": H. Miller, 17, 25–26. "Magic must predominate": Nin, a.q. Stroman, 30. "Man is

Notes 389

nourished...vanity": Varda, *Uncle*. Partch and sexuality: Alves and Campbell; Gilmore, 76. Snyder, Watts, and marijuana: McCorkle, "An Oral History." Snyder and Druid Heights: Snyder biographical essay in Gonnerman; Snyder, in Killion and Snyder, 104–5. "East'll meet West": Kerouac, *Dharma Bums*, 231. "I advocate...silly": Killion and Snyder, 19.

Chapter 9: "Know these words": Ginsberg, a.q. Schumacher, 27. "I'll be a genius": Ginsberg, a.q. Schumacher, 16. "The jobless, wandering": publication statement in "Our Country and Our Culture," *Partisan Review* XIX (September–October 1952), 586. "ugly spirit": Burroughs, a.q. B. Miles. "accelerated a process...relationship to reality": Ginsberg, a.q. Torgoff, 142–43. "I guess you might": Kerouac, a.q. Holmes, *Declare*. "domineering": Kerouac, a.q. Morgan, 177. "All in all": Ginsberg, a.q. Morgan, 177. "'Doctor, I don't think'": Ginsberg, a.q. Kramer, 42. "I saw the best": Ginsberg, a.q. Morgan, 203. "the first time I sat": Ginsberg, a.q. Morgan, 203. "an act of sympathy": Ginsberg, *Howl*, 152. "installed wall panels": J. Ryan; Karlstrom, "Hedrick." "It was exactly": Ryan, a.q. Aukeman, 102. "we started it": Hedrick, a.q. Aukeman, 104. "to improvise organized": Karlstrom, "Hedrick." "6 Poets at": Ginsberg, *Howl*, 165. The reading: McClure, *Scratching*, 13. "the sacredness of plant": Schneider, Kindle loc. 509. "really interested": Whalen, a.q. Schneider, Kindle loc. 494. "surprised at his own": Ginsberg, *Howl*, 165. "gone beyond a point": McClure, *Scratching*, 12–13. "ambiguity, tension": Davidson, 35. "Clown": *SF Chronicle*, June 6, 1957. "decision sound and clear": *SF Chronicle*, October 7, 1957. "the ravings of a lunatic": Hollander, "Poetry Chronicle," *Partisan Review* no. 24, 1957, 297. "a new *kind*": Holmes, *Declare*. "worships primitivism": Norman Podhoretz, "Know Nothing," *Partisan Review*, Spring 1958. "In its glorification": Podhoretz, a.q. Wakefield, 179. "people keep seeing": Ginsberg, a.q. Schumacher, 273.

Chapter 10: Nixon, Parks, a.q. D. Williams, 47. "The arc of the moral": Farrell, 83. "It was the best": Nixon, a.q. D. Williams, 255. "an instinctive individuality": Holmes, *Declare*, 110. "the music of inner...destroying it": Holmes, *Declare*, 124. "the Beat Generation": Ginsberg, a.q. Schumacher, 333. "sentimental as a lollipop...or a bard": Mailer, a.q. Wakefield, 166. "Perhaps it was": Wakefield, 166. "You're Beat": Garcia interview. Rock 'n' roll "riots": see Martin and Segrave. "the basic, heavy-beat": a.q. Martin and Segrave, 41. "a world of citizens": Greenfield, a.q. Oakley, 280. Youth cultural attitudes: Oakley, 287; see also Miller and Nowack. "They were stereotyped...submissive": Oakley, 292. "Naturally, we fell": J. Johnson, xxxiii. "in the curative": J. Johnson, 128. "I hate Jack's": J. Johnson, 133. "For me, too": J. Johnson, 137.

Chapter 11: "his wartime experiences...Baghdad by the Bay": Starr, 127. "the richest portrait": Conroy, in introduction to Conrad. DeFeo: Karlstrom, "DeFeo." Hopps and Newman: see Hopps. "was totally engaged": DeFeo, a.q. Desmarais, "A Lifetime." "paternal": Karlstrom, "DeFeo." "I would just have": Karlstrom, "Hedrick." "there was this marvelous": DeFeo, a.q. Aukeman. "slight, self-effacing": Albright, 95. "mystical": Brown, a.q. Foley, 16. "In our conscious alliance": Duncan, a.q. Albright, 95. "always been involved": a.q. Thomas Albright, "Meet Bruce Conner," *Rolling Stone*, March 9, 1968. "constellation of attitudes": Albright, 81. *Child*: Karlstrom, "Conner." "primal angst": Aukeman. "living theater...culture in action": Albright, 99. "sent letters out": Conner, a.q. Aukeman. RBPA: Aukeman; Foley, 19. "people who were making": Conner, a.q. Aukeman. *A MOVIE*: see Duncan and McKenna. "possible to have": di Prima, 266. "magic grotto": Frankenstein, a.q. Foley, 12. "Bruce was in": Villa, a.q. Foley, 8. "I wanted to create": Karlstrom, "DeFeo," 12. "funky or primitive": Karlstrom, "DeFeo," 3. "a burst of white": Lucy Lippard, a.q. Green and Levy, 57. "The room itself": Conner, a.q. Aukeman, 145. "She was dealing": McClure, a.q. Aukeman, 57. "*The Rose* itself": Getz interview. "simply being in that dome...exquisite instrument": Jacobs, a.q. Youngblood, 388, 389, 389. "We could tint": Belson, a.q. Youngblood, 389. "limitless, incomprehensively": Frankenstein. "the effects of a": McConville.

Chapter 12: Rationing: Frame, 43. Coffee: Levy; M. Green. "London's rendezvous": Frame, 120. "It was history": Frame, 94. "Although it came": Korner, a.q. Frame, 97. "We were beatniks": Pilgrim, a.q. Frame, 116. "all British rock": Frame, 116. Press and rock: Frame, 188. "It is not autocracy": Frame, 291. "it was lucky": Foster, 94. *Lady Chatterley*: Levy, 21. "bitter cold": Frame, 347–48. "vaguely left-wing": Sue Miles, a.q. J. Green, 24. "Contrary

Notes

391

to our headmaster's": J. Green, 7. "I grew up not wanting": Quant, a.q. Levy, 45. Chelsea Set: Levy. "We work hard": Stamp, a.q. Levy, 57. "Cuban-heeled boots": Levy, 17. *Queen*: see Levy.

Chapter 13: "[Ed] Kienholz was my...speaking to me": Hopps, 76. "always a mystery": Hopper, a.q. Duncan and McKenna, 333. "short, angular": Hopps, 75. Berman and jazz: Berman. "craved anonymity like": Berman, 29. "crucial to me": Hopps, 74. "just stood, for me": Brown, a.q. Duncan and McKenna, 11. "both ocular and occultic...gestural painting": Meltzer, a.q. Duncan and McKenna, 26. "transcend the 'monster'": Duncan and McKenna, 30. "infused with nostalgia": Duncan and McKenna, 9. "We were not taking": McClure, a.q. Torgoff, 281. "Light is eternity": McClure, "Peyote Poem," *Meat*. "biological mysticism": Stephen Fredman, a.q. Duncan and McKenna, 42. "They were used": Hopps, 31. "dark-side-of-the-moon": Hopps, 73. Cause of Berman arrest: see Berman; Berman interview. *Soup Cans*: Cain; Hopps. "Escalator is the backfire": Rexroth and Lipton, a.q. Rosemont, 160. "I was capable": Lipton, a.q. Maynard, 23. "not so much a book": Maynard, 40. "Sentimental...long words": Rexroth, a.q. Maynard, 44. "not to be spoken": Maynard, 68. "Come and stand here": Ginsberg, a.q. Maynard, 58. "Mentor of the Holy...Squaresville": Lipton, a.q. Maynard, 108–9. "like any other consumer": Maynard, 197.

Chapter 14: Grove Press: Ortenberg and O'Connor. "laugh sensation": a.q. Ortenberg and O'Connor. "existential impasse...*is* our meaning": Lahr. "do something useful": Pound, a.q. "James Laughlin," Poetry Foundation, https://www.poetryfoundation.org/poets/james-laughlin. "who knew what we": di Prima, *Memoirs*, 175. "broken ground for all": di Prima, *Memoirs*, 176. "In the striving": di Prima, *Recollections*, 101–2. *Floating Bear*: di Prima, *Recollections*, 101–2. "a glimpse of wonders": Stone, a.q. Jarnow, *Heads*, 42. "Given your general animus": Mailer, a.q. Wakefield, 143. "A practice of loving": Day, a.q. Kent, 90. Anti–air raid demonstrations: Farrell. "rude young man": Malina, 6/20/55, 370. "These people, by their conduct": a.q. Malina, 371. "They call Lenny Bruce": Caen, a.q. Conrad, 67. "What I want": Bruce, a.q. Collins and Skover, 21. "If [Bruce] ever": a.q. Collins and

392 **Notes**

Skover, 168. "If you haven't": a.q. Krassner, 82. Living Theatre building: John Lyon Archive. "symptomatic of the errors": a.q. Tytell, 155. "The junk merchant": Burroughs, introduction to *Naked Lunch*. "a great labyrinth": B. Miles, 244. "telling is equated": Harry Oliver, a.q. Lawlor, 37. "a point... where": a.q. B. Miles, 277.

Chapter 15: "nontheistic mode": Fields, 63. "not only the last frontier": Ferlinghetti, a.q. Allen and Tallman. "if you can imagine": Watts, *IMOW*, 305. "we were to meet": Watts, a.q. Gidlow. "studies of humanity's": Gidlow, 360. "puritanical and uninteresting": Gidlow, 71. "felt fresh, young": Gidlow, 200. "timeless time": Watts, *Cloud*, 3–4. "rural slum...poisons": Gidlow, 354. Psychedelics and Druid Heights: Gidlow; Broughton. East-West house: Dalenberg. "You can rush": Kerouac, *Big Sur*, a.q. Schneider, Kindle loc. 2335. "I was living...available in English": Kyger, "Interviews." "The first night": Goertz. "In the beginners' mind": a.q. Fields, 230. "We just observed": Weitsman interview. "Robert Duncan was there...so appealing": Kyger, "Interviews." "total trust": di Prima, *Recollections*, 319.

Chapter 16: "Let's do something": Newfield. Bay Area response: Rossman, 86. "as though the act": Conrad, 94. "Our eyes were opening": Rossman, 34. "America's lushest": Didion, a.q. Starr, 371. "courageous, dedicated": Harrington, introduction to Newfield, 13. "mysticism, anarchy...black Awakening": Newfield, 47, 30. "What are the dangers": a.q. Rosenfeld, 72. HUAC in San Francisco: see Rosenfeld; Rossman; Dorman; Free Speech Movement (FSM) Archives, https://fsm-a.org; Anderson and Biggs. "Honorable beaters...you are insane": Mandel, a.q. Nolte. "bunch of Beatniks": Anderson and Biggs, 33. Longshoremen march: Jenkins. *Operation Abolition*: Rosenfeld, 95. Meisenbach trial: Anderson and Biggs; Carolyn Anspacher, "No Student Riot, Say 5 Witnesses," *San Francisco Chronicle*, April 25, 1961. "depersonalization that reduces": Hayden, "Port Huron Statement," Wikisource, https://en.wikisource.org/wiki/Port_Huron _Statement. Enovid: Halberstam, *Fifties*. "a deep pool": a.q. Halberstam, *Fifties*, 595. "I was different...fit in": Lerner interview.

Notes 393

Chapter 17: hungry i: see Bush; Starr, 104. Harry Smith: Szwed, passim. "magic, cabalistic": a.q. Szwed, Kindle loc. 3010. "It was our": a.q. Szwed, Kindle loc. 2465. Cambridge folk scene: Von Schmidt and Rooney. "a one-man folk": Von Schmidt and Rooney, 31. "You could be loose": a.q. Von Schmidt and Rooney, 65. Cabale: Von Schmidt and Rooney; Rothman. "a rough, tough beatnik": Hicks, 69. Joplin: George-Warren; Echols. "hard-lipped folk": Dylan, 6. "milk and sugar...big trick": Dylan, 34–35. "We all play": a.q. Dylan, 95. "played these songs": Dylan, 70. "our motivation was": a.q. Von Schmidt and Rooney, 198.

Chapter 18: In general, see Bernstein. First days of TMC: Ramón Sender, "The SFTMC—A Report, 1964," in Bernstein, 43–44. "It just knocked": Sender, "Desert Ambulance." "Well...there's a guy": a.q. Sender, *Home*. "deep listening": Oliveros, UCB OHP. Oliveros bio: Bernstein. "a landscape of sound": Subotnick essay in Bernstein, "Music as Studio Art," 112. "frying eggs, a game": K. Potter. "organic rather than representational": Halprin, a.q. Ross, 87. "ordinary and extraordinary": Ross, xiv. "was to declare": Howard, a.q. Whiting. "being in nature": Halprin, a.q. Bernstein, 230. "designed as a sensory": "Anna Halprin, John Graham, Lynn Palmer, and A. A. Leath in 'The Five Legged Stool,'" Anna Halprin Digital Archive, https://annahalprindigitalarchive.omeka.net/exhibits/show/san-francisco-dancers -workshop/item/321. Sonics series: Bernstein. "thirty-five-foot": Bernstein, 11. "Can I play": Sender interview. "I brought a bowl...low and slow": Sender interview. "dancers sitting": Bernstein, 15. "We said, 'We'll'": Sender, "Desert Ambulance." "sandpaper, rubber bands": Martin, a.q. Bernstein, 160. "to look more carefully": Sender, a.q. Bernstein, 64. Art and the gang members: Sender, a.q. Bernstein, 17. Lucy Lewis: Lewis interview. "one of those": Hunter, a.q. Marks, "Hippies." "I used the cartridge": Hunter, a.q. Marks, "Hippies." Olsen: Olsen interview. "At specific times": Halprin, a.q. Bernstein, 227. Halprin in Paris: Bernstein; Green interview.

Chapter 19: "a madman show": Davis, 24. "individual prerogatives": Robert Scheer, a.q. introduction to Davis. "not merely to entertain": Davis, 13. "Unencumbered by party": Davis, 28. "Sunday nights, they'd": Ham interview.

"the first neighborhood": Ham interview. Ham: Marks, "Lightman." "Meet Brother Walter": a.q. Bernstein, 165. *In C*: Weitsman interview. "Tell a story… hypnotic music…trumpet": Lesh, 38. "a vehicle of mercy": a.q. Bernstein, 24. "aural pop art": Bernstein, 24. "avant-garde…academia": Breuer interview. "was decades": Breuer, a.q. Bernstein, 16. "rehearsal time": Ham interview. "was decades ahead": Breuer essay in Bernstein, 16. "controlled, minimal": Ham interview. Magic Theater: Ham interview; Lewis interview. "lived my life backwards": Sender interview. "a parade of changes": Ross, 182. "ceremony of trust": Ann Murphy, "Parades and Changes Over the Past 43 Years: An Interview with Anna Halprin," Dancers' Group, January 1, 2013, https://dancersgroup.org/2013/01/parades-and-changes-over-the-past-43-years-an-interview-with-anna-halprin/. Blue Unicorn: "A coffeehouse is…for the lost": Fallon, "New Hip Hangout." "a revolution of individuality": C. Perry, 20. LeMar: Aldrich interview. "I am starting": Aldrich interview. Helms: Helms, a.q. Erlewine.

Chapter 20: "people are going": Halberstam, *Children*. "We've been cooling off": Halberstam, *Children*. "race, freedom rider…transcendent experience": Hayden, 55, 97. "Until I": Vincent, "Students." Mel's Drive-In: Starr; Rossman, 88; Freeman, "Freedom." Sheraton-Palace: "Sheraton-Palace Hotel Protests," SFSU, https://history.sfsu.edu/socialjusticeproject/sheraton-palace-hotel-protests#:~:text=One%20of%20the%20most%20dramatic,the%20swanky%20Sheraton%2DPalace%20Hotel. "hymn chanting": Sy Beubis, "Police Break Up Palace Picket Line," *San Francisco Examiner*, March 2, 1964. Victory: Rosenfeld, 177; "BIG PALACE SIT-IN," *San Francisco Chronicle*, March 7, 1964, 1. Savio: Rosenfeld, 177. Boise bust: http://boiselifeworks.info/#death. Freedom Summer: see Hinman-Smith. "Don't come to Mississippi": a.q. Hinman-Smith, 69. "dialogue and open-ended": Hinman-Smith, 6. List of arrests: Hinman-Smith, 143, from Mary King, *Freedom Song* (New York: Morrow, 1987). "because of interference": "Chronology of the Free Speech Controversy on the Berkeley Campus," Free Speech Movement Archives, https://fsm-a.org/stacks/FSM_faculty_chrono.html. "It was the common supposition…Civil Rights work": Rossman, 90–91. "There is no place": a.q. Hinman-Smith, 274. "There's a time": a.q.

Rossman, 121. "we can live differently": Waters, 91. "Freedom is indivisible": a.q. Hinman-Smith, 359. "For sixties activists": Lee and Shlain, 127–28. "When a young person": a.q. Lee and Shlain, 129. "facing, alone and then": "Looking Back at the Berkeley Free Speech Movement," Michael Rossman website, http://www.mrossman.org/fsm/fsmindex.html.

Chapter 21: "not beatnik": Bailey, a.q. Levy, 26. Carnaby Street: Levy. Origin of the name Beatles: see Mark Lewisohn, *The Beatles: All These Years* (Boston: Little, Brown, 2013). Beatles in 1963: Levy, 78. "targets, chevrons": a.q. J. Green, 63. "We were missionaries": a.q. Booth, 38. "The Beatles were thugs": a.q. Oldham, 256. "the group parents": Oldham, 293. "used them as a conduit": a.q. Oldham, 293. Crime in New York: Norman, 224. "optimistic, exuberant": a.q. Foreman. "We liked him because": a.q. Taylor, 86. "maybe the only pure": Levy, 122. "streets were painted": Alexander Walker, a.q. Levy, 162. "Swinging London personified": Norman, 248. "They were all so hip": Faithfull, 42. "you effect a sort of": Nuttall, a.q. J. Green, 15. "really started the scene": a.q. Kubernik, 95. "You can mark": a.q. Hassett, *Hitchhiker*, 55. Royal Albert Hall poetry: Whiteside. "Satisfaction": L. Hutchinson.

Chapter 22: Owsley: see Greenfield. "You perform a process": Owsley, a.q. Eisner. LSD general: see Stevens; Lee and Shlain. "the weirder the better": John Wilcock, a.q. Maynard, 16. "fantasy much like": a.q. Schumacher, 311. "the whole fucking…purpose of life": Schumacher, 328, 332. Sharing it with artists: Stevens; Kramer; Lee and Shlain; Schumacher. Mary Pinchot: Stevens; Lee and Shlain. "holy or wise": a.q. Stevens, 165. "We began to see": a.q. Stevens, 150. "borderline personality types": Stevens, 150. "a school, a commune": Stevens, 208. LSD prank: Kleps, 75. "Psychedelic visionary": Kleps, 15. "stud duck…won us": McMurtry. Perry Lane: Stevens, 226. "opened up doors": Kesey in Alison Ellwood and Alex Gibney, dirs., *Magic Trip* (New York: History Channel Films, 2011). "Suddenly people were stripped": Kesey, 175. "the yoga of a man": Kesey, 200. "Kerouac drew": a.q. Hassett, *How the Beats*, 12. "And Neal would *still*": a.q. Quarnstrom, 106. "wanted to go beyond": a.q. Christensen, 145. "was the kind of guy…rocket sled": Gans, *Conversations*, 299. "I feel like I'm": Garcia interview. "they

396   **Notes**

weren't just playing...the invisible": a.q. Christensen, 143–44. "It always seemed": a.q. Reich and Wenner. "the real work": Snyder, *Earth House Hold*, 127. "For one thing": a.q. Jackson, *Garcia*.

Chapter 23: "there are more beards": Gruen, "The New Bohemia," *New York Herald Tribune*, November 29, 1964. "powerhouse of perversion": Collins and Skover, 243. Committee on Poetry letter: Schumacher, 411. "I feel terrible": a.q. Collins and Skover, 363. "hinge": K. Potter, 54. "1. The line between": a.q. F. Turner, Kindle loc. 4003. "My intentions in these works": Stern, UCB OHP. "I will fight": a.q. F. Turner, Kindle loc. 634. Classes at State: Markoff, *Whole Earth*, 121. "I actually burst": a.q. Kubernik, 83. "a rhythm thing": a.q. Siegel. "the rebels were like": Boyd, 106–7.

Chapter 24: "I can remember": a.q. Hjort, 19. Paulekas: Priore, 75. "ad hoc assemblage": Romano, 42. "The Byrds have gone": Robbins, *Los Angeles Free Press*, April 23, 1965. "like they had just": a.q. Hjort, 33. "dreamed of what... below my waist": Des Barres. *Folk-rock*: see M. Walker, *Laurel Canyon Billboard*: Unterberger, 133. "a great mimic": Hjort. "fabulous flower pattern": Cher, 96. "the muumuu": a.q. Edelstein. Buffalo Springfield: Einarson; McDonough. "one long parade": Einarson, 14. "looser and freer...at the same time": Manzarek, 67. "writing some songs": Manzarek, 94. Sunset Strip "riots": Hjort, 112. "There are over": Hjort, 112. CAFF: Taylor, 174. Valley benefit: Hjort, 121.

Chapter 25: "I speak tonight": Cydney Adams, "March 15, 1965: LBJ Speaks Before Congress on Voting Rights," CBS, https://www.cbsnews.com/news /on-this-day-march-15-1965-president-lyndon-b-johnson-speaks-before -congress-on-voting-rights-act/. "an indictment of America": a.q. Glaude, 14. "like he'd just stepped": a.q. Sculatti and Seay, 29. "George's mother": a.q. Marks, "Hippies." "a musical and visual": Sculatti and Seay, 28. "and this car pulls": a.q. Marks, "Hippies." "You're in a B movie": Loughlin interview. "Check my gun...Sheriff": Olsen interview. Light show machine: Ham interview. "You better be able": Gleason, 127. "I came from": Casady interview. "very open, per se": a.q. Gleason, 187. "that all these people": a.q. Gleason, 224, 248. "peacenik communes": Newton. "painters in one room": a.q. Jackson, 245–46. "1984, monopoly capitalism": a.q. Echols, 123. "the theater

Notes

of LSD": R. Jacopetti interview. "A time has come": a.q. C. Perry, 22–23. "A rare cultural epiphany": Coyote, *Sleeping*, 39. "far too much vulgarity": a.q. Selvin, *Summer*, 12. "Ladieeeees": a.q. S. Mason, 12. "the world's first psychedelic": Sculatti and Seay, 43. "a mural by": Gleason, 30. Longshoremen shows: Selvin, *Summer*. "a pleasure city…".: a.q. Gleason, 1. "feast day or saint's": Gleason, 2. "velvet Lotta Crabtree": Gleason, 6. "exhilarating sense": a.q. Sculatti and Seay, 48.

Chapter 26: "turned away from": F. Turner, Kindle loc. 960. "Most of the creative": a.q. Brand. "If I were to tell": a.q. C. Perry, 43. "didn't seem to fit": R. Jacopetti interview. "a tapestry, a mandala": a.q. Reich and Wenner. "Dr. Lao would…for more people…quality of the music": Gleason, 18–20. Union complaint: Anthony, 111. Freeway revolt: see Issel. "coffeehouse atmosphere": Caserta, 75. Caserta and bell-bottoms: Caserta. "found out that the people": a.q. Wolf, 217. "made the hair": J. Thelin interview. "It didn't change… rebirth": J. Thelin interview. "They were all guys…explosion of consciousness": M. Thelin interview. "There's a whole new": a.q. Wolf, 219. "what the world needs": J. Thelin interview. "the tyranny of money": a.q. Wolf, 216. "Go down on Haight…quit [his] job…mysticism, spiritual…austere": J. Thelin interview. Blind Jerry's: Strauch interview. "seekers in the H-A…protective and sympathetic": H. Perry, 7, 21–22. "I get up early": Graham interview. "the Fillmore and Avalon": a.q. Anthony, 6. "Bill was the best": a.q. Marks, "From Folk." "He would do anything": a.q. Kubernik, 14. "I suppose by nature": a.q. Taylor, 138. "Everybody was dancing": a.q. Noble, "Artists Liberation Front." "glorious temple": Marks, "Lightman." "that wild mercury sound": Dylan, a.q. Rosenbaum.

Chapter 27: "a game…difficult to read": a.q. Hathaway. "Crazy films… Kool-Aid bowl": Van Meter interview. "open up and explode": a.q. Van Meter and Lyons. "He gave us": Silverberg interview. A POOR MAN's: *Berkeley Barb*, May 13, 1966. ALF: Noble, "Artists Liberation Front." *The Beard*: see Cándida Smith. "To be a dramatist": Friedrich Nietzsche, *The Birth of Tragedy* (New York, Penguin, 1994). 55. "deviance, like difference": Howard Becker and Irving Horowitz, a.q. N. Boyd, 1. Compton's Cafeteria: Stryker and Silverman. "a pact": Getz interview. "She knocked us out": a.q.

Notes

George-Warren, 141. Joplin and freedom: George-Warren, 136. "A seed or roach": Don Hyde, email to author, July 20, 2020. "an exercise in...*Here Now*": Slick, 27, 92, 97.

Chapter 28: Hollingshead: see Stevens. "Great...second sight": a.q. Levy, 245. "Arcadian strain...than the apocalyptic": Levy, 245–46. "Eton and Soho": Levy, 100. "serious conductor of lightning": a.q. Levy, 96. "Robert wanted to break": a.q. Levy, 100. Indica: see J. Green. "Indica...was the place": a.q. Taylor, 184. "it had absolutely": Taylor, 185. "I hung out with Miles...had the books": a.q. J. Green, 77. "put up the shelves": a.q. J. Green, 75. "Lettered it all up": a.q. J. Green, 76. John Hopkins: see J. Green. "we'd won the lottery": a.q. Schaffner, 7. Notting Hill: see J. Green. Pink Floyd: see N. Mason. "Who will be there?": Schaffner, 9. "You had to pay": a.q. Schaffner, 9. *Time*: Levy, 222. "a veritable witches...world of adulthood": Faithfull, 59. "Make me sound": a.q. Emerick. "a silky, dreamy": Martin, 79. "Let's call it": B. Miles and S. Miles, a.q. J. Green, 118–19. "Pop / Op": Schaffner, 39. "everybody's friend": Taylor, 155. "a gloomy, low-ceilinged": J. Boyd, 143. Lights: N. Mason. "the Floyd were": a.q. J. Green, 111.

Chapter 29: Hunter's Point: C. Perry; John Ross at Shaping San Francisco Oral, "John Ross on the 1966 Armory Riot," July 7, 2015, Internet Archive, https://archive.org/details/Clip12ArmoryRiot. "white equivalent": Berg, a.q. Babcock, "Guiding Vision." "Time to Forget...marketeers...lonely dropout": see "Time to Forget," flyer, Digger Archives, https://www.diggers.org/images /dp006_m.jpg. Origins of name: Murcott, a.q. Holben, footnote 911. "Take a Cop": "The Early Digger Papers," Digger Archives, https://www.diggers.org /digger_sheets.htm. "baptism": Berg, a.q. Glotfelty and Quesnel. *Il Candelaio*: Berg, a.q. Babcock, "Guiding Vision." "not an act of charity": Coyote, *Sleeping*, 71. "Free to be conditioned...obscenity": "A-Political Or, Criminal Or Victim Or...," DP 004, Digger Archives, https://www.diggers.org/digger_sheets .htm#A-Political%20Or. "explore this notion": Berg, a.q. Babcock, "Guiding Vision." "life...you describe": Berg, a.q. Babcock, "Guiding Vision." "Trip Without a Ticket": "Trip Without a Ticket," Digger Archives, https://www .diggers.org/digpaps68/twatdp.html. "challenged ourselves to imagine... *authenticity*": Coyote, *Rainman*, 131. "Commodities are tools": Coyote,

Notes 399

a.q. Wolf, 118. "ludicrous promises…curriculum": Coyote, *Sleeping*, 12, 15. "Well, most everyone…mentioned": a.q. Wolf. "From our point of view": Coyote, *Sleeping*, 69. The 700 block of Ashbury Street: Strauch interview. "They looked angry": a.q. Taylor, 167. "We wanted to create…of being": a.q. Anthony, 118. "We saw the vitality": a.q. Taylor, 167. "We knew we had": Lee and Shlain, 160. Cooke: Lee and Shlain, 157. "We hold these experiences": a.q. Krassner, 108. "the color gold": Handbill, John Lyon Archives.

Chapter 30: *Oracle* origins: see A. Cohen. "more innovative…dualisms": A. Cohen. "an attempt to break": a.q. Anthony, 59. "to provide guidance": A. Cohen. "Institutional Buddhism…need both": Snyder, *Earth House Hold*, 90, 92. "the organic unity": A. Cohen. "you never interfere…in-things": Wise, a.q. Wolf, 241–42 "the *Time* magazine": Coyote, a.q. Wolf, 130. "It's free because": George Metevsky [*sic*], "Delving the Diggers," Digger Archives, https://www.diggers .org/diggers/digart1.html#Delving. "This is gonna…I don't think so": Willner, a.q. Babcock. "going beyond acid": a.q. Wolfe, *Electric*. "were looking at them… outside?": Willner, a.q., "For the Duration," Babcock. Arrests and photo: Minault, a.q. Babcock, "We're Gonna Do." Gleason on Diggers: "New Youth," *Chronicle*, November 11, 1966. Kandel: Wolf. "When I read *Howl*": a.q. Wolf, 250. "Hip and middle-class…do you, Mr. Jones?": George Metesky, "The Ideology of Failure," Digger Archives, https://www.diggers.org/diggers/digart1 .html#Ideology. "The street scene": Zapata, "In Search of a Frame," Digger Archives, https://www.diggers.org/diggers/digart1.html#Frame. "planetary frame": Coyote, *Sleeping*, 95. *Death of Money*: see Anthony; Lee and Shlain. "Well *I'm* a biker": Willner interview. "have created…absurdity of the future": Hertzberg, 439–40. "the high sign": "Nitty Gritty," *Newsweek*, December 29, 1966.

Chapter 31: "a sideshow of gnawing": *EVO*, October 1965, 3. "We belong to a party": "The New Civilization," *EVO*, August 1–15, 1966, 2. "an open war": "Active + Anxiety = Chaos," *EVO*, August 1–15, 1966, 3. "Beatniks are nice": *EVO*, May 15–30, 1966. "I first knew Walter…the name 'dada'": Ed Sanders, "Ed Sanders on EVO and 'The New Vision,'" *EVO*, http://eastvillageother.org /recollections/sanders. "Walter…told me…good to me…was a hit": Rattiner. "I went to his loft…style to the newspaper": Reed. "thugs to monitor": Reed. "amoral, a facile…to the limit": a.q. J. Stein, 168. "charming, well-born":

400   Notes

J. Stein, 183. "Dylan liked Edie": J. Stein, 283. "on an acoustic guitar": a.q. Heylin, xii. "Maybe they're tuning": a.q. Heylin, 38. "a repetition of the concrete": Grace Glueck, *New York Times*, a.q. Heylin, 4. "their concern was with": a.q. Heylin, xxvi. "plastic: sterile...better thing to say": a.q. Heylin, 18. "the most prophetic": David Fricke, "The Velvet Underground," *Rolling Stone*, March 14, 1985. "But the Velvets' music": a.q. Heylin, xi. "America has everything": a.q. McNeill, 80. "leveled...in a funny way": a.q. McNeill, 83. "Like every great": a.q. Stevens, 326. "We had no way...meeting center": Hoffman, 92. "a sacramental meeting place": a.q. McNeill, 5. "the musical children": a.q. Sanders, *Fug You*, 206. "neither art nor": Sanders, *Fug You*, 209–10.

Chapter 32: Origin of "Be-In": Brand. Gerd Stern: Markoff, *Whole Earth*, 136. "new and strong": *Berkeley Barb*, January 6, 1967, 1. "We emphasized the unity": A. Cohen, 139. "Beats, LSD": A. Cohen, a.q. Klassen, 25. "our Mark 1...new human culture": Rossman, 76. "The days of fear": John Lyon Archive. "If he starts to preach": a.q. Kramer, 6. *pradakshina*: Furlong, 181. "that belonged to me": a.q. Wolf, 34. "We can't go down": a.q. Gleason, 42. "Everyone was smiling": Des Barres. "This is just like": Brigden interview. "swinging": a.q. Gleason, 43. "What if we're": a.q. Schumacher, 480. "No fights...was full": Gleason, 43. "the Be-In was a blossom": a.q. Lee and Shlain, 162. "There was a...sense": Thompson, 7. "nothing happened at": Edd Denson, "What Happened at the Hippening," *Berkeley Barb*, January 20, 1967, 5. "journal of arts and letters": A. Cohen, 139. "use the presses": A. Cohen, 142. "As poet I hold": Courtesy of John Suiter, author of a Snyder biography in progress with Counterpoint Press. "the ancient shamanistic... humanity": Snyder, *Earth House Hold*, 105. "open one of those...But that garden...people learn...cutting down...dig a hole...just a probe": "Houseboat Summit," Library of Consciousness.

Chapter 33: "That means if": a.q. Kramer, 102–3. Poets fundraiser: Handbill, John Lyon Archive. "GENUINELY multi-...involved with": Babcock, "'We're Gonna Do.'" "just involved us actualizing": a.q. Wolf, 124. "Now wait a minute": Babcock, "Guiding Vision." "embrace of conditions...Still, they realized...a boundless hunger...Something had been...between liberation and destruction": C. Williams, 83–84, 90–91. "Fuck the Church...believe it anyhow": C. Williams, 103–4. "tools, lumber": H. Perry, 144. "content to report": Wolf, xvi. Graham denies interview: Robert Hurwitt, "Ramparts' 'Hippie' Article Raises Row," *Berkeley Barb*, June 9–15, 1967. "a distinctly fascistic…when that is done…traditional forms of leadership": Hinckle, "Social History." "50 times without": Slick, 107. "the half-step movement": Casady interview. "A long-haired girl": Silverstein. "the hippies jarred": Wainwright. "Berkeley Coed, 19": *New York Times*, February 27, 1967, 19. "Villagers…are for…rock 'n' roll music": Martin Arnold, *New York Times*, May 5, 1967, 40. "But they are still": Herb Gold, "Where the Action Is," *New York Times*, February 19, 1967, 28. Hunter Thompson: Hunter Thompson "'The Hashbury' Is the Capital of the Hippies," *New York Times Magazine*, May 5, 1967. "noisy, swarming": Bernard Weinraub, "10,000 Chant 'L-O-V-E,'" *New York Times*, March 27, 1967, 1. "Layers of inhibitions": McNeill, 8. "spiked popcorn": Clapton, 90. "fantastic!": Weinraub, "10,000 Chant. "it is the only": Hoffman, 166. "acting, for real": Doctorow, a.q. by Eric Foner in introduction to Raskin, xvii. "just as singers…put-ons": Hoffman, 116–17. "a parody of left-wing": Rubin, 98.

Chapter 34: "people came because": a.q. Echols, 157. "runaways": Quarnstrom, 212. "outrageous pamphleteers": Kunkin. "Pretty little 16-year-old": a.q. Wolf, xl. "San Francisco last weekend": Kunkin. "disperse…Much of Cal": Lew Welch, Com/Co., March 29, 1967, John Lyon Archive. Father Leon Harris and All Saints: see Holben. "squares for hippies": a.q. Holben, 279. "residents of the Haight…we are becoming": a.q. Holben, 279. "A congregation": a.q. Holben, 8. "Well, the time": a.q. Kunkin. "to discourage new arrivals": "Blunt Warning by Cahill on Hippie 'Pilgrims,'" *SF Chronicle*, March 23, 1967, 1. Health Department and Haight: "Health Crusade to 'Clean Up' the Hippies," *SF Chronicle*, March 25, 1967, 1. "Mayor Acts," *SF Chronicle*, March 24, 1967, 1. Health Department raid: "INSIDE HIPPIES' PADS," *SF Chronicle*, March 28, 1967, 1. Easter Sunday: A. Cohen. Gray Line: H. Perry, 164, 186–87. Haight Independent Proprietors: Strauch interview; McDaniel interview. "[the hippies] have some": a.q. Holben, 280. Haight Street: Jeff Jassen, "The Year of the Shuck," *Berkeley Barb*, May 5, 1967, 3. Los Angeles police: Ken Hansen, "Police Fear Inundation by 70,000 Hippies," *Los Angeles Times*, June 4, 1967. "They laughed at us": a.q. McNeill,

402   **Notes**

103. "many of the hippies": McNeill, 104. "What…in fact happened": Berg to Babcock, "Guiding Vision." "health care is a right": Smith interview; Schoenfeld interview. "Why isn't rock": a.q. Gleason.

Chapter 35: Hendrix jams with Cream: Needs, "Regent Polytechnic." Hendrix bio: Henderson; Cross. Name change: Needs, "Café Wha?" "No, but I sure": a.q. Cross, 132. Chas Chandler: Cross. "phase shifts, double-tracking": Henderson, 133. "if we don't have to tour": a.q. Emerick, 132. "We had this fantastic": a.q. Taylor, 21. "stunning Mellotron line": Emerick, 136. Recording "Strawberry Fields": see G. Martin. "the lurking schmaltz": G. Martin, 34. "I'm a bit disappointed": a.q. Kubernik, 27. "Let's make the session": a.q. Emerick, 154. "multicoloured flowing": G. Martin, 58. "a pure watercolour": a.q. Sheff. "touching show of unity": Emerick, 182. "You've given a concert": a.q. G. Martin, 147. "utopian, ironic": a.q. Kubernik, 84. "a revelation": Lee and Shlain, 182. "It was Beethoven": a.q. Taylor, 165. "Tim Leary stood up": Barlow and Greenfield, 53–54.

Chapter 36: Monterey Pop Board: Hjort, 128. "the philosophy of New": Ralph Gleason, *Parsley, Sage, Rosemary and Thyme* liner notes (New York: Columbia Records, 1966). "I said it nicely": Coyote, *Sleeping*, 99. "to help your work": Coyote, *Sleeping*, 100. "The hip malapropisms": Scully, 112. "Paul Simon is the spiritual": Scully, 120. "Be free; wear flowers": a.q. Echols, 163. "an outgrowth of Sunset…excess": Priore, 259. "Virtually everyone who played": a.q. Lucky, 72. "county fair for": Schaeffer interview. "tent-alley bazaar": Cooke, 26. "You gotta get": a.q. J. Thelin interview. "rock 'n' roll for": a.q. Carlin, 147. "Don't fuck it up": a.q. George-Warren, 151. "Those were real": a.q. Echols, 169. "being in contact": a.q. Echols, 165. Bloomfield on his performance: Wolkin, 146. Owsley: Greenfield, 102. "a celebration of an industry": Sidran, 109. "perfect…excellent": Slick, 132. "We were all shamans": a.q. Goldberg. "When I got to the Fairgrounds": Hochanadel interview. "a group that will destroy": *Monterey Pop* film soundtrack. "the best guitar playing": Christgau, 30. "I saw him take": a.q. Cooke, 36. "the English and American…I just want to grab…get mad, no": *Monterey Pop* film soundtrack. "A short while back": Bob Weir & RatDog, "Two Djinn," lyrics by Gerrit Graham, Just After Midnight Music C/O TRI, Inc., 2000.

Afterword: "The new consciousness": Ferlinghetti and Peters, 198–99. "it's a pain": Berg, a.q. Glotfelty and Quesnel. Food: see Kauffman. "preindustrial roots...dietary prophets": Kauffman, 7. Organic food industry: Kauffman; Klassen. "formality and beauty": Waters, 148. Jeanne Rose: Rose interview. Brand and computers: see Markoff, *Dormouse.*

INDEX

Abrams, Jerry, 156
Ackerman, Gerald, 7, 325
Adam, Helen, 8, 70, 148, 325
Adler, Lou, 204, 205, 309–313, 314
Adler, Stella, 28, 52
Agee, James, 27, 37, 110, 325
Albin, Peter, 213, 237, 325
Albin, Rodney, 213
Albrecht, Bob, 321
Albright, Thomas, 82, 85, 86, 325
Alexander, Bob, 84, 103
Allen, Don, 110, 123, 124, 252, 325
Alpert, Richard, 184–185, 224, 275
American Academy of Asian Studies
	(AAAS), 45–47, 121–123, 280
Anderson, Chester, 290
Anderson, Margaret, 2, 25, 325
Anger, Kenneth, 41, 104, 200, 326
Animals (band), 300–301, 313
Anslinger, Harry, 26, 50, 158, 326
Antonioni, Michelangelo, 177
Arensberg, Louise, 21, 103–104, 326
Arensberg, Walter, 21, 103–104, 326
Arminger, Priscilla (Vickie Russell),
	67, 343
Arnold, Martin, 286–287
Artaud, Antonin, 86, 102
Arthur, Gavin, 275

Artists Liberation Front (ALF),
	234–235, 253, 259, 283, 290
Asawa, Ruth, 36, 326
Asch, Moe, 135
Ashberry, John, 32–33, 36, 326
Aspinall, Neil, 306
Auden, W. H., 19, 29, 31, 70

Baez, Joan, 136, 137, 140, 168, 326
Bailey, David, 99, 171
Baillie, Bruce, 156, 239
Baker, Chet, 150, 174
Baldwin, James, x, 169, 193, 210, 224
Balin, Marty, 211–212, 216, 223, 228
Ballard, Roy, 292
Bamberger, Rosalie "Rose," 130–131
Banducci, Harry Charles "Enrico,"
	134, 326
Barber, Chris, 92, 94
Barlow, John, xii, 307, 326
Barrett, Syd, 244–245, 248
Batman Gallery, 87
Beach Boys (band), 201, 303
Beatles (band)
	American musical response to, 199
	beginnings and British Invasion of,
		172–176
	Byrds and, 202–203, 241

405

Index

Beatles (band) (*cont.*)
  Des Barres and, 204
  Dylan and, 176, 246
  mind-opening experiences of, 241,
    242–243, 246–247, 301–302
  Rolling Stones as foil to, 174–176
  Sgt. Pepper, 301–307
  "Swinging London" and, 177
Beck, Jeff, 229, 299
Beck, Julian, 27–29, 326
  Day and, 113
  Ginsberg and, 69
  Living Theatre of, 28, 35–37, 115–116
Beckett, Samuel, 54–55, 85, 109–110,
    151, 322
"Be-In," 275–280
Belafonte, Harry, 133, 293
Belson, Jordan, 88–90, 148, 156, 326
Bendich, Albert, 72
Berg, Peter, 214, 234, 249–253,
    261–262, 295, 310, 320, 326–327
Berio, Luciano, 145, 150, 154
Berkson, Bill, 32, 327
Berman, Shirley, 85
Berman, Wallace, 85, 101–106, 152,
    242, 254, 327
Berry, Chuck, 78, 173, 196, 210, 327
Besant, Annie, 18, 327
Bierman, Arthur, 222
Bierman, Sue, 222
Big Brother and the Holding Company
    (band)
  activism of, 254
  formation of, 213–214
  Getz and, 88, 237, 331
  Joplin and, 237–238, 313–314,
    316, 336
  Monterey festival and, 310, 313–314,
    316
  poster art for, 231–232
  Trips Festival and, 221
Bigarini, William, 59–60
Bischoff, Elmer, 13, 41, 69–70, 327

Black Mountain College, 36, 43, 59,
    123, 194–195
Blackstone, Elliot, 237
Blake, Peter, 306–307
Blaser, Robin, 8, 148, 327
Blau, Herbert, x, 53–55, 72
Bloomfield, Michael, 197, 227, 229,
    312, 314
Blum, Irving, 105
Boise, Ron, 165
Bono, Sonny, 205–206
Booker T. and the MG's (band), 201,
    315
Bowart, Walter, 266–267
Bowen, Michael, 249–250, 254–255,
    258, 275–276, 285
Boyd, Joe, 197, 244, 248
Brady, Mildred, 7
Brakhage, Stan, 41, 156
Brand, Stewart, 195, 219–220, 253,
    321–322
Brando, Marlon, 52–53
Brautigan, Richard, 146, 281
Brecht, Bertolt, 21, 28, 35, 54, 140, 148
Bremser, Bonnie, 192
Bremser, Ray, 192
Breton, André, 6, 37
Breuer, Lee, 55, 151–153, 155–157
Bridges, Harry, xi, 164
Broughton, James, 3, 8–9, 41–43, 47,
    121, 146
Brown, Archie, 128
Brown, James, 196, 316
Brown, Joan, 83, 85–87, 102, 146
Brown, Pat, 126, 222–223
Brown, Willie, 234
Bruce, Lenny, 114–115, 134, 192–193
Bruchlos, Barron, 112
Bruno, Giordana, 251
Bucher, Brooks, 261
Buffalo Springfield, 206–207, 208, 311,
    316
Burdon, Eric, 313, 317

Index 407

Burroughs, William, 66–68, 114, 116–117, 192, 242, 269
Byrds (band), 202–204, 206, 229, 241, 309, 311

Caen, Herb, 82, 114, 127, 129, 223, 327
CAFF (Community Action for Facts and Freedom), 208, 309
Cage, John, 21, 26–28, 34–36, 327
  Ashbery and, 33
  background of, 21
  California studies and work of, 21
  Cunningham and, 21, 27, 36
  enduring influence of, 112, 145, 157, 194, 247
  Greenwich Village community of, 30
  Gruen and, 32
  "happening" presented by, 36
  Harrison and, 27–28
  musical premise of, 26
  religious interests of, 30, 34, 36
Cage, Xenia, 27
Cahill, Thomas, 292
Cahn, Rolf, 137
Cale, John, 194, 270
California School of Fine Arts (CFSA), 9–16, 328
  bohemian outlets and, 59
  Garcia as student at, 13, 188
  Jess and, 14, 40–41
  as jewel of city, 82–83
  King Ubu Gallery and, 41
  Painterland and, 83–90
Callahan, Michael, 147, 148, 194–195, 327
Cameron (artist), 104–105
Campbell, Joseph, 18, 27, 29–30, 37, 45, 327
Capote, Truman, 270
Carmichael, Stokely, 288, 293
Carpenter, John, 227
Carr, Lucien, 65–67
Carter, Asa, 79

Casady, Jack, 212, 239, 286
Caserta, Peggy, 223
Cassady, Neal, 60, 67–68, 69, 186–187, 189, 192, 328
Castell, Luria, 153, 159, 163, 215–218, 328
Catholic Worker Movement, 113–114
Chandler, Chas, 300–301
Charlatans (band), 210–211, 216
Chauduri, Haridas, 45, 46, 47
Chávez, César, 163, 259
Cher, 205–206
Chessman, Caryl, 126–127
Christgau, Robert, 313, 317
Christopher, George, 81
Cieciorka, Frank, 253
Cipollina, John, 217
City Lights (bookstore), 57–59, 72–74
Clapton, Eric, 241, 287–288, 299
Clark, Gene, 202
Clarke, Kenny, 25–26
Clarke, Michael, 202
Clurman, Harold, 52
Cocteau, Jean, 102–103, 111
Cohen, Allen, 328
  arrest of, 262
  Be-In and, 276
  confrontation averted by, 293
  Love Pageant Rally of, 254–255, 258
  LSD supplied by, 224
  Oracle newspaper of, 257–259, 276, 278–279
Cohen, Bob, 153, 211, 227, 328
Collins, Burgess (Jess), 40–41, 70, 144–145, 148, 242, 336
Collins, Judy, 139, 293, 314
Coltrane, John, 111, 154, 189, 195, 197, 225, 229, 237
Colyer, Bill, 92–93
Colyer, Ken, 92–93, 97, 328
Com/Co, 290–292
Congress of Racial Equality (CORE), 161–162, 167–169

408 **Index**

Conner, Bruce, x, 85–88, 328
  collaboration with musicians and
    dancers, 145, 146, 147
  filmmaking of, 86, 156, 232–233
  Fraser and, 242
  influence and tradition of, 307
  Oracle centerfold on, 258
Connor, Eugene "Bull," 161, 163
Conroy, Pat, 82
Constable, Rosalind, 183
Cooke, John, 312
Corso, Gregory, 139, 243
Country Joe and the Fish, 217, 253,
    286, 314
Cowell, Henry, 21, 27, 28, 328
Coyote, Peter, 214, 251–253, 282,
    310–311, 328
Crane, Sue, 247
Crawford, Cheryl, 52
Cream (band), 287–288, 299, 301, 316
Creeley, Robert, 36
Crosby, David, 202, 229, 310, 316
Crowley, Aleister, 41, 104
Crumb, Charles, 208
Cuccia, Vincent, 193
Cullen, Countee, 2, 329
Cunningham, Imogen, 121, 329
Cunningham, Merce, 21, 27, 36, 329
Curry, Francis, 237
Curtis, Walter, 187

Dalenberg, Claude, 121, 329
Dane, Barbara, 137
Darin, Bobby, 218
Davis, Clive, 314–315
Davis, Miles
  Greenwich Village and, 27, 31, 111
  influence of, 174, 202, 225, 286
  Newport Jazz Festival and, 197
  San Francisco scene and, 41, 132
Davis, Ronnie, x, 55, 148, 151–156,
    214–215, 234, 251, 329
Day, Dorothy, 113–114, 329

de Angulo, Jaime, 40, 43, 285, 329
de Freitas, Michael (Michael X), 244
de Kooning, Elaine, 30
de Kooning, Willem, 33, 115, 116,
    269, 329
Dean, James, 53, 105
DeFeo, Mary Joan "Jay," x, 83–88, 329
  Capp Street church and, 152
  Conner and, 85, 86
  Hopps and, 104
  masterpiece of (*The Rose*), 87–88
  shows at the Place, 59, 83
DeLoach, Cartha, 128, 329
Denby, Edwin, 33
Densmore, John, 207
Des Barres, Pamela, 203–204, 277
Desnos, Robert, 2, 330
Dewey, Ken, 148, 150, 152, 330
di Prima, Diane, 80, 87, 111–112, 124,
    192, 330
Dick, Philip K., 7, 330
Dickson, Jim, 202, 208, 309
Didion, Joan, 127
Diebenkorn, Richard, 15, 104, 330
Diggers (activist group), 249–253, 257,
    259–264, 290–294
  as climate activists, 320
  Grogan as "Jesus of," 295
  Hoffman influenced by, 288
  Invisible Circus of, 281–284
  opposition to association with
    Monterey festival, 310–311
  origin of name, 250
  Thompson's admiration for, 287
Doctorow, E. L., 288
Doda, Carol, 166
Doherty, Denny, 205
Donahue, Tom, 215, 296–297, 330
Donegan, Tony "Lonnie," 92–93, 94
Donovan (singer), 177, 241, 309
Doors (band), 206–207, 208
Dreiser, Theodore, 2, 330
Dryden, Spencer, 212

Index

409

Duchamp, Marcel, 14, 15, 21, 101, 103, 330
Dugan, Judy, 223
Dunbar, John, 243
Duncan, Gary, 213, 217, 330
Duncan, Robert, x, xii, 1–4, 7–8
   Berman and, 85, 102
   at Black Mountain College, 36
   Coyote and, 252
   Ginsberg and, 68
   Interplayers and, 42
   Jess as partner of, 40–41
   and King Ubu Gallery, 40–41
   Oliveros and, 144–145
   politics of, 29
   publishers of, 15, 110
   readings of works, 9
   6 Gallery and, 70
   Tape Music Center and, 148
   world intuited by/legacy of, 222, 275, 313
Durkee, Steve, 195, 275
Dylan, Bob, 330
   activism and protest songs of, 193, 195–197
   American exceptionalism rejected by, ix
   Beatles and, 176, 246
   Blonde on Blonde, 218, 229, 300
   Byrds and, 202, 203
   electric music of, 197, 218
   folk music beginnings and success of, 139–140
   Hendrix and, 300
   influences on, 117, 135, 140, 195–196
   "Like a Rolling Stone," 196–197
   Pennebaker's documentary on, 177, 311–312
   support for Bruce, 193
   "Swinging London" and, 177–178
   Warhol's circle and, 270

Eastman, Max, 25, 113
Eggemeier, Lowell, 158

Eisenhower, Dwight D., 50–51, 125
Elder, Muldoon, 165
Elliot, Cass, 205
Elliott, Helen, 193
Elmore, Greg, 217
Emerick, Geoff, 246, 302, 305, 306
English, Michael, 248
Eno, Brian, 271
Epstein, Brian, 173, 174, 246, 303
Erdman, Jean, 27, 30, 34, 330
Erickson, Robert, 144–145
Evans, Mal, 303, 304–305
Evans-Wentz, Walter, 20
Evarts, Connor, 200
Everett, Ruth Fuller. *See* Sasaki, Ruth Fuller
Everson, William, 5, 9, 331

Faithfull, Marianne, 177–178, 241–243, 246, 304
Fallon, Michael, 157–158
Family Dog group, 215–218
Farmer, James, 161, 162, 168–169
Ferguson, Michael, 156, 210, 211, 331
Ferlinghetti, Lawrence, x, 57–59, 331
   Asian influence on, 120
   English connections of, 178
   Evergreen Review and, 110
   Hopps and, 104
   obscenity case against, 72–74
   rock shows and, 228
   Sender and, 144
Ferus Gallery, 83, 84, 101–106, 254
Fields, Rick, 119
Fonda, Peter, 106, 208, 241
Ford, Gordon Onslow, 14–15, 46, 62, 331
Ford, Jaqueline, 62
Foster, Mo, 96
Foster, Paul, 286
Frame, Peter, 94, 95, 97, 331
Francois, Terry, 164
Frankenstein, Alfred, 14, 41, 90, 155, 194, 331

410 **Index**

Franklin, Aretha, 316
Fraser, Robert, 242, 243, 306–307
freaks, ix–x, 218
Free Speech Movement (FSM),
166–169, 200, 259
Freed, Alan, 79
Freiberg, David, 217, 312
Freilicher, Jack, 31–33
Freilicher, Jane, 31–33, 331
Friedan, Betty, 131
Fritsch, Bill "Sweet William," 252,
310
Fugs (band), 193, 217, 273–274
Furay, Richie, 206

Gainsborough, Louis, 45
Gaither, Thomas, 126
Garcia, Jerry, 13, 78, 135, 188–189,
221, 331
Garcia, Sara, 221
Gee, S. Paul "Sam," 132
Gelber, Jack, 115–116
Gerrans, Arthur, 292
Getz, Dave, 88, 237, 331
Gidlow, Elsa, 2, 28, 120–121, 331
Gillespie, Dizzy, 25–26, 184, 277,
310, 331
Gilmour, David, 244–245
Ginsberg, Allen, x, 26, 27, 65–74,
331
activism of, 192–193, 217, 234
on Beat, 77
Be-In and, 276–278
Burroughs and, 116–117
at Cedar Tavern, 27
di Prima influenced by, 111
Dylan and, 196, 218
early Beat days of, 65–68
East Village home of, 191
EVO poster of, 266
Grove Press and, 109
heckler and, 107
Hendrix's representation of, 318

jazz and, 26
Living Theatre and, 116
LSD use by, 183
mainstream criticism of, 73–74
obscenity case against, 72–74
Oracle discussion and, 279
protest of marijuana laws, 158
Snyder and, 70–72, 280
"Swinging London" and, 178
writing and performing "Howl,"
69–74
Glass, Philip, 155, 269
Gleason, Madeline, 8–9, 331
Gleason, Ralph, 332
on Be-In, 277–278
competition for and resignation of,
284–285
on Family Dog shows, 216–217
as jazz critic, 82, 110
liner notes for Simon &
Garfunkel, 310
Monterey festival and, 311, 312
on Mother's (club), 215
as rock critic, 212
on Trips Festival, 221–222
underground radio and, 296
Gold, Herb, 287
Good, Jack, 96–97
Goodman, Paul, 7, 29, 35–36, 37, 332
Goodwin, Tom, 269
Gordon, Elizabeth, 16, 332
Gordon, Lorraine (née Stein, aka
Lorraine Lion), 110–111
Gordon, Max, 110–111
Gordy, Berry, 200–201
Gorky, Arshile, 12, 332
Gottlieb, Lou, 220, 238
Goya-Lukich, Jorge, 14
Graham, Bill, 217–218, 220, 227–232,
234, 260, 285, 332
Graham, Gerrit, 318
Graham, John, 147, 149
Graham, Martha, 27

Index

Grateful Dead (band)
  activism of, 234, 293
  Be-In performance, 277
  clothing of, 223
  first East Coast show of, 295
  formation of, 188–189, 217
  Haight residence of, 253
  Kesey and, 260
  Love Pageant Rally, 254
  LSD (acid tests) and, 188–189,
    217–218, 220
  Monterey festival and, 310–311,
    317–318
  Olompali residence of, 238
  poster art for, 232
  Trips Festival and, 220–222
Gravenites, Linda, 289
Graves, Morris, 27, 332
Green, Debbie, 137
Green, Luther "Spike," 233–234
Greene, Herb, 224
Greenfield, Jeff, 79–80
Greenhill, Manny, 136
Gregory, Dick, 134, 164, 253, 332
Griffin, Rick, 232
Grogan, Emmett, 249–253, 332
  arrest of, 261
  as "conscience of hippie
    community," 285
  Hoffman influenced by, 288
  Invisible Circus of, 281–284
  as "Jesus of the Diggers," 295
  money-making opposed by, 281
  opposition to association with
    Monterey festival, 310–311
  Oracle criticized by, 259
Gropius, Walter, 36, 332
Grossman, Albert, 137, 138, 140, 314, 332
Grove Press, 109–110, 114
Gruen, John, 31–33, 191, 266, 332
Guggenheim, Peggy, 27, 332
Gurley, Jim, 213–214, 232, 237
Guthrie, Woody, 133, 139, 140

Haag, John, 200
Hagen, Mike, 219
Haley, Bill, 78
Hall, Manly B., 18, 333
Hallinan, Matthew, 164
Hallinan, Patrick, 166
Hallinan, Terence, 164, 333
Hallinan, Vincent, 164, 278
Halprin, Ann, 143, 145–150, 152, 157,
    220–221, 234, 276, 333
Ham, Bill, 152–156, 211, 215, 227,
    233, 253
Hammond, John, 140
Hanrahan, William, 72, 333
Hardwick, Elizabeth, 274
Harmon, Ellen, 153, 156, 215–218
Harrington, Michael, 27, 51, 113, 127
Harris, Leon, 291, 294, 333
Harrison, George, 172–176, 202,
    302–307
Harrison, Lou, 21, 27–28, 32, 34–35,
    39–40, 145, 253
Hart, Mickey, 189
Hasegawa, Saburo, 46, 280
Haselwood, Dave, 85, 122
Hasted, John, 95, 97
Hawken, Paul, 320
Haworth, Jann, 306–307
Hayden, Tom, 130, 162–163, 333
Haynes, Jim, 247
Hayward, Claude, 290
Haywood, Bill, 2, 333
Heap, Jane, 25
Heard, Gerald, 18–20, 22, 24,
    182–183, 333
Hedrick, Wally, x, 83–86, 333–334
  Beat and, 78, 84
  Capp Street church and, 152
  as CFSA student, 13, 14
  Conner and, 86
  funk art of, 14, 83
  Garcia as student of, 13, 188
  as Ghost House resident, 41

412 Index

Hedrick, Wally (*cont.*)
  shows at the Place, 59
  and 6 Gallery, 70, 83
Heliczer, Kate, 244
Heller, Joseph, 115
Helms, Chet, 158–159, 334
  Big Brother and the Holding
    Company and, 213–214, 237
  Family Dog show and, 216
  London scene and, 248
  Monterey festival and, 312
  rock promotion by, 227–229,
    231–232
Hendricks, "Chocolate George," 263
Hendricks, Jim, 205
Hendrix, Jimi, 299–301, 310, 312,
  316–318, 334
Hennacy, Ammon, 7, 334
Hentoff, Nat, 112, 114, 314
Hertzberg, Hendrik, 263
Hesse, Hermann, 85, 103, 104, 156, 185
Hesseman, Howard, 138, 297
Hicks, Dan, 138
Hicks, Tommy, 96
Hill, Lewis Kimball, 42, 334
Hillman, Chris, 202, 204
Hillyard, Roger, 224–225,
  232–233, 320
Hinckle, Warren, 284–285
Hipp, Travis T., 137
hippies, ix, 158, 218, 257
Hochanadel, Mike, 315–316
Hoffman, Abbie, 272–273, 288,
  307, 334
Hofmann, Albert, 22, 334
Hofmann, Hans, 31, 334
Hofstadter, Richard, 51
Hogan, Frank, 115, 193
Hogan, William, 72
Hollander, John, 73
Hollingshead, Michael, 184, 241, 334
Holmes, John Clellon, 26, 68, 73,
  77, 334

Hoover, J. Edgar, 50, 127–128, 130,
  162, 334
Hopkins, John "Hoppy," 243–244,
  247–248
Hopper, Dennis, 101–102, 105–106,
  208, 334
Hopps, Walter, 83–84, 88, 101–106,
  334–335
Horn, Clayton, 72–73
House, Son, 138, 141
Hoving, Thomas, 88
Howard, Rachel, 146
"Howl"/*Howl and Other Poems*
  (Ginsberg), 65, 69–74, 111
Hubbard, Al, 24, 335
Huerta, Dolores, 163, 259
Hughes, Langston, 2, 37, 335
Hughes, Lynn, 211, 216
Huncke, Herbert, 67, 69, 192, 335
Hunter, Alberta, 2, 335
Hunter, George, 149–150, 210–211, 335
Hurt, John, 140–141
Huxley, Aldous, 17–20, 22–24, 184,
  335
Hyde, Don, 238

Indica Books, 178, 242–243, 247–248
Interplayers, 40, 41–42
Irving, Jules, 53–55
Isherwood, Christopher, 18–20, 54, 335

Jackson, Clay, 136
Jacob, Abe, 228
Jacobs, Henry "Sandy," 89–90, 335
Jacobus, Harry, 41
Jacopetti, Ben, 214, 220, 239, 335
Jacopetti, Rain, 214, 220, 239, 335
Jagger, Mick, 175, 242, 300, 304, 309
Jahrmarkt, Billy "Batman," 87
James, Billy, 208
Janiger, Oscar, 182
Jeffers, Robinson, 4, 5, 29, 61, 275,
  335–336

Index

Jefferson Airplane, 336
  Family Dog show and, 216–217
  formation of, 211–213
  Graham's shows and, 217–218,
    227–228
  Monterey festival and, 311–312, 315
  seamstress for, 321
  Slick joining, 239
  social impact of and Haight scene,
    285–286
Jenner, Peter, 244, 245, 248
Jess (Burgess Collins), 14, 40–41, 70,
  144–145, 148, 242, 336
Joans, Ted, 37, 139, 336
Jobs, Steve, 321
Johns, Jasper, 83, 105, 116
Johnson, Jimhmi, 300
Johnson, Joyce, 80, 336
Johnson, Lyndon B., 209
Johnson, Matthew "Peanut," 249
Jones, Brian, 202, 246, 300, 304, 314
Jones, Elvin, 195, 207, 336
Jones, LeRoi, 111–112, 140, 192, 336
Joplin, Janis, 138, 237–238, 313–314,
  316, 336

Kael, Pauline, 7, 43, 336
Kahn, Herman, 113, 114
Kalina, Joyce, 136
Kallman, Chester, 29, 31
Kammerer, David, 66–67, 69
Kandel, Lenore, 192, 252, 262, 277,
  281–284, 336
Kandinsky, Wassily, 12, 21
Kantner, Paul, 211
Kaprow, Allan, 112, 194
Karpen, Julius, 314
Katz, Matthew, 213, 315
Katzman, Allen, 266–267
Kauffman, Jonathan, 320
Kaufman, Bob "Bomkauf," 59–60, 336
Kaukonen, Jorma "Jerry," 138, 211–212,
  286, 336

Keith, Linda, 300
Kelley, Alton, 153, 215–218,
  231–232, 336
Kelley, Paula, 136
Kennedy, John F., 130, 174
Kennedy, Robert F., 162
Kerouac, Jack, 337
  on Beat generation, 68
  Buddhism and, 120, 122
  Burroughs and, 116–117
  Cassady and, 67–68
  cultural impact of, 65
  early days of Beat, 66–68
  Garcia influenced by, 188
  Ginsberg's "Howl" and, 69, 71
  inspiration from Black culture, 77–78
  jazz culture and, 26
  Johnson and, 80
  Kesey influenced by, 186
  mainstream criticism of, 73
  Manzarek influenced by, 207
  Podhoertz's libel of, 285
  publishers of, 110
  Snyder and, 63, 120
  success of *On the Road*, 76–78
  weiss and, 60
  writing *On the Road*, 68
Kerr, Clark, 167–168
Kesey, Ken, 186–189, 195, 218,
  219–220, 253, 260–261, 337
Kienholz, Ed, 101, 104–105, 254
Kimmel, Marjorie Cameron Parsons,
  104–105
King, Andrew, 244–245
King, Hayward, 69–70
King, Martin Luther, Jr., 76, 162,
  164, 293
King Ubu Gallery, 40–41, 70
Klee, Paul, 12, 21
Kleps, Art, 185
Kline, Franz, 36, 116
Kooper, Al, 197, 314
Korngold, Murray, 182

Index

KPFA (radio station), 42–44, 121, 137, 143–145
Kramer, Eddie, 301
Krasner, Lee, 29, 33, 337
Krassner, Paul, 115, 273
Kreutzmann, Bill, 189
Krieger, Robby, 207
Krishnamurta, Jiddu, 18, 20, 337
Kunkin, Art, 199, 290–291, 337
Kupferberg, Tuli, 193
Kyger, Joanne, 122–124

Lahr, John, 109–110
Lamantia, Philip, 6, 7, 15, 41, 69–71, 192, 337
Lancaster, Joyce, 41–42
Laughlin, Chandler "Chan," 137, 210–211
Laughlin, James, 6, 110, 337
LaVigne, Robert, 55, 148, 337
Lawrence, D. H., 5, 19, 97, 114
Lead Belly, 94, 95, 110, 133, 139
Leary, Timothy, 183–185, 241, 259, 272, 276–280, 307, 337–338
Leite, George, 6, 338
Lennon, John, 172–176, 246, 253, 301–307, 314, 338
Leonard, Mike, 244–245
Lesh, Phil, 154–155, 188–189, 217, 338
Lewis, Lucy, 149–150, 156, 338
Lindsay, Vachel, 2, 338
Lipton, Lawrence, 106–107, 200, 338
Lisch, Arthur, 291–292
Little Richard, 79, 203, 300
Living Theatre, 28, 35–37, 111, 115–116, 140, 192
Lloyd, Charles, 277
Locks, Seymour, 152–153
Love Pageant Rally, 254–255, 258, 285
Lovell, Vik, 186
Lovin' Spoonful (band), 204, 205
Low, Jackson Mac, 29, 338
Luce, Clare Booth, 182

Luce, Henry, 182–183
Luhan, Mabel Dodge, 25, 338

MacAgy, Douglas, 12, 16, 338
MacLise, Angus, 194, 270
MacPhee, Chester, 72
Maguire, Michael, 128–129
Mailer, Norman, 77, 112, 114, 193, 338
Maleczech, Ruth, 55, 151–153, 155
Malina, Judith, 27–30, 34–37, 338
    Cage's music and, 34–36
    Day and, 113–114
    Ginsberg and, 69
    Living Theatre of, 28, 35–37, 115–116
    Perkoff and, 106–107
Mamas & the Papas (band), 204–205, 311
Mandel, William, 129
Mander, Jerry, 220–221
Manzarek, Ray, 207
Marchbank, Pearce, 174
Marinello, Frank, 314
Marks, Ben, 229
Martin, Flo, 296
Martin, George, 173, 247, 302–305, 338
Martin, Peter, 57
Martin, Tony, 148, 155, 222, 232, 234, 339
Masekela, Hugh, 208, 315
Mason, Kathy, 132
Mason, Nick, 244–245, 299
Maurin, Peter, 113
Maynard, John, 107
McCarthy, Joseph, 50, 51
McCartney, Paul, 172–176, 242–243, 246–247, 302–307, 309–310, 339
McClure, Joanna, 83, 84
McClure, Michael, 339
    arts collaboration and, 148
    Be-In and, 276–278
    Berman and, 102–103
    Blue Unicorn and, 158
    Conner and, 85

Index

DeFeo and, 88
di Prima and, 87
Dylan and, 218
Ginsberg and, 70
Halprin and, 146
Invisible Circus and, 282
North Beach described by, 59
Painterland and, 83–85, 87, 88
peyote use by, 103
as playwright, 235, 262
rock shows described by, 228
Sender and, 144
6 Gallery and, 70–72
McConville, David, 90
McCorkle, Locke, 44, 62–63, 339
McCoy, Don, 238
McCoy, Paula, 238, 253
McDaniel, Stan, 293–294
McGhee, Brownie, 137, 210
McGuinn, Jim, 197, 202, 206, 310, 312
McGuire, Barry, 204, 205
McKay, Claude, 2, 339
McKernan, Ron "Pigpen," 189
McKinney, Eleanor, 42
McLuhan, Marshall, 194, 272, 280
McMurtry, Larry, 186
McNair, Archie, 98
McNeill, Don, 272, 287, 295, 339
Meisenbach, Robert, 129
Mekas, Jonas, 156, 191, 200, 271, 339
Meltzer, David, 103, 148, 339
Meltzer, Richard, xii
Melvin, Milan, 297
Meredith, James, 163
Merry Pranksters, 186–189, 219–220, 260
Metesky (Metevsky), George, 251, 259, 262
Metzner, Ralph, 184
Meyerson, Martin, 169
Mezzrow, Mezz, 310
Michael X (Michael de Freitas), 244

Miles, Barry, 97, 178, 242–243, 245, 247, 339
Miles, Josephine, 8, 9, 339
Miles, Sue, 97
Milk, Harvey, 236
Miller, Henry, 4–6, 14–15, 61, 110, 114, 339–340
Miller, Stanley "Mouse," 231–232, 276
Mills, C. Wright, 51, 162, 340
Millstein, Gilbert, 76–77, 80
Minault, Kent, 251, 261, 282
Minton, Henry, 25–26, 340
Mitchell, Bobby, 215
Mitchell, Joan, 109
Mitchell, John, 244
Monk, Thelonious, 25–26, 41, 111, 140, 174, 184, 197, 340
Monroe, Harriet, 2, 340
Monterey International Pop Festival, 299, 309–318
Moon, Keith, 317
Moore, Fred, 127, 321
Morley, Grace McCann, 11–12, 340
Morrell, Lady Ottoline, 19, 340
Morrison, Jim, 207
Moscoso, Victor, 232
Moses, Robert Parris, 162, 166
Moss, Jerry, 314–315
Motherwell, Robert, 12, 36, 340
Motown, 174, 199, 200–201
Mullen, Frances, 20–21, 340
Murao, Shigeyoshi, 58, 72, 341
Murcott, Billy, 249–253
Murphy, Michael, 46
Muszalski, Ronald, 262

Naked Lunch (Burroughs), 114, 116–117, 192
Nathan, Leonard, 226
Needham, Sherry, 266–267
Nelson, Robert, 156, 214
Neri, Manuel, 86, 146
Neuwirth, Bob, 136, 341

416 **Index**

New Lost City Ramblers (band), 135, 137, 139
New School, 28, 52, 112
Newfield, Jack, 127
Newhall, Scott, 82, 222–223
Newman, Jim, 83–84, 103
Newport Folk Festival, 140–141, 197
Newton, Huey, 311
Nin, Anaïs, 6, 15, 42, 61, 104, 341
Nomland, Kemper, 58
Nord, Eric "Big Daddy," 59, 134
Norse, Harold, 29, 34, 341
Nuttall, Jeff, 178
Nys, Maria, 19, 341

O'Day, Anita, 310
Odetta, 136–137, 138, 341
O'Hara, Frank, 31–33, 36, 341
Oldham, Andrew Loog, 174–175, 341
Oliveros, Pauline, 143–145, 147–149, 154, 155, 157, 214, 341
Olivier, Barry, 137
Olsen, Richie, 150, 210, 341
Olson, Charles, 36, 112, 192, 341
On the Road (Kerouac), 65, 68, 76–78, 186, 207
Ono, Yoko, 112, 194
Osmond, Humphrey, 23–24, 183–184, 341
Ostin, Mo, 314–315

Paglia, Camille, 53
Painterland, 83–90
Pariser, Alan, 208, 309
Park, David, 13, 41, 69–70, 341
Parker, Charlie, 25–26, 37, 342
Partch, Harry, 6, 61–62, 145, 200, 342
Patchen, Kenneth, 5, 58, 342
Paul Butterfield Blues Band, 197, 227, 314
Paulekas, Szou, 202
Paulekas, Vito, 202–203
Peabody, Elizabeth Palmer, 119

Peale, Norman Vincent, 51
Pearl, Ed, 138
Peitchel, Samuel, 164
Pennebaker, D. A., 177, 311–312, 314, 342
Perkoff, Stuart, 106–107
Perry, Charles, 158
Perry, Helen Swick, 226–227
Peter, Paul and Mary, 140, 208
Phillips, John, 204–205, 309–313, 314, 342
Phillips, Michelle, 204–205, 309–310
Pickett, Wilson, 201, 287
Pilgrim, Johnny, 95
Pink Floyd, 244–245, 246, 247–248, 299
Piscator, Erwin, 28
Podhoertz, Norman, 73–74, 285
Pollock, Jackson, 12, 29, 33, 186, 342
Ponch, Martin, 41–42
Porter, Bern, 6, 15–16, 342
Pound, Ezra, 8, 110
Powers, Chester (Dino Valenti), 217
Presley, Elvis, 78–79, 94, 95–96, 138, 172
Price, Richard, 46
Priore, Domenic, 311
Psychedelic Shop, 223–225, 257, 262, 294

Quant, Mary, 98, 171–172, 174, 175–176, 206
Quarnstrom, Lee, 187, 289
Quicksilver Messenger Service (band), 217, 238, 277, 310, 314

Ramakrishna Paramahamsa, 20
Rattiner, Dan, 266–267
Rauschenberg, Robert, 36, 83, 116, 243, 269
Reagan, Ronald, 169, 208, 261–262, 342
Redding, Otis, 174, 201, 300, 313, 315–316

Index

Reed, Ishmael, 266–268
Reed, Lou, 270
Reich, Steve, 147, 150, 151, 153–155, 156, 214, 342
Rembar, Charles, 114
Remington, Deborah, 69–70
Reps, Paul, 18
Resner, Bill, 233–234
Resner, Hillel, 233–234
Rexroth, Kenneth, x, xii, 1–7, 342
    arts collaboration and, 148
    Buddhism and, 6, 43, 119–120
    Chicago roots of, 2
    Ginsberg and, 68, 72
    hippie in vocabulary of, 218
    KPFA and, 42, 43
    Lipton and, 106, 107
    Living Theatre's production of work, 35
    poets and writers drawn to and influenced by, 4–7, 47, 195, 251
    political activism of, 2–3, 6–7
    Porter and, 15
    publishers of, 58, 110
    readings of works, 9
    relationship with Duncan, 1, 3
    salons of, 7, 47, 58, 60, 68
    6 Gallery readings and, 70–71
    Velleman and, 58–59
    visits to Ghost House, 41
    world intuited by/legacy of, 222, 275, 313
Rexroth, Marie, 6, 342
Richard, Cliff, 96–97
Richards, Keith, 174, 178–179, 300, 304, 342
Richards, M. C., 36, 194–195, 342–343
Richer, Arthur, 152
Rifkin, Danny, 253, 278, 312, 313
Riley, Terry, 145, 147, 150, 154, 343
Riservato, Pino, 93
Rivers, Johnny, 309, 311, 313
Rivers, Larry, 31, 33, 269, 343

Robbins, Paul Jay, 203, 271
Robinson, Peter, 136
Robinson, William "Smokey," 200–201, 287, 309
Rodd, John, 295
Rodriguez, Richard, 294–295
Rodriguez de Montalvo, Garci, xi
Rohan, Brian, 278
Rohé, Fred, 320
Rolling Stones (band), 174–179, 199, 204, 241–242, 246, 300
Romero, Elias, 148, 152–153, 155–156, 343
Rose, Jeanne, 321
Rosenberg, Davey, 166
Rosset, Barney, 109–110, 184, 343
Rossman, Michael, 127, 167, 169, 276, 343
Rothko, Mark, 12, 104, 343
Rothkop, David, 226
Roxon, Lillian, 271
Rubin, Jerry, 276–277, 288
Rukeyser, Muriel, 6, 343
Ruscha, Ed, 105, 242
Rush, Loren, 145, 147–148
Russell, Ross, 102
Russell, Sanders, 7, 343
Russell, Vickie (Priscilla Arminger), 67, 343
Ryan, John, 36, 59, 69–70, 343

Sackheim, Eric, 136
Saijo, Albert, 122
Samwell, Ian, 96–97
San Francisco Art Institute (SFAI), 344. *See also* California School of Fine Arts
San Francisco Mime Troupe, 55, 150–156, 214–215
    benefit for legal defense fund of, 217–218
    collaborations of, 148
    Com/Co and, 290

Index

San Francisco Mime Troupe (*cont.*)
  Diggers and, 249–253
  guerilla theater of, 234
Sanders, Ed, 158, 191–193, 265–267, 273, 343
Sanger, Margaret, 131
Sarria, José, 40, 344
Sasaki, Ruth Fuller, 44, 46, 47, 122, 344
Sasaki, Shigetsu, 44
Sassoon, Vidal, 171–172
Sausalito Six, 15
Savio, Mario, 165, 167–168, 320–321, 344
Schafer, Andrée, 2, 6, 344
Scherr, Max, 259, 296
Scheyer, Galka, 21
Schoenberg, Arnold, 21, 344
Schoenfeld, Eugene L., 296
Schwartz, Delmore, 27, 270
Scott, Chloe, 186, 253
Scully, Rock, 163, 311, 312, 344
Sebastian, John, 205
Sedgwick, Edie, 269–270
Seeger, Pete, 136, 137, 139
Seeland, Esther, 226
Seeland, Jerry, 226
Seidemann, Bob, 317
Seigenthaler, John, 162
Sender, Ramón, x, 143–144, 147–148, 154–157, 220, 238–239, 344
Senzaki, Nyogen, 18, 121–122, 344
Shankar, Ravi, 225, 229, 306, 309, 316
Shapiro, Benny, 202, 208, 309
Sheets, Kermit, 41–42
Shelley, John, 222–223, 234
Shepp, Archie, 225, 268
Sheridan, Arthur, 234
Shrimpton, Jean, 171
Shubb, Rick, 138
Sidran, Ben, 315
Siggins, Bob, 136
Signer, Ethan, 136
Silverberg, Lenny, 226, 233

Silverstein, Shel, 286
Simon, Paul, 204, 309–311, 344
Simon & Garfunkel (band), 204, 309, 313
Simpson, David, 69–70
Sims, Terry, 165
6 Gallery, 70–72, 83, 84, 110, 152
Slick, Grace, 216, 239, 286, 315
Sloan, P. F., 204
Smith, Bessie, 138
Smith, David, 296
Smith, Harry, 135, 136, 345
Smith, Hassel, 41, 104
Smith, Jack, 192
Smith, Norman, 246
Smith, Richard Cándida, 235
Snyder, Gary, 345
  acid tests and, 189
  background and studies of, 46–47
  Be-In and, 275–280
  "The Circumambulation of Mt. Tamalpais," 280
  Diggers and, 281
  Ginsberg and, 70–72, 280
  Kerouac and, 63, 120
  Kyger as wife of, 122
  Leary challenged by, 279
  Manzarek and, 207
  McCarthyism and, 49
  Oracle coverage of, 258, 279
  Sausalito home as bohemian center, 62–64
  Thompson and, 287
  values and vision of, 63–64, 279–280
  Village Voice article on, 272
Solomon, Howard, 192
Somers, Roger, 120–121
Sommerville, Ian, 241, 243
Sonnabend, Casey, 276
Sonny and Cher (band), 205–206
Southern, Terry, 242
Sox, Ellis D., 292
Spellman, Francis, 193

Index

Spencer, Fumi, 152, 154, 155
Spencer, William, 153, 155
Spicer, Jack, 7, 59, 70, 145, 345
Spiegelberg, Frederic, 44, 45, 195, 345
Spohn, Clay, 14, 345
Stamp, Terence, 98, 172
Stanislavski, Konstantin, 52
Stanley, Owsley "Bear," 181–182, 188, 233, 257, 277, 314, 345
Starr, Kevin, 82
Starr, Ringo, 172–176, 253, 302–307
Stax/Volt, 199, 200–201, 316
Steele, Tommy, 96
Stein, Gertrude, 21, 32
Stella, Frank, 83, 105
Stepanian, Michael, 278
Stephen, John, 172
Stern, Gerd, 43, 62, 121, 194–195, 275, 345
Stewart, Jim, 201
Still, Clyfford, 12–13, 41, 60, 104, 345
Stills, Stephen, 206–207
Stockhausen, Karlheinz, 145, 247, 346
Stolaroff, Myron, 182–183, 322, 346
Stone, Robert, 112, 186
Strachwitz, Chris, 137
Strasberg, Lee, 28, 52
Strauch, Hyla, 226
Strauch, Tsvi, 226, 293–294
Strummer, Joe, 178
Stubbs, Bob, 157–158
Student Nonviolent Coordinating Committee (SNCC), 126, 161–163, 166, 273
Students for a Democratic Society, 130, 162–163
Subotnick, Morton, 55, 143–148, 150, 154, 156–157, 346
Sullivan, Redd, 95
Sunshine, Monty, 92–93
Suzuki, D. T., 20, 30, 34, 46, 47, 346
Suzuki, Shunryu Shogaku, 122–124, 277, 346

Swami Vivekananda, 20
Syndell Gallery, 83–84, 104
Syracuse, Russ "the Moose," 216

Tape Music Center, 143–150, 154–157
Taplin, Jonathan, 197, 270
Taylor, Cecil, 112, 192
Taylor, Derek, 203, 208, 243, 247, 307, 309–311, 346
Thelin, Jay, 223–225, 232, 262, 276, 294, 313, 346
Thelin, Marsha, 224–225, 232
Thelin, Ron, 223–225, 257, 294, 346
Thompson, Bill, 212–213
Thompson, Hunter, 278, 287
Thomson, Virgil, 32, 346
Thoreau, Henry David, x, 119, 224
Thornton, Big Mama, 313
Tinker, Carol, 234
Tobase, Hodo, 46, 121, 122
Tobey, Mark, 27, 46
Todd, Charlotte, 252–253
Toly, Signe, 211, 239
Toropov, Yuri, 234
Towle, Jack, 153, 215–218
Towle, Katherine, 166–167
Townshend, Pete, 176, 303, 316–317, 346
Tudor, David, 36, 195, 346
Tzara, Tristan, 2, 346

University of California Berkley
folk music at, 137–138
Free Speech Movement at, 166–169
student activism at, 126–130

Valenti, Dino, 217
Van Doren, Mark, 57–58
Van Meter, Ben, 156, 232–233, 346
Van Ronk, Dave, 135, 139, 140, 346–347
Varda, Jean, 14–15, 46, 61, 69–70, 195, 347

420 **Index**

Velleman, Silvio, 58–59
Velvet Underground (band), 270–271
Villa, Carlos, 87
Vincent, Stephen, 163
Vollmer, Joan, 67, 68

W. E. B. Du Bois Club, 153,
    163–164, 215
Wagner, Robin, 55
Wainwright, Loudon, 286, 294
Waiting for Godot (Beckett), 54–55,
    109–110
Wakefield, Dan, 77
Warhol, Andy, 101, 105–106, 232, 243,
    269–271
Wasson, R. Gordon, 183, 184, 234
Waterman, Dick, 141
Waters, Alice, 168, 320–321
Waters, Roger, 244–245
Watson, Bob, 95
Watts, Alan, 43–47, 63, 115, 120, 277,
    279, 347
Watts, Charlie, 179, 300
Waymouth, Nigel, 248
Weaver, Helen, 193
Weavers (band), 133–134
Webb, George, 92
Webb, Harry (Cliff Richard), 96–97
Wein, George, 136–137, 197
Weinberg, Jack, 167, 168
Weir, Bob, 189, 220, 307, 318
weiss, ruth, 60, 347
Weitsman, Mel, x, 12–13, 41, 60, 71,
    123, 154, 347
Welch, Lew, 121–122, 207, 281, 291
Weldon, Ann, 283–284
Werber, Frank, 134, 347
Wexler, Jerry, 314–315

Whalen, Philip, 46–47, 70–71, 121,
    207, 280
Wheeler, William, 128
White, George, 23, 347
Whitman, Walt, 25, 275–276
Who (band), 174, 176, 287, 303, 316–317
Whyton, Wally, 95
Wiley, William, 151
Wilhelm, Mike, 210
Williams, Cecil, 236, 282–284
Williams, Tennessee, 29, 32, 53, 54,
    110, 347
Williams, William Carlos, 6, 7, 35, 110
Willis, Ellen, 271
Willner, Phyllis, 260, 261, 263
Willson, Peter Wynne, 248
Wilson, Adrian, 41–42
Wilson, Brian, 201, 303
Wilson, Tom, 197, 204
Wilson, Wes, 231–232
Wise, Shirly, 259
Witt-Diamant, Ruth, 9, 347
Wohl, Barbara, 228
Wolfe, Tom, 51, 187, 261, 347
Wozniak, Steve, 321
Wright, Rick, 244–245
Wyckoff, Carrie Mead, 20, 347
Wyman, Bill, 300

Yancey, Jimmy, 2, 348
Yardbirds (band), 174, 229, 299
Yates, Francis, 104
Yates, Peter, 20–21, 62, 104, 348
Young, La Monte, 145, 194, 270, 348
Young, Lester, 26, 348
Young, Neil, 206–207, 316

Zellerbach, Harold, 234